Search ⸻ ith ASP.NET

Professional
Search Engine Optimization with ASP.NET
A Developer's Guide to SEO

Cristian Darie

Jaimie Sirovich

BICENTENNIAL
1807
WILEY
2007
BICENTENNIAL

Wiley Publishing, Inc.

Professional Search Engine Optimization with ASP.NET:
A Developer's Guide to SEO

Published by
Wiley Publishing, Inc.
10475 Crosspoint Boulevard
Indianapolis, IN 46256
www.wiley.com

Copyright © 2007 by Wiley Publishing, Inc., Indianapolis, Indiana

Published simultaneously in Canada

ISBN: 978-0-470-13147-3

Manufactured in the United States of America

10 9 8 7 6 5 4 3 2 1

Library of Congress Cataloging-in-Publication Data: Available from Publisher.

About the Authors

Cristian Darie is a software engineer with experience in a wide range of modern technologies, and the author of numerous books and tutorials on AJAX, ASP.NET, PHP, SQL, and related areas. Cristian currently lives in Bucharest, Romania, studying distributed application architectures for his PhD. He's getting involved with various commercial and research projects, and when not planning to buy Google, he enjoys his bit of social life. If you want to say "Hi," you can reach Cristian through his personal web site at http://www.cristiandarie.ro.

Jaimie Sirovich is a search engine marketing consultant. He works with his clients to build them powerful online presences. Officially Jaimie is a computer programmer, but he claims to enjoy marketing much more. He graduated from Stevens Institute of Technology with a BS in Computer Science. He worked under Barry Schwartz at RustyBrick, Inc., as lead programmer on all eCommerce projects until 2005. At present, Jaimie consults for several organizations and administrates the popular search engine marketing blog, SEOEgghead.com.

Credits

Senior Acquisitions Editor
Jim Minatel

Development Editor
Kenyon Brown

Technical Editor
Doug Parsons

Production Editor
Angela Smith

Copy Editor
Kim Cofer

Editorial Manager
Mary Beth Wakefield

Production Manager
Tim Tate

Vice President and Executive Group Publisher
Richard Swadley

Vice President and Executive Publisher
Joseph B. Wikert

Project Coordinator, Cover
Lynsey Osborn

Compositor
Happenstance Type-O-Rama

Proofreader
Sossity Smith

Indexer
Jack Lewis

Anniversary Logo Design
Richard Pacifico

Acknowledgments

The authors would like to thank the following people and companies, listed alphabetically, for their invaluable assistance with the production of this book. Without their help, this book would not have been possible in its current form.

Dan Kramer of Volatile Graphix for generously providing his cloaking database to the public — and even adding some data to make our cloaking code examples work better.

Doug Parsons, the Technical Editor of this book, for carefully checking our code and helping out with great improvement suggestions.

Kim Krause Berg of The Usability Effect for providing assistance and insight where this book references usability and accessibility topics.

MaxMind, Inc., for providing their free GeoLite geo-targeting data — making our geo-targeting code examples possible.

Ruben Cordoba Castillo, an ASP.NET developer from Spain, for offering his feedback on several topics covered by this book.

Seth Yates, the creator of UrlRewriter.NET, for developing such a useful product, and for checking that we didn't make technical mistakes when presenting its usage.

Stefan Schackow, author of *Professional ASP.NET 2.0 Security, Membership, and Role Management* (Wiley Publishing, Inc., 2006), for pointing out a few subtle errors that only a man with his experience could have spotted.

Yaroslav Govorunov of Helicon Tech, the creators of ISAPI_Rewrite, for checking the technical accuracy of our coverage of their product.

Family and friends of both Jaimie and Cristian — for tolerating the endless trail of empty cans of (caffeinated) soda left on the table while writing this book.

Contents

Contents

Contents

Contents

Contents

Introduction

Welcome to *Professional Search Engine Optimization with ASP.NET: A Developer's Guide to SEO*!

Search engine optimization has traditionally been only the job of a marketing staff. With this book, we place search engine optimization in a brand new light, asserting that SEO should be a consideration of the programmer as well.

For maximum efficiency in the search engine optimization efforts, developers and marketers should work together, starting from the web site's inception and technical and visual design and throughout its development lifetime. We provide developers and IT professionals with the information they need to create and maintain a search engine friendly web site and avoid common pitfalls that confuse search engines. This book discusses in depth how to facilitate site spidering and discusses the various technologies and services that can be leveraged for site promotion.

Who Should Read This Book

Professional Search Engine Optimization with ASP.NET: A Developer's Guide to SEO is mainly geared toward web developers because it discusses search engine optimization in the context of web site programming. One does not need to be a programmer by trade to benefit from this book, but some programming background is important for *fully* understanding and following the technical exercises.

We also tried to make this book friendly for the search engine marketer with some IT background who wants to learn about a different, more technical angle of search engine optimization. Usually, each chapter starts with a less-technical discussion on the topic at hand and then develops into the more advanced technical details. Many books cover search engine optimization, but few delve at all into the meaty technical details of *how* to design a web site with the goal of search engine optimization in mind. Ultimately, this book does just that.

Where programming *is* discussed, we show code with explanations. We don't hide behind concepts and buzzwords; we include hands-on practical exercises instead. Contained within this reference are fully functional examples of using XML-based sitemaps, social-bookmarking widgets, and even working implementations of cloaking and geo-targeting.

What Will You Learn from This Book?

In this book, we have assembled the most important topics that programmers and search engine marketers should know about when designing web sites.

Getting the Most Out of This Book

You may choose to read this book cover-to-cover, but that is strictly not required. We recommend that you read Chapters 1–6 first, but the remaining chapters can be perused in any order. In case you run into technical problems, a page with chapter-by-chapter book updates and errata is maintained by Cristian Darie at www.cristiandarie.ro/seo-asp/. You can also search for errata for the book at www.wrox.com, as is discussed later in this introduction.

If you have any feedback related to this book, don't hesitate to contact either Cristian or Jaimie! This will help to make everyone's experience with this book more pleasant and fulfilling.

At the end of **Chapter 1, "You: Programmer and Search Engine Marketer,"** you will create the environment where you'll be coding away throughout the rest of the book. Programming can be tricky at times; in order to avoid most configuration and coding errors you may encounter, we will instruct you how to prepare the working folder and your database.

> If you aren't ready for these tasks yet, don't worry! You can come back at any time, later. All programming-related tasks in this book are explained step-by-step to minimize the chances that anyone gets lost on the way.

Chapter 2, "A Primer in Basic SEO," is a primer in search engine optimization tailored for the IT professional. It stresses the points that are particularly relevant to the programmer from the perspective of the programmer. You'll also learn about a few tools and resources that all search engine marketers and web developers should know about.

Chapter 3, "Provocative SE-Friendly URLs," details how to create (or enhance) your web site with improved URLs that are easier for search engines to understand and more persuasive for their human readers. You'll even create a URL factory, which you will be able to reuse in your own projects.

Chapter 4, "Content Relocation and HTTP Status Codes," presents all of the nuances involved in using HTTP status codes correctly to relocate and indicate other statuses for content. The use of these status codes properly is essential when restructuring information on a web site.

Chapter 5, "Duplicate Content," discusses duplicate content in great detail. It then proposes strategies for avoiding problems related to duplicate content.

Chapter 6, "SE-Friendly HTML and JavaScript," discusses search engine optimization issues that present themselves in the context of rendering content using HTML, JavaScript and AJAX, and Flash.

Chapter 7, "Web Feeds and Social Bookmarking," discusses web syndication and social bookmarking. Tools to create feeds and ways to leverage social bookmarking are presented.

Chapter 8, "Black Hat SEO," presents black hat SEO from the perspective of preventing black hat victimization and attacks. You may want to skip ahead to this chapter to see what this is all about!

Chapter 9, "Sitemaps," discusses the use of sitemaps — traditional and XML-based — for the purpose of improving and speeding indexing.

Chapter 10, "Link Bait," discusses the concept of link bait and provides an example of a site tool that could bait links.

Chapter 11, "Cloaking, Geo-Targeting, and IP Delivery," discusses cloaking, geo-targeting, and IP delivery. It includes fully working examples of all three.

Chapter 12, "Foreign Language SEO," discusses search engine optimization for foreign languages and the concerns therein.

Chapter 13, "Coping with Technical Issues," discusses the various issues that an IT professional must understand when maintaining a site, such as how to change web hosts without potentially hurting search rankings.

Chapter 14, "Case Study: Building an E-Commerce Store," rounds it off with a fully functional search engine optimized e-commerce catalog incorporating much of the material in the previous chapters.

Chapter 15, "Site Clinic: So You Have a Web Site?," presents concerns that may face a preexisting web site and suggests enhancements that can be implemented in the context of their difficulty.

We hope that you will enjoy reading this book and that it will prove useful for your real-world search engine optimization endeavors!

Contacting the Authors

Jaimie Sirovich can be contacted through his blog at http://www.seoegghead.com. Cristian Darie can be contacted from his web site at http://www.cristiandarie.ro.

Conventions

To help you get the most from the text and keep track of what's happening, we've used a number of conventions throughout the book.

> **Boxes like this one hold important, not-to-be forgotten information that is directly relevant to the surrounding text.**

Tips, hints, tricks, and asides to the current discussion are offset and placed in italics like this.

As for styles in the text:

- ❏ We *highlight* new terms and important words when we introduce them.
- ❏ We show keyboard strokes like this: Ctrl+A.
- ❏ We show file names, URLs, and code within the text like so: `persistence.properties`.
- ❏ We present code in two different ways:

```
In code examples we highlight new and important code with a gray background.
The gray highlighting is not used for code that's less important in the present
context, or has been shown before.
```

Source Code

As you work through the examples in this book, you may choose either to type in all the code manually or to use the source code files that accompany the book. All of the source code used in this book is available for download at `http://www.wrox.com`. Once at the site, simply locate the book's title (either by using the Search box or by using one of the title lists) and click the Download Code link on the book's detail page to obtain all the source code for the book.

> *Because many books have similar titles, you may find it easiest to search by ISBN; this book's ISBN is 978-0-470-13147-3.*

Once you download the code, just decompress it with your favorite compression tool. Alternatively, you can go to the main Wrox code download page at `http://www.wrox.com/dynamic/books/download.aspx` to see the code available for this book and all other Wrox books.

Errata

We make every effort to ensure that there are no errors in the text or in the code. However, no one is perfect, and mistakes do occur. If you find an error in one of our books, like a spelling mistake or faulty piece of code, we would be very grateful for your feedback. By sending in errata you may save another reader hours of frustration and at the same time you will be helping us provide even higher quality information.

To find the errata page for this book, go to `http://www.wrox.com` and locate the title using the Search box or one of the title lists. Then, on the book details page, click the Book Errata link. On this page you can view all errata that has been submitted for this book and posted by Wrox editors. A complete book list including links to each book's errata is also available at `www.wrox.com/misc-pages/booklist.shtml`.

If you don't spot "your" error on the Book Errata page, go to `www.wrox.com/contact/techsupport.shtml` and complete the form there to send us the error you have found. We'll check the information and, if appropriate, post a message to the book's errata page and fix the problem in subsequent editions of the book.

p2p.wrox.com

For author and peer discussion, join the P2P forums at p2p.wrox.com. The forums are a Web-based system for you to post messages relating to Wrox books and related technologies and interact with other readers and technology users. The forums offer a subscription feature to e-mail you topics of interest of your choosing when new posts are made to the forums. Wrox authors, editors, other industry experts, and your fellow readers are present on these forums.

At http://p2p.wrox.com you will find a number of different forums that will help you not only as you read this book, but also as you develop your own applications. To join the forums, just follow these steps:

1. Go to p2p.wrox.com and click the Register link.

2. Read the terms of use and click Agree.

3. Complete the required information to join as well as any optional information you wish to provide and click Submit.

4. You will receive an e-mail with information describing how to verify your account and complete the joining process.

> *You can read messages in the forums without joining P2P but in order to post your own messages, you must join.*

Once you join, you can post new messages and respond to messages other users post. You can read messages at any time on the Web. If you would like to have new messages from a particular forum e-mailed to you, click the Subscribe to this Forum icon by the forum name in the forum listing.

For more information about how to use the Wrox P2P, be sure to read the P2P FAQs for answers to questions about how the forum software works as well as many common questions specific to P2P and Wrox books. To read the FAQs, click the FAQ link on any P2P page.

1

You: Programmer and Search Engine Marketer

Googling for information on the World Wide Web is such a common activity these days that it is hard to imagine that just a few years ago this verb did not even exist. Search engines are now an integral part of our lifestyle, but this was not always the case. Historically, systems for finding information were driven by data organization and classification performed by humans. Such systems are not entirely obsolete — libraries still keep their books ordered by categories, author names, and so forth. Yahoo! itself started as a manually maintained directory of web sites, organized into categories. Those were the good old days.

Today, the data of the World Wide Web is enormous and rapidly changing; it cannot be confined in the rigid structure of the library. The format of the information is extremely varied, and the individual bits of data — coming from blogs, articles, web services of all kinds, picture galleries, and so on — form an almost infinitely complex virtual organism. In this environment, making information *findable* necessitates something more than the traditional structures of data organization or classification.

Introduce the ad-hoc query and the modern search engine. This functionality reduces the aforementioned need for organization and classification; and since its inception, it has been become pervasive. Google's popular email service, GMail, features its searching capability that permits a user to find emails that contain a particular set of keywords. Microsoft Windows Vista now integrates an instant search feature as part of the operating system, helping you quickly find information within any email, Word document, or database on your hard drive from the Start menu regardless of the underlying file format. But, by far, the most popular use of this functionality is in the World Wide Web search engine.

These search engines are the exponents of the explosive growth of the Internet, and an entire industry has grown around their huge popularity. Each visit to a search engine potentially generates business for a particular vendor. Looking at Figure 1-1 it is easy to figure out where people in Manhattan are likely to order pizza online. Furthermore, the traffic resulting from non-sponsored, or organic, search results cost nothing to the vendor. These are highlighted in Figure 1-1.

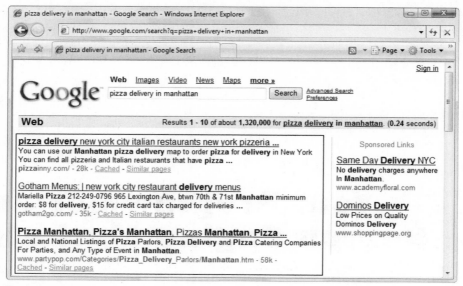

Figure 1-1

The less obvious effect of the search engine explosion phenomenon is that web developers are now directly involved in the search engine marketing process. To rank well in these organic results, it may not be enough to "write relevant content," as the typical search engine marketing tutorial drones. Rather, the web application developer must work together with the marketing team, and he or she must build a web site fully aware that certain features or technologies may interfere with a search engine marketing campaign. An improperly designed web site can interfere with a search engine's need to periodically navigate and index the information contained therein. In the worst case, the search engine may not be able to index the content at all.

So, ironically, while users are becoming less interested in understanding the structure of data on the Internet, the structure of a web site is becoming an increasingly important facet in search engine marketing! This structure — the architecture of a web site — is the primary focus of this book.

We hope that this brief introduction whets your appetite! The remainder of this chapter tells you what to expect from this book. You will also configure your development machine to ensure you won't have any problems following the technical exercises in the later chapters.

Who Are You?

Maybe you're a great programmer or IT professional, but marketing isn't your thing. Or perhaps you're a tech-savvy search engine marketer who wants a peek under the hood of a search engine optimized web site. Search engine marketing is a field where technology and marketing are both critical and interdependent, because small changes in the implementation of a web site can make you or break you in search engine rankings. Furthermore, the fusion of technology and marketing know-how can create web site features that attract more visitors.

The mission of this book is to help web developers create web sites that rank well with the major search engines, and to teach search engine marketers how to use technology to their advantage. We assert that neither marketing nor IT can exist in a vacuum, and it is essential that they not see themselves as opposing forces in an organization. They *must* work together. This book aims to educate both sides in that regard.

The Story

So how do a search engine marketer from the USA (Jaimie) and a programmer from Romania (Cristian) meet? To answer, we need to tell you a funny little story. A while ago, Jaimie happened to purchase a book that shall remain nameless written by Cristian, and was not pleased with one particular aspect of its contents. Jaimie proceeded to grill him with some critical comments on a public web site. Ouch!

Cristian contacted Jaimie courteously, and explained most of it away. No, we're not going to tell you the name of the book, what the contents were, or whether it is still in print. But things did eventually get more amicable, and we started to correspond about what we do for a living. Jaimie is a web site developer and search engine marketer, and Cristian is a software engineer who has published quite a few books in the technology sector. As a result of those discussions, the idea of a technology-focused search engine optimization book came about. The rest is more or less history.

What Do You Need to Learn?

As with anything in the technology-related industry, one must constantly learn and research to keep apprised of the latest news and trends. *How exhausting!* Fortunately, there are fundamental truths with regard to search engine optimization that are both easy to understand and probably won't change in time significantly — so a solid foundation that you build now will likely stand the test of time.

We remember the days when search engine optimization was a black art of analyzing and improving on-page factors. Search engine marketers were obsessed over keyword density and which HTML tags to use. Many went so far as to recommend optimizing content for different search engines individually, thusly creating different pages with similar content optimized with different densities and tags. Today, that would create a problem called *duplicate content*.

The current struggle is creating a site with interactive content and navigation with a minimal amount of duplicate content, with URLs that do not confuse web spiders, and a tidy internal linking structure. There is a thread on SearchEngineWatch (http://www.searchenginewatch.com) where someone asked which skill everyone reading would like to hone. Almost all of them enumerated programming as one of the skills (http://forums.searchenginewatch.com/showthread.php?t=11945). This does not surprise us. Having an understanding of both programming and search engine marketing will serve one well in the pursuit of success on the Internet.

When people ask us where we'd suggest spending money in an SEO plan, we always recommend making sure that one is starting with a sound foundation. If your web site has architectural problems, it's tantamount to trumpeting your marketing message atop a house of cards. *Professional Search Engine Optimization with ASP.NET: A Developer's Guide to SEO* aims to illustrate how to build that foundation.

To get the most out of this journey, you should be familiar with a bit of web programming (ideally, with ASP.NET and C#). Some of the examples also use databases, so a bit of experience with SQL Server 2005 would also be very useful. You can also get quite a bit out this book by only reading the explanations. And another strategy to reading this book is to do just that — then hand this book to the web developer with a list of concerns and directives in order to ensure the resulting product is search engine optimized. In that case, don't get bogged down in the exercises — just skim them.

We cover a quick introduction to SEO in Chapter 2, which should nail down the foundations of that subject. However, ASP.NET, C#, and SQL Server are vast subjects; and this book cannot afford to teach them. The code samples are explained step by step, but if you have never built an ASP.NET application, or have never written an SQL command before, you should consider reading a tutorial for these technologies, such as the following:

❑ *Build Your Own ASP.NET 2.0 Web Site Using C# & VB* by Cristian Darie and Zak Ruvalcaba (Sitepoint, 2006)

❑ *Beginning ASP.NET 2.0* by Chris Hart & co. (Wiley Publishing, Inc., 2005)

SEO and the Site Architecture

A web site's architecture is what grounds all future search engine marketing efforts. The content rests on top of it, as shown in Figure 1-2. An optimal web site architecture facilitates a search engine in traversing and understanding the site. Therefore, creating a web site with a search engine optimized architecture is a major contributing factor in achieving and maintaining high search engine rankings.

Architecture should also be considered throughout a web site's lifetime by the web site developer, alongside other factors such as aesthetics and usability. If a feature of a web site does not permit a search engine to access the content, hinders it, or confuses it, the effects of good content may be reduced substantially. For example, a web site that uses Flash or AJAX technologies inappropriately may obscure the majority of its content from a search engine.

We do not cover copywriting concepts in detail, or provide much coaching as to how to create persuasive page titles. These are also very important topics, which are masterfully covered by Bryan and Jeffrey Eisenberg in *Persuasive Online Copywriting: How to Take Your Words to the Bank* (Wizard Academy Press, 2002), and by John Caples and Fred E. Hahn in *Tested Advertising Methods, 5th edition* (Prentice Hall, 1998). Shari Thurow also has an excellent section on creating effective titles in her book, *Search Engine Visibility, 2nd edition* (New Riders Press, 2007). Copy and titles that rank well are obviously not really successful if they do not convert or result in click-throughs, respectively. We do give some pointers, though, to get you started.

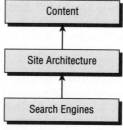

Figure 1-2

We also do not discuss concepts related to search engine optimization such as usability and user psychology in depth, though they are strong themes throughout the book.

Optimizing a site's architecture frequently involves tinkering with variables that also affect usability and the overall user perception of your site. When we encounter such situations, we alert you to why these certain choices were made. Chapter 5, "Duplicate Content," highlights a typical problem with breadcrumbs and presents some potential solutions. Sometimes we find that SEO enhancements run counter to usability. Likewise, not all designs that are user friendly are search engine friendly. Either way, a compromise must be struck to satisfy both kinds of visitors — users and search engines.

SEO Cannot Be an Afterthought

One common misconception is that search engine optimization efforts can be made after a web site is launched. This is frequently incorrect. Whenever possible, a web site can and should be designed to be search engine friendly as a fundamental concern.

Unfortunately, when a preexisting web site is designed in a way that poses problems for search engines, search engine optimization can become a larger and more difficult task. If a web site has to be redesigned, or even partially redesigned, the migration process frequently necessitates special technical considerations. For example, if URLs are changed, old URLs must be *properly* redirected to new ones with similar relevant content.

The majority of this book documents best practices for design from scratch as well as how to mitigate redesign problems and concerns. The rest is dedicated to discretionary enhancements.

Communicating Architectural Decisions

The aforementioned scenario regarding URL migration is a perfect example of how the technical team and marketing team must communicate. The programmer must be instructed to add the proper redirects to the web application. Otherwise, existing search rankings may be hopelessly lost forever. Marketers must know that such measures must be taken in the first place.

In a world where organic rankings contribute to the bottom line, a one-line redirect command in a web server configuration file may be much more important than one may think. This particular topic, URL migration, is discussed in Chapter 4.

Architectural Minutia Can Make or Break You

So you now understand that small mistakes in implementation can be quite insidious. Another common example would be the use of JavaScript-based navigation, and failing to provide an HTML-based alternative. Spiders would be lost, because they, for the most part, do not interpret JavaScript.

The search engine spider is "the third browser." Many organizations will painstakingly test the efficacy and usability of a design in Internet Explorer and Firefox with dedicated QA teams. *Unfortunately, many fall short by neglecting to design and test for the spider.* Perhaps this is because you have to design in the abstract for the spider; we don't have a Google spider at our disposal after all, and we can't interview it afterwards with regard to what it thought of our "usability." However, that does not make its assessment any less important.

The Spider Simulator tool located at http://www.seochat.com/seo-tools/spider-simulator/ shows you the contents of a web page from the perspective of a hypothetical search engine. The tool is very simplistic, but if you're new to SEO, using it can be an enlightening experience.

Preparing Your Playground

This book contains many exercises, and all of them assume that you've prepared your environment as explained in the next few pages. You will install the following applications:

❑ Visual Web Developer 2005 Express Edition. This is a free and powerful tool from Microsoft that you can use to develop ASP.NET 2.0 web sites. It includes features such as IntelliSense (Microsoft's code auto-completion technology), code formatting, database integration with the ability to design databases visually, debugging, and much more. All the features of Visual Web Developer are also supported by the more complex (and expensive) Visual Studio 2005 — so you can use that one instead if you have access to it.

❑ SQL Server 2005 Express Edition is the free, but fully functional version of SQL Server 2005, Microsoft's RDBMS (Relational Database Management System) product. It is a powerful database server that we'll use to store the data for our applications in this book that require database functionality.

❑ SQL Server Management Studio Express is a free SQL Server management interface. Although you can also interact with your databases using Visual Web Developer, using SQL Server Management Studio Express is preferable because its interface has been built solely for the purpose of working with SQL Server databases.

After installing the necessary software, you'll learn how to configure IIS (Internet Information Services) and the seoasp web site. All exercises you build in this book will be accessible on your machine through http://seoasp/. We'll create a simple test page in this application to ensure that your machine has been installed and configured properly.

Lastly, you'll prepare a SQL Server database named seoasp, which will be required for a few of the exercises in this book. The database isn't a necessity right now, so you can leave this task for when you'll actually need it in an exercise.

Installing Visual Web Developer 2005 Express Edition

Install Visual Web Developer 2005 Express Edition by following these simple steps:

1. Browse to http://msdn.microsoft.com/vstudio/express/vwd/.

2. Click the Download Now link. In the new page, click Download. You'll download a file named vwdsetup.exe.

3. Execute the downloaded file.

4. Accept the default options. At one moment you'll be asked about installing Microsoft MSDN 2005 Express Edition, which is the product's documentation. It wouldn't hurt to install it, but you need to be patient, because it's quite big. You will also be offered the option to install SQL

Server 2005 Express. If you choose to do so, you can skip the following section on installing the database server, except for the steps where you're instructed to install product updates.

5. Install the Visual Web Developer Service Pack 1. This is a separate download that can be found on the Visual Web Developer downloads page.

If you use Windows Vista, you should install the Service Pack 1 for Windows Vista.

6. Start Visual Web Developer to ensure it installed correctly. Its welcome screen should look similar to Figure 1-3.

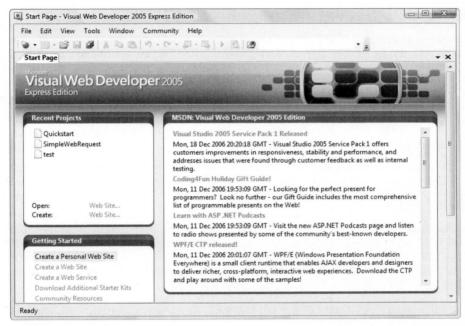

Figure 1-3

Installing SQL Server 2005 Express Edition

Install SQL Server 2005 Express Edition by following these steps:

1. Navigate to `http://msdn.microsoft.com/vstudio/express/sql/` and click the Download Now link.

2. You can choose between SQL Server 2005 Express Edition and SQL Server 2005 Express Edition with Advanced Services. In this book we won't use any of the advanced services from the second package, so either package would do the job.

3. Click Download. You'll download an installer file called `SQLEXPR.EXE`.

4. Execute the file and follow the steps to install the product. It's safe to use the default options all the way through.

5. Provided that everything goes well, at the end of the installation you will have a new SQL Server 2005 instance up and running, named `(local)\SqlExpress`.

> If you're using Windows Vista, you must also install SQL Server 2005 Service Pack 2, which solves the authentication-related problems that occur in Vista. Find it at `http://www.microsoft.com/sql/downloads/2005/default.mspx`. After installing the service pack, reboot your system or start the SQL Server 2005 process manually.

Installing SQL Server Management Studio Express

In order to use your SQL Server 2005 instance effectively, you'll need some sort of administration tool to work with your databases. SQL Server Management Studio Express is a free tool provided by Microsoft that allows you to manage your instance of SQL Server 2005. To install it, follow these steps:

1. Navigate again to `http://msdn.microsoft.com/vstudio/express/sql/` and click the Download Now link.

2. Download the SQL Server Management Studio Express edition that corresponds to the SQL Server 2005 version that you installed previously.

3. After the download completes, execute the file and follow the steps to install the product.

Installing IIS

IIS (Internet Information Services) is the web server included by Microsoft in its server-capable Windows versions. These are Windows Vista Business, Windows XP Professional, Windows XP Media Center Edition, Windows 2000 Professional, Server, Advanced Server, and Windows Server 2003, but it's not installed automatically in all versions. IIS isn't available (and can't be installed) with Windows XP Home Edition, Windows Vista Home Basic, or Windows Vista Home Premium.

To follow the examples in the book, you can use either IIS, or the web server included in Visual Web Developer 2005 — Cassini. Whenever possible, we suggest that you use IIS, because this resembles more accurately the environment in which an ASP.NET application would run on a web server.

To install IIS under Windows XP, follow these steps:

1. In the Control Panel, select Add or Remove Programs.

2. Choose Add/Remove Windows Components (in Windows XP).

3. In the list of components, select Internet Information Services, then click the Details button and make sure the IIS Frontpage Extensions node is checked.

4. Click Next or OK. Windows may prompt you to insert the Windows CD or DVD.

5. The final step involves configuring ASP.NET with IIS. Start a command-line console (Start ➪ Run ➪ cmd), and type the following commands:

```
cd C:\Windows\Microsoft.NET\Framework\v2.0.50727
aspnet_regiis.exe -i
```

Installing IIS under Windows Vista is a little bit different:

1. In the Control Panel, select Programs and Features.

2. Choose Turn Windows features on or off.

3. In the list of components, check Internet Information Services. Then select the following options:

- ❑ World Wide Web Services ⇨ Application Development Features ⇨ ASP.NET

- ❑ Web Management Tools ⇨ IIS 6 Management Compatibility, and the IIS Metabase and IIS 6 configuration compatibility and IIS 6 WMI Compatibility sub-nodes

- ❑ World Wide Web Services ⇨ Security ⇨ Windows Authentication

Figure 1-4 shows these settings.

4. Click OK.

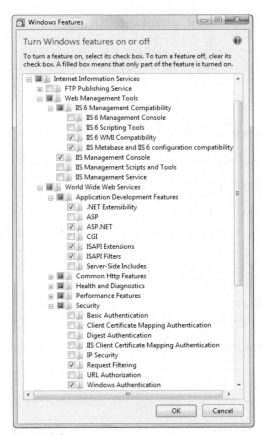

Figure 1-4

Creating the seoasp Web Site

To keep your hard drive tidy, we'll use a single web application for all the exercises in this book, which will be located in the C:\seoasp\ folder. (Of course, you can use a different folder or location if you prefer.) We'll cover the web application setup steps for Windows Vista and Windows XP.

IIS 7 in Windows Vista supports multiple root web sites on the same web server, so we'll create a web site called http://seoasp/, which will point to the C:\seoasp\ folder that you create for your application. This way, your new web site will not interfere with the existing http://localhost/.

IIS in Windows XP doesn't support multiple web sites, so we'll modify the http://localhost/ web site to point to the C:\seoasp\ folder that you create. For Windows XP we chose not to use a different host name (as in http://seoasp/) to avoid some common web site authentication problems. For the examples in the upcoming chapters, if using Windows XP, you should reference the web server using http://localhost/, not http://seoasp/.

Windows Vista: Creating the seoasp Application

If you're running Windows Vista, follow these steps to prepare your seoasp web site.

1.   First, you need to add the seoasp host to the Windows hosts file. This will tell Windows that all domain name resolution requests for seoasp should be handled by the local machine instead of your configured DNS. Open the hosts file, which is located by default in C:\Windows\System32\drivers\etc\hosts, and add this line to it:

```
127.0.0.1        localhost
::1              localhost
127.0.0.1        seoasp
```

2.   Next, create a folder named seoasp on C:\.

3.   Open the IIS Manager tool from the Administrative Tools section of the Control Panel. Browse to the Default Web Site by navigating in the Connections tab, or by clicking the ViewWeb Sites link in the Actions tab — see Figure 1-5.

4.   Right-click the Web Sites node, and select Add Web Site... from the context menu.

5.   Type **seoasp** for the Web site name and for Host header, and C:\seoasp for its Physical path. Then click Select... and choose the Classic .NET AppPool. In the end, the Add Web Site dialog should look like Figure 1-6. Then click OK.

6.   The seoasp web site will show up as a child node under the Web Sites node. Select the seoasp node, double-click the Authentication icon, and enable Windows Authentication.

Congratulations! Your work is now done here. Feel free to close the IIS Manager.

Figure 1-5

Figure 1-6

Windows XP: Preparing the seoasp Web Application

1. Create a folder named seoasp in C:\.

2. Open the Internet Information Services tool from the Administrative Tools section of the Control Panel. Expand the node of your local computer, and then expand the Web Sites node, as shown in Figure 1-7.

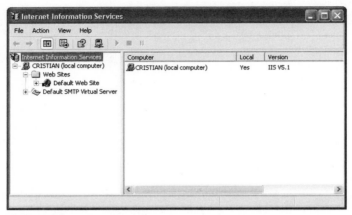

Figure 1-7

3. Right-click the Default Web Site node and select Properties.

4. Select the Home Directory tab and click the Browse button.

5. On the dialog window that shows up, select the C:\seoasp\ folder that you created earlier and click OK.

Congratulations! Your work is now done here. Feel free to close the Internet Information Services tool.

Creating the seoasp Web Application

Here we'll create the seoasp web application at http://seoasp/ (if you're using Windows Vista), or http://localhost/ (if you're using Windows XP). If you decided to use Visual Web Developer's integrated web server (Cassini), at step 2 you'll need to select File System in the Location tab, and load your application from the file system rather than through the web server (IIS).

1. Start Visual Web Developer.

> **If you're using Windows Vista with the User Account Control feature activated, you'll need to run Visual Web Developer as Administrator.**

2. Select File ⇨ New Web Site…. Leave the default ASP.NET Web Site template selected, and change the Location to the web location you've set up for your application — this should be

either **http://seoasp/** or **http://localhost/**. In this book we'll use Visual C# for the language, so be sure the language option is correctly selected, as shown in Figure 1-8. (Should your favorite language be Visual Basic .NET, the code should be reasonably simple to translate.)

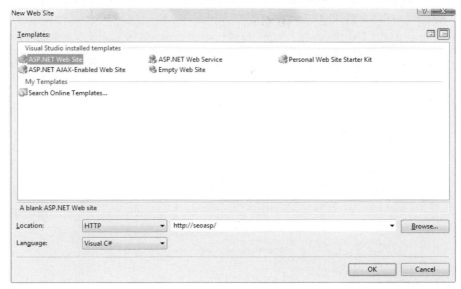

Figure 1-8

> All the application screenshots in this book have been taken using Windows Vista and the `http://seoasp/` web location. You may need to adjust the web location depending on your specific setup.

3. After you click OK, Visual Web Developer will create a new project at the selected location. The initial window looks like that shown in Figure 1-9.

4. Modify the default content of `Default.aspx` like this:

```
<html xmlns="http://www.w3.org/1999/xhtml" >
<head runat="server">
  <title>Professional Search Engine Optimization with ASP.NET</title>
</head>
<body>
  <form id="form1" runat="server">
  <div>
    Welcome to Professional Search Engine Optimization with ASP.NET: A Developer's
Guide to SEO!
  </div>
  </form>
</body>
</html>
```

5. To ensure your system is properly configured to run and debug your project, hit **F5**. This is the default keyboard shortcut for the Start Debugging command, which means it starts your project in debug mode. The first time you start the project with debugging, Visual Web Developer will offer to create a configuration file for you (named Web.config), and activate the option that enables debugging for you — see Figure 1-10.

6. After you click OK, the default browser of your system will be launched to load your web application at http://seoasp/, as shown in Figure 1-11. (No matter what your preference is regarding web browsers, we generally recommend that you use Internet Explorer when you need to debug ASP.NET applications, because of the browser's tight integration with Visual Web Developer.)

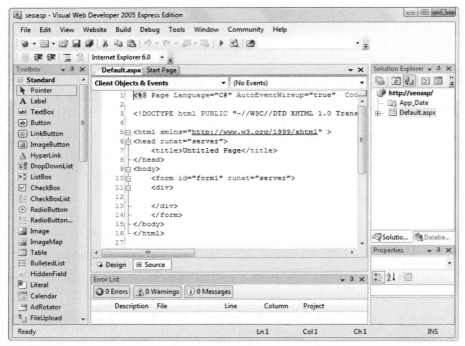

Figure 1-9

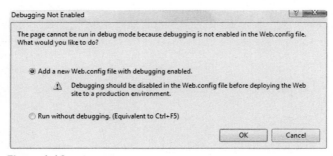

Figure 1-10

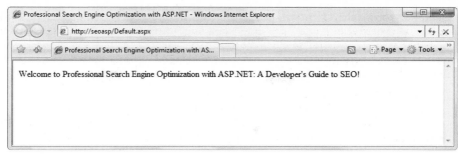

Figure 1-11

Congratulations! If your page loaded successfully, you're ready to move on. If you encountered any errors, verify that you have correctly followed all the steps of the exercises, and that your machine is configured correctly.

Creating the seoasp SQL Server Database

The final task for this chapter is to test your SQL Server 2005 installation, and create a database named seoasp.

You will be using this database only for the exercises in Chapter 11 and Chapter 14, so you can skip this database installation for now if desired.

As mentioned earlier, it is possible to use Visual Web Developer to connect to your SQL Server 2005 instance. However, we prefer to use SQL Server Management Studio Express, because it's more powerful and better suited for certain database operations. Follow these steps:

1. Start SQL Server Manager Express from Start ➪ Programs ➪ Microsoft SQL Server 2005 ➪ SQL Server Management Studio Express.

> **If you're using Windows Vista with the User Account Control service activated, you'll need to run the program using administrator privileges.**

2. When executed, it will first ask for your credentials, as shown in Figure 1-12.

3. By default, when installed, SQL Server 2005 will only accept connections through Windows Authentication, meaning that your Windows user account will be used for logging in. Because you're the user that installed SQL Server 2005, you will already have full privileges to the instance. Click Connect to connect to your SQL Server 2005 instance. After connecting to SQL Server, you'll be shown an interface that offers you numerous ways to manage your server and databases — see Figure 1-13.

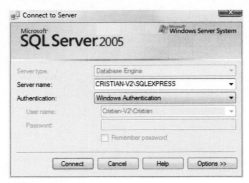

Figure 1-12

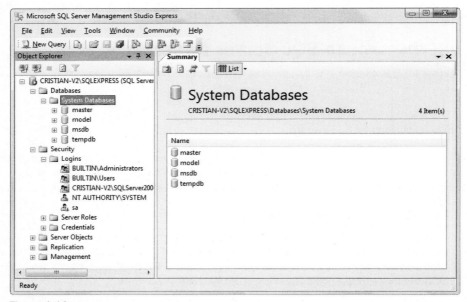

Figure 1-13

4. By default, SQL Server only allows connections using Windows Authentication, which uses the credentials of your logged-in Windows user — this is the method that you've just used to connect to your server using the SQL Server Management Studio. In most real-world scenarios, you'll connect to the database using a SQL Server user ID and password, and we'll use this method in our examples as well. To enable SQL Server authentication, right-click the root node in the Object Explorer window and select Properties. In the dialog that appears, select the Security page, and select the SQL Server and Windows Authentication mode, as shown in Figure 1-14.

5. Click OK to save the change. You'll be notified that you may need to restart SQL Server in order for the change to take effect. You can do so now by right-clicking the server node (the root node) in the Object Explorer pane and selecting Restart.

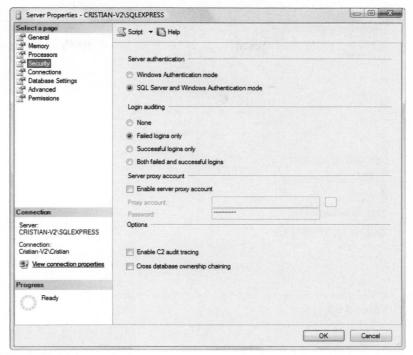

Figure 1-14

6. Let's create the `seoasp` database now. Right-click the Databases node and choose New Database.... Type **seoasp** for the name of the new database, and leave all the options to their defaults, as shown in Figure 1-15.

7. After clicking OK, the new database will be created. The last task is to create a SQL Server user name, which will have access to our newly created database. Using the system administrator account (sa by default) is not indicated. Expand the Security ⇨ Logins node in Object Explorer, right-click the Logins node, and select New Login....

8. In the dialog that shows up, select SQL Server authentication and type seouser for the user name and seomaster for the password. Unselect the Enforce password policy, Enforce password expiration, and User must change password at the next login checkboxes. Though these options are very important to be selected in a real-world scenario, we're deactivating them for our exercises in this book. Finally, change the Default database to **seoasp**. The required settings are described in Figure 1-16.

9. We want our new user to have full access to the `seoasp` database. This can be done after creating the user, but we can also do it from the New Login window. Select User Mapping from the Select a page pane, check the seoasp table from the list, and check the db_owner role, as shown in Figure 1-17. This will give your seouser login permissions to do all the necessary tasks on the `seoasp` database.

10. Click OK, and wait for your user to be created.

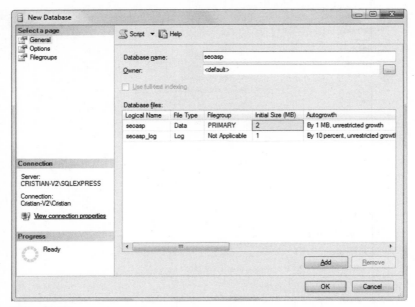

Figure 1-15

Figure 1-16

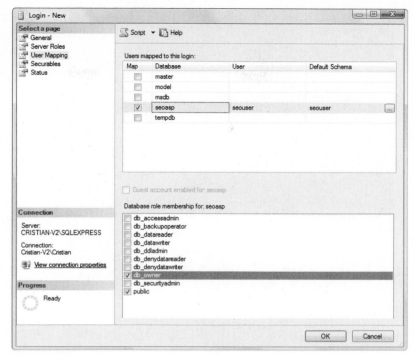

Figure 1-17

That's it for now! To test that your new user was created successfully, you can restart the SQL Server Management Studio, and log in using SQL Server authentication, and the seouser login name with the seomaster password. This time you won't be allowed to create new users, or perform other administrative tasks — instead, you'll have full privileges only to the seoasp database, which is exactly what we want. You'll meet SQL Server Management Studio and our database again in Chapters 11 and 14.

Summary

Congratulations; and thank you for having the patience to go through the boring, but necessary setup tasks. You've installed many powerful software products, and even worked with them a little bit — but you'll have a lot more fun in the next chapters, we promise! The next chapter takes you through a quick SEO tutorial, and builds the foundation for the chapters to come.

2

A Primer in Basic SEO

Although this book addresses search engine optimization primarily from the perspective of a web site's architecture, you, the web site developer, may also appreciate this handy reference of basic factors that contribute to site ranking. This chapter discusses some of the fundamentals of search engine optimization.

If you are a search engine marketing veteran, feel free to skip to Chapter 3. However, because this chapter is relatively short, it may still be worth a skim. It can also be useful to refer back to it, because our intent is to provide a brief guide about what does matter and what probably does not. This will serve to illuminate some of the recommendations we make later with regard to web site architecture.

This chapter contains, in a nutshell:

❑ A short introduction to the fundamentals of SEO.

❑ A list of the most important search engine ranking factors.

❑ Discussion of search engine penalties, and how you can avoid them.

❑ Using web analytics to assist in measuring the performance of your web site.

❑ Using research tools to gather market data.

❑ Resources and tools for the search engine marketer and web developer.

Introduction to SEO

Today, the most popular tool that the users employ to find products and information on the web is the search engine. Consequently, ranking well in a search engine can be very profitable. In a search landscape where users rarely peruse past the first or second page of search results, poor rankings are simply not an option.

> **Search engine optimization aims to increase the number of visitors to a web site from unpaid, "organic" search engine listings by improving rankings.**

Knowing and understanding the exact algorithms employed by a search engine would offer an unassailable advantage for the search engine marketer. However, search engines will never disclose their proprietary inner workings — in part for that very reason. Furthermore, a search engine is actually the synthesis of thousands of complex interconnected algorithms. Arguably, even an individual computer scientist at Google could not know and understand everything that contributes to a search results page. And certainly, deducing the exact algorithms is impossible. There are simply too many variables involved.

Nevertheless, search engine marketers are aware of several ranking factors — some with affirmation by representatives of search engine companies themselves. There are positive factors that are generally known to improve a web site's rankings. Likewise, there are negative factors that may hurt a web site's rankings. Discussing these factors is the primary focus of the material that follows in this chapter.

> *You should be especially wary of your sources in the realm of search engine optimization. There are many snake oil salesmen publishing completely misleading information. Some of them are even trying to be helpful — they are just wrong. One place to turn to when looking for answers is reputable contributors on SEO forums. A number of these forums are provided at the end of this chapter.*

Many factors affect search engine rankings. But before discussing them, the next section covers the concept of "link equity," which is a fundamental concept in search engine marketing.

Link Equity

Without links, the World Wide Web would just be a collection of unrelated documents. Links provide structure and provide both implicit and explicit information in the aggregate. For example, if a web page is linked from many web sites, it usually implies that it is a more important page than one that has fewer incoming links. Moreover, if the anchor text of those links contains the word "cookie," this indicates to search engines that the cited page is about cookies.

Links assign value to web pages, and as a result they have a fundamental role in the search engine optimization. This book frequently references a concept called *URL equity* or *link equity*. Link equity is defined as the equity, or value, transferred to another URL by a particular link. For clarity, we will use the term *link equity* when we refer to the assigning or *transferring* of equity, and *URL equity* when we refer to the actual equity contained by a given URL.

Among all the factors that search engines take into consideration when ranking web sites, link equity has become paramount. It is also important for other reasons, as we will make clear. Link equity comes in the following forms:

1. **Search engine ranking equity.** Modern search engines use the quantity and quality of links to a particular URL as a metric for its quality, relevance, and usefulness. A web site that scores well in this regard will rank better. Thus, the URL contains an *economic* value in tandem with the content that it contains. That, in turn, comprises its URL equity. If the content is moved to a new URL, the old URL will eventually be removed from a search engine index. However, doing so alone will

not result in transference of the said equity, unless all the incoming links are changed to target the new location on the web sites that contain the links (needless to say, this is not likely to be a successful endeavor). The solution is to inform the search engines about the change using redirects, which would also result in equity transference. Without a proper redirect, there is no way for a search engine to know that the links are associated with the new URL, and the URL equity is thusly entirely lost.

2. **Bookmark equity.** Users will often bookmark useful URLs in their browsers, and more recently in social bookmarking web sites. Moving content to a new URL will forgo the traffic resulting from these bookmarks unless a redirect is used to inform the browser that the content has moved. Without a redirect, a user will likely receive an error message stating that the content is not available.

3. **Direct citation equity.** Last but not least, other sites may cite and link to URLs on your web site. That may drive a significant amount of traffic to your web site in itself. Moving content to a new URL will forgo the traffic resulting from these links unless a redirect is used to inform the browser that the content has moved.

Therefore, before changing any URLs, log files or web analytics should be consulted. One must understand the value in a URL. Web analytics are particularly useful in this case because the information is provided in an easy, understandable, summarized format. If a URL must be changed, one may want to employ a 301-redirect. This will transfer the equity in all three cases. Redirects are discussed at length in Chapter 4, "Content Relocation and HTTP Status Codes."

Google PageRank

PageRank is an algorithm patented by Google that measures a particular page's importance relative to other pages included in the search engine's index. It was invented in the late 1990s by Larry Page and Sergey Brin. PageRank implements the concept of link equity as a ranking factor.

> **PageRank considers a link to a page as a vote, indicating importance.**

PageRank approximates the likelihood that a user, randomly clicking links throughout the Internet, will arrive at that particular page. A page that is arrived at more often is likely more important — and has a higher PageRank. Each page linking to another page increases the PageRank of that other page. Pages with higher PageRank typically increase the PageRank of the other page more on that basis. You can read a few details about the PageRank algorithm at http://en.wikipedia.org/wiki/PageRank.

To view a site's PageRank, install the Google toolbar (http://toolbar.google.com/) and enable the PageRank feature, or install the SearchStatus plugin for Firefox (http://www.quirk.biz/searchstatus/). One thing to note, however, is that the PageRank indicated by Google is a cached value, and is usually out of date.

> **PageRank values are published only a few times per year, and sometimes using outdated information. Therefore, PageRank is not a terribly accurate metric. Google itself is likely using a more current value for rankings.**

PageRank is just one factor in the collective algorithm Google uses when building search results pages (SERPs). It is still possible that a page with a lower PageRank ranks above one with a higher PageRank for a particular query. PageRank is also relevance agnostic, in that it measures overall popularity using links, and not the subject shrouding them. Google currently also investigates the relevance of links when calculating search rankings, therefore PageRank should not be the sole focus of a search engine marketer. Building relevant links will naturally contribute to a higher PageRank. Furthermore, building too many irrelevant links solely for the purpose of increasing PageRank may actually hurt the ranking of a site, because Google attempts to detect and devalue irrelevant links that are presumably used to manipulate it.

PageRank is also widely regarded by users as a trust-building factor, because users will tend to perceive sites with a high value as more reputable or authoritative. Indeed this is what PageRank is designed to indicate. This perception is encouraged by the fact that Google penalizes spam or irrelevant sites (or individual pages) by reducing or zeroing their PageRank.

Google PageRank isn't the only link-related ranking algorithm, but it is one of the most popular. Other algorithms include:

- The Hilltop algorithm (`http://www.cs.toronto.edu/~georgem/hilltop/`)
- ExpertRank of Ask.com (`http://about.ask.com/en/docs/about/ask_technology.shtml`)
- HITS (`http://en.wikipedia.org/wiki/HITS_algorithm`)
- TrustRank (`http://en.wikipedia.org/wiki/TrustRank`)

A Word on Usability and Accessibility

Web site usability is defined as the ease of use exhibited by a web site. Web site accessibility addresses the same concerns, but focuses on those users who have impairments such as limited vision or hearing. The search engine marketer can analogize usability and accessibility as "user optimization."

Having a web site that ranks well is paramount. But the search engine is only one of the consumers of a web site's contents, and your users must also appreciate your web site once they arrive. Developers especially tend to ignore this factor, and they often cower in fear when they hear words like "usability" and "accessibility." Kim Krause Berg of *The Usability Effect* (`http://www.usabilityeffect.com`) suggests an explanation:

> *"This is because, and they [developers] are not alone in this belief, they fear someone is about to put some serious limitations on their work. Graphic artists often react the same way."*

As a hybrid developer and search engine marketer, you must have a wiser reaction. The implementation of a web site must incorporate search engine optimization concerns, as well as usability and accessibility concerns. Where interests conflict, a careful compromise must be struck. "User optimization" must not be forgotten.

Sometimes search engine optimization and usability concerns coincide; other times they hopelessly clash. Ultimately, your users will appreciate attention to usability and accessibility in the form of more conversions. If you want more information on this subject, Steve Krug's *Don't Make Me Think, 2nd edition* (New Riders Press, 2005) is a classic that covers these concepts in detail. *Prioritizing Web Usability* (New

Riders Press, 2006) by Jakob Nielsen and Hoa Loranger is also a great book, addressing the areas where usability problems typically present themselves.

Search Engine Ranking Factors

The algorithms used by Google, Yahoo!, or MSN Live Search to calculate search results can change at any time, therefore we generally avoid citing specific details regarding particular search engines and their algorithms. Search engines have been known to occasionally modify their algorithms and, as a result, turn the SERPs upside down. Examples of this include Google's Florida and BigDaddy updates. A great place to peruse to see the latest trends are the forums mentioned at the end of this chapter.

Historically, search engine marketers created optimized pages for each particular search engine. This is no longer viable, as mentioned in Chapter 1, because it yields duplicate content. Rankings must be achieved in all search engines using the same web pages. Furthermore, calculations such as "optimal keyword density" and "optimal page content length" for the various search engines are almost entirely obsolete. Calculations like these demonstrate a gross oversimplification of modern search engine information retrieval algorithms.

With these disclaimers out of the way, it is time to briefly discuss the most important and consistently considered factors as a quick primer for the web site developer. We group the factors that affect search engine rankings into the following general categories:

- ❑ Visible on-page factors
- ❑ Invisible on-page factors
- ❑ Time-based factors
- ❑ External factors

> You can find a great synopsis of the relevance of the various factors, in the opinion of a number of various experts, at `http://www.seomoz.org/articles/search-ranking-factors.php`.

On-Page Factors

On-page factors are those criteria of a web page that are dictated by the contents of a web page itself. They are critical to a search engine marketing campaign, but less so than they were historically, because they are very easy to manipulate. Because there are obvious incentives for spammers to do so, search engines have begun to place importance on other factors as well. That is *not* to say that on-page factors are not important, however.

It is useful to further divide on-page factors into two categories — those that are visible and those that are invisible. The former are much more important than the latter. Many search engine marketers believe that the latter are now devalued to the extent that they are mostly not worth bothering with. This is because they can be so easily manipulated without influencing page presentation at all. Spam can be carefully hidden in a web page in this way. A search engine's confidence in such factors being honest or accurate, therefore, is low. In short, the search engine's algorithms regard visible content with more confidence, because the user will actually see this content.

> Any content that is hidden using CSS or other forms of subterfuge, regardless of intent, may be regarded as an invisible factor and devalued. At worst, if employed excessively, the page or site may be penalized as a whole.
>
> Note, however, that in the context of an ASP.NET application this shouldn't be confused with the `Visible` property of controls, or with other forms of hiding content at server-side. Content that is hidden this way isn't sent to the client at all, which makes it effectively invisible for the web spider.

Visible On-Page Factors

The visible on-page factors covered here are the following:

- ❑ Page title
- ❑ Page headings
- ❑ Page copy
- ❑ Outbound links
- ❑ Keywords in URLs and domain name
- ❑ Internal link structure and anchors
- ❑ Overall site topicality

Page Title

The page title is a string of text, defined by contents of the `<title>` element in the `<head>` section of the HTML document. The title is visible both in the title bar of a browser window, as well as the headline of a search engine result. It is arguably one of the most important factors in search engine optimization because it is both an important factor in search engine rankings, as well as a critical call to action that can enhance the click-through rate (CTR). Vanessa Fox of Google states "Make sure each page has a descriptive `<title>` tag and headings. The title of a page isn't all that useful if every page has the same one."

> *One of the biggest mistakes web developers make is to set the title for all pages on a web site to the same generic text. Frequently, this text is the company name and/or a slogan. In this case, at best your pages will be indexed poorly. At worst, the site could receive a penalty if the search engines see the pages as duplicate content. Be sure all pages on a dynamic site have unique and relevant titles.*

When writing titles, it is also wise to insert some targeted keywords. You should not lose sight, however, that a title is also a call to action. Even if a title successfully influences a search engine to rank a page highly, that ranking effectiveness is then multiplied by your CTR. Keyword stuffed titles are not always effective for CTR, though they may rank well. As a reminder, these keywords should also appear in the document's copy.

People will also frequently use a page title for the anchor text of an inbound link. Anchor text is an important off-page factor, and its beneficial effect is discussed later in this chapter.

Page Headings

Page headings are sections of text set off from web page copy to indicate overall context and meaning. They are usually larger in size than the other copy within the document. They are typically created using <Hx> tags in HTML, where x is a number between 1 and 6. They have been abused in the past to manipulate search rankings, but they are still an important on-page factor, and they also serve to help the user navigate a page.

Page Copy

It is intuitively clear that a page that contains the keywords that a user is looking for should be relevant to his or her search query. Search engine algorithms take this into account as well. Keyword insertion, however, should not be done in the excess. Mentioning the keywords in various inflections (plural, singular, past, present, and so on) is likely beneficial, as well as varying word order ("chocolate chip cookies" versus "cookies with chocolate chips"). Excessive and contrived keyword repetition — "keyword stuffing" — however, could actually be perceived as spam.

> *Because the search engine algorithms are unknown, "excessive" is an unfortunately vague qualifier. This is one of the times we will reference something requisitely in an imprecise manner.*

SEO copywriting aims to produce content on a web site in such a way that it reads well for the surfer, but also targets specific search terms in search engines. It is a process that legitimately, without the use of spamming techniques, seeks to achieve high rankings in the search engines. SEO copywriting is an art, and it takes time to master. There is no magic solution that will make it easy to create copy that is persuasive, contains relevant keywords a few times, and sounds like it is not contrived specifically to do so. There are a few tricks, and a few useful hints, however.

> *One of our favorite tricks is to use the end and beginning of a sentence to repeat a keyword subtly. Example: "Miami Hotels: You may want to try one of our fine hotels in **Miami. Hotel** accommodations at the Makebelieve Hotel will exceed your wildest expectations."*

The copy should also contain words that are related, but not necessarily inflections of your targeted key phrase. For example, a search engine algorithm would likely see a page on cookies that also contains the words "chocolate chip" or "cakes" as relevant. This tends to happen naturally with well-written prose, but it is worth mentioning.

Outbound Links

Search engines will evaluate the links that a document contains. A related link on a web page is valuable content in and of itself, and is treated as such by search engines. However, links to totally irrelevant or spam content can potentially hurt the rankings of a page. Linking to a "bad neighborhood" of spam sites or even lots of irrelevant sites can hurt a site's rankings.

Keywords in Page URL and Domain Name

It is likely that keywords contained by a URL, both in the domain name or in the file name, do have a minor but apparent positive effect on ranking. It also likely has an effect on CTR because keywords in the URL may make a user more likely to click a link due to an increase in perceived relevance. The URL, like the page title, is also often selected as the anchor text for a link. This may have the same previously mentioned beneficial effect.

Internal Link Structure and Anchors

Search engines may make the assumption that pages not linked to, or buried within a web site's internal link structure are less important, just as they assume that pages that are not linked well from external sources are less important than those that are. Linking from the home page to content that you would like to rank can improve that page's rankings, as well as linking to it from a sitemap and from various related content within the site. This models real-world human behavior as well. Popular products are often prominently featured in the front of a store.

One horrible way to push pages down the link hierarchy is to implement pagination using "< prev" and "next >" links, without linking directly to the individual pages. Consider the example of the fourth page of an article that is split into four parts. It is reached like this:

Home Page ⇨ Article Part 1 ⇨ Article Part 2 ⇨ Article Part 3 ⇨ Article Part 4

This fourth page is harder to reach not only by humans (who need to click at least four times), but also by search engines, which would probably consider the content in that page as less important. We call the effect of this link structure "death by pagination," and we suggest two possible approaches for mitigating the problem:

1. Don't use simple pagination. Page with "< prev" and "next >" links, but also add links to the individual pages, that is, "< prev 1 2 3 4 next >." This creates a better navigation scheme to all pages.

2. Add a sitemap with links to all the pages.

This technique is also demonstrated in the e-commerce case study in Chapter 14. You learn more about sitemaps in Chapter 9.

Overall Site Topicality

The fact that a web page is semantically related to other pages within a web site may boost the rankings of that particular page. This means other related pages linked within a site may be used to boost the rankings of the web site as a whole. This tends to happen naturally when writing quality content for a web site regardless.

Invisible On-Page Factors

Invisible on-page factors are, as you correctly guessed, parts of a web page that are not visible to the human readers. They can be read, however, by a search engine parsing a web site. Invisible page factors include:

❑ Meta description

❑ Meta keywords

❑ Alt and title attributes

❑ Page structure considerations

Meta Description

For the most part, the importance of a meta description lies in the fact that search engines may choose to use it in the SERPs, instead of displaying relevant bits from the page (this is not guaranteed, however). Speaking from a marketing point of view, this may improve CTR. A meta description may also have a minor effect on search engine rankings, but it is definitely not a critical factor in that regard. Here is an example:

```
<head>
  <meta name="description" value="The secrets to baking fresh, chewy chocolate chip
cookies that make you wish thousands of calories were actually good for you!" />
  ...
</head>
```

Meta Keywords

This criterion is widely regarded as totally unimportant because it is completely invisible and subject to manipulation. It is wise to place a few major keywords as well as their misspellings in the meta keywords tag, but the effectiveness of targeting misspellings this way has been disputed:

```
<head>
  <meta name="keywords" value="chocolate chip cookies, baking chocolate chip
cookies, choclate, cokies" />
  ...
</head>
```

Alt and Title Attributes

Because these tags are mostly invisible, they are likely not an important ranking factor. Many assert that their value is higher on hyperlinked images. They are important, however, for screen readers and text-based browsers — that is, for accessibility and usability in general, so they should not be ignored for that reason alone. Neither of these attributes will make or break you, but blind visitors using screen readers will thank you in any case. This is a case where accessibility, usability, and search engine optimization coincide. The descriptions should be short. Keyword stuffing in an `alt` tag will irk blind users using screen readers, and possibly "irk" the search engines as well. Alt tags can only be used in image tags, whereas title attributes can be used in most tags. Here is an example of the `alt` attribute in an image:

```
<img src="/images/chocolate_chip_cookie.jpg" alt="a picture of a really big
chocolate chip cookie">
```

And the `title` attribute on a link:

```
<a href="/chocolate_chip_cookie.html" title="a really big chocolate chip cookie">
```

Page Structure Considerations

Search engines use block-level elements, for example `<div>`, `<p>`, or `<table>` elements to group related text. Using block-level elements indiscriminately for layout, as illustrated in the following example, may be harmful:

```
<div>Dog</div>
<div>food</div> is likely to be less relevant than:
<div>dog food</div>.
```

Time-Based Factors

Try as you might, but the only criterion that cannot be manipulated in any way is time. Old men and women are often sought for their knowledge and experience. And the price of wine is directly proportional to its age for a reason.

This is a useful analogy. Because time cannot be cheated, an old site that slowly accumulates links over time and regularly adds new knowledge is what we term "fine wine." Search engines tend to agree, and give the deserved credit to such fine wines.

Many users previously purchased expired domain names that used to house an older popular web site in the interest of tricking search engines into thinking a site is not new. Search engines are now aware of this practice and reset the "aging-value" of any site that is housed by an expired domain name, as well as devalue its preexisting links. In fact, there may also be a penalty applied to such expired domain names, as discussed later in this chapter in the section "The Expired Domain Penalty." There are still opportunities, however, in buying domains directly from users with old existing web sites.

The time-based factors that are used as ranking factors are the site and page age, and the age of the links referring to it. The registration length of a domain name may also influence rankings.

Site and Page Age

A web site that has existed for many years is likely to rank better than a new site, all other variables held constant. Over time, a web site that gradually adds valuable content acquires trust. This models human behavior as well — a shopper is more likely to shop at a store that has existed for many years and provided good service than a new store with no reputation at all.

Likewise, a page that has existed for a long time may rank better, both because it probably acquired links over the years, and because search engines may consider age a factor on the page level as well. There are some conflicting views on this, however, and many also suggest changing and updating content on a page over time as well, because it indicates that the site is active and includes fresh content.

Link Age

Links that are present on other sites pointing to a web site acquire more value over time. This is another instance of the "fine wine" analogy. Over time, a link actually appreciates in value.

Domain Registration Length

Search engines may view a long domain name registration as an indication that a web site is not engaging in spam. Domain names are relatively inexpensive on a yearly basis, and spammers frequently use them in a disposable fashion. The domains eventually get permanently banned and must be abandoned. A search engine spammer would typically not register a domain name for more than one year, because registering for more than that disrupts the economics of spamming. Search engines are aware of this. Therefore, if possible, it may be wise to register your domain name for more than one year. It certainly cannot hurt.

External Factors

Many external factors can influence the search engine rankings of a web site. The following pages discuss these:

- ❏ Quantity, quality, and relevance of inbound links
- ❏ Link churn
- ❏ Link acquisition rate
- ❏ Link anchor text and surrounding copy
- ❏ Reciprocal links
- ❏ Number of links on a page
- ❏ Semantic relationships among links on a page
- ❏ IP addresses of cross-linked sites
- ❏ TLD of domain name for a link
- ❏ Link location
- ❏ Web standards compliance
- ❏ Detrimental "red-flag" factors

Quantity of Inbound Links

A site with many inbound links is likely to be relevant because many people voted for it by placing the link on their sites. There are some caveats here with regard to whether the links are detected to be part of an artificial link scheme, and quality is also a concern as explained in the next section. However, more is generally better.

Quality of Inbound Links

A popular web site that links to you prominently that itself has many inbound links and a good reputation is likely to mean more than a link from a random page from an unimportant web site with few links. There is no absolute definition that describes "quality." Search engines themselves struggle with this definition and use very complicated algorithms that implement an approximation of the human definition. Use your judgment and intuition.

There are certain exceptions to this rule, as MySpace.com (or other similar social web sites with user-generated content) may have many links pointing to it as a whole, but a link, even from a popular MySpace profile sub page may not yield the results that would seem reasonable from a direct interpretation of link popularity. The same may also be true for Blogger.com blogs and other subdomain-based sites. This may be because search engines treat such sites as exceptions to stem artificial manipulation.

Relevance of Inbound Links

A search engine is likely to view a link from a semantically related web page or site as more valuable than a link from a random unrelated one. Usually, a series of links with very similar anchor text from unrelated sources is an indicator of an artificial link scheme, and they may be devalued. Too many links from irrelevant sources may result in a penalty. This has led to speculation that competitors can hurt your web site by pointing many such links to your web site. Google states in its Webmaster Help Center, however, that there is "almost nothing a competitor can do to harm your ranking or have your site removed from our index" (`http://www.google.com/support/webmasters/bin/answer.py?answer=34449`). The verdict is out on MSN Live Search, as documented at `http://www.seroundtable.com/archives/006666.html`.

Link Churn

Links that appear and disappear on pages are likely to be part of a linking scheme. The rate at which these links appear and disappear is termed "link churn." If this happens frequently, it may be regarded as spam. Those links will either be devalued, or at worst your web site will be regarded as spam and penalized. Unless you are participating in such a scheme, this should probably not be a concern.

Link Acquisition Rate

An algorithm may view the acquisition of many thousands of links by a new site as suspicious, if not also accompanied by relevant highly ranked authority sites. Usually this is an indicator of a linking scheme. This consideration was affirmed by Google engineer Matt Cutts in one of his videos at `http://www.mattcutts.com/blog/more-seo-answers-on-video/`.

Link Anchor Text and Surrounding Copy

Inbound links that contain semantically related anchor text to the content they point to have a positive effect on rankings. The copy surrounding the link, if present, may also do the same. Some even posit that this copy is as important as the link anchor text itself. Links with such surrounding copy are widely believed to be valued more by search engines, because links without copy surrounding it are frequently purchased and/or less indicative of a vote.

> *Manipulating link anchor text and the surrounding copy, if done en masse, can be used to manipulate search results by creating a phenomenon called "Google bombing"* (`http://en.wikipedia.org/wiki/Google_bomb`). *One popular example of this is illustrated, at the time of writing, with a query to Yahoo!, Google, or MSN, with the keyword "miserable failure." The top result is the White House's official biographical page for President George W. Bush, which doesn't contain either of the words "miserable" or "failure" in the copy, but is linked from many sites that contain the words "miserable failure." This particular Google bomb, and a few related ones, are described at* `http://en.wikipedia.org/wiki/Miserable_failure`.

Reciprocal Links

A long time ago, webmasters used to trade links strategically to achieve radical improvements in rankings. This created an artificial number of self-serving votes. Over time, search engines became wiser and they devalued such reciprocal links. In response, search engine marketers created link-exchanging schemes with multiple parties to avoid detection. Modern search engines can detect such simple subterfuge as well. That is not to say that reciprocal linking is bad, but it should be balanced by several one-way links as well. The combination of the two models something more natural-looking and will result in higher ranking.

Number of Links on a Page

A link on a page with few outbound links is generally worth more than a link on a page with many outbound links. This concept is also implied by the formula for Google's PageRank.

Semantic Relationship among Links on a Page

A search engine may assume that a page with many links to pages that are not semantically related is a links page, or some sort of page designed to manipulate rankings or trade links. It is also believed that even naming a page with the word "links" in it, such as `links.aspx`, may actually devalue links contained within that particular page.

IP Addresses of Cross-Linked Sites

It is sometimes useful to think of an IP address as you do a phone number. For this example's sake, format a hypothetical phone number, (123) 555-1212, differently — as if it were an IP:

```
123.555.1212
```

The first number, 123, is the area code, the second, 555, is the exchange, and the third, 1212, is the number within that exchange. The numbers go from most significant to least significant. 123 probably indicates "somewhere in this or that state." 555 means "some county in the state," and so on. So we can assert that the person answering the phone at 123.555.1212 is in the same neighborhood as 123.555.1213.

Likewise, IP addresses located in the same C class — that is, addresses that match for the first three octets (`xxx.xxx.xxx.*`) — are very likely to be nearby, perhaps even on the same server.

When sites are interlinked with many links that come from such similar IP addresses, they will be regarded suspiciously, and those links may be devalued. For example, a link from `domainA` on `100.100.1.1` to `domainB` on `100.100.1.2` is a link between two such sites. Done excessively, this can be an indicator for artificial link schemes meant to manipulate the rankings of those web sites. Matt Cutts affirms that Google scrutinizes this sort of interlinking in his video at `http://www.mattcutts.com/blog/seo-answers-on-google-video/`.

Perhaps you host quite a few sites with similar themed content for whatever reason, and do not wish to worry about this. There are a few vendors that offer hosting in multiple C classes. We don't have experience working with any of these providers, and do not make any recommendations. This is just a list of hosting services that we've found that offer this particular service. Many of them also offer custom nameserver and netblock information.

- ❑ `http://www.dataracks.net/`
- ❑ `http://www.gotwebhost.com/`
- ❑ `http://www.seowebhosting.net/`
- ❑ `http://www.webhostforseo.com/`

TLD of Domain Name for a Link

It is widely believed that `.edu` and `.gov` domain names are less susceptible to manipulation and therefore weighed more heavily. This is disputed by some search engine marketers as the actual factor, and they assert that the same effect may be as a result of the age (most schools and governmental agencies have had sites for a while), and amount of links that they've acquired over time. Matt Cutts coincides with this view (http://www.mattcutts.com/blog/another-two-videos/). It is mostly irrelevant, however, what the underlying reason is. Getting a link from a site that fits this sort of profile is very desirable — and most .edu and .gov domains do.

Link Location

Links prominently presented in content near the center of the page may be regarded by the search engines as more important. Links embedded in content presented near the bottom of a page are usually less important; and external links at the bottom of a page to semantically unrelated sites may, at worst, be a criterion for spam-detection. Presentation location is different than *physical* location. The physical location within the document was historically important, but is less of a factor more recently. Ideally, the primary content of a page should be early in the HTML source of a web page, as well as prominently displayed in the center region of a web page. More on this topic is discussed in Chapter 6, "SE-Friendly HTML and JavaScript."

Web Standards Compliance

Standards compliance and cleanliness of code is historically unimportant, but the recent accessibility work may eventually make it become a small ranking factor. That said, Matt downplays it because 40% of the web doesn't validate (http://www.mattcutts.com/blog/more-seo-answers-on-video/). Content on google.com itself does not validate, at the moment of writing this text. You can use the W3C Markup Validation Service at http://validator.w3.org/ to test your web pages for compliance.

Detrimental "Red-Flag" Factors

Obviously writing spammy content, launching thousands of spammy doorway pages simultaneously, or soliciting spammy links that actually get detected as such are detrimental in nature, but we will not continue in that vein. Some of these factors are discussed in more detail in Chapter 8, "Black Hat SEO."

Potential Search Engine Penalties

A penalized web site is much less likely to show up in a SERP, and in some cases it may not appear at all. This section discusses the following:

- ❏ The Google "sandbox effect"
- ❏ Expired domain penalty
- ❏ Duplicate content penalty
- ❏ The Google supplemental index

The Google "Sandbox Effect"

Many search engine optimization experts hypothesize that there is a virtual "purgatory" that all newly launched sites must pass through in order to rank well in Google. In fact, many new sites seem to pass through this stage, and many find that the period is remarkably close to six months. Matt Cutts states in an interview with Barry Schwartz that there may be "things in the algorithm that may be perceived as a sand-box that doesn't apply to all industries" (http://www.seroundtable.com/archives/002822.html).

We believe that while Google may not explicitly have a "sandbox," the effect itself is real. For this reason it is termed an "effect," and not a "penalty." It may be the collective side effect of several algorithms — not an explicit "sandbox algorithm." Some sites seem to be exceptions to the rule, especially those that acquire links from several authority sites early on. A few links from CNN.com and other prominent web sites, for example, may exempt a web site from the sandbox effect.

Some hypothesize that Yahoo! has a similar algorithmic factor, but that it is less severe and pronounced. MSN Search does not appear to have anything similar implemented.

The Expired Domain Penalty

Using a previously expired domain to launch a new web site used to evade this dreaded "sandbox effect." This was likely because Google was unaware that the site was new. Google put a stop to this loophole a while ago, and now it seems to be quite the opposite situation at times.

An expired domain name may now be subject to a temporary penalty. This is important, because it implies an additional delay before a site begins to rank well. In some cases Google will even refuse to index the pages at all during that period, leaving a web site vulnerable to content theft. Content theft is discussed at length in Chapter 5, "Duplicate Content."

It is also likely that Google devalues any links that are acquired before the re-registration of the domain. At the time of writing, other search engines do not appear to penalize previously expired domains.

Duplicate Content Penalty

Search engines attempt to avoid indexing multiple copies of the same content — duplicate content. Many search engine optimization experts hypothesize that not only does a search engine not index such pages, but it also penalizes a site for having the duplicated content.

This is a subject of much debate, but in any case, having duplicate content will not improve the rankings of a site in any of the major search engines. Therefore, duplicate content should be avoided, and this book devotes an entire chapter to the subject.

The Google Supplemental Index

This is not strictly a penalty in and of itself, but it may be the result of one. Google stores its crawled search data in two indexes: the primary index and the *supplemental index*. The supplemental index stores pages that are less important to Google for whatever reason. Results from the supplemental index typically appear at the end of the results for a Google query (unless the query is very specific), and the results are marked as supplemental results.

Figure 2-1 shows how a supplemental result is denoted in a Google search results page. Factors that lead to inclusion of that link in the supplemental index rather than the primary index are the lack of signifi-cant unique content or a lack of inbound links to the said content. It may also be as a result of explicit penalization.

Figure 2-1

Resources and Tools

There are many tools, web sites, and practices that serious search engine marketers must be aware of. As a web developer concerned with SEO, you should also be knowledgeable of at least the most important of them. The rest of this chapter highlights a few such resources that can be helpful in your search engine marketing quest.

Web Analytics

Web analytics measure traffic and track user behavior on a particular web site. Typically web analytics are used for the purpose of optimizing business performance based on various metrics such as conversion rate and return on investment. They are particularly relevant for tracking return on investment for PPC advertising, where there is a particular cost for each click. However, they are also used to track which keywords from organic traffic are leading to conversions. This informs the search engine marketer which key phrases he or she should target when performing search engine optimization — both to improve and to maintain current positioning.

Google Analytics

Google Analytics is a free and robust web service that performs web analytics. It is located at `http://www.google.com/analytics/`. The service is complex enough to merit its own book; feel free to check out *Google Analytics* by Mary E. Tyler and Jerri L. Ledford (Wiley Publishing, Inc., 2006). Figure 2-2 shows one of the many reports Google Analytics can deliver.

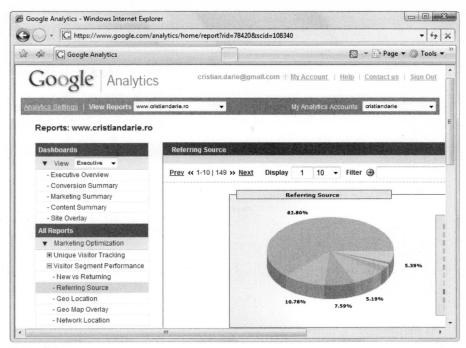

Figure 2-2

Other Web Analytics Tools

Google Analytics is just one of the many analytics tools available today. Here are a few others:

❏ ClickTracks (http://www.clicktracks.com/)

❏ CoreMetrics (http://www.coremetrics.com/)

❏ HitTail (http://www.hittail.com/)

A detailed list of web analytics tools has been aggregated by Carsten Cumbrowski at http://www .cumbrowski.com/webanalytics.html.

Market Research

Just as it is important to know data about your web site, it's equally important to know the market and your competitors. The first skill to learn is how to use the built-in features of the search engines. For example, to find all the pages from http://www.seoegghead.com indexed by Google, Yahoo!, or MSN, you'd need to submit a query for site:www.seoegghead.com. Figure 2-3 shows the results of this query in Google.

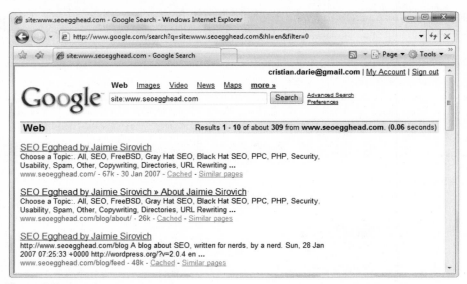

Figure 2-3

Yahoo! Site Explorer

Yahoo! Site Explorer shows what pages of a web site were indexed by Yahoo!, and what other pages link to it. A query of linkdomain:www.cristiandarie.ro brings you to the Yahoo! Site Explorer page shown in Figure 2-4.

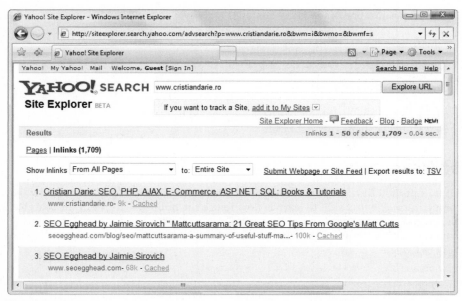

Figure 2-4

Google and MSN Live Search also contain this functionality. It can be accessed in both using the same `linkdomain:` syntax, but at the time of writing they don't provide very accurate information.

Google Trends

Google Trends is a tool from Google that provides the statistics regarding the volume of keyword searches over various time periods. Data are available going back to 2004.

The Google Trends service lets you partition data by language and region and plot multiple key phrases on one graph. This can be used to track and anticipate traffic for a particular period (see Figure 2-5). The service is available at `http://www.google.com/trends`.

Figure 2-5 shows the Google Trends report for "SEO" and "ASP.NET" as of February 2, 2007.

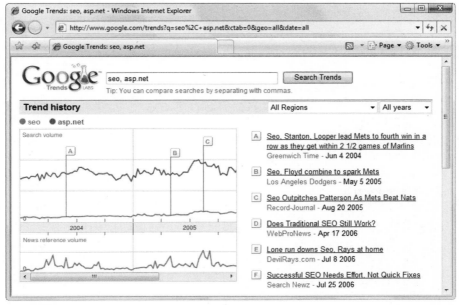

Figure 2-5

Alexa Rankings

Alexa Rankings attempt to rank all web sites globally by quantity of traffic. The traffic rankings use statistics based on data gathered from the Alexa Toolbar and other tools connected to the service. The service is provided by Alexa Internet, a subsidiary of Amazon Incorporated. Yahoo! is ranked number one at the time of this book's writing.

The statistics aren't generally accepted as accurate, and many speculate that the rankings are subject to manipulation and skewing as a result of a limited dataset. In general, the statistics are more accurate with higher ranking sites (those with *lower* numerical rankings). Despite these caveats, Alexa Rankings can be used to get a handle on increasing traffic trends, and they are generally fun to watch.

Figure 2-6 shows the Alexa Rankings page for `http://www.seoegghead.com`, at the date of February 2, 2007.

Figure 2-6

Researching Keywords

Brainstorming keywords that seem relevant to your web site may help to identify keywords to target in a search engine marketing campaign. However, the actual keywords used by web searchers may be surprising more often than not. Fortunately, tools are available that mine available search data and conveniently allow one to peruse both related keywords as well as their respective query volumes. Such services include:

❑   Wordtracker (`http://www.wordtracker.com`)

❑   Keyword Discovery (`http://www.keyworddiscovery.com`)

❑   The Yahoo! Search Marketing Keyword Tool (`http://inventory.overture.com/`)

Both Wordtracker and Keyword Discovery are fee-based tools that tap into various smaller search engines to assemble their data. The latter is a free tool that uses the data from Yahoo! Search Marketing's pay-per-click network; Figure 2-7 shows this tool in action for the keyword "seo."

Because none of these tools are immune to data anomalies — and even deliberate manipulation — it may be wise to use two tools and some intuition to assess whether the data is real. For more information on using keyword research tools effectively, we recommend reading *Search Engine Optimization An Hour a Day* (Wiley Publishing, Inc., 2006) by Jennifer Grappone and Gradiva Couzin.

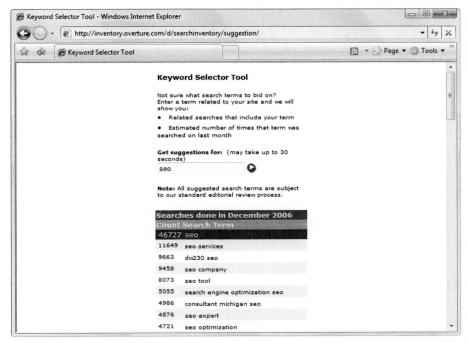

Figure 2-7

Browser Plugins

The Search Engine Marketer may be aided by some Search Engine Optimization tools. Table 2-1 reveals the ones that we've found particularly useful.

Table 2-1

Tool Name	Browser	Web Site	Description
SearchStatus	Firefox	`http://www.quirk.biz/searchstatus/`	This plugin shows both PageRank and Alexa Ranking in the Firefox status bar.

Continued

Table 2-1 (*continued*)

Tool Name	Browser	Web Site	Description
SEO for Firefox	Firefox	`http://www.seobook.com/archives/001741.shtml`	This plugin modifies Google and Yahoo! SERPs to display various metrics regarding a site, such as PageRank, Alexa Ranking, and number of links broken down by several criteria.
Web Developer Extension	Firefox	`http://chrispederick.com/work/webdeveloper/`	A must-have tool for all web developers; the list of features is too long to mention here.
RefControl	Firefox	`http://www.stardrifter.org/refcontrol/`	The plugin lets you control what gets sent as the HTTP REFERER on a per-site basis.
View HTTP Headers	Firefox	`http://livehttpheaders.mozdev.org/`	Displays HTTP headers.
View HTTP Headers	Internet Explorer	`http://www.blunck.info/iehttpheaders.html` or `http://www.blunck.se/iehttpheaders/iehttpheaders.html`	Displays HTTP headers.

Community Forums

There are a few great places where you can ask your SEO-related questions. It is advisable to search and peruse the forum archives before asking questions, because many of them are likely answered already. Table 2-2 shows resources we find consistently helpful.

Table 2-2

Resource	Link
Digital Point Forums	`http://forums.digitalpoint.com/`
Cre8asiteforums	`http://www.cre8asiteforums.com/`
WebmasterWorld Forums	`http://www.webmasterworld.com/`
SearchEngineWatch Forums	`http://forums.searchenginewatch.com/`
Search Engine Roundtable Forums	`http://forums.seroundtable.com/`

Search Engine Blogs and Resources

Table 2-3 lists a number of blogs that are good to read to stay current. You'll discover many more, and eventually make your own list of favorites. This is just *our* list.

Table 2-3

Resource	Link
SearchEngineWatch	http://searchenginewatch.com/
SEO Book	http://www.seobook.com/
Matt Cutts' blog	http://www.mattcutts.com/blog/
Search Engine Roundtable	http://www.seroundtable.com/
ThreadWatch	http://www.threadwatch.org/
SEO Black Hat	http://seoblackhat.com/
Google Blog	http://googleblog.blogspot.com/
Google Blogoscoped	http://blog.outer-court.com/
John Battelle	http://battellemedia.com/
Copyblogger	http://www.copyblogger.com/
Yahoo! Search Blog	http://www.ysearchblog.com/
Carsten Cumbrowski	http://www.cumbrowski.com/
… and let's not forget SEO Egghead	http://www.seoegghead.com

Summary

Although much of what you've read in this chapter is common sense, we are sure you have learned at least a few new things about the factors that influence the rankings of your web site in modern search engines.

Starting with Chapter 3, we're putting on our programmer hats. So put on your hat and grab a can of Red Bull. Lots of technical content is ahead!

3

Provocative SE-Friendly URLs

"**Click me!**" If the ideal URL could speak, its speech would resemble the communication of an experienced salesman. It would grab your attention with relevant keywords and a call to action; and it would persuasively argue that one should choose it instead of the other one. Other URLs on the page would pale in comparison.

URLs are more visible than many realize, and a contributing factor in CTR. They are often cited directly in copy, and they occupy approximately 20% of the real estate in a given search engine result page. Apart from "looking enticing" to humans, URLs must be friendly to search engines. URLs function as the "addresses" of all content in a web site. If confused by them, a search engine spider may not reach some of your content in the first place. This would clearly reduce search engine friendliness.

Creating search engine friendly URLs becomes challenging and requires more forethought when developing a dynamic web site. A dynamic web site with poorly architected URLs presents numerous problems for a search engine. On the other hand, search engine friendly URLs containing relevant keywords may both increase search engine rankings, as well as prompt a user to click them.

This chapter discusses how well-crafted URLs can make the difference between highly ranked web pages and pages at the bottom of the search results. It then illustrates how to generate optimized URLs for dynamic web sites using the various URL-rewriting modules in coordination with application code written in ASP.NET. Lastly, this chapter considers some common caveats — and addresses how to avoid them.

By the end of this chapter you will acquire the skills that will enable you to employ search engine friendly URLs in a dynamic ASP.NET-based web site. More specifically, in the rest of this chapter you will:

❑   Understand the differences between static URLs and dynamic URLs.

❑   Understand the benefits of URL rewriting.

❑ Follow exercises to practice rewriting numeric and keyword-rich URLs, and media file URLs.

❑ Implement URL rewriting using ISAPI_Rewrite, UrlRewriter.NET, HTTP handlers, and HTTP modules.

❑ Learn how to work with regular expressions.

❑ Create a "link factory" class to help you maintain consistency among the URLs in your site.

Why Do URLs Matter?

Many search engine marketers have historically recommended placing relevant keywords in URLs. The original rationale was that a URL's contents are one of the major criteria in search engine ranking.

Over time, this has changed. It is now a less important criterion with regard to search engine ranking. On top of that, dynamic sites make employing such URLs more difficult. That does not mean, however, that creating such URLs with relevant keywords is obsolete and unnecessary!

So let's enumerate all of the benefits of placing keywords in URLs:

1. Doing so still has a small beneficial effect on search engine ranking in and of itself.

2. The URL is roughly 20% of the real estate you get in a SERP result. It functions as a call to action and increases perceived relevance.

3. The URL appears in the status bar of a browser when the mouse hovers over anchor text that references it. Again — it functions as a call to action and increases perceived relevance.

4. Keyword-based URLs tend to be easier to remember than `?ProductID=5&CategoryID=2`.

5. Query keywords, including those in the URL, are highlighted in search result pages.

6. Often, the URL is cited as the actual anchor text, that is:

```
<a href="http://www.example.com/foo.html">http://www.example.com/foo.html</a>
```

Obviously, a user is more likely to click a link to a URL that contains relevant keywords, than a link that does not. Also, because keywords in anchor text *are* a decisive ranking factor, having keywords in the URL-anchor-text *will* help you rank better for "foos."

To sum up these benefits in one phrase:

> **Keyword-rich URLs are more aesthetically pleasing and more visible, and are likely to enhance your CTR and search engine rankings.**

For a real-world example, see Figure 3-1, where I was searching for "Mickey Mouse t-shirt."

Figure 3-1

Static URLs and Dynamic URLs

Initially, the World Wide Web was comprised predominantly of static web sites. Each URL within a web site pointed to an actual physical file located on a web server's file system. Therefore, a search engine spider had very little to worry about. The spider would crawl throughout the web site and index every URL in a relatively straightforward manner. Problems such as duplicate content and spider traps did not typically exist.

Today, dynamic web sites dominate the World Wide Web landscape. Unfortunately, they frequently present problems when one looks at their URLs from a search engine's perspective — especially with regard to spidering.

For example, many dynamic web sites employ query string parameters that generate different URLs that host very similar or identical content. This is interpreted as *duplicate content* by search engines, and this can get the pages penalized. The use of many URL parameters may also result in *spider traps* (http://en .wikipedia.org/wiki/Spider_trap), or in linking structures that are hard to follow by a search engine. Needless to say, both scenarios reduce the web site's ranking performance with the search engines.

Because the web developers reading this book are architecting dynamic sites, these subjects must be examined in depth. And we start by categorizing URLs into two groups based on their anatomy:

❑   Static URLs

❑   Dynamic URLs

Static URLs

Static URLs do *not* include a query string. By this definition, a URL referencing an `.aspx` page *without* parameters is still static. Two examples of static URLs are as follows:

```
http://www.example.com/about-us.html
http://www.example.com/SiteMap.aspx
```

Static URLs — even those generated by an ASP.NET application — typically pose no challenges for a search engine.

Dynamic URLs

Dynamic URLs are those that include a query string, set off by a question mark, `?`. This string is used to pass various parameters to an ASP.NET page. Multiple parameters are delimited by `&` and then appended to the query string. A typical dynamic URL looks like the following:

```
http://www.example.com/Product.aspx?CategoryID=1&ProductID=2
```

In this example, `Product.aspx` is the name of a physical file on a web server. The highlighted section is the query string. When a web browser makes a request to the ASP.NET page with a particular query string, the page may then present differing content based on the various parameters.

> **Because the query string values affect the page contents, a search engine typically considers the same file name with a differing query strings as completely different web pages, despite the fact that those pages originate from the same physical file.**

However, the script does not necessarily have to present different content based on different permutations of the query string — which is the basis of the most common cause of duplicate content. The most trivial example of this is when one adds a parameter that does not change the presented content at all, such as in these examples:

```
http://www.example.com/Product.aspx?ProductID=2&Param=123
http://www.example.com/Product.aspx?ProductID=2&AnotherParam=456
```

Session IDs and various other tracking IDs are two very common culprits. In the worst case, a search engine may not index such URLs at all. Therefore, the use of such parameters should be avoided as much as possible.

Dynamic URLs — especially those with more than two parameters, may pose problems for search engines, due to the increased difficulty ascertaining how to spider the site. Matt Cutts of Google affirms all of this on his blog at `http://www.mattcutts.com/blog/seo-answers-on-google-video/`. Lastly, a dynamic URL may look less appealing or relevant than a well-constructed static URL to a human user.

In some cases, search engines may attempt to eliminate an extra parameter — such as a session-related parameter, and index site URLs without it. Depending on this functionality is neither realistic nor wise, however.

Fortunately, there are many ways to improve URLs with regard to indexability as well as aesthetics. This typically involves eliminating any unnecessary parameters, and/or obscuring the dynamic parameters using keyword-rich static URLs.

The solution to the latter is to use IIS or ASP.NET-specific techniques to map static URLs to dynamic URLs. This is a process called *URL rewriting*, and is detailed later in this chapter.

Dynamic URLs may also benefit from some of the concepts in this chapter, such as using functions to generate URLs to enhance URL consistency, and strategies to reduce the number of parameters — rewritten or not — required for site navigation.

URLs and Duplicate Content

As mentioned earlier, if a search engine establishes that many different URLs in a web site contain the same content, it may not index them at all; in the worst case, if it is done excessively, it may designate the site as a spam site and penalize it.

Unfortunately, many web sites have been "forced" to create duplicate content because of technical considerations and business rules. However, sometimes there are better solutions to these considerations and rules. The concepts of the URLs and duplicate content are intimately related. This chapter and the next discuss the technicalities related to URL rewriting and redirection, and Chapter 5 analyzes the concept of duplicate content.

URLs of the Real World

Before proceeding to write code, let's look at three examples of URLs that you see frequently while browsing, and discuss the technical details involved in creating these URLs. This will help you understand where we're heading, and why you'll write the code from the exercises in this chapter. This section shows examples with:

- ❑ Dynamic URLs
- ❑ Numeric rewritten URLs
- ❑ Keyword-rich URLs

Example #1: Dynamic URLs

Data displayed by dynamic web sites is usually stored in some sort of backend database. Typically, a numeric ID is associated with a data row of a database table, and all database operations with the table (such as selecting, inserting, deleting, or updating rows) are done by referencing that ID.

More often than not, the same ID used to identify an item in the database is also used in ASP.NET code to refer to that particular item — such as a product in an e-commerce web site, or an article of a blog, and so on. In a dynamic URL, these IDs are passed via the query string to a script that presents differing content accordingly.

Figure 3-2 shows a page from `http://www.cristiandarie.ro/BalloonShop/`. This is a demo e-commerce site presented in one of Cristian's books, and employs dynamic URLs. As you can see, the page is composed using data from the database, and the ID that identifies the data item is taken from the dynamic URL.

Figure 3-2

This is probably the most common approach employed by dynamic web sites at present, as you frequently meet URLs such as the following:

- ❏   `http://www.example.com/Catalog.aspx?CatID=1`
- ❏   `http://www.example.com/Catalog.aspx?CatID=2&ProdID=3&RefID=4`

This approach is certainly the easiest and most straightforward when developing a dynamic site. However, this is about the only benefit these URLs bring. Dynamic URLs come with three important potential draw-backs, however:

- ❏   They are frequently sub-optimal from a search engine spider's point of view.
- ❏   They don't provide relevant keywords or a call to action to a human viewing the URL, therefore reducing the CTR.
- ❏   They aren't easy to remember, or communicate to other parties in the offline world.

Some programmers also tend to use extra parameters freely. For example, if the parameter `RefID` from the previous example is used for some sort of tracking mechanism, and search engine friendliness is a priority, it should be removed. Lastly, any necessary duplicate content should be excluded from search engines' view using a `robots.txt` file or a `robots` meta tag (this topic is discussed in Chapter 5).

> If URLs on your site are for the most part indexed properly, it may not be wise to restructure URLs. However, if you decide that you must, please also read Chapter 4, which teaches you how to make the transition smoother. Chapter 4 shows how to preserve link equity by properly redirecting old URLs to new URLs. Also, not all solutions to URL-based problems require restructuring URLs; as mentioned earlier, duplicate content can be excluded using the `robots.txt` file or the `robots` meta tag.

Example #2: Numeric Rewritten URLs

An improved version of the previous example is a modified URL that removes the dynamic parameters and hides them in a static URL. This static URL is then mapped, using one of the techniques you'll learn later, to a dynamic URL. The `RefID` parameter previously alluded to is also not present, because those types of tracking parameters usually can and should be avoided.

- ❏   `http://www.example.com/Products/1/`
- ❏   `http://www.example.com/Products/2/1/`

The impact of numeric URL rewriting will likely be negligible with the search engines on pages with a single parameter, but it may be significant on pages with two parameters or more. For humans, using numeric URLs can be beneficial when the context makes the URLs *hackable*, giving those numbers a special meaning. The best example is with blogs, which are frequently employing numeric URLs to reflect the date of the content; for example, `http://blog.example.com/2007/07/17/` will contain the post or posts from July 17th, 2007.

This form of URL is particularly well-suited to the adaptation of existing software. Retrofitting an application for keyword-rich URLs, as discussed in the next section, may present additional difficulty in implementation.

Example #3: Keyword-Rich Rewritten URLs

Finally, here are two ideal keyword-rich URLs:

```
http://www.example.com/High-Powered-Drill-P1.html
http://www.example.com/Tools-C2/High-Powered-Drill-P1.html
```

This is the best approach to creating URLs, but also presents an increased level of difficulty in implementation — especially if you are modifying preexisting source code for software. In that case this solution may not have an easy and apparent implementation, and it requires more interaction with the database to extract the copy for the URLs.

The decision whether to use the `.html` *suffix in the URL is mostly a non-issue. You could also use a URL such as* `http://www.example.com/High-Powered-Drill-P1/` *if you prefer the look of directories.*

This "ideal" URL presents a static URL that indicates both to the search engine and to the user that it is topically related to the search query. Usually the keyword-rich URLs are created using keywords from the name or description of the item presented in the page itself. Characters in the keyword string that are not alphanumeric need to be removed, and spaces should be converted to a delimiting character. Dashes are desirable over underscores as the delimiting character because most search engines treat the dash as a space, and the underscore as an actual character, though this particular detail is probably not terribly significant. On a new site, dashes should be chosen as a word-delimiter.

Don't Obsess!

Don't get URL-obsessive! Many times, it's not worth removing URLs that have acquired value over time. For example, it would not be recommended to change underscores to dashes in existing URLs in an existing web site, all other things left equal. However, in the initial design phase it would be wise to use the dash rather than the programmer's tendency to prefer the underscore character. The effects of this "optimization" are marginal at best, and changing URLs for marginal gains is not recommended because the side effects may cause more harm than the gains — even if everything is done properly. Use your best judgment when deciding whether to change your current URL structure.

Maintaining URL Consistency

No matter if your URLs are static or dynamic, it's important to maintain consistency. In the case of dynamic URLs, it's important to maintain consistent parameter order in URLs with more than one parameter.

In ASP.NET, the parameters of a query string are typically accessed by name rather than by ordinal. The order in which the parameters appear does not affect the output of the ASP.NET page, unless your script is specifically written to take parameter order into consideration. Here is an example where an ASP.NET web site would generate the exact same content, but using different URLs:

```
http://www.example.com/Catalog.aspx?ProductID=1&CategoryID=2
http://www.example.com/Catalog.aspx?CategoryID=2&ProductID=1
```

If `Catalog.aspx` reads the parameters as `Request.QueryString["ProductID"]` and `Request.QueryString["CategoryID"]`, respectively, these two different URLs would generate the same content. There's no standard specifying that URL parameters are commutative. If both dynamic links are used within the web site, search engines may end up parsing different URLs with identical content, which could get the site penalized.

The programmer should also try to use consistent capitalization on file names and query strings. Search engines resolve such simple differences, especially because file names in Windows are not case sensitive, but the following URLs are technically different in both Windows and Unix operating systems:

```
http://www.example.com/products.aspx?color=red
```

and

```
http://www.example.com/PRODUCTS.ASPX?color=RED
```

Your script may recognize the equivalence of those URLs, but a search engine may not. Again, maintaining a consistent style is desirable. The developer should also try to reference directories in a web site with the trailing "/" consistently. For example, if you're using numeric rewritten URLs, it would be best to avoid referencing a particular product using both of the following links, even if your script can successfully parse them:

```
http://www.example.com/Products/1/
```

and

```
http://www.example.com/Products/1
```

In practice, search engines *can* resolve many of these ambiguities. Matt Cutts asserts that Google can "*do things like keeping or removing trailing slashes, [and try] to convert urls with upper case to lower case*" (http://www.mattcutts.com/blog/seo-advice-url-canonicalization/), but this is only a subset of the aforementioned ambiguities. It is best to remove all of the offending ambiguities regardless.

To enforce consistency as a whole, you can create a function for each type of URL required by a site. Through the logic in that function URLs are consistently formatted. Consistency also makes it easier to exclude files in robots.txt, as the preceding problems having to do with ordering and casing also apply there.

For example, if you're building an e-commerce web site, you could create a function such as the following:

```
public static string CreateLink(int categoryId, int productId)
{
   return "Product.aspx?CategoryID=" + categoryId + "&ProductID=" + productId;
}
```

Calling this function providing 5 and 6 as parameters, it will return Product.aspx?CategoryID=5&ProductID=6. Using this function throughout the web site will ensure all your links follow a consistent format.

This implementation of CreateLink() is overly simplistic and not really useful for real-world scenarios. If you want to improve your URLs more significantly, you need to utilize more advanced functions in coordination with URL rewriting. The benefits of URL consistency will also apply there. So without further ado, let's learn about this subject.

Implementing URL Rewriting

From this moment on, this chapter discusses URL rewriting. Of particular importance is Scott Guthrie's ASP.NET URL rewriting article, which you can read at http://weblogs.asp.net/scottgu/archive/2007/02/26/tip-trick-url-rewriting-with-asp-net.aspx. Another interesting article is "URL Rewriting in ASP.NET" by Scott Mitchell, available at http://msdn2.microsoft.com/en-us/library/ms972974.aspx.

The hurdle we must overcome to support keyword-rich URLs like those shown earlier is that they don't actually exist anywhere in your web site. Your site still contains a script — named, say, Product.aspx —

which expects to receive parameters through the query string and generate content depending on those parameters. This script would be ready to handle a request such as this:

```
http://www.example.com/Product.aspx?ProductID=123
```

but your web server would normally generate a 404 error if you tried any of the following:

```
http://www.example.com/Products/123.html
http://www.example.com/my-super-product.html
```

URL rewriting allows you to transform the URL of such an incoming request (which we'll call the *original URL*) to a different, existing URL (which we'll call the *rewritten URL*), according to a defined set of rules. You could use URL rewriting to transform the previous nonexistent URLs to `Product.aspx?ProductID=123`, which *does* exist.

If you happen to have some experience with the Apache web server, you probably know that it ships by default with the mod_rewrite module, which is the standard way to implement URL rewriting in the LAMP (Linux/Apache/MySQL/PHP) world. That is covered in the PHP edition of this book.

Unfortunately, IIS doesn't ship by default with such a module. IIS 7 contains a number of new features that make URL rewriting easier, but it will take a while until all existing IIS 5 and 6 web servers will be upgraded. Third-party URL-rewriting modules for IIS 5 and 6 do exist, and also several URL-rewriting libraries, hacks, and techniques, and each of them can (or cannot) be used depending on your version and configuration of IIS, and the version of ASP.NET. In this chapter we try to cover the most relevant scenarios by providing practical solutions.

To understand why an apparently easy problem — that of implementing URL rewriting — can become so problematic, you first need to understand how the process really works. To implement URL rewriting, there are three steps:

1. **Intercept the incoming request.** When implementing URL rewriting, it's obvious that you need to intercept the incoming request, which usually points to a resource that doesn't exist on your server physically. This task is not trivial when your web site is hosted on IIS 6 and older. There are different ways to implement URL rewriting depending on the version of IIS you use (IIS 7 brings some additional features over IIS 5/6), and depending on whether you implement rewriting using an IIS extension, or from within your ASP.NET application (using C# or VB.NET code). In this latter case, usually IIS still needs to be configured to pass the requests we need to rewrite to the ASP.NET engine, which doesn't usually happen by default.

2. **Associate the incoming URL with an existing URL on your server.** There are various techniques you can use to calculate what URL should be loaded, depending on the incoming URL. The "real" URL usually is a dynamic URL.

3. **Rewrite the original URL to the rewritten URL.** Depending on the technique used to capture the original URL and the form of the original URL, you have various options to specify the real URL your application should execute.

The result of this process is that the user requests a URL, but a different URL actually serves the request. The rest of the chapter covers several ways to implement each of the preceding steps, including:

❑   URL rewriting with IIS and ISAPI_Rewrite

❑   URL rewriting using URLRewriter

❑   Writing a custom URL rewriting handler

❑   URL rewriting with IIS 7

For background information on how IIS processes incoming requests, we recommend Scott Mitchell's article "How ASP.NET Web Pages are Processed on the Web Server," located at `http://aspnet` `.4guysfromrolla.com/articles/011404-1.aspx`.

URL Rewriting with IIS and ISAPI_Rewrite

If your IIS web server, no matter if it's IIS 5, 6, or 7, has an ISAPI rewriting filter installed, we encourage you to use it, because it's likely to be the most efficient and practical method to implement URL rewriting. When such a filter is used, rewriting happens right when the request hits your web server, before being processed by the ASP.NET ISAPI extension. This has the following advantages:

❑   Simple implementation. Rewriting rules are written in configuration files; you don't need to write any supporting code.

❑   Task separation. The ASP.NET application works just as if it was working with dynamic URLs. Apart from the link building functionality, the ASP.NET application doesn't need to be aware of the URL rewriting layer of your application.

❑   You can easily rewrite requests for resources that are not processed by ASP.NET by default, such as those for image files, for example.

To process incoming requests, IIS works with ISAPI extensions, which are code libraries that process the incoming requests. IIS chooses the appropriate ISAPI extension to process a certain request depending on the extension of the requested file. For example, an ASP.NET-enabled IIS machine will redirect ASP.NET-specific requests (which are those for `.aspx` files, `.ashx` files, and so on), to the ASP.NET ISAPI extension, which is a file named `aspnet_isapi.dll`.

To intercept incoming requests on an IIS 6–based server, you can create your own URL rewriting ISAPI filter or use an existing one. Creating your own ISAPI filter is too complex a process to cover in this book, but fortunately existing products are available:

❑   ISAPI_Rewrite by Helicon Tech (`http://www.isapirewrite.com/`)

❑   ISAPI Rewrite by Ionic — IIRF (`http://cheeso.members.winisp.net/IIRF.aspx`)

❑   IIS Rewrite by QuerkSoft (`http://www.qwerksoft.com/products/iisrewrite/`)

Figure 3-3 describes how an ISAPI Rewrite filter, such as those just listed, fits into the picture. Its role is to rewrite the URL of the incoming requests, but doesn't affect the output of the ASP.NET script in any way.

> **At first sight, the rewriting rules can be added easily to an existing web site, but in practice there are other issues to take into consideration. For example, as we'll show a bit later, you'd also need to modify the existing links within the web site content. In Chapter 4 you continue by learning how to properly redirect old links to the new links in a preexisting web site, to preserve their equity.**

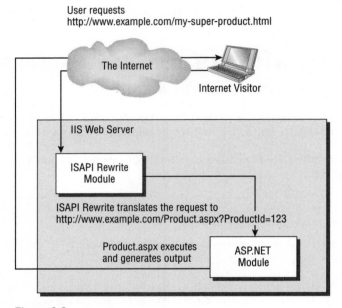

Figure 3-3

ISAPI rewriting filters can be invaluable tools to web developers tasked with architecting complex dynamic sites that are still search engine friendly. They allow the programmer to easily declare a set of rules that are applied by IIS on-the-fly to map incoming URLs requested by the visitor to dynamic query strings sent to various ASP.NET pages. As far as a search engine spider is concerned, the URLs are static.

The following few pages demonstrate URL rewriting functionality by using Helicon's ISAPI_Rewrite filter. You can find its official documentation at http://www.isapirewrite.com/docs/. Ionic's ISAPI rewriting module has similar functionality.

In the first exercise we'll create a simple rewrite rule that translates my-super-product.html to Product.aspx?ProductID=123. This is the exact scenario that was presented in Figure 3-3.

The Product.aspx Web Form is designed to simulate a real product page. The script receives a query string parameter named ProductID, and generates a very simple output message based on the value of this parameter. Figure 3-4 shows the sample output that you'll get by loading http://seoasp/ Product.aspx?ProductID=3.

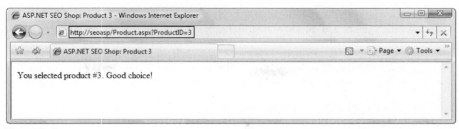

Figure 3-4

In order to improve search engine friendliness, we want to be able to access the same page through a static URL: `http://seoasp/my-super-product.html`. To implement this feature, we'll use — you guessed it! — URL rewriting, using Helicon's ISAPI_Rewrite.

As you know, what ISAPI_Rewrite basically does is to translate an input string (the URL typed by your visitor) to another string (a URL that can be processed by your ASP.NET code). In this exercise we'll make it rewrite `my-super-product.html` to `Product.aspx?ProductID=123`.

> **This book covers ISAPI_Rewrite version 2. At the moment of writing, ISAPI_Rewrite 3.0 is in beta testing. The new version comes with an updated syntax for the configuration files and rewriting rules, which is compatible to that of the Apache mod_rewrite module, which is the standard rewriting engine in the Apache world. Please visit Cristian's web page dedicated to this book,** `http://www.cristiandarie.ro/seo-asp/`**, for updates and additional information regarding the following exercises.**

Using Helicon's ISAPI_Rewrite

1. The first step is to install ISAPI_Rewrite. Navigate to `http://www.helicontech.com/download.htm` and download ISAPI_Rewrite Lite (freeware). The file name should be something like `isapi_rwl_x86.msi`. At the time of writing, the full (not freeware) version of the product comes in a different package if you're using Windows Vista and IIS 7, but the freeware edition is the same for all platforms.

2. Execute the MSI file you just downloaded, and install the application using the default options all the way through.

    If you run into trouble, you should visit the Installation section of the product's manual, at `http://www.isapirewrite.com/docs/#install`*. If you run Windows Vista, you need certain IIS modules to be installed in order for ISAPI_Rewrite to function. If you configured IIS as shown in Chapter 1, you already have everything you need, and the installation of ISAPI_Rewrite should run smoothly.*

3. Make sure your IIS web server is running and open the `http://seoasp/` web site using Visual Web Developer.

4. Create a new Web Form named `Product.aspx` in your project, with no code-behind file or Master Page. Then modify the generated code as shown in the following code snippet. (Remember that you can have Visual Web Developer generate the `Page_Load` signature for you by switching to Design view, and double-clicking an empty area of the page or using the Properties window.)

```
<%@ Page Language="C#" %>
<!DOCTYPE html PUBLIC "-//W3C//DTD XHTML 1.0 Transitional//EN"
"http://www.w3.org/TR/xhtml1/DTD/xhtml1-transitional.dtd">

<script runat="server">
  protected void Page_Load(object sender, EventArgs e)
  {
    // retrieve the product ID from the query string
    string productId = Request.QueryString["ProductID"];

    // use productId to customize page contents
    if (productId != null)
    {
      // set the page title
      this.Title += ": Product " + productId;

      // display product details
      message.Text =
        String.Format("You selected product #{0}. Good choice!", productId);
    }
    else
    {
      // display product details
      message.Text = "Please select a product from our catalog.";
    }

  }
</script>

<html xmlns="http://www.w3.org/1999/xhtml" >
<head runat="server">
  <title>ASP.NET SEO Shop</title>
</head>
<body>
  <form id="form1" runat="server">
    <asp:Literal runat="server" ID="message" />
  </form>
</body>
</html>
```

5. Test your Web Form by loading `http://seoasp/Product.aspx?ProductID=3`. The result should resemble Figure 3-4.

6. Let's now write the rewriting rule. Open the `Program Files/Helicon/ISAPI_Rewrite/httpd.ini` file (you can find a shortcut to this file in Programs), and add the following high-lighted lines to the file. Note the file is read-only by default. If you use Notepad to edit it, you'll need to make it writable first.

```
[ISAPI_Rewrite]
```

```
# Translate /my-super.product.html to /Product.aspx?ProductID=123
RewriteRule ^/my-super-product\.html$ /Product.aspx?ProductID=123
```

7.   Switch back to your browser again, and this time load `http://seoasp/my-super-product`
`.html`. If everything works as it should, you should get the output that's shown in Figure 3-5.

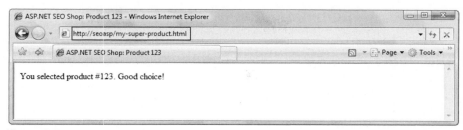

Figure 3-5

Congratulations! You've just written your first rewrite rule using Helicon's ISAPI_Rewrite. The free edition of this product only allows server-wide rewriting rules, whereas the commercial edition would allow you to use an application-specific `httpd.ini` configuration file, located in the root of your web site. However, this limitation shouldn't affect your learning process.

An alternative to Helicon's ISAPI_Rewrite is Ionic's ISAPI Rewrite Filter (IIRF), which is completely free. The URL rewriting syntax isn't similar to that of mod_rewrite, and the product is newer and less-proven. If you don't mind these potential drawbacks, and if you're looking for a completely free IIS rewriting engine, we encourage you test IIRF.

The exercise you've just finished features a very simplistic scenario, without much practical value — at least compared with what you'll learn next! Its purpose was to install ISAPI_Rewrite, and to ensure your working environment is correctly configured.

You started by creating a very simple ASP.NET Web Form that takes a numeric parameter from the query string. You could imagine this is a more involved page that displays lots of details about the product with the ID mentioned by the `ProductID` query string parameter, but in our case we're simply displaying a text message that confirms the ID has been correctly read from the query string.

`Product.aspx` is indeed very simple! It starts by reading the product ID value:

```
protected void Page_Load(object sender, EventArgs e)
{
    // retrieve the product ID from the query string
    string productId = Request.QueryString["ProductID"];
```

Next, we verify if the value we just read is `null`. If that is the case, then `ProductID` doesn't exist as a query string parameter. Otherwise, we display a simple text message, and update the page title, to confirm that `ProductID` was correctly read:

```
    // use productId to customize page contents
    if (productId != null)
    {
        // set the page title
        this.Title += ": Product " + productId;
```

```
          // display product details
        message.Text =
          String.Format("You selected product #{0}. Good choice!", productId);
    }
    else
    {
        // display product details
        message.Text = "Please select a product from our catalog.";
    }
```

URL Rewriting and ISAPI_Rewrite

As Figure 3-3 describes, `Product.aspx` is accessed *after* the original URL has been rewritten. This explains why `Request.QueryString["ProductID"]` reads the value of `ProductID` from the *rewritten* version of the URL. This is helpful, because the script works fine no matter if you accessed `Product.aspx` directly, or if the initial request was for another URL that was rewritten to `Product.aspx`.

The `Request.QueryString` collection, as well as the other values you can read through the `Request` object, work with the rewritten URL. For example, when requesting `my-super-product.html` in the context of our exercise, `Request.RawUrl` will return `/Product.aspx?ProductID=123`.

The rewriting engine allows you to retrieve the originally requested URL by saving its value to a server variable named `HTTP_X_REWRITE_URL`. You can read this value through `Request.ServerVariables["HTTP_X_REWRITE_URL"]`. This is helpful whenever you need to know what was the original request initiated by the client.

The `Request` class offers complete details about the current request. The following table describes the most commonly used `Request` members. You should visit the documentation for the complete list, or use IntelliSense in Visual Web Developer to quickly access the class members.

Server Variable	Description
`Request.RawURL`	Returns a string representing the URL of the request excluding the domain name, such as `/Product.aspx?ID=123`. When URL rewriting is involved, `RawURL` returns the rewritten URL.
`Request.Url`	Similar to `Request.RawURL`, except the return value is a `Uri` object, which also contains data about the request domain.
`Request.PhysicalPath`	Returns a string representing the physical path of the requested file, such as `C:\seoasp\Product.aspx`.
`Request.QueryString`	Returns a `NameValueCollection` object that contains the query string parameters of the request. You can use this object's indexer to access its values by name or by index, such as in `Request.QueryString[0]` or `Request.QueryString[ProductID]`.

Server Variable	Description
Request.Cookies	Returns a NameValueCollection object containing the client's cookies.
Request.Headers	Returns a NameValueCollection object containing the request headers.
Request.ServerVariables	Returns a NameValueCollection object containing IIS variables.
Request.ServerVariables[HTTP_X_REWRITE_URL]	Returns a string representing the originally requested URL, when the URL is rewritten by Helicon's ISAPI_Rewrite or IIRF (Ionic ISAPI Rewrite).

For a visual example of how the predefined server variables are interpreted, see Figure 3-6.

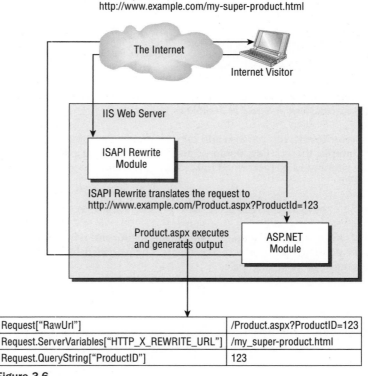

Request["RawUrl"]	/Product.aspx?ProductID=123
Request.ServerVariables["HTTP_X_REWRITE_URL"]	/my_super-product.html
Request.QueryString["ProductID"]	123

Figure 3-6

After testing that `Product.aspx` works when accessed using its physical name (`http://seoasp/Product.aspx?ProductID=123`), we moved on to access this same script, but through a URL that doesn't physically exist on your server. We implemented this feature using Helicon's ISAPI_Rewrite.

As previously stated, the free version of Helicon's ISAPI_Rewrite only supports server-wide rewriting rules, which are stored in a file named `httpd.ini` in the product's installation folder (`\Program Files\Helicon\ISAPI_Rewrite`). This file has a section named `[ISAPI_Rewrite]`, usually at the beginning of the file, which can contain URL rewriting rules.

We added a single rule to the file, which translates requests to `/my-super-product.html` to `/Product.aspx?ProductID=123`. The line that precedes the `RewriteRule` line is a comment; comments are marked using the # character at the beginning of the line, and are ignored by the parser:

```
# Translate my-super.product.html to /Product.aspx?ProductID=123
RewriteRule ^/my-super-product\.html$ /Product.aspx?ProductID=123
```

In its basic form, `RewriteRule` takes two parameters. The first parameter *describes* the original URL that needs to be rewritten, and the second specifies what it should be rewritten to. The pattern that describes the form of the original URL is delimited by ^ and $, which mark the beginning and the end of the matched URL. The pattern is written using *regular expressions*, which you learn about in the next exercise.

In case you were wondering why the `.html` extension in the rewrite rule has been written as `\.html`, we will explain it now. In regular expressions — the programming language used to describe the original URL that needs to be rewritten — the dot is a character that has a special significance. If you want that dot to be read as a literal dot, you need to escape it using the backslash character. As you'll learn, this is a general rule with regular expressions: when special characters need to be read literally, they need to be escaped with the backslash character (which is a special character in turn — so if you wanted to use a backslash, it would be denoted as `\\`).

At the end of a rewrite rule you can also add one or more flag arguments, which affect the rewriting behavior. For example, the `[L]` flag, demonstrated in the following example, specifies that when a match is found the rewrite should be performed immediately, without processing any further `RewriteRule` entries:

```
RewriteRule ^/my-super-product\.html$ /Product.aspx?ProductID=123 [L]
```

These arguments are specific to the `RewriteRule` command, and not to regular expressions in general. Table 3-1 lists the possible `RewriteRule` arguments. The rewrite flags must always be placed in square brackets at the end of an individual rule.

Table 3-1

RewriteRule Option	Significance	Description
I	Ignore case	The regular expression of the `RewriteRule` and any corresponding `RewriteCond` directives is performed using case-insensitive matching.

Table 3-1 (*continued*)

RewriteRule Option	Significance	Description
F	Forbidden	In case the `RewriteRule` regular expression matches, the web server returns a `404 Not Found` response, regardless of the format string (second parameter of `RewriteRule`) specified. Read Chapter 4 for more details about the HTTP status codes.
L	Last rule	If a match is found, stop processing further rules.
N	Next iteration	Restarts processing the set of rules from the beginning, but using the current rewritten URL. The number of restarts is limited by the value specified with the `RepeatLimit` directive.
NS	Next iteration of the same rule	Restarts processing the rule, using the rewritten URL. The number of restarts is limited by the value specified with the `RepeatLimit` directive, and is calculated independently of the number of restarts counted for the N directive.
P	Proxy	Immediately passes the rewritten URL to the ISAPI extension that handles proxy requests. The new URL must be a complete URL that includes the protocol, domain name, and so on.
R	Redirect	Sends a 302 redirect status code to the client pointing to the new URL, instead of rewriting the URL. This is always the last rule, even if the L flag is not specified.
RP	Permanent redirect	The same as R, except the 301 status code is used instead.
U	Unmangle log	Log the new URL as it was the originally requested URL.
O	Normalize	Normalize the URL before processing by removing illegal characters, and so on, and also deletes the query string.
CL	Lowercase	Changes the rewritten URL to lowercase.
CU	Uppercase	Changes the rewritten URL to uppercase.

Also, you should know that although `RewriteRule` is arguably the most important directive that you can use for URL rewriting with Helicon's ISAPI_Rewrite, it is not the only one. Table 3-2 quickly describes a few other directives. Please visit the product's documentation for a complete reference.

Table 3-2

Directive	Description
RewriteRule	This is the directive that allows for URL rewriting.
RewriteHeader	A generic version of `RewriteRule` that can rewrite any HTTP headers of the request. `RewriteHeader URL` is the same as `RewriteRule`.
RewriteProxy	Similar to `RewriteRule`, except it forces the result URL to be passed to the ISAPI extension that handles proxy requests.
RewriteCond	Allows defining one or more conditions (when more `RewriteCond` entries are used) that must be met before the following `RewriteRule`, `RewriteHeader`, or `RewriteProxy` directive is processed.

Introducing Regular Expressions

Before you can implement any really useful rewrite rules, it's important to learn about regular expressions. We'll teach them now, while discussing ISAPI_Rewrite, but regular expressions will also be needed when implementing other URL-related tasks, or when performing other kinds of string matching and parsing — so pay attention to this material.

Many love regular expressions, whereas others hate them. Many think they're very hard to work with, whereas many (or maybe not so many) think they're a piece of cake. Either way, they're one of those topics you can't avoid when URL rewriting is involved. We'll try to serve a gentle introduction to the subject, although entire books have been written on the subject. The Wikipedia page on regular expressions is great for background information (`http://en.wikipedia.org/wiki/Regular_expression`).

> **Appendix A of this book is a generic introduction to regular expressions. You should read it if you find that the theory in the following few pages — which is a fast-track introduction to regular expressions in the context of URL rewriting — is too sparse. For comprehensive coverage of regular expressions we recommend Andrew Watt's** *Beginning Regular Expressions* **(Wiley Publishing, Inc., 2005).**

A regular expression (sometimes referred to as a *regex*) is a special string that describes a text *pattern*. With regular expressions you can define rules that match groups of strings, extract data from strings, and transform strings, which enable very flexible and complex text manipulation using concise rules. Regular expressions aren't specific to ISAPI_Rewrite, or even to URL rewriting in general. On the contrary, they've been around for a while, and they're implemented in many tools and programming languages, including the .NET Framework — and implicitly ASP.NET.

To demonstrate their usefulness with a simple example, we'll assume your web site needs to rewrite links as shown in Table 3-3.

If you have 100,000 products, without regular expressions you'd be in a bit of a trouble, because you'd need to write just as many rules — no more, no less. *You don't want to manage a configuration file with 100,000 rewrite rules!* That would be unwieldy.

Table 3-3

Original URL	Rewritten URL
Products/P1.html	Product.aspx?ProductID=1
Products/P2.html	Product.aspx?ProductID=2
Products/P3.html	Product.aspx?ProductID=3
Products/P4.html	Product.aspx?ProductID=4
...	...

However, if you look at the Original URL column of the table, you'll see that all entries follow the same *pattern*. And as suggested earlier, regular expressions can come to rescue! Patterns are useful because with a single pattern you can match a theoretically infinite number of possible input URLs, so you just need to write a rewriting rule for every *type* of URL you have in your web site.

In the exercise that follows, we'll use a regular expression that matches `Products/Pn.html`, and we'll use ISAPI_Rewrite to translate URLs that match that pattern to `Product.aspx?ProductID=n`. This will implement exactly the rules described in Table 3-3.

Working with Regular Expressions

1. Open the `httpd.ini` configuration file and add the following rewriting rule to it.

```
[ISAPI_Rewrite]

# Defend your computer from some worm attacks
RewriteRule .*(?:global.asa|default\.ida|root\.exe|\.\.).* . [F,I,O]

# Translate my-super.product.html to /Product.aspx?ProductID=123
RewriteRule ^/my-super-product\.html$ /Product.aspx?ProductID=123

# Rewrite numeric URLs
RewriteRule ^/Products/P([0-9]+)\.html$ /Product.aspx?ProductID=$1 [L]
```

2. Switch back to your browser, and load `http://seoasp/Products/P1.html`. If everything works as planned, you will get the output that's shown in Figure 3-7.

3. You can check that the rule really works, even for IDs formed of more digits. Loading `http://seoasp/Products/P123456.html` would give you the output shown in Figure 3-8.

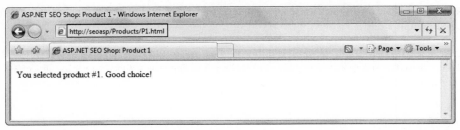

Figure 3-7

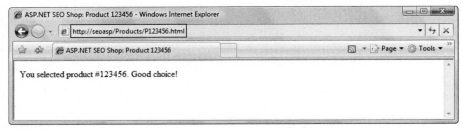

Figure 3-8

Note that by default, regular expression matching is case sensitive. So the regular expression in your `RewriteRule` *directive will match* `/Products/P123.html`, *but will not match* `/products/` `p123.html`, *for example. Keep this in mind when performing your tests. To make the matching case sensitive, you need to use the* `[I]` `RewriteRule` *flag, as you'll soon learn.*

Congratulations! The exercise was quite short, but you've written your first "real" regular expression! Let's take a closer look at your new rewrite rule:

```
RewriteRule ^/Products/P([0-9]+)\.html$ /Product.aspx?ProductID=$1 [L]
```

If this is your first exposure to regular expressions, it must look scary! Just take a deep breath and read on: we promise, it's not as complicated as it looks.

> **Appendix A contains a gentler introduction to regular expressions.**

As you learned in the previous exercise, a basic `RewriteRule` takes two arguments. In our example it also received a special flag — `[L]` — as a third argument. We'll discuss the meaning of these arguments next.

The first argument of `RewriteRule` is a regular expression that describes the *matching* URLs we want to rewrite. The second argument specifies the destination (*rewritten*) URL — this is *not* a regular expression. So, in geek-speak, the `RewriteRule` line from the exercise basically says: "rewrite any URL that *matches* the `^/Products/P([0-9]+)\.html$` pattern to `/Product.aspx?ProductID=$1`." In English, the same line can be roughly read as: "delegate any request to a URL that looks like `/Products/Pn.html` to `/Product.aspx?ProductID=n`."

In regular expressions, most characters, including alphanumeric characters, are read literally and simply match themselves. Remember the first `RewriteRule` you've written in this chapter to match `my-super-product.html`, which was mostly created of such "normal" characters. However, what makes regular expressions so powerful (and sometimes complicated), are the special characters (or *metacharacters*), such as `^`, `.`, or `*`, which have special meanings. Table 3-4 describes the most frequently used metacharacters.

Table 3-4

Metacharacter	Description
`^`	Matches the beginning of the line. In our case, it will always match the beginning of the URL. The domain name isn't considered part of the URL, as far `RewriteRule` is concerned. It is useful to think of `^` as "anchoring" the characters that follow to the beginning of the string, that is, asserting that they be the first part.
`.`	Matches any single character.
`*`	Specifies that the preceding character or expression can be repeated zero or more times — not at all to an infinite number of times.
`+`	Specifies that the preceding character or expression can be repeated one or more times. In other words, the preceding character or expression must match at least once.
`?`	Specifies that the preceding character or expression can be repeated zero or one time. In other words, the preceding character or expression is optional.
`{m,n}`	Specifies that the preceding character or expression can be repeated between *m* and *n* times; *m* and *n* are integers, and *m* needs to be lower than *n*.
`( )`	The parentheses are used to define a *captured expression*. The string matching the expression between parentheses can be then read as a variable. The parentheses can also be used to group the contents therein, as in mathematics, and operators such as `*`, `+`, or `?` can then be applied to the resulting expression.
`[ ]`	Used to define a character class. For example, `[abc]` will match any of the characters a, b, c. The - character can be used to define a range of characters. For example, `[a-z]` matches any lowercase letter. If - is meant to be interpreted literally, it should be the last character before `]`. Many metacharacters lose their special function when enclosed between `[` and `]`, and are interpreted literally.
`[^ ]`	Similar to `[ ]`, except it matches everything except the mentioned character class. For example, `[^a-c]` matches all characters except a, b, and c.
`$`	Matches the end of the line. In our case, it will always match the end of the URL. It is useful to think of it as "anchoring" the previous characters to the end of the string, that is, asserting that they be the last part.

Continued

Table 3-4 (*continued*)

Metacharacter	Description
\	The backslash is used to escape the character that follows. It is used to escape metacharacters when we need them to be taken for their literal value, rather than their special meaning. For example, \. will match a dot, rather than "any character" (the typical meaning of the dot in a regular expression). The backslash can also escape itself — so if you want to match C:\Windows, you'll need to refer to it as C:\\Windows.

Using Table 3-4 as reference, let's analyze the expression ^/Products/P([0-9]+)\.html$. The expression starts with the ^ character, matching the beginning of the requested URL (remember, this doesn't include the domain name). The characters /Products/P assert that the next characters in the URL string match those characters.

Let's recap: the expression ^/Products/P will match any URL that starts with /Products/P.

The next characters, ([0-9]+), are the crux of this process. The [0-9] bit matches any character between 0 and 9 (that is, any digit), and the + that follows indicates that the pattern can repeat one or more times, so we can have an entire number rather than just a digit. The enclosing round parentheses around [0-9]+ indicate that the regular expression engine should store the matching string (which will be a digit or number) inside a variable called $1. (We'll need this variable to compose the rewritten URL.)

Finally, we have \.html$, which means that string should end in .html. The \ is the escaping character that indicates that the . should be taken as a literal dot, not as "any character" (which is the significance of the . metacharacter). The $ matches the end of the string.

The second argument of RewriteRule, /Product.aspx?ProductID=$1, plugs the digit or number extracted by the matching regular expression into the $1 variable. If the regular expression matched more than one string, the subsequent matches could be referenced as $2, $3, and so on. You'll meet several such examples later in this book.

> *The second argument of* RewriteRule *isn't written using the regular expression language. Indeed, it doesn't need to, because it's not meant to match anything. Instead, it simply supplies the form of the rewritten URL. The only part with a special significance here are the variables ($1, $2, and so on) whose values are extracted from the expressions written between parentheses in the first argument of* RewriteRule.

As you can see, this rule does indeed rewrite any request for a URL that looks like /Products/Pn.html to Product.aspx?ProductID=n, which can be executed by our Product.aspx page. The [L] makes sure that if a match is found, the rewriting rules that follow won't be processed.

```
RewriteRule ^/Products/P([0-9]+)\.html$ /Product.aspx?ProductID=$1 [L]
```

This is particularly useful if you have a long list of RewriteRule commands, because using [L] improves performance and prevents ISAPI_Rewrite from processing all the RewriteRule commands that follow once a match is found. This is usually what we want regardless.

Helicon's ISAPI_Rewrite ships with a regular expression tester application, which allows you to verify if a certain rewriting rule matches a test string. The application is named RXTest.exe, and is located in the product's installation folder (by default Program Files\Helicon\ISAPI_Rewrite\).

Rewriting Numeric URLs with Two Parameters

What you've accomplished in the previous exercise is rewriting numeric URLs with one parameter. We'll now expand that little example to also rewrite URLs with two parameters. The URLs with one parameter that we support looks like http://seoasp/Products/Pn.html. Now we'll assume that our links need to support links that include a category ID as well, in addition to the product ID. The new URLs will look like:

```
http://seoasp/Products/C2/P1.html
```

The existing Product.aspx script will be modified to handle links such as:

```
http://seoasp/Product.aspx?CategoryID=2&ProductID=1
```

As a quick reminder, here's the rewriting rule you used for numeric URLs with one parameter:

```
RewriteRule ^/Products/P([0-9]+)\.html$ /Product.aspx?ProductID=$1 [L]
```

For rewriting two parameters, the rule would be a bit longer, but not much more complex:

```
RewriteRule ^/Products/C([0-9]+)/P([0-9]+)\.html$ ↵
/Product.aspx?CategoryID=$1&ProductID=$2 [L]
```

Let's put this to work in a quick exercise.

Rewriting Numeric URLs

1. Modify your Product.aspx page that you created in the previous exercise, like this:

```
<%@ Page Language="C#" %>
<!DOCTYPE html PUBLIC "-//W3C//DTD XHTML 1.0 Transitional//EN"
"http://www.w3.org/TR/xhtml1/DTD/xhtml1-transitional.dtd">

<script runat="server">
  protected void Page_Load(object sender, EventArgs e)
  {
    // retrieve the product ID and category ID from the query string
    string productId = Request.QueryString["ProductID"];
    string categoryId = Request.QueryString["CategoryID"];

    // use productId to customize page contents
    if (productId != null && categoryId == null)
    {
      // set the page title
      this.Title += ": Product " + productId;
```

```
      // display product details
      message.Text =
        String.Format("You selected product #{0}. Good choice!", productId);
    }
    // use productId and categoryId to customize page contents
    else if (productId != null && categoryId != null)
    {
      // set the page title
      this.Title +=
        String.Format(": Product {0}: Category {1}", productId, categoryId);

      // display product details
      message.Text =
        String.Format("You selected product #{0} in category #{1}. Good choice!",
                    productId, categoryId);
    }
    else
    {
      // display product details
      message.Text = "Please select a product from our catalog.";
    }

  }
</script>

<html xmlns="http://www.w3.org/1999/xhtml" >
<head runat="server">
  <title>ASP.NET SEO Shop</title>
</head>
<body>
  <form id="form1" runat="server">
    <asp:Literal runat="server" ID="message" />
  </form>
</body>
</html>
```

2. Test your script with a URL that contains just a product ID, such as `http://seoasp/Products/P123456.html`, to ensure that the old functionality still works. The result should resemble Figure 3-8.

3. Now test your script by loading `http://seoasp/Product.aspx?CategoryID=5&ProductID=99`. You should get the output shown in Figure 3-9.

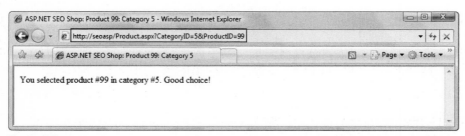

Figure 3-9

4. Add a new rewriting rule to the `httpd.ini` file as shown here:

```
[ISAPI_Rewrite]

# Defend your computer from some worm attacks
RewriteRule .*(?:global.asa|default\.ida|root\.exe|\.\.).* . [F,I,O]

# Translate my-super.product.html to /Product.aspx?ProductID=123
RewriteRule ^/my-super-product\.html$ /Product.aspx?ProductID=123

# Rewrite numeric URLs that contain a product ID
RewriteRule ^/Products/P([0-9]+)\.html$ /Product.aspx?ProductID=$1 [L]

# Rewrite numeric URLs that contain a product ID and a category ID
RewriteRule ^/Products/C([0-9]+)/P([0-9]+)\.html$ ↵
/Product.aspx?CategoryID=$1&ProductID=$2 [L]
```

Note that the entire `RewriteRule` *command and its parameters must be written on a single line in your* `httpd.ini` *file. If you split it in two lines as printed in the book, it will not work.*

5. Load `http://seoasp/Products/C5/P99.html`, and expect to get the same output as with the previous request, as shown in Figure 3-10.

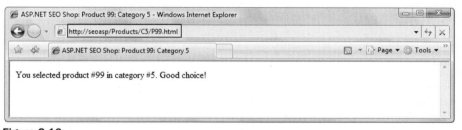

Figure 3-10

In this example you started by modifying `Product.aspx` to accept URLs that accept a product ID and a category ID. Then you added URL rewriting support for URLs with two numeric parameters. You created a rewriting rule to your `httpd.ini` file, which handles URLs with two parameters:

```
RewriteRule ^/Products/C([0-9]+)/P([0-9]+)\.html$ ↵
/Product.aspx?CategoryID=$1&ProductID=$2 [L]
```

The rule looks a bit complicated, but if you look carefully, you'll see that it's not so different from the rule handling URLs with a single parameter. The rewriting rule has now two parameters — `$1` is the number that comes after `/Products/C`, and is defined by `([0-9]+)`, and the second parameter, `$2`, is the number that comes after `/P`.

Figure 3-11 is a visual representation of how this rewrite rule matches the incoming link.

The result is that we now delegate any URL that looks like `/Products/Cm/Pn.html` to `/Product.aspx?CategoryID=m&ProductID=n`.

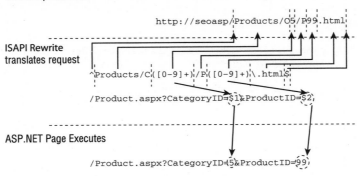

Figure 3-11

Rewriting Keyword-Rich URLs

Here's where the real fun begins! This kind of URL rewriting is a bit more complex, and there are more strategies you could take. When working with rewritten numeric URLs, it was relatively easy to extract the product and category IDs from a URL such as `/Products/C5/P9.html`, and rewrite the URL to `Product.aspx?CategoryID=5&ProductID=9`.

A keyword-rich URL doesn't necessarily have to include any IDs. Take a look at this one:

```
http://www.example.com/Products/Tools/Super-Drill.html
```

(You met a similar example in the first exercise of this chapter, where you handled the rewriting of `http://seoasp/my-super-product.html`.)

This URL refers to a product named "Super Drill" located in a category named "Tools." Obviously, if you want to support this kind of URL, you need some kind of mechanism to find the IDs of the category and product the URL refers to.

One solution that comes to mind is to add a column in the product information table that associates such beautified URLs to "real" URLs that your application can handle. In such a request you could look up the information in the Category and Product tables, get their IDs, and use them. We demonstrate this technique in an exercise later in this chapter.

We also have a solution for those who prefer an automated solution that doesn't involve a lookup database. This solution still brings the benefits of a keyword-rich URL, while being easier to implement. Look at the following URLs:

```
http://www.example.com/Products/Super-Drill-P9.html
http://www.example.com/Products/Tools-C5/Super-Drill-P9.html
```

These URLs include keywords. However, we've sneaked IDs in these URLs, in a way that isn't unpleasant to the human eye, and doesn't distract attention from the keywords that matter, either. In the case of the first URL, the rewriting rule can simply extract the number that is tied at the end of the product name (-P9), and ignore the rest of the URL. For the second URL, the rewriting rule can extract the category ID (-C5) and product ID (-P9), and then use these numbers to build a URL such as `Product .aspx?CategoryID=5&ProductID=9`.

> *This book generally uses such keyword-rich URLs, which also contain item IDs. Later in this chapter, however, you'll be taught how to implement ID-free keyword-rich URLs as well.*

The rewrite rule for keyword-rich URLs with a single parameter looks like this:

```
RewriteRule ^/Products/.*-P([0-9]+)\.html?$ /Product.aspx?ProductID=$1 [L]
```

The rewrite rule for keyword-rich URLs with two parameters looks like this:

```
RewriteRule ^/Products/.*-C([0-9]+)/.*-P([0-9]+)\.html$ ↵
/Product.aspx?CategoryID=$1&ProductID=$2 [L]
```

Let's see these rules at work in an exercise.

Rewriting Keyword-Rich URLs

1. Modify the `httpd.ini` configuration file like this:

```
[ISAPI_Rewrite]

# Rewrite numeric URLs that contain a product ID
RewriteRule ^/Products/P([0-9]+)\.html$ /Product.aspx?ProductID=$1 [L]

# Rewrite numeric URLs that contain a product ID and a category ID
RewriteRule ^/Products/C([0-9]+)/P([0-9]+)\.html$ ↵
/Product.aspx?CategoryID=$1&ProductID=$2 [L]

# Rewrite keyword-rich URLs with a product ID and a category ID
RewriteRule ^/Products/.*-C([0-9]+)/.*-P([0-9]+)\.html$ ↵
/Product.aspx?CategoryID=$1&ProductID=$2 [L]

# Rewrite keyword-rich URLs with a product ID
RewriteRule ^/Products/.*-P([0-9]+)\.html$ /Product.aspx?ProductID=$1 [L]
```

2. Load `http://seoasp/Products/Tools-C5/Super-Drill-P9.html`, and voila, you should get the result that's shown in Figure 3-12.

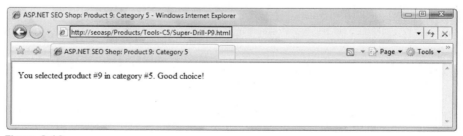

Figure 3-12

3. To test the rewrite rule that matches product keyword-rich URLs that don't include a category, try loading `http://seoasp/Products/Super-Drill-P9.html`. The result should be the expected one.

> There's one interesting gotcha for you to keep in mind when developing web applications, especially when they use URL rewriting. Your web browser sometimes caches the results returned by your URLs — which can lead to painful debugging experiences — so we recommend that you disable your browser's cache during developing.

You now have two new rules in your `httpd.ini` file, and they are working beautifully! The first rule handles keyword-rich URLs that include a product ID and a category ID, and the second rule handles keyword-rich URLs that include only a product ID. Note that the order of these rules is important, because the second rule matches the URLs that are meant to be captured by the first rule. Also remember that because we didn't use the `[I]` flag, the matching is case sensitive.

The first new rule matches URLs that start with the string `/Products/`, then contain a number of zero or more characters (`.*`), followed by `-C`. This is expressed by `^/Products/.*-C`. The next characters must be one or more digits, which as a whole are saved to the `$1` variable, because the expression is written between parentheses — `([0-9]+)`. This first variable extracted from the URL, `$1`, is the category ID.

After the category ID, the URL must contain a slash, then zero or more characters (`.*`), then `-P`, as expressed by `/.*-P`. Afterwards, another captured group follows, to extract the ID of the product, `([0-9]+)`, which becomes the `$2` variable. The final bit of the regular expression, `\.html$`, specifies the URL needs to end in `.html`.

The two extracted values, `$1` and `$2`, are used to create the new URL, `/Product.aspx?CategoryID=$1&ProductID=$2`. Figure 3-13 describes the process visually.

The second rewrite rule you implemented is a simpler version of this one.

This exercise concludes the first part of this chapter. We'll now continue by teaching you how to implement the same functionality using C# code in your ASP.NET web application.

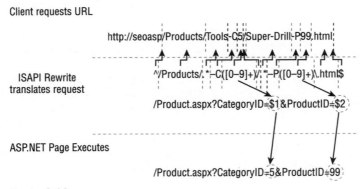

Client requests URL

http://seoasp/Products/Tools-C5/Super-Drill-P99.html

ISAPI Rewrite translates request

`^/Products/.*-C([0-9]+)/.*-P([0-9]+)\.html$`

`/Product.aspx?CategoryID=$1&ProductID=$2`

ASP.NET Page Executes

`/Product.aspx?CategoryID=5&ProductID=99`

Figure 3-13

URL Rewriting with ASP.NET and UrlRewriter.NET

Whenever possible, we suggest implementing URL rewriting using an ISAPI filter, because this is usually the fastest and trouble-free way. However, especially when using a shared host environment, you may not have this option, so you need to handle URL rewriting using C# or VB.NET code in your web application.

Just as with ISAPI filters, you have the option to write your own code or use an existing library. The two URL rewriting libraries that we know of at the moment of writing this book are those at UrlRewriter.net and UrlRewriting.net. No matter if you write your own code or you use one of these projects, you should be aware of some limitations related to ASP.NET URL rewriting with IIS 5 or 6 (IIS 7 is discussed separately later in this chapter):

❑ **Only user requests handled by your ASP.NET application can be rewritten.** This probably sounds obvious, but it's frequently overlooked, because web developers tend to forget that not all requests are passed to the ASP.NET ISAPI extension. Indeed, this extension is configured to take only requests for ASP.NET-specific file extensions, such as .aspx, .asmx, .ashx, and so on. Other kinds of requests are passed to other ISAPI extensions, depending on the file type. In other words, unless IIS is specifically configured to act otherwise, requests for image files, or CSS files, for example, cannot by intercepted (and rewritten) by your ASP.NET application.

❑ **Rewriting folder requests needs special considerations.** If you want to rewrite URLs such as http://www.example.com/MYFOLDER/ and MYFOLDER doesn't exist, you need to configure IIS to pass all requests (*) to the ASP.NET ISAPI extension. An alternative would be to create a folder named MYFOLDER that contains an empty Default.aspx file. This would be enough to put the ASP.NET mechanism in motion when the folder is requested, and allow it to intercept and rewrite the request.

❑ **It is easy to associate additional file extensions with the ASP.NET ISAPI extension.** You will want to ask your shared web hosting service to do this if they don't offer an ISAPI Rewrite filter, and you need to rewrite requests for folders, or for file extensions that aren't normally associated with ASP.NET.

❑ **You should code specialized ASP.NET handling modules for specific extension requests.** For example, it's not efficient to have an .aspx page — which inherits all its functionality from the Page class — to handle requests for image files.

Configuring IIS to Pass All Requests to ASP.NET

As hinted earlier, if you only intend to use ASP.NET to rewrite requests for ASP.NET file extensions, you don't need to make any changes to your web server. However, if you need to rewrite other file extensions, such as .html, .jpg, .png, and so on, you need to configure IIS to pass requests to such files to the ASP.NET ISAPI extension.

You can also configure IIS to pass *all* incoming requests to the ASP.NET ISAPI extension, which allows your application to rewrite them. This should be done with caution though, because it can have unwanted side effects. More specifically, if you attempt to rewrite a request for a file extension that has its own registered ISAPI extension (say, .php) this approach falls apart on IIS 5. In IIS 5, once a request is mapped to an ISAPI extension, that extension owns the request for its entire lifetime. IIS 6, on the other hand, allows transferring the request from one ISAPI extension to another.

If you decide to configure IIS to pass all the requests to the ASP.NET ISAPI extensions, here are the steps you need to follow.

Configuring IIS on Windows XP and Windows 2000 Server

1. Open the Internet Information Services tool and navigate to the **Home Directory** tab.

2. Select **Configuration**.

3. Click **Add** and type the path to aspnet_isapi.dll in the **Executable** box, such as C:\WINDOWS\ Microsoft.NET\Framework\v2.0.50727\aspnet_isapi.dll.

4. Type .* for the file extension, and unselect the "Check that file exists" check box.

5. Click **OK** to close all open dialogs.

Configuring IIS on Windows 2003 Server

1. Open the Internet Information Services (IIS) Manager tool.

2. Right-click the web site you need to configure and select **Properties**.

3. Click the **Home Directory** tab.

4. Click the **Configuration** button.

5. Click **Insert...**, and type the path to aspnet_isapi.dll in the **Executable** box, such as C:\WINDOWS\Microsoft.NET\Framework\v2.0.50727\aspnet_isapi.dll.

6. Click **OK** to close all open dialogs.

Configuring IIS 7

IIS 7 is much more flexible than its previous versions, and can be easily configured to pass certain requests to your own HTTP modules *from within your web application*. Scott Guthrie nicely lists the new features in his article at http://weblogs.asp.net/scottgu/archive/2006/04/20/Cool-new-IIS7-Features-and-APIs.aspx. When using UrlRewriter.NET in the following exercises, you'll learn how to configure IIS 7 to pass the requests.

> *At the time of writing, Windows Longhorn Server is in beta phase. Should the final version of the product affect the information presented in this chapter, you'll find any updates at* http://www .cristiandarie.ro/seo-asp/.

Using UrlRewriter.NET

UrlRewriter.NET is an open-source URL rewriting component for ASP.NET 1.1 and 2.0. It provides similar capabilities as the URL rewriting ISAPI filters, except that it works in environments that don't allow installing such IIS add-ons. Basically, this product has similar features to those of ISAPI_Rewrite, but this time the rewriting is implemented at the ASP.NET level, rather than the IIS level. Let's learn how to install and use it by going through an exercise.

Using UrlRewriter.NET

1.   Before starting off this exercise, please comment out all rewrite rules you may have implemented in the ISAPI_Rewrite exercises. Open `httpd.ini`, and prefix all the `RewriteRule` lines with the comment symbol (#).

2.   Visit `http://www.urlrewriter.net`, click the **Download** button, and download the latest release of the product.

3.   The product package contains a folder named `UrlRewriter`. Unzip the package to a folder on your hard disk, different than your `seoasp` web site folder. For the purposes of this exercise we'll assume you've extracted `UrlRewriter` in `C:\`.

4.   Open the `http://seoasp/` web site in Visual Web Developer.

5.   Add a reference to the `Intelligencia.UrlRewriter` assembly. To do this, right-click the root entry of your project in Solution Explorer (the entry should read `http://seoasp/`), and choose **Add Reference...**. In the dialog that opens, click the Browse tab, and browse to `UrlRewriter\bin\Release\Intelligencia.UrlRewriter.dll`. Select the file and click **OK**.

6.   Open your `Web.config` file in your web project, and add the following configuration section handler that enables UrlRewriter.NET to read its configuration from a configuration node named `rewriter`:

```
<?xml version="1.0"?>
<configuration>
  <configSections>
    <section name="rewriter" requirePermission="false"
type="Intelligencia.UrlRewriter.Configuration.RewriterConfigurationSectionHandler,
Intelligencia.UrlRewriter" />
  </configSections>
...
```

The `configSections` *element must be the first child of the* `configuration` *element.*

7.   Now configure the `UrlRewriter` HTTP module, which allows UrlRewriter.NET to intercept incoming requests (and rewrite them):

```
<system.web>
  <httpModules>
    <add type="Intelligencia.UrlRewriter.RewriterHttpModule,
Intelligencia.UrlRewriter" name="UrlRewriter" />
  </httpModules>
...
```

8.   Excellent, now UrlRewriter.NET is ready to use! In our first test, let's have it rewrite incoming requests for `/my-super-product.aspx` to `/Product.aspx?ProductID=123`. Add the highlighted configuration elements in the `<configuration>` section of `Web.config`:

```
<configuration>
  <rewriter>
    <rewrite url="/my-super-product.aspx" to="/Product.aspx?ProductID=123" />
  </rewriter>
...
```

Note that in this first exercise we're rewriting an .aspx file, and not an .html file as we did in the first ISAPI_Rewrite example. This allows the URL rewrite process to work as expected even if you haven't configured IIS to pass all incoming requests to the ASP.NET ISAPI extension.

9. Load `http://seoasp/my-super-product.aspx`, and expect to see the output in Figure 3-14. Note that this exercise relies on the `Product.aspx` page developed earlier in this chapter. If you didn't follow the previous exercises, you should take it from the code download.

Figure 3-14

As this exercise hinted, UrlRewriter.NET allows you to perform the same functionality from inside your ASP.NET application, which can be extremely helpful when you can't install an ISAPI rewriting filter in your IIS machine.

After setting up your `Web.config` file as required, all you have to do is add your rewriting rules to the `<rewriter>` section. After following the ISAPI_Rewrite exercises, the meaning of this configuration line should be pretty obvious to you:

```
<rewriter>
    <rewrite url="/my-super-product.aspx" to="/Product.aspx?ProductID=123" />
</rewriter>
```

The value of the `url` attribute of the `rewrite` element supports regular expressions, and we'll test this soon. The documentation of UrlRewriter.NET includes details about all the rewriting options you have, and you can access it at `http://urlrewriter.net/index.php/support/`. For your quick reference, we've included in Table 3-5 details about the most useful actions performed by UrlRewriter.NET, and Table 3-5 lists the possible conditions you can use in these actions.

Table 3-5

Element	Example	Description
rewrite	`<rewrite url="^/P-([0-9]+).aspx$" to="/Product.aspx?ID=$1" processing= "stop" />`	Rewrites the incoming request. The `url` attribute specifies the matching regular expression, and `to` specifies the rewritten URL. The value of the optional `processing` attribute specifies that if a match is found, the processing should `continue` (the default), `stop`, or `restart`.

Table 3-5 (*continued*)

Element	Example	Description
redirect	`<redirect url="^/P-(.+).html$" to="/Product.aspx?ID=$1" permanent="true" />`	Redirects the incoming request. If `permanent` is `true` (the default), a 301 redirect is performed, otherwise a 302 redirect is used. Refer to Chapter 4 for more details about the HTTP status codes.

If	`<if address="192.168.0.1" />`
	`    <forbidden />`
	`</if>`
		Allows grouping one or more directives, which are parsed if the condition is true.

unless	`<unless address="127.0.0.1" />`
	`    <set cookie="Visited" value="true" />`
	`</if>`
		Allows grouping one or more directives, which are parsed if the condition is false.

set status	`<set status="500" />`	Sets the status code to return to the client. If the status code is equal or greater than 300, the action is final, otherwise the following directives are processed in sequence. Refer to Chapter 4 for more details about the HTTP status codes.

set property	`<if url="^/P-([0-9]+).aspx$">`
	`    <set property="ProductID" value="$1" />`
	`</if>`
		Sets a property in `HttpContext.Current.Items` using the last performed match. The example sets a property named `Rewriter.ProductID`.

set cookie	`<set cookie="Visited" value="true" />`	Adds a cookie to the collection of cookies sent to the client.
add header	`<add header="X-Powered-By" value="UrlRewriter.NET" />`	Adds a header value.
forbidden	`<forbidden />`	Returns a 403 Forbidden status code.

not-found	`<if url="^/old/.*$">`
	`    <not-found />`
	`</if>`
		Returns a 404 Not Found response to the client.

not-allowed	`<if method="DELETE">`
	`    <not-allowed />`
	`</if>`
		Returns a 405 Method Not Allowed response to the client

Continued

Table 3-5 (*continued*)

Element	Example	Description

gone	`<if url="^/old/.*$">`
	`  <gone />`
	`</if>`
		Returns a 410 Gone response to the client.

not-implemented	`<if header="User-Agent"`
	`match="MSIE" />`
	`  <not-implemented />`
	`</if>`
		Returns a 501 Not Implemented response to the client.

We'll let you discover the finer details of UrlRewriter.NET's capabilities in its documentation, at `http://urlrewriter.net/index.php/support/`. Before moving on to other topics, let's see how to rewrite keyword-rich URLs of the following form:

```
http://www.example.com/Products/Tools-C5/Super-Drill-P9.html
```

Yes, this is the same scenario as the last one discussed for Helicon's ISAPI_Rewrite, except this time we're implementing the feature using UrlRewriter.NET.

Rewriting Numeric and Keyword-Rich URLs

1. To be able to rewrite requests that contain non-existent folders, you need to configure IIS as described in "Configuring IIS to Pass All Requests to ASP.NET," earlier in this chapter. If you use IIS 7, you need to edit the `Web.config` file of your project by adding the following `system.webServer` entry. This ensures that the `RewriterHttpModule` module has access to all incoming requests.

```
<configuration>
...
  <system.webServer>
    <modules runAllManagedModulesForAllRequests="true">
      <add name="UrlRewriter" type="Intelligencia.UrlRewriter.RewriterHttpModule" />
    </modules>
    <validation validateIntegratedModeConfiguration="false" />
  </system.webServer>
```

The `<configSections>` *element must be the first child of* `<configuration>`. *Keep this in mind when adding new elements to* `<configuration>`.

2. If you're running Windows Vista and IIS 7, you were instructed in Chapter 1 to switch your web site to use Classic .NET AppPool, so that you can run your project in debug mode. In order for the configuration element you added earlier to work correctly, you need to switch your application back to DefaultAppPool, from the Advanced Settings dialog of your web site, in the Internet Information Services (IIS) Manager application.

3. Modify the `<rewriter>` element in `Web.config` by adding the following rewrite rules.

```
<rewriter>
    <!-- Group rewrite rules that deal with product URLs -->
    <if url="^/Products/.*">

      <!--Rewrite numeric URLs that contain a productID and a category ID -->
      <rewrite url="^/Products/C([0-9]+)/P([0-9]+).html$"
               to="/Product.aspx?CategoryID=$1&amp;ProductID=$2"
               processing="stop" />

      <!-- Rewrite numeric URLs that contain a product ID -->
      <rewrite url="^/Products/P([0-9]+).html$"
               to="/Product.aspx?ProductID=$1"
               processing="stop" />

      <!-- Rewrite keyword-rich URLs with a product ID and a category ID -->
      <rewrite url="^/Products/.*-C([0-9]+)/.*-P([0-9]+).html$"
               to="/Product.aspx?CategoryID=$1&amp;ProductID=$2"
               processing="stop" />

      <!-- Rewrite keyword-rich URLs with a product ID -->
      <rewrite url="^/Products/.*-P([0-9]+).html$"
               to="/Product.aspx?ProductID=$1"
               processing="stop" />
    </if>
</rewriter>
```

4. Alright, it's time to do some testing! First, load `http://seoasp/Products/P123456.html`, and verify that it has the same output as that in Figure 3-8. Then load `http://seoasp/Products/C5/P99.html`, and you should get the result as the one in Figure 3-10.

5. To test keyword-rich URLs, load `http://seoasp/Products/Tools-C5/Super-Drill-P9.html`. If everything works as expected, you should get the same page as that in Figure 3-12.

Now you've achieved the same functionality using UrlRewriter.NET as you previously did using an ISAPI filter. Because both can be used to achieve the same features, choosing one over the other depends on your server configuration, and to some extent to your personal taste.

> **The URL rewriting component you can download at** `http://www.urlrewriting.net` **has similar features as that at** `http://www.urlrewriter.net`, **and it includes a friendly tutorial in PDF format.**

You'll meet these URL rewriting products again later. For now, it's time to move one and learn more about the basics of URL rewriting with ASP.NET. This time, you learn how to write your own rewriting code.

Using UrlRewriter.NET on a Web Hosting Account

The real advantage of an ASP.NET rewriting engine such as UrlRewriter.NET is that you can easily use it with a shared hosting account, or with production web servers whose software configuration cannot be easily changed.

To use UrlRewriter.NET with your ASP.NET application all you have to do is copy its DLL file to the Bin folder of the application, and add the necessary configuration elements to Web.config — just as shown in the previous exercises.

Additionally, if you need to rewrite file extensions that aren't associated by default with ASP.NET, or requests for folders, you need to ask your hosting provider to associate those extensions for you, or use their control panel if it has this feature. To support folder rewriting without creating the folders on your disk, you need to send all the incoming requests to ASP.NET.

Creating Your Own Rewriting Code

Though using a solid, tested product like those described earlier is preferable to writing your own rewriting code, it's still important to understand what happens behind the scenes. Here we cover the basic URL rewriting techniques, which will help you build complete applications that employ URL rewriting.

The workhorse of the ASP.NET URL rewriting mechanism lies in the RewritePath method of the HttpContext object. The easiest way to test this method is by using it in the Global.asax file, which handles application-wide events. One of these event handlers is Application_BeginRequest, which is executed each time the application receives a client request. Let's walk through a simple exercise where we use these tools to implement a simple rewriting, hand-made mechanism.

URL Rewriting with ASP.NET and Global.asax

1. Start by making sure that none of the products you've worked with earlier rewrite requests to /my-super-product.aspx, because this is the URL we intend to rewrite in this exercise.

2. Open the http://seoasp/ project in Visual Web Developer, right-click the root node of your project in Solution Explorer, and choose **Add New Item...**. From the list of templates select **Global Application Class**. Its name should be automatically set to Global.asax. Then click **OK**.

3. If you open Global.asax, you'll notice that it already implements empty handlers for a few of the supported application-wide events. Add the following method to the file:

```
void Application_BeginRequest(object sender, EventArgs e)
{
  // get the current HttpContext object
  HttpContext context = HttpContext.Current;

  // get the current location
  string currentLocation = context.Request.Path.ToLower();

  // rewrite /my-super-product.aspx
  if (currentLocation == "/my-super-product.aspx")
```

```
    {
      context.RewritePath("~/Product.aspx?ProductID=SUPER");
      return;
    }
  }
```

4. Save the changes, and load `http://seoasp/my-super-product.aspx`. With the risk of boring you with the same image over and over again, we present Figure 3-15, which confirms that your little rewriting code worked as expected.

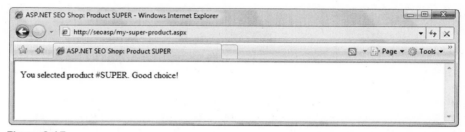

Figure 3-15

Congratulations, you've performed URL rewriting with your own, brand new code! This exercise served to give you the taste of performing URL rewriting yourself. However, writing efficient URL rewriting code that knows how to handle more rewriting scenarios and file types takes more effort than that. Also keep in mind that using `Global.asax` is not the ideal place to keep your URL rewriting code. Using ASP.NET HTTP modules allow for a cleaner code structure — we'll work with these soon as well.

Given that free products such as UrlRewriter.NET and UrlRewriting.net already implement ASP.NET URL rewriting best practices, the motivation to create your own code from scratch, in a production environment, is low. Later in this chapter we'll see how to create custom HTTP handlers and modules in the context of enabling ID-free URL rewriting, but if you're interested in building a complete URL rewriting engine from scratch, we suggest that you consult advanced ASP.NET books, on a variety of topics, to have all your bases covered. One such great book is Stefan Schackow's *Professional ASP.NET 2.0 Security, Membership, and Role Management* (Wiley Publishing, Inc., 2006).

Technical Considerations

Apart from basic URL rewriting, no matter how you implement it, you need to be aware of additional technical issues you may encounter when using such techniques in your web sites:

❑   If your web site contains ASP.NET controls or pages that generate postback events that you handled at server-side, you need to perform additional changes to your site so that it handles the postbacks correctly.

❑   You need to make sure the relative links in your pages point to the correct absolute locations after URL rewriting.

Let's deal with these issues one at a time.

Handling Postbacks Correctly

Although they appear to be working correctly, the URL-rewritten pages you've loaded in all the exercises so far have a major flaw: they can't handle postbacks correctly. Postback is the mechanism that fires server-side handlers as response of client events by submitting the ASP.NET form. In other words, a postback occurs every time a control in your page that has the `runat="server"` attribute fires an event that is handled at server-side with C# or VB.NET code.

To understand the flaw in our solution, add the following button into the form in `Product.aspx`:

```
<body>
  <form id="form1" runat="server">
    <asp:Literal runat="server" ID="message" />
    <asp:Button ID="myButton" runat="server" Text="Click me!" />
  </form>
</body>
```

Switch the form to Design view, and double-click the button in the designer to have Visual Web Developer generate its `Click` event handler for you. Then complete its code by adding the following line:

```
protected void myButton_Click(object sender, EventArgs e)
{
    message.Text += "<br />You clicked the button!";
}
```

Alright, you have one button that displays a little message when clicked. To test this button, load `http://seoasp/Product.aspx`, and click the button to ensure it works as expected. The result should resemble that in Figure 3-16. (Note that clicking it multiple times doesn't display additional text, because the contents of the `Literal` control used for displaying the message is refreshed on every page load.)

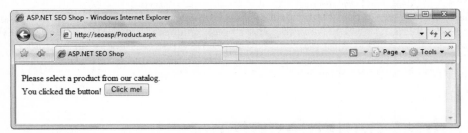

Figure 3-16

Now, load the same `Product.aspx` form, but this time using a rewritten URL. I'll choose `http://seoasp/Products/Super-AJAX-PHP-Book-P35.html`, which should be properly handled by your existing code and rewritten to `http://seoasp/Product.aspx?ProductID=35`. Then click the button. Oops! You'll get an error, as shown in Figure 3-17.

If you look at the new URL in the address bar of your web browser, you can intuit what happens: the page is unaware that it was loaded using a rewritten URL, and it submits the form to the wrong URL — in this example, `http://seoasp/Products/Product.aspx?ProductID=35`. The presence of the `Products` folder in the initial URL broke the path to which the form is submitted.

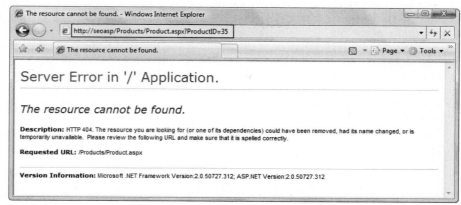

Figure 3-17

The new URL doesn't exist physically in our web site, and it's also not handled by any rewrite rules. This happens because the `action` attribute of the form points back to the name of the physical page it's located on, which in this case is `Products.aspx` (this behavior isn't configurable via properties). This can be verified simply by looking at the HTML source of the form, before clicking the button:

```
<form name="form1" method="post" action="Product.aspx?ProductID=35" id="form1">
```

When this form is located on a page that contains folders, the action path will be appended to the path including the folders. When URL rewriting is involved, it's easy to intuit that this behavior isn't what we want. Additionally, even if the original path doesn't contain folders, the form still submits to a dynamic URL, rendering our URL rewriting efforts useless.

To overcome this problem, there are three potential solutions. The first works with any version of ASP.NET, and involves creating a new `HtmlForm` class that removes the `action` attribute, like this:

```
namespace ActionlessForm
{
  public class Form : System.Web.UI.HtmlControls.HtmlForm
  {
    protected override void RenderAttributes(System.Web.UI.HtmlTextWriter writer)
    {
      Attributes.Add("enctype", Enctype);
      Attributes.Add("id", ClientID);
      Attributes.Add("method", Method);
      Attributes.Add("name", Name);
      Attributes.Add("target", Target);
      Attributes.Render(writer);
    }
  }
}
```

If you save this file as `ActionlessForm.cs`, you can compile it into a library file using the C# compiler, like this:

```
csc.exe /target:library ActionlessForm.cs
```

The default location of the .NET 2.0 C# compiler is `\windows\microsoft.net\framework\v2.0 .50727\csc.exe`. Note that you may need to download and install the Microsoft .NET Software Development Kit to have access to the C# compiler. To create libraries you can also use Visual C# 2005 Express Edition, in which case you don't need to compile the C# file yourself. Copying the resulted file, `SuperHandler.dll`, to the `Bin` folder of your application would make it accessible to the rest of the application. Then you'd need to replace all the `<form>` elements in your Web Forms and Master Pages with the new form, like this:

```
<%@ Page Language="C#" %>
<!DOCTYPE html PUBLIC "-//W3C//DTD XHTML 1.0 Transitional//EN"
"http://www.w3.org/TR/xhtml1/DTD/xhtml1-transitional.dtd">

<%@ Register TagPrefix="af" Namespace="ActionlessForm" Assembly="ActionlessForm" %>

...

<html xmlns="http://www.w3.org/1999/xhtml" >
<head id="Head1" runat="server">
  <title>ASP.NET SEO Shop</title>
</head>
<body>
  <af:form id="form1" runat="server">
    <asp:Literal runat="server" ID="message" />
    <asp:Button ID="myButton" runat="server" Text="Click me!"
OnClick="myButton_Click" />
  </af:form>
</body>
</html>
```

Needless to say, updating all your Web Forms and Master Pages like this isn't the most elegant solution in the world, but it's the best option you have with ASP.NET 1.x. Fortunately, ASP.NET 2.0 offers a cleaner solution, which doesn't require you to alter your existing pages, and it consists of using the ASP.NET 2.0 Control Adapter extensibility architecture. This method is covered by Scott Guthrie in his article at http://weblogs.asp.net/scottgu/archive/2007/02/26/tip-trick-url-rewriting-with-asp-net.aspx.

The last solution implies using `Context.RewritePath` to rewrite the current path to `/?`, effectively stripping the `action` tag of the form. This technique is demonstrated in the case study in Chapter 14, but as you'll see, it's not recommended that you use it in more complex applications because of the restrictions it implies on your code, and its potential side effects.

Absolute Paths and ~/

Another potential problem when using URL rewriting is that relative links will stop working when folders are used. For example, a link to `/image.jpg` in `Product.aspx` would be translated to `http://seoasp/image.jpg` if read from `Product.aspx?ProductID=10`, or to `http://seoasp/`

`Products/image.jpg` if read through a rewritten URL such as `http://seoasp/Products/P-10.html`. To avoid such problems, you should use at least one of the following two techniques:

❑   Always use absolute paths. Creating a URL factory library, as shown later in this chapter, can help with this task.

❑   Use the ~ syntax supported by ASP.NET controls. The ~ symbol always references the root location of your application, and it is replaced by its absolute value when the controls are rendered by the server.

Rewriting ID-Free URLs

To rewrite URLs that don't contain IDs, you need to learn how to implement your own little rewriting engine. This way, you can analyze the URL, and eventually use data from a database to associate the incoming URL with a real URL from your web site.

We'll discuss two techniques you can use for your own URL rewriting code. The first involves using ASP.NET generic handlers, and the second uses ASP.NET HTTP modules. To make good use of any of these techniques you need to know how to handle .NET regular expressions, so we'll start with a quick presentation of them.

.NET Regular Expressions

You can find a quick and useful introduction to regular expressions in C# at `http://www.regular-expressions.info/dotnet.html`. Andrew Watt's *Beginning Regular Expressions* also contains detailed coverage of .NET's regular expressions implementation. Here we'll only learn the necessary bit of theory required the exercises in this book.

Microsoft .NET packs all its regular expressions functionality in six classes and one delegate, which are described in Table 3-6. All these classes are part of the `System.Text.RegularExpressions` namespace.

Table 3-6

Class	Description
Regex	Class that performs regular expression operations. It can be instantiated to represent a compiled instance of a regular expression, or you can use its static methods to perform the same actions.
Capture	Represents the result of a single match.
CaptureCollection	Represents a collection of `Capture` objects.
Group	Represents the results of a capturing group (an expression written between parentheses in the regular expression), in the form of a `CaptureCollection` object.

Continued

Table 3-6 (*continued*)

Class	Description
GroupCollection	Represents a collection of Group objects.
Match	Represents the result of a single regular expression match. The captures are available via the Captures member, which returns a CaptureCollection object, and the captured groups are available via the Groups member, which is a GroupCollection object.
MatchCollection	Represents a collection of Match objects.
MatchEvaluator	A delegate that can be used during regular expression–based text replacement operations. A delegate represents a reference to a method, and you can use delegates to pass methods references as parameters. This particular delegate helps in replacement operations, when the replacement string for each match must be calculated using C# code depending on the match. In those cases, instead of providing a simple replacement string, you pass an instance of MatchEvaluator. You'll meet an example in Chapter 8.

When instantiating the Regex class, you get an object that represents a regular expression. That object can then be used to perform matches or string replacement operations. Here's a simple example of using Regex, Match, and Group:

```
Regex regex = new Regex("^/Products/(.+).html$");
Match match = regex.Match("/Products/Link-Juice.html");
Group group = match.Groups[1];
string productName = group.Value;
```

After this code executes, productName will contain Link-Juice. The Captures collection contains the matching strings. In our case this collection has a single member, whose value is /Products/Link-Juice.html.

The captured groups — the expressions written between parentheses — are accessible via the Groups collection. The first element of the collection contains the entire matching string (/Products/Link-Juice.html). For retrieving the product name, which is captured by the (.+) expression, we've read the second group from the Match object — match.Groups[1].

When creating a Regex object, the object stores the regular expression internally in a specific, "compiled" format, which helps improve the performance for any subsequent operations the object will perform. When a certain match or replace operation is performed only once, you can use the static methods of Regex, which create a Regex object for you, use it to perform the required operation, and destroy it afterwards. Here's an example:

```
Match match = Regex.Match("/Products/Link-Juice.html", "^/Products/(.+).html$");
Group group = match.Groups[1];
string productName = group.Value;
```

In practice, when needing to extract data from matching groups, instead of accessing the groups by index, we prefer using named groups. In the following example you can see how we've given a name to the group that captures the product's name, and then we accessed the group by its name:

```
Match match = Regex.Match("/Products/Link-Juice.html",
                         "^/Products/(?<PRODUCTNAME>.+).html$");
Group group = match.Groups["PRODUCTNAME"];
string productName = group.Value;
```

Table 3-7 describes the most frequently used methods of Regex.

Table 3-7

Regex Method	Description
Match	Searches for a regular expression in a string and returns the first match in the form of a Match object.
Matches	Searches for a regular expression in a string and returns a MatchCollection object that contains all matches.
IsMatch	Returns a Boolean value indicating whether a match has been found.
Replace	Performs a regular expression string replacing operation. The replacement text can contain variables named $1, $2, and so on, representing the values of the captured groups from the matching regular expression. Overloads of Replace allow providing a MatchEvaluator instance instead of the replacement string, in which case the method referenced by the MatchEvaluator is called for each match, and its return value is used as the string replacement value.
Split	Splits a string in the places matched by the regular expression.

Many of the Regex methods receive as parameter a RegexOptions value, which can affect the behavior of the regular expressions parser. Table 3-8 describes the members of the enumeration.

Table 3-8

RegexOptions Member	Description
Compiled	Searches for a regular expression in a string and returns the first match in the form of a Match object.
CultureInvariant	Searches for a regular expression in a string and returns a MatchCollection object that contains all matches.
ECMAScript	Returns a Boolean value indicating whether a match has been found.

Continued

Table 3-8 (*continued*)

RegexOptions Member	Description
ExplicitCapture	Specifies that all captures must be marked explicitly using the (?<name>) syntax. It is helpful when the expression contains many parentheses that don't need to be captured.
IgnoreCase	Performs a case-insensitive match.
IgnorePatternWhitespace	Instructs the parser to ignore spaces or tabs in the regular expression, except when they appear in a character class, such as [ ]. This is helpful when writing a pattern over multiple lines, to make it easier to read.
Multiline	In Multiline mode, the ^ and $ characters will match the beginning and end, respectively, of any line of text.
None	Doesn't alter the parser in any way.
RightToLeft	The matching will be done right-to-left.
Singleline	In Singleline mode, the dot metacharacter matches every character, including \n.

Two or more enumeration members can be combined using the bitwise OR operator, like this:

```
Regex regex = new Regex("^/Products/(.+).html$",
                RegexOptions.IgnoreCase | RegexOptions.Compiled);
```

Rewriting ID-Free URLs Using Generic Handlers

The rewriting exercises presented so far in this chapter promote an easy implementation that takes advantage of the fact that the article IDs are sneaked in the URLs. However, if you prefer not to have IDs in your URLs at all, this is possible as well. First we'll teach you how to implement ID-free URLs using generic handlers, and then we'll see how to do the same using ASP.NET HTTP modules.

For a short tutorial dedicated to HTTP modules and handlers, see the article "Extending ASP.NET with HttpHandlers and HttpModules," which you can find at http://www.devx.com/dotnet/Article/ 6962/. A *generic handler* is a special kind of HTTP handler, which instead of being implemented as a C# class and associated with a certain file extension, it's always implemented as a file with the .ashx extension.

In our proposed implementation that uses generic handlers, we begin by rewriting incoming URLs that follow a certain pattern, or even all URLs, to a local script that receives the original URL as a parameter. For example, assume that the visitor requests this URL:

```
http://www.example.com/Articles/AJAX-PHP-Book-Review.html
```

This request can be rewritten using a rule such as this one:

```
RewriteRule ^/Articles/(.*)$ /Loader.ashx?Page=$1
```

Processed by this rule, the request would become:

```
http://www.example.com/Loader.ashx?Page=AJAX-PHP-Book-Review.html
```

At this point, `Loader.ashx` is responsible for displaying the content depending on the `Page` parameter it receives. Typically, the script would use a lookup table to find the article ID based on the URL, and generate the output depending on that ID. Let's test this technique by going through a simple exercise.

Supporting ID-Free URLs

1. Open `http://seoasp/` in Visual Web Developer, right-click the root node, and choose **Add New Item...**. Choose the **Generic Handler** template, type `Loader.ashx` for the name (see Figure 3-18), and click **Add**.

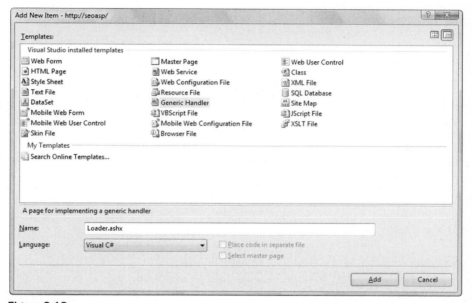

Figure 3-18

2. Modify the automatically generated code as shown in the following code snippet:

```
<%@ WebHandler Language="C#" Class="Loader" %>

using System;
using System.Web;
using System.Web.UI;

public class Loader : IHttpHandler
{
  public void ProcessRequest(HttpContext context)
  {
```

```
      // get the value of the Page parameter
      string pageName = context.Request.QueryString["Page"];

      // stop if there's no Page parameter
      if (pageName == null || pageName == "") return;

      // rewrite the URL depending on the requested page
      if (pageName.ToLower() == "ajax-php-book-review.html")
      {
        // assume the ID of the AJAX-PHP-Book-Review.html article is 35
        context.RewritePath("/Product.aspx?ProductID=35");

        // create an compiled instance of the page we want to load
        IHttpHandler handler = PageParser.GetCompiledPageInstance("Product.aspx",
null, context);

        // load the new page
        handler.ProcessRequest(context);
      }
      else
      {
        // return a 404 status code if the article name wasn't recognized
        context.Response.Status = "404 Not Found";
      }
    }
```

```
  public bool IsReusable
  {
    get
    {
      return true;
    }
  }
}
```

3. Use your favorite tool to rewrite requests to `^/Articles/(.*)$` to `/Loader.ashx?Page=$1`. If using Helicon's ISAPI_Rewrite, the rule should be the following:

```
# ID-free URL rewriting test
RewriteRule ^/Articles/(.*)$ /Loader.ashx?Page=$1
```

If using UrlRewriter.NET, the configuration element would look like this:

```
<!-- ID-free URL rewriting test -->
<rewrite url="^/Articles/(.*)$" to="/Loader.ashx?Page=$1" processing="stop" />
```

4. Load `http://seoasp/Articles/AJAX-PHP-Book-Review.html`. You should get a page showing the results generated by `Product.aspx?ProductID=35` (see Figure 3-19).

5. Now try loading an unknown article, such as `http://seoasp/Articles/test.html`. Because we didn't output any content, you should get the default 404 template of the browser, such as that shown in Figure 3-20.

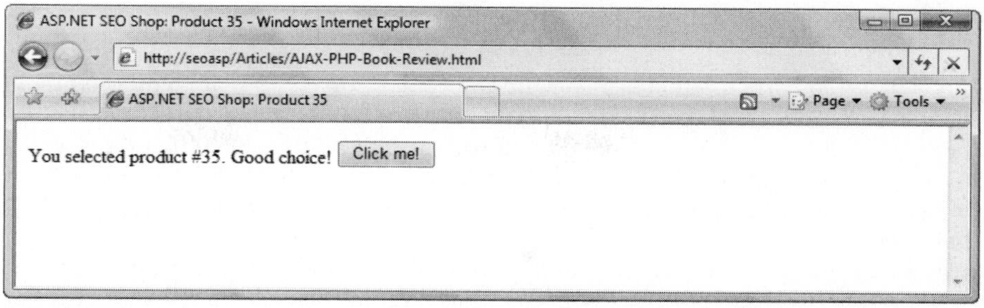

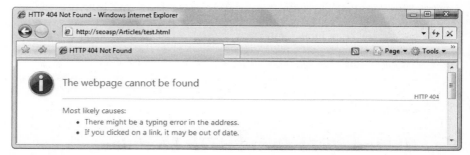

Figure 3-19

Figure 3-20

The purpose of this exercise was to demonstrate how you can create a script that associates incoming URLs with product IDs, without requiring the URLs to contain any IDs. Note that using an HttpModule would still be the most efficient technical way of implementing URL rewriting with ASP.NET. However, the easier implementation demonstrates a concept that applies to any URL rewriting scenario, even when using products such as ISAPI_Rewrite and UrlRewriter.NET.

In a real-world web site, if you don't introduce product IDs in the URL, you can't use generic regular expressions to rewrite incoming all URLs to their destination URLs. Instead, you need to use lookup tables that associate possible incoming URLs with real pages. This is typically done using a database, but for the purpose of this exercise we've simply verified if the incoming link is for AJAX-PHP-Book-Review.html, and in case it is, load Product.aspx?ProductID=35 instead. The code achieved to do this was quite simple:

```
// rewrite the URL depending on the requested page
if (pageName.ToLower() == "ajax-php-book-review.html")
{
  // assume the ID of the AJAX-PHP-Book-Review.html article is 35
  context.RewritePath("/Product.aspx?ProductID=35");
}
```

This code is executed by a generic handler file named Loader.ashx. A generic handler is an ASP.NET-supported file type that can be used to write scripts that don't need the full functionality of .aspx Web Forms. In our case we only needed a simple script that is able to load different other pages depending on the parameter received as the query string.

> ### ASPX versus ASHX
>
> ASP.NET Web Forms — that is, files with the `.aspx` extension — are represented by classes that derive from `System.Web.UI.Page`. This is a very powerful class that contains all the functionality needed to render web pages, and includes support for features such as Master Pages, controls, code-behind files, and so on. ASP.NET generic handlers — which are files with the `.ashx` extension — are also files that are processed by ASP.NET, but they don't derive from `System.Web.UI.Page`. This makes them perfect for creating web-accessible functionality without the overhead implied by inheriting from `Page`. So while it is perfectly possible to create `.aspx` Web Forms that generate images, RSS feeds, or other non-HTML output, it is often much more efficient to use a generic handler instead.
>
> Generic handlers must inherit the `System.Web.IHttpHandler` interface. Interfaces don't contain any functionality, but they declare a set of members that the inheriting classes must implement. In particular, `IHttpHandler` contains two members: the `IsReusable` Boolean property, which specifies if the handler instance can be reused for more requests, and the `ProcessRequest()` method, which is executed when the handler is loaded. When creating a new generic handler in Visual Web Developer, you get a very simple handler template, which simply outputs "Hello World".

Rewriting ID-Free URLs Using HTTP Modules

Technically, the most efficient implementation of ASP.NET URL rewriting is done using HTTP modules. They allow intercepting the incoming request right from the beginning of its life cycle, when the `BeginRequest` event is fired. This approach is generally better than using HTTP handlers for URL rewriting, because by the time the handler runs, the front half of the entire ASP.NET request pipeline — which includes authentication, authorization, output caching — has already run. A complete URL rewriting engine using HTTP modules is presented in the article at `http://www.15seconds.com/Issue/030522.htm`.

Earlier in this chapter you used the `Global.asax` file to attach code to the `BeginRequest` event. When using HTTP modules, you can use a delegate to attach another event handler to that event, so you can achieve the same functionality without touching `Global.asax`.

An HTTP module is a class that implements the `IHttpModule` interface, which defines two member methods: `Init()` and `Dispose()`. When implementing URL rewriting, we use the `Init()` method to define a handler from the `BeginRequest` event, and we use that handler to rewrite the request. The `PageLoader` handler presented earlier would be implemented as an HTTP module like this:

```
using System;
using System.Web;
using System.Web.UI;
using System.Text.RegularExpressions;

public class PageLoader : IHttpModule
{
  // static Regex that extracts the article name
  Regex regex = new Regex("/Articles/(.+)$");
```

```
   // required by IHttpModule
   public void Init(HttpApplication app)
   {
     // add a new handler for application's BeginRequest event
     app.BeginRequest += new System.EventHandler(this.BeginRequest);
   }

   // performs URL rewriting
   public void BeginRequest(object s, EventArgs e)
   {
     // get the current context
     HttpContext context = HttpContext.Current;

     // this module only rewrites article requests
     Match match = regex.Match(context.Request.FilePath);
     if (match.Groups.Count < 2) return;

     // get the article name
     string pageName = match.Groups[1].Value;

     // rewrite the URL depending on the requested page
     if (pageName.ToLower() == "ajax-php-book-review.html")
     {
       // assume the ID of the AJAX-PHP-Book-Review.html article is 35
       context.RewritePath("~/Product.aspx?ProductID=35");
     }
     else
     {
       // return a 404 status code if the article name wasn't recognized
       context.Response.Status = "404 Not Found";
     }
   }

   // required by IHttpModule
   public void Dispose()
   {
     //  add clean-up code here if required
   }
 }
```

This time we used a regular expression to parse the incoming URL and extract the name of the article, but other than that, the code is identical to that of the previous exercise. Note that before testing this module, you should remove the rewrite rules that send article requests to Loader.ashx. After creating the module, you need to configure the module in your application's Web.config file:

```
<system.web>
  <httpModules>
    <add type="PageLoader" name="PageLoader" />
    ...
  </httpModules>
```

If using IIS 7, you should also configure the PageLoader module to process all requests, as you did for UrlRewriter.NET. With IIS 5 or 6 you need to configure the file extensions you intend to rewrite (.html in this case) for the ASP.NET ISAPI extension.

```
<system.webServer>
  <modules runAllManagedModulesForAllRequests="true">
    <add name="UrlRewriter" type="Intelligencia.UrlRewriter.RewriterHttpModule" />
    <add name="PageLoader" type="PageLoader" />
  </modules>
  <validation validateIntegratedModeConfiguration="false" />
</system.webServer>
```

After this is set, loading `http://seoasp/Articles/AJAX-PHP-Book-Review.html` should display the output you saw earlier in Figure 3-19.

Rewriting Images and Streaming Media

Some recommend using keywords not only in HTML document names, but also embedded in the image and media file names. If you are in the image and streaming media distribution business, this detail may be especially important.

Depending on your particular application, you may find it easier to use proper physical file names, rather than rewriting requests. However, if you want to rewrite the incoming requests for image files, you can. Rewriting can be accomplished here with little effort. In the exercise that follows, we place the image files in one directory with their IDs, plus the extension, as their file names (that is, `1.jpg`, `2.jpg`, and so on) — no extensions. We delegate the requests *directly* to physical files on the file system.

> **There are circumstances when you need to generate the images on-the-fly by altering existing images on your file system, or by retrieving the images from a database. In those cases simply rewriting the requests won't do it — instead, you must deliver the image file yourself. An example with this technique is provided in Chapter 10, "Link Bait," when you generate fortune cookie images with random messages on every request.**

Rewriting Image Files

1. Copy the `Media` folder from the code download to your `seoasp` folder. In your `seoasp/Media` folder, you should have five files named 1, 2, 3, 4, and 5. These are jpeg image files.

2. If you're using Helicon's ISAPI_Rewrite, add the following rewrite rule to `httpd.ini`:

```
# Rewrite Cartoons.html to Cartoons.aspx
RewriteRule ^/Cartoons.html$ /Cartoons.aspx [L]

# Rewrite media files
RewriteRule ^/.*-M(.+)$ /Media/$1 [L]
```

If you're using UrlRewriter.NET, you should add these rules to the `<rewriter>` node in `Web.config`:

```
<rewriter>
  <!-- Rewrite Cartoons.html to Cartoons.aspx -->
  <rewrite url="^/Cartoons.html$" to="/Cartoons.aspx" processing="stop" />
```

```
        <!-- Rewrite media files -->
        <rewrite url="^/.*-M(.+)$" to="/Media/$1" processing="stop" />
    </rewriter>
```

3. Create a new Web Form in your project named `Cartoons.aspx`. Then modify the automatically generated code like this:

```
<%@ Page Language="C#" %>
<!DOCTYPE html PUBLIC "-//W3C//DTD XHTML 1.0 Transitional//EN"
"http://www.w3.org/TR/xhtml1/DTD/xhtml1-transitional.dtd">

<html xmlns="http://www.w3.org/1999/xhtml">
<head>
  <title>URL Rewriting Media Files</title>
</head>
<body>
  <form id="form1" runat="server">

    <img src="http://seoasp/Tweety-M1.jpg" alt="Tweety" />
    <img src="http://seoasp/Toy-Story-M2.jpg" alt="Toy Story" />
    <img src="http://seoasp/Tweety-Sylvester-M3.jpg" alt="Tweety & Sylvester" />
    <img src="http://seoasp/Mickey-M4.jpg" alt="Mickey" />
    <img src="http://seoasp/Minnie-M5.jpg" alt="Minnie" />
  </form>
</body>
</html>
```

4. Load `http://seoasp/Cartoons.html`, and expect to see five images, as shown in Figure 3-21.

This was a simple exercise where we tested that requests for image files can also be rewritten. The regular expression used is pretty simple:

```
RewriteRule ^/.*-M(.+)$ /Media/$1 [L]
```

The rule matches any random set of characters followed by -M (`^.*-M`), followed by a group of characters that is captured as $1 — `(.+)`. In English, this rule matches URLs such as `Some-Media-Name-Mn.extension`, and rewrites them directly to a physical file `/media/n.extension`.

Figure 3-21

97

When creating the Link factory, in the next exercise we'll include methods that generate beautified image links. In case you want to use search engine friendly image file names, you should either give them proper names from the start, or use the URL factory together with the rewriting rule to ensure consistency throughout the web site.

Building a Link Factory

Back in the days when you worked only with dynamic URLs, it was easy to build the URLs right in the application code without much planning. You cannot do that here. If you want to use keyword-rich URLs in your web site, just having a `RewriteRule` in your `httpd.ini` file isn't enough! You also need to ensure that all the links in your web site use these keyword-rich versions consistently throughout the web site. Obviously, including the URLs manually in the web site is not an option — it's a dynamic site after all, and the link management task would quickly become impossible to handle when you have a large number of products in your catalog!

Fortunately, there's a very straightforward solution to this problem, which as soon as it's put in place, takes away any additional link management effort. The solution we're proposing is to use a function to generate the new URLs based on data already existing in your database, such as product or category names. As we mentioned before, this also enforces consistency.

Say that you have a product called Super Drill, located in the category Tools. You know the product ID is 9, and the category ID is 5. It's quite easy to create a C# method that uses this data to generate a link such as `/Products/Tools-C5/Super-Drill-P9.html`. In the exercise that follows we'll create a class named `LinkFactory`, which will generate these links.

Building the Link Factory

1. In the `<appSettings>` node of `Web.config`, add a key named `SiteDomain`, whose value is your domain name. This will be used by our link factory to create absolute URLs.

```
<configuration>
  <appSettings>
    <add key="SiteDomain" value="http://seoasp" />
  </appSettings>
```

2. Open your `seoasp` application in Visual Web Developer, and create a new folder named `App_Code`. The easiest way to do this is by right-clicking the root node in Solution Explorer and choosing **Add ASP.NET Folder > App_Code**.

3. Right-click the `App_Code` folder, select **Add New Item...**, choose the **Class** template, and type **LinkFactory** for the name of the new class. Then click **Add**.

4. Transform `LinkFactory` into a static class, and add the `MakeCategoryProductUrl`, `MakeMediaUrl`, and `prepareUrlText` methods:

```
using System;
using System.Web;
using System.Configuration;
using System.Text.RegularExpressions;
```

```csharp
/// <summary>
/// LinkFactory creates absolute links to locations in our site
/// </summary>
public static class LinkFactory
{
  // regular expression that removes characters that aren't a-z, 0-9, dash,
underscore or space
  private static Regex purifyUrlRegex = new Regex("[^-a-zA-Z0-9_ ]",
RegexOptions.Compiled);

  // regular expression that changes dashes, underscores and spaces to dashes
  private static Regex dashesRegex = new Regex("[-_ ]+", RegexOptions.Compiled);

  // builds a link to a product page
  public static string MakeCategoryProductUrl(
    string categoryName, string categoryId, string productName, string productId)
  {
    // prepare the product name and category name for inclusion in URL
    categoryName = prepareUrlText(categoryName);
    productName = prepareUrlText(productName);

    // read the site domain from configuration file
    string siteDomain = ConfigurationManager.AppSettings["SiteDomain"];

    // build the keyword-rich URL
    string url = String.Format("{0}/Products/{1}-C{2}/{3}-P{4}.html",
      siteDomain, categoryName, categoryId, productName, productId);

    // return the URL
    return HttpUtility.UrlPathEncode(url);
  }

  // builds a link to a media file
  public static string MakeMediaUrl(string name, string extension, string id)
  {
    // prepare the medium name for inclusion in URL
    name = prepareUrlText(name);

    // read the site domain from configuration file
    string siteDomain = ConfigurationManager.AppSettings["SiteDomain"];

    // build the keyword-rich URL
    string url = String.Format("{0}/{1}-M{2}.{3}",siteDomain,name,id,extension);

    // return the URL
    return HttpUtility.UrlPathEncode(url);
  }

  // prepares a string to be included in an URL
  private static string prepareUrlText(string urlText)
  {
    // remove all characters that aren't a-z, 0-9, dash, underscore or space
    urlText = purifyUrlRegex.Replace(urlText, "");
```

```
      // remove all leading and trailing spaces
      urlText = urlText.Trim();

      // change all dashes, underscores and spaces to dashes
      urlText = dashesRegex.Replace(urlText, "-");

      // return the modified string
      return urlText;
   }
}
```

5. Add a Web Form to your project, named `Catalog.aspx`, with these contents:

```
<%@ Page Language="C#" %>
<!DOCTYPE html PUBLIC "-//W3C//DTD XHTML 1.0 Transitional//EN"
"http://www.w3.org/TR/xhtml1/DTD/xhtml1-transitional.dtd">

<html xmlns="http://www.w3.org/1999/xhtml">
<head runat="server">
   <title>The SEO Egghead Shop</title>
</head>
<body>
   <form id="form1" runat="server">
      <h1>Products on Promotion at SEO Egghead Shop</h1>
      <p><a href="<%=LinkFactory.MakeCategoryProductUrl("Carpenter's Tools", "12",
"Belt Sander", "45")%>">Carpenter's Tools: Belt Sander</a>

      <p><a href="<%=LinkFactory.MakeCategoryProductUrl("SEO Toolbox", "6", "Link
Juice", "31")%>">SEO Toolbox: Link Juice</a></p>

      <p><a href="<%=LinkFactory.MakeCategoryProductUrl("Bookstore", "2", "ASP.NET
2.0 E-Commerce", "42")%>">Bookstore: ASP.NET 2.0 E-Commerce</a></p>

      <p>Featured product images:</p>
      <img src="<%=LinkFactory.MakeMediaUrl("Tweety", "jpg", "1")%>" alt="Tweety" />
      <img src="<%=LinkFactory.MakeMediaUrl("Toy Story", "jpg", "2")%>" alt="Toy
Story" />
      <img src="<%=LinkFactory.MakeMediaUrl("Tweety & Sylvester", "jpg", "3")%>"
alt="Tweety & Sylvester" />
      <img src="<%=LinkFactory.MakeMediaUrl("Mickey", "jpg", "4")%>" alt="Mickey" />
      <img src="<%=LinkFactory.MakeMediaUrl("Minnie", "jpg", "5")%>" alt="Minnie" />
   </form>
</body>
</html>
```

6. Finally, let's rewrite `Catalog.html` to `Catalog.aspx`. If you're using Helicon's ISAPI_Rewrite, add this rule to `httpd.ini`:

```
# Rewrite Catalog.html
RewriteRule ^/Catalog.html$ /Catalog.aspx [L]
```

If you're using UrlRewriter.NET, this rule should be added to the `<rewriter>` element in `Web.config` like this:

```
<!-- Rewrite Catalog.html to Catalog.aspx -->
<rewrite url="^/Catalog.html$" to="/Catalog.aspx" processing="stop" />
```

7. Load `http://seoasp/Catalog.html` in your web browser. You should be shown a page like the one in Figure 3-22.

8. For the links to be functional, you need to have the `Product.aspx` script you created in the earlier exercises. Click one of the links to ensure the product links have been created correctly. Figure 3-23 shows the page loaded when clicking **Bookstore: ASP.NET 2.0 E-Commerce**.

Figure 3-22

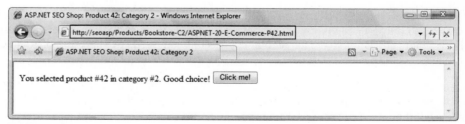

Figure 3-23

So what happened in this exercise? If you take a look in `Catalog.aspx`, you can see that you didn't hard-code any links. Instead, you've used the `LinkFactory` class to create product links and media links by using product, category, and media file data — which in a real-world scenario would come from a database. Take, for example, this method call:

```
LinkFactory.MakeCategoryProductUrl("SEO Toolbox", 6, "Link Juice", 31)
```

If you look at the HTML output generated by `Catalog.aspx`, you can see this was transformed to:

```
http://seoasp/Products/SEO-Toolbox-C6/Link-Juice-P31.html
```

Similarly, `MakeMediaUrl` creates media links. Take this example:

```
LinkFactory.MakeMediaUrl("Tweety & Sylvester", "jpg", 3)
```

This produces the following output:

```
http://seoasp/Tweety-Sylvester-M3.jpg
```

As you can see, now it's very easy to use the data you already have in your database, to create search-engine friendly and user-friendly links. The `LinkFactory` class contains the following static methods:

❑   `prepareUrlText` receives as parameter a string, such as a product or category name, and trans-forms it into a form that can be included in a URL. All characters except alphanumeric characters, the dash, underscore, and the space are removed, and dashes are added as word separators. For example, this function would transform Super Drill to Super-Drill.

❑   `MakeCategoryProductUrl` takes as parameters the names and IDs of a product and a category, and uses `prepareUrlText` to generate a link such as `http://seoasp/Products/Tools-C5/Super-Drill/P9.html`. The `HttpUtility.UrlPathEncode()` method is used to ensure that all characters are properly encoded to be included in a URL.

❑   `MakeMediaUrl` takes as parameters the name, file extension, and ID of a media file, and uses `prepareUrlText` to generate media links such as `http://seoasp/Minnie-M5.jpg`. The `HttpUtility.UrlPathEncode()` method is used to ensure that all characters are properly encoded to be included in a URL.

The `LinkFactory` class also has two *static* Regex members: `purifyUrlRegex` and `dashesRegex`. These objects are used only by `prepareUrlText`, but we're storing them as static members for performance reasons: it's more efficient to have the regular expressions compiled once and stored as static members, rather than re-creating them every time `purifyUrlRegex` executes.

`prepareUrlText` starts by using the first regular expression, `purifyUrlRegex` - [^-a-zA-Z0-9_], to delete all characters that aren't alphanumerical, dash, space, or underscore, ensuring there are no characters left that could break our URL.

```
// prepares a string to be included in an URL
private static string prepareUrlText(string urlText)
{
    // remove all characters that aren't a-z, 0-9, dash, underscore or space
    urlText = purifyUrlRegex.Replace(urlText, "");
```

Static Class Members

As opposed to instance class members, which always belong to a class instance (an object, that is), static class members belong to the class as a whole. Static members can only be accessed through the class name — such as in `Math.Sin()`, and are typically used when creating generic functionality that isn't tied to a particular instance. A class can contain both static and instance members (such as `Regex`), but a class that is declared `static` can only contain static members. The static class fields can be initialized in the static constructor, which is executed only once in the application lifetime — just before the first static field, property, or method is accessed. Undercover, the static members are called upon a global instance of the class, which is created the first time a static member is accessed. For more information about static class members please read an OOP C# tutorial, such as that that can be downloaded from Cristian Darie's web site at `http://www.cristiandarie.ro/downloads/`.

The `Replace` method of `Regex` is available as both a static method and as an instance method. Here we used its instance version to replace the string portions matched by the regular expression with an empty string. In this case, the regular expression `[^-a-zA-Z0-9_ ]` matches all characters not (`^`) in the set of letters, numbers, dashes, underscores, or spaces. We indicate that the matching characters should be replaced with `""`, the empty string, effectively removing them.

Then we continue by removing the leading and trailing spaces from the string it receives as parameter, using the `String.Trim()` function:

```
// remove all leading and trailing spaces
urlText = urlText.Trim();
```

Finally, we use the dashesRegex regular expression `-[-_ ]+` to transform any groups of spaces, dashes, and underscores to dashes. For example, a string such as `SEO___Toolbox` (note there are three underscores) would be replaced to `SEO-Toolbox`. Then we return the transformed URL string:

```
// change all dashes, underscores and spaces to dashes
urlText = dashesRegex.Replace(urlText, "-");

// return the modified string
return urlText;
}
```

`prepareUrlText()` is used by `MakeCategoryProductUrl()` and `MakeMediaUrl()` to create product URLs. It's worth noting that these methods use the site domain saved in `Web.config` to create absolute URLs, and that `HttpUtility.UrlPathEncode()` is used to ensure that no unaccepted characters appear in the final URLs. In this case the URL should be sanitized already, but using `UrlPathEncode()` is a good programming practice nevertheless.

The entire application should be retrofitted with `MakeCategoryProductUrl()`, `MakeMediaUrl()`, and similar methods, to ensure URL consistency throughout the web site. In the exercise you just finished, the product and category data was hard-coded in `Catalog.aspx`, but the URL methods can be called just as easily from `GridView` or `DataList` templates, for example, using database information to generate the links. For example, imagine this list of products is generated by a `DataList` control like this:

```
<asp:DataList ...>
  <ItemTemplate>
    <asp:HyperLink ID="HyperLink1" Runat="server"
      NavigateUrl='<%# "~/Product.aspx?CategoryID=" + Eval("CategoryID") +
"&ProductID=" + Eval("ProductID") %>'
      Text='<%# Eval("CategoryName") : Eval("ProductName") %>'
      ToolTip='<%# Eval("CategoryName") : Eval("ProductName") %>'>
    </asp:HyperLink>
  </ItemTemplate>
</asp:DataList>
```

In this case, you'd update the `NavigateUrl` property of the `Hyperlink` control, like this:

```
<asp:DataList ...>
  <ItemTemplate>
    <asp:HyperLink ID="HyperLink1" Runat="server"
      NavigateUrl='<%=LinkFactory.MakeCategoryProductUrl(Eval("CategoryName"),
Eval("CategoryID"), Eval("ProductName"), Eval("ProductID"))%>'
      Text='<%# Eval("CategoryName"): Eval("ProductName") %>'
      ToolTip='<%# Eval("CategoryName"): Eval("ProductName") %>'>
    </asp:HyperLink>
  </ItemTemplate>
</asp:DataList>
```

Problems Rewriting Doesn't Solve

URL rewriting is not a panacea for all dynamic site problems. In particular, URL rewriting in and of itself does not solve any duplicate content problems. If a given site has duplicate content problems with a dynamic approach to its URLs, the problem would likely also be manifest in the resulting rewritten static URLs as well. In essence, URL rewriting only obscures the parameters — however many there are, from the search engine spider's view. This is useful for URLs that have many parameters as we mentioned. Needless to say, however, if the varying permutations of obscured parameters *do not* dictate significant changes to the content, the same duplicate content problems remain.

A simple example would be the case of rewriting the page of a product that can exist in multiple categories. Obviously, these two pages would probably show duplicate (or very similar content) even if accessed through static-looking links, such as:

```
http://www.example.com/College-Books-C1/Some-Book-Title-P2.html
http://www.example.com/Out-of-Print-Books-C2/Some-Book-Title-P2.html
```

Additionally, in the case that you have duplicate content, using static-looking URLs may actually exacerbate the problem. This is because whereas dynamic URLs make the parameter values and names obvious, rewritten static URLs obscure them. Search engines are known to, for example, attempt to drop a parameter it heuristically guesses is a session ID and eliminate duplicate content. If the session parameter were rewritten, a search engine would not be able to do this at all.

There are solutions to this problem. They typically involve removing any parameters that can be avoided, as well as excluding any of the remaining duplicate content. These solutions are explored in depth in the chapter on duplicate content.

A Last Word of Caution

URLs are much more difficult to revise than titles and descriptions once a site is launched and indexed. Thus, when designing a new site, special care should be devoted to them. Changing URLs later requires one to redirect all of the old URLs to the new ones, which can be extremely tedious, and has the potential to influence rankings for the worse if done improperly and link equity is lost. Even the most trivial changes to URL structure should be accompanied by some redirects, and such changes should only be made when it is absolutely necessary.

This is a relatively simple process. In short, you use the URL factory that we just created to create the new URLs based on the parameters in the old dynamic URLs. Then you employ what is called a "301-redirect" to the new URLs. The various types of redirects are discussed in the following chapter.

So, if you are retrofitting a web application that is powering a web site that is already indexed by search engines, you must redirect the old dynamic URLs to the new rewritten ones. This is especially important, because without doing this every page would have a duplicate and result in a large quantity of duplicate content. You can safely ignore this discussion, however, if you are designing a new web site.

Summary

We covered a lot of material here! We detailed how to employ static-looking URLs in a dynamic web site step-by-step. Such URLs are both search engine friendly and more enticing to the user. This can be accomplished through several techniques, and you've tested the most popular of them in this chapter. A "URL factory" can be used to enforce consistency in URLs. It is important to realize, however, that URL rewriting is not a panacea for all dynamic site problems — in particular, duplicate content problems.

Content Relocation
and HTTP Status Codes

One of the perks of ASP.NET is that it abstracts away many low-level implementation details from the web developer. It does such a great job, in fact, that one can typically build complex web applications without understanding much at all about the protocol web servers use to speak to the world, HTTP (HyperText Transport Protocol).

Though most of the time this ignorance is bliss, it is sometimes not so with regard to search engine optimization. Using the protocol improperly has the potential to wreak havoc for search engine rankings. On the other hand, knowing how to use it effectively can be of great help to the very same end.

HTTP status codes are a small but critical part of this protocol. They provide information regarding the state of an HTTP request. One may use them, for example, to indicate that the requested information should be retrieved from a different location henceforth. In modern search engines, doing so also may result in a transference of link equity to that new location. This example alone highlights the importance of knowing how to use these codes.

In this chapter you:

❑ Learn about the HTTP status codes that are pertinent to the search engine marketer.

❑ Understand how to use the redirection status codes properly, how to signal deleted pages, and how to avoid indexing errors.

❑ Learn how to implement redirection using ASP.NET, ISAPI_Rewrite, and UrlRewriter.NET.

❑ Follow step-by-step exercises to implement automatic URL correction and canonicalization.

The HTTP Status Codes

Each time a user agent requests a URL from a web site, the server replies with a set of HTTP headers; the requested content follows after them. Most users never see this part of the communication, however, because web browsers do not normally display them.

If you've never seen how these headers look, it's time to get your feet wet. The easiest way to get started is to use a web-based tool that does all of the work for you. One such tool is located at `http://www .seoegghead.com/tools/view-http-headers.php`.

Figure 4-1 shows the results of using this tool for `http://www.cristiandarie.ro`. The status code is highlighted in the figure.

A more convenient way to view these headers is by using a plugin for your browser. One plugin you can use with Firefox is `LiveHTTPHeaders` (`http://livehttpheaders.mozdev.org/`). For Internet Explorer you can use `ieHTTPHeaders` (`http://www.blunck.se/iehttpheaders/iehttpheaders.html`). Figure 4-2 shows `LiveHTTPHeaders` in action.

The part of the HTTP headers we're predominantly interested in for the purpose of this chapter is the line containing the *status code* of the request, as indicated in the figure. The most common status code is `200`, which specifies the request was processed by our web server successfully without any surprises, and that the content the user requested follows.

Figure 4-1

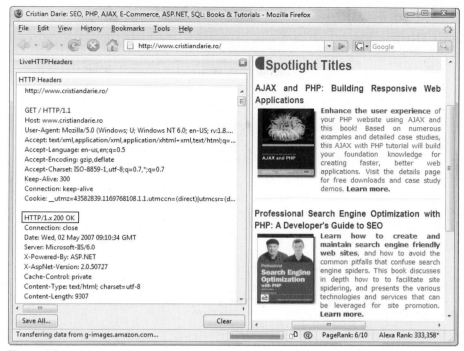

Figure 4-2

However, there are many other status codes you need to know about as a search engine marketer. The status codes we'll consider in this chapter are:

- ❏ Redirection: 301 and 302
- ❏ Removal: 404
- ❏ Server Error: 500

The official descriptions for all HTTP status codes are available at `http://www.w3.org/Protocols/rfc2616/rfc2616-sec10.html`.

Redirection Using 301 and 302

301 and 302 are the HTTP status codes used for redirection. These codes indicate that another request must be made in order to fulfill the HTTP request — the content is located elsewhere. When a web page replies with either of these codes, it does not return any HTML content, but includes an additional `Location:` HTTP header that indicates another URL where the content is found.

Figure 4-3 shows an example of how redirects occur in practice. As you can see, when a redirect occurs, the URL that issues the redirect doesn't return any content, but indicates the new URL that should be referenced instead.

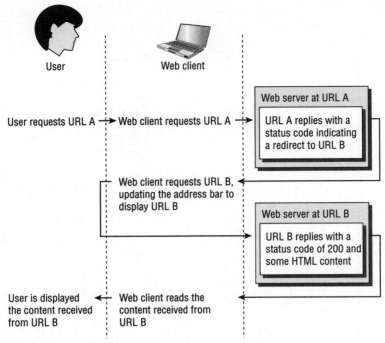

Figure 4-3

Note that in the case that the user agent is a search engine spider or a software application, there is not a user involved in the process, as shown in Figure 4-3. Search engines follow the same basic process to update SERPs when they encounter a redirect.

Redirections can be chained, meaning that one redirect can point to a page that, in turn, redirects again. However, multiple redirects should be avoided to the extent that it is possible. A maximum of five redirections was stipulated by an older version of RFC 2616, but that limit was later lifted. Regardless, it is wise to avoid chained redirects because they can slow down site spidering — spiders may only *schedule* the result of the redirection for spidering instead of immediately fetching it.

There are actually many redirection status codes in the HTTP standard. They are listed in Table 4-1.

Table 4-1

Status Code	Description
300	Multiple choices
301	Moved permanently
302	Found

Table 4-1 (*continued*)

Status Code	Description
303	See other
304	Not modified
305	Use Proxy
307	Temporary Redirect

In practice only the 301 and 302 status codes are used for redirection. Furthermore, because browsers are known to struggle with certain of the other status codes, it is probably wise to avoid the others, even if they seem more relevant or specific. It can only be assumed that search engines may also struggle with them, or at least that it is not entirely understood how they should be interpreted.

301

The 301 status code indicates that a resource has been permanently moved to the new location specified by the `Location:` header that follows. It indicates that the old URL is obsolete and should replace any references to the old URL with the indicated URL.

Let's take as an example a fictional page named `http://www.example.com/OldPage.aspx`, which returns this header:

```
HTTP/1.1 301 Moved Permanently
Date: Wed, 02 May 2007 09:50:39 GMT
Server: Microsoft-IIS/6.0
X-Powered-By: ASP.NET
Location: http://www.example.com/NewPage.aspx
Content-Length: 0
Connection: close
Content-Type: text/html; charset=utf-8
```

When loading the page in web browser, one will be automatically redirected to the new location specified by the `Location` header. After the redirection, the back button in your browser won't reference the initially requested page, as a result of the old page being *permanently* redirected.

The 301 status code also indicates to search engines that link equity from the previous URL should be credited to the new one. In theory, the new page will inherit the rankings of the original page. In practice, however, it may take some time for this to occur. It would be wise not to frivolously change URLs regardless, if this is a concern.

301 is arguably the most important status code when it comes to search engine optimization. The largest part of this chapter is dedicated to working with this status code, and to exercises demonstrating its use. But let's also examine the 302, 404, and 500 status codes. These are important to understand as well.

302

The 302 status code is a bit ambiguous in meaning. It indicates that a resource is "temporarily" moved. The old URL is not obsolete at all, and clients will not cache the result unless indicated explicitly by a `Cache-Control` or `Expires` header. To confuse things even further, 302 is also used for some paid advertising links, but that is not the usage we will discuss here.

The big problem with the 302 status code is that its meaning for search engines depends on its context. In practice, it is worth dividing them into *internal* temporary redirects, that is, from a page on domain A to another page on domain A, and *external* temporary redirects, or from a page on domain A to a page on domain B.

Browsers always abide by the definition cited previously for interpreting a 302 redirect. However, today, most search engines (Google and Yahoo! included) only use it for an *internal* 302. For an internal 302 redirect, then, search engines will not cache the result of the redirect, and continue to list domain A in the SERPs. This is consistent with the definition.

External 302 redirects are more of a problem. Matt Cutts of Google states that more than 99% of the time, Google will list the result with the destination result, that is, domain B instead of domain A. This is against the standard, and Google behaves like this to mitigate a vulnerability called "302 hijacking."

302 hijacking refers to the practice of using a page on domain A to reference a page on domain B, which has fresh quality content. Typically, that page would rank well based on that "stolen" fresh content from domain B, and employ a form of cloaking to redirect users to another page. This practice became prevalent enough to warrant a change in policy from both Google and Yahoo!, and, according to Matt Cutts, *"Google is moving to a set of heuristics that return the destination page more than 99% of the time. Why not 100% of the time? Most search engines reserve the right to make exceptions when we think the source page will be better for users, even though we'll only do that rarely."*

In the article at `http://www.mattcutts.com/blog/seo-advice-discussing-302-redirects/`, Matt Cutts discusses external 302s. In this case, the RFC definition is not the rule — it is the exception! For the most part, external 302s are treated as 301s, but they do not effect the transference of link equity.

In practice, on a dynamic site, one should evaluate whether 302s are necessary anyway. If you want a URL to host some different content than the usual temporarily, it is better to change the content transparently. Possible implementations include using application code, rewriting the old URL to the new URL, or fetching and displaying the alternative content remotely, sometimes obviating the need for the 302 in the first place.

Removing Deleted Pages Using 404

Everyone has seen the 404 status code at some point. It means that the URL you requested does not exist. However, there are a few technical details related to this status code that are less obvious.

First of all, it's less understood that along with a 404 status code, the web server can also deliver any HTML content — just like it does with the 200 status code. Indeed, people usually associate 404 with the generic error pages generated by the web servers, or with the generic 404 page displayed by the web browser when the web server doesn't return any content along with the status code. However, it's advisable to customize your 404 page to enhance the user experience. Advanced web sites may even try to give the visitors suggestions as to what they might have meant based on the keywords in the invalid URL.

Regardless of whether a 404 page is generic or custom, it always tells search engines the page does not exist; and if so, that it should be removed from the index. The content delivered together with a 404 status code isn't indexed.

> Search engines *never* index a page that arrives with the 404 status code.

For a static site, presenting a 404 error is automatic — simply delete the file. Unfortunately, many dynamic sites abandon the concept of 404s, because it takes some extra effort to implement. Typically when a product is deleted from a database, the product's page is no longer linked from the other pages of the web site. The product's page may, however, be linked from pages from external web sites, have acquired link equity, and remain indexed by search engines.

The worst thing you can do is return a page with a 200 status code — as happens often when an item ID no longer exists in a database. This will result in a number of blank pages indexed by a search engine over time, resulting in duplicate content. Instead, one should return a 404 status code, perhaps with a friendly error message as well.

> **A common mistake is to deliver a "page not found" message that is meant to handle 404, but with a 200 status code instead. Web hosting services often allow setting a custom 404 page — that is, the page that is to be fed when a nonexistent URL is requested. However, they may not set the 404 status code correctly. This can result in a theoretically infinite number of duplicate pages in your web site. One can verify that the correct headers are sent using the tools cited earlier in this chapter.**

The moral of the story? Keep a tidy shop. Return 404s for all deleted pages. Some search engine marketers suggest redirecting old products to semantically related products instead of 404ing. This preserves link equity, whereas a 404 does not. We will demonstrate techniques for doing this later in this chapter.

In Chapter 3, you went through an exercise where you set the 404 status code programmatically, using C# code. Setting the status code of a page is simple — you just need to set the `Status` property of the `HttpContext.Response` object to the status code you want to return:

```
// send back a 404 page if the page doesn't exist
context.Response.Write("Sorry, the requested page doesn't exist.");
context.Response.Status = "404 Not Found";
return;
```

Instead of setting the `Status` property as a string, you can use `StatusCode`, which is a numeric property:

```
context.Response.StatusCode = 404;
```

Avoiding Indexing Error Pages Using 500

Once upon a time, in a place far away, your web server is chugging along; everything is fine and dandy. Then, all of a sudden, something terrible happens, and the database goes down. Because this is an unanticipated error condition (all of us could do better error checking!), many pages return erroneous blank pages or perhaps 404s. Perhaps the web server goes down altogether. Worse still, you don't have a hot standby to replace it. Meanwhile, search engines are trying to index your pages, not finding anything, getting blank pages, and so on. Let's go through the possibilities:

❑ *Returning 404s or blank pages.* This is a real problem. If a server returns a 404, a search engine will de-list your pages. If a search engine sees blank pages, or pages full of errors, it may do the same. This should be avoided at all costs.

❑ *Not finding anything (no connection).* This is actually more desirable than it sounds in terms of indexing. Though this makes you look unprofessional to a human visitor, a search engine is likely to assume that there are intermittent connectivity problems and try again later. From a spider's point of view, as long as this is resolved in a day or so, there is no major problem.

So what is the proper solution during a server crisis? It's actually fairly simple. A "500" status code can be returned, along with a custom page describing the error. This indicates to search engines that there is a temporary technical problem. Perhaps the site is down for maintenance. Say it politely and provide the time it will be back up. Or perhaps there was a national disaster as in the case of certain web servers in the New Orleans area. Put up a global error page for every URL with a polite message, and wait for things to clear up. One could also do this automatically if, for example, the database cannot be accessed.

To do this in ASP.NET you simply need to set the response status code to 500. It's also advisable to generate some output that informs human visitors that you're encountering technical difficulties:

```
// send back a 500 page during a server error
context.Response.Write("The bank is closed until the scary aliens leave on their
space ship; sorry for the inconvenience, thank you for being a Bank of Mars
customer.");
context.Response.Status = "500 Internal Server Error";
return;
```

Building Custom Error Pages

When an unhandled exception is thrown by your ASP.NET application, the 500 status code is correctly used. Take, for example, the error generated by a test script — `ErrorTest.aspx` — that tries to divide a number by 0. When the page is loaded from the local machine, by default ASP.NET generates a detailed debug message that is sent with the 500 status code — this is shown in Figure 4-4. The default output received by external users differs (it doesn't include the debugging details by default), but it's still returned with a 500 status code.

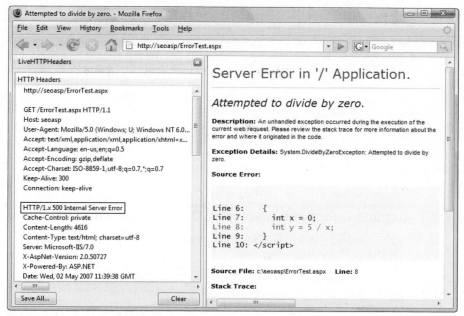

Figure 4-4

When developing a real-world application, as part of your error handling strategy, you'll generally want to:

❑ Generate custom pages that would be displayed on certain errors. You should have at least custom 404 and 500 pages.

❑ Log errors so that your developers can prevent them from happening in the future. This step is particularly important when dealing with errors that don't occur frequently, and only affect a few visitors of your site. These errors would likely go unnoticed unless an error reporting feature is used.

Perhaps the best place to log the application errors is the Global.asax file. As you learned in Chapter 3, this includes handlers for global application events. One of those handlers is named Application_Error(), which is fired when a server error occurs. Possible logging methods include emailing the error details to the site administrator, saving them to the event log, or even saving them into the database. (This latter method shouldn't be used alone, because it may not be able to log database-related errors.)

You can use this method to log your error, like this:

```
void Application_Error(Object sender, EventArgs e)
{
  // log error details
}
```

An example of real error logging code is provided in the exercise that follows.

ASP.NET lets you configure pages for certain status codes easily through the `<customErrors>` element in `Web.config`. For example, you can specify what pages the request should be redirected to for certain status codes. We generally recommend creating a custom 404 page that suggests to your visitors other pages they can visit on your web site. This page can be as simple as an `.html` page linking to your site's home page, or as complex as a script that suggests possible pages depending on what the visitor might have been looking for. The 500 page should be as simple as possible, with no code — ideally a simple `.html` page. Your web server is already having problems, and you should avoid having it execute any additional code.

The following exercise quickly demonstrates how you can set up custom 404 and 500 pages using ASP.NET, and how to send the error details by email.

Logging Errors and Displaying Custom 404 and 500 Pages

1. Load `http://seoasp/` in Visual Web Developer, and add a Web Form named `ErrorTest.aspx` in your project, with the following code:

```
<%@ Page Language="C#" %>
<!DOCTYPE html PUBLIC "-//W3C//DTD XHTML 1.0 Transitional//EN"
"http://www.w3.org/TR/xhtml1/DTD/xhtml1-transitional.dtd">

<script runat="server">
  protected void Page_Load(object sender, EventArgs e)
  {
    int x = 0;
    int y = 5 / x;
  }
</script>

<html xmlns="http://www.w3.org/1999/xhtml" >
<head runat="server">
  <title>Testing ASP.NET Errors</title>
</head>
<body>
  This text will not show up in your browser because of the error in the code.
</body>
</html>
```

2. Open your `Web.config` configuration file and search for an element named `<customErrors>`, and edit it like this:

```
<customErrors mode="On" defaultRedirect="~/ServerError.aspx">
  <error statusCode="404" redirect="~/NotFound.aspx" />
  <error statusCode="500" redirect="~/ServerError.aspx" />
</customErrors>
```

3. Add a Web Form named `ServerError.aspx` to your project, with these contents:

```
<%@ Page Language="C#" %>
<!DOCTYPE html PUBLIC "-//W3C//DTD XHTML 1.0 Transitional//EN"
"http://www.w3.org/TR/xhtml1/DTD/xhtml1-transitional.dtd">
```

```
<script runat="server">
  protected void Page_Load(object sender, EventArgs e)
  {
    // set the 500 status code
    Response.Status = "500 Internal Server Error";
  }
</script>

<html xmlns="http://www.w3.org/1999/xhtml" >
<head>
  <title>Example.com Server Error</title>
</head>
<body>
  <h1>Sorry!</h1>
  <p>We're currently experiencing technical difficulties, and can't display the
    page you requested. Please accept our apologies, and visit us at
    <asp:HyperLink Text="<%$ AppSettings:SiteDomain %>"
            NavigateUrl="<%$ AppSettings:SiteDomain %>" runat="server" />
    soon.</p>
</body>
</html>
```

4.   Now add a Web Form named `NotFound.aspx` to your project, and type this code in:

```
<%@ Page Language="C#" %>
<!DOCTYPE html PUBLIC "-//W3C//DTD XHTML 1.0 Transitional//EN"
"http://www.w3.org/TR/xhtml1/DTD/xhtml1-transitional.dtd">

<script runat="server">
  protected void Page_Load(object sender, EventArgs e)
  {
    // set the 404 status code
    Response.Status = "404 Not Found";
  }
</script>

<html xmlns="http://www.w3.org/1999/xhtml" >
<head runat="server">
  <title>Example.com Page Not Found</title>
</head>
<body>
  <form id="form1" runat="server">
    <h1>SEO Egghead Shop</h1>
    <p>The page you requested doesn't exist on our web site. Please visit our
<asp:HyperLink Text="home page" NavigateUrl="<%$ AppSettings:SiteDomain %>"
runat="server" />, and check out our best selling products:</p>

<img src="<%=LinkFactory.MakeMediaUrl("Tweety", "jpg", "1")%>" alt="Tweety" />
<img src="<%=LinkFactory.MakeMediaUrl("Toy Story", "jpg", "2")%>"
alt="Toy Story" />
<img src="<%=LinkFactory.MakeMediaUrl("Minnie", "jpg", "5")%>" alt="Minnie" />
  </form>
</body>
</html>
```

5. Open `Global.asax`, and add the following code to the `Application_Error` method. This code will email you the details of the error when a 404 or 500 page is displayed to the visitor. If you don't care for this feature, you can skip this step and the next.

```
<%@ Application Language="C#" %>
<%@ Import Namespace="System.Net" %>
<%@ Import Namespace="System.Net.Mail" %>
<%@ Import Namespace="System.Configuration" %>

<script runat="server">
...

  void Application_Error(Object sender, EventArgs e)
  {
    // get the exception details
    Exception ex = Server.GetLastError();
    if (ex.InnerException != null) ex = ex.InnerException;

    // get the current date and time
    string dateTime = DateTime.Now.ToLongDateString() + ", at "
                    + DateTime.Now.ToShortTimeString();

    // build the error message
    string errorMessage = "Exception generated on " + dateTime;
    System.Web.HttpContext context = System.Web.HttpContext.Current;
    errorMessage += "\n\n Page location: " + context.Request.RawUrl;
    errorMessage += "\n\n Message: " + ex.Message;
    errorMessage += "\n\n Source: " + ex.Source;
    errorMessage += "\n\n Method: " + ex.TargetSite;
    errorMessage += "\n\n Stack Trace: \n\n" + ex.StackTrace;

    // email the error details
    string mailServer = ConfigurationManager.AppSettings["EmailServer"];
    string from = ConfigurationManager.AppSettings["ErrorEmailFrom"];
    string to = ConfigurationManager.AppSettings["ErrorEmailTo"];
    string smtpUser = ConfigurationManager.AppSettings["SmtpHostUserName"];
    string smtpPassword = ConfigurationManager.AppSettings["SmtpHostPassword"];

    string subject = "Example.com error report";
    try
    {
      SmtpClient mailClient = new SmtpClient(mailServer);
      MailMessage mailMessage = new MailMessage(from, to, subject, errorMessage);
      mailClient.Credentials = new NetworkCredential(smtpUser, smtpPassword);
      mailClient.Send(mailMessage);
    }
    catch(Exception myex) { /* ignore errors */ }
  }

</script>
```

6. Add these settings in `Web.config`, changing the highlighted values to those of the email server you want to use for sending error logging emails:

```
<appSettings>
  <add key="SiteDomain" value="http://seoasp" />
  <add key="EmailServer" value="mail.example.com" />
  <add key="ErrorEmailFrom" value="errors@example.com" />
  <add key="ErrorEmailTo" value="admin@example.com" />
  <add key="ErrorEmailSmtpUserName" value="myUsername" />
  <add key="ErrorEmailSmtpPassword" value="myPassword" />
</appSettings>
```

> Make sure that you set correct email data, otherwise the email function will not work.

7. Let's test the new features now. Load `http://seoasp/ErrorTest.aspx`. If you run the project in Debug mode, the `DivideByZeroException` will first be caught by the debugger, and the offending line of code will be highlighted in Visual Web Developer, as shown in Figure 4-5. If this was a "real" error, now you'd normally use debugging windows such as Locals or Watch (accessible through the Debug > Windows menu) to investigate the error. Instead, just press **F5** to let the application continue its execution, in spite of the error.

8. After the unhandled exception is raised (`DivideByZeroException`), the execution is passed immediately to the `Application_Error()` handler in `Global.asax`. This method executes and sends the details of the error over email. (Alternatively, you could save the error details to the Windows Event Log, or save them to a text file on your file system.) Finally, the request is redirected to `ServerError.aspx` (as configured in `Web.config`), as shown in Figure 4-6. Figure 4-7 shows the message you can expect to receive in your mailbox when making this test.

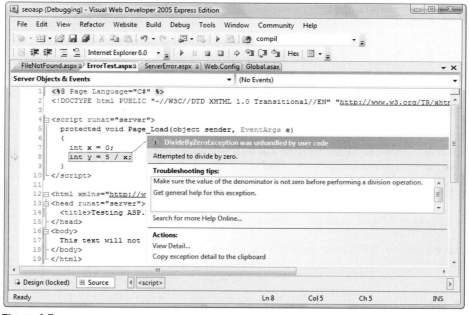

Figure 4-5

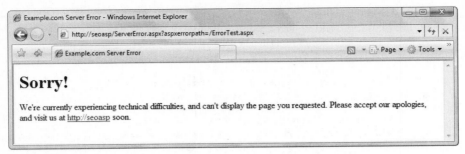

Figure 4-6

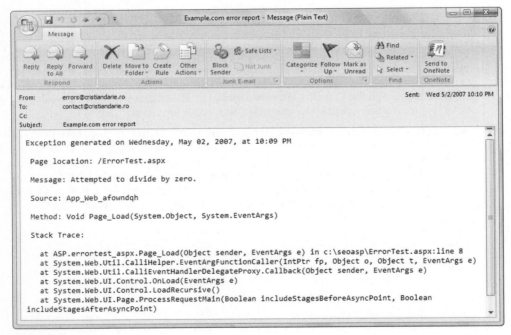

Figure 4-7

So you wrote quite a bit of code for your 404 and 500 pages, and for the supporting error logging code. These are loaded automatically by the ASP.NET runtime when necessary, but at times you'll want to redirect or rewrite the incoming request to these pages yourself. Take, for example, this `RewriteRule` ISAPI_Rewrite directive, which rewrites requests for `ProductRemoved.aspx` to `NotFound.aspx`.

```
RewriteRule ^/ProductRemoved.aspx$ /NotFound.aspx
```

In Figure 4-8 you can see that the request for `ProductRemoved.aspx` is correctly rewritten, and you get back a page with the 404 status code. This way, search engines will know not to index the retrieved contents.

Figure 4-8

However, typically ASP.NET applications don't rely entirely on URL rewriting to display the 404 and 500 pages. This is because the `<customErrors>` element supported by `Web.config` makes it easy to define your 404 and 500 pages (and pages for other status codes as well), to which the response is automatically **302 redirected to** when necessary. Take, for example, a request to `http://seoasp/Gimme404` `.aspx`. This URL doesn't exist on your server, and is not rewritten by any rewrite rules — so the following `Web.config` setting redirects the request to `NotFound.aspx`:

```
<customErrors mode="On" defaultRedirect="~/ServerError.aspx">
  <error statusCode="404" redirect="~/NotFound.aspx" />
  <error statusCode="500" redirect="~/ServerError.aspx" />
</customErrors>
```

Indeed, as highlighted in Figure 4-9, the request isn't rewritten to `NotFound.aspx`, but 302 redirected to it. Rewriting the request is the cleaner way to do this from an SEO perspective, but unfortunately the functionality of `<customErrors>` isn't customizable (despite its name).

> You learned in Chapter 3 that by default, IIS will only pass to the ASP.NET ISAPI extension requests for ASP.NET file extensions — such as `.aspx`. As a consequence, your ASP.NET web application can only intercept 404 errors for file-not-found requests made for those files. Unless you configured your server to pass all requests to ASP.NET, you should also define a 404 page through IIS, which would be displayed for file-not-found requests for non-ASP.NET file extensions. The 404 page that is configured through IIS should have its own logging mechanism, if you need one. This is necessary because a 404 page loaded by IIS will not be regarded as an error by ASP.NET, so the `Application_Error` event — which is necessary for the presented logging mechanism — won't fire.

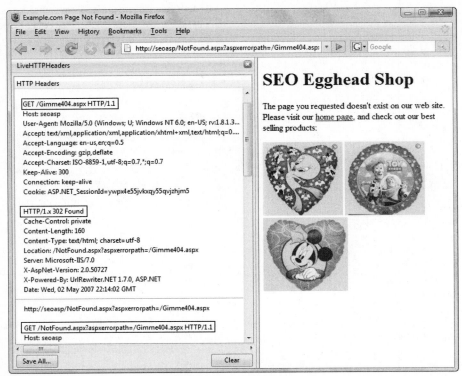

Figure 4-9

Let's highlight the relevant technical implementation details before moving on to the next subject:

❑ In our 404 and 500 pages, we set the appropriate status code using `Response.Status`. Similar functionality can be achieved by setting `Response.StatusCode` to the integer value of the code we want to set.

❑ Any errors that happen when sending the email are ignored, using the empty `catch` block. This behavior is by design — if `Application_Error()` is executed, you already have an error in your application, so you don't want to risk causing others.

❑ If you're using UrlRewriter.NET and Windows Vista/IIS 7, you may have set your application to use the `DefaultAppPool` to enable rewriting for all files. To be able to debug your application, you'll need to temporarily switch your application to Classic .NET AppPool.

❑ Because by default the errors that can happen when sending the email are ignored, while developing your application you'll need to make sure the email feature works.

❑ `Application_Error()` is executed not only when an exception it thrown away by your own code, but also when other errors happen — such as File Not Found (404). Your error logging feature will then catch these errors too.

❑ In `Application_Error()`, we get the exception that caused the problem using `Server`
`.GetLastError()`. In case the exception was raised by your code, the real exception you're
interested in can be retrieved through this exception's `InnerException` property. This is why
when `InnerException` is something different than null, we take the exception details from
there.

❑ As noted earlier, in case ASP.NET doesn't process all incoming requests, you should also set a
404 page through IIS. This feature isn't available for the 500 page. As per the documentation, the
following status codes aren't customizable through IIS 6: 400, 403.9, 411, 414, 500, 500.11, 500.14,
500.15, 501, 503, and 505.

Redirecting with ASP.NET and IIS

From now on, we will primarily be discussing uses of the 301 HTTP status code. You can implement 301
redirects using ISAPI Rewriting modules, products like UrlRewriter.NET, or from within your ASP.NET
code by setting the appropriate header data.

When using ISAPI_Rewrite, redirecting is implemented similarly to URL rewriting, except that you specify a redirection status code as a parameter. The following rule does a 301 redirect to `Catalog.aspx` when
the initial request is for `Catalog.html`:

```
# 301 Redirect Catalog.html to Catalog.aspx
RewriteRule ^/Catalog.html$ http://seoasp/Catalog.aspx [RP]
```

The `[RP]` option of the rewrite rule specifies that a permanent redirect (301) should be made. If you want
to use a temporary redirect (302), `[R]` should be used instead.

> Note the specification requires you to specify absolute URLs in redirect instructions. For example, in
> this example we redirected to `http://seoasp/Catalog.aspx`, and not to `/Catalog.aspx`. Most
> clients will understand relative paths as well, but ideally you'd always specify absolute locations for
> redirection. Future versions of ISAPI_Rewrite are planned to add the missing parts of the URL auto-
> matically, but the current version at the time of writing this book, 2.11, does not. The redirection syntax
> may also be updated. Any changes that affect the theory in the book will be documented at `http://www`
> `.cristiandarie.ro/seo-asp/`.

Except for the new `[RP]` option at the end, there's nothing new for you here — but that option represents
an important difference! With or without the `[R]` or `[RP]` option, the visitor would end up seeing the content provided by `Catalog.aspx`. However, when redirection is used, the user's web client actually makes
two calls to the web server. First it asks for `Catalog.html`; as a response, it gets a 301 (in case of `[RP]`)
or a 302 (in case of `[R]`) redirect code in the HTTP header, indicating `Catalog.aspx` as the new location.
Then the web client requests `Catalog.aspx`, and informs the user that a new URL has been loaded by
updating the URL displayed in the address bar.

Redirecting using UrlRewriter.NET is equally easy:

```
<redirect url="^/Catalog.html$" to="/Catalog.aspx" permanent="true" />
```

When the `permanent` attribute is `false` the redirect uses the 302 status code, otherwise a 301 redirect is made.

If you want to implement the redirect yourself, you need to manipulate the response headers using the Response object provided by your current HttpContext object. Here's how to 301 redirect `Catalog.html` to `Catalog.aspx` yourself:

```
if (context.Request.Path == "/Catalog.html")
{
  context.Response.Status = "301 Moved Permanently";
  context.Response.AddHeader("Location", "http://www.example.com/Catalog.aspx");
}
```

> **When just the `Location` header is mentioned without explicitly mentioning the status code, a *302* temporary redirect is implied. Keep this in mind.**

In practice, when a site redesign involves changing URLs, the webmaster should at least 301 redirect the most important URLs to their new counterparts. Otherwise link equity of the old URLs will be lost.

In the remainder of this chapter we analyze to the most common problems web sites face today that can be solved using HTTP redirection. We discuss:

❑ URL correction

❑ Dealing with multiple domain names

❑ URL canonicalization and eliminating `Default.aspx`

URL Correction

The great advantage with our current keyword-rich URLs is that we aren't really relying on the product or category names to find their data, but rather only on their IDs, which are subtly inserted in the URLs. This works great because the text in the URL can change without disabling it.

One potential problem with these links, though, is that when the text for a product or category name changes, its link will automatically be changed as well. As you already know, this has the potential to generate duplicate content problems, and that's certainly not something that you want!

With our current site, there are an infinite number of variations that lead to the same content. Take these three different URLs, which currently generate the same content:

```
http://seoasp/Product.aspx?CategoryID=6&ProductID=31
http://seoasp/Products/SEO-Toolbox-C6/Link-Juice-P31.html
http://seoasp/Products/SEO-Toolbox-C6/New-Link-Juice-With-Vitamin-L-P31.html
```

The solution we're proposing is to choose a standard version of the URL, and 301 redirects all the other URLs that refer to that content to the standard URL. This avoids duplicate content problems that can result from multiple URLs returning the same content. This process is also critical during a migration to keyword-rich URLs on a preexisting web site, in order to preserve URL equity.

Note that rewriting engines can't help here, because they don't have access to your product database. You can use regular expressions to transform `/SEO-Toolbox-C6/` into `?CategoryID=6`, but you can't do the transformation the other way around unless you know the name of the category with the ID of 6. That's why redirecting dynamic URLs to keyword-rich URLs needs to be taken care of in your ASP.NET application.

The exercise that follows demonstrates how to do exactly that.

Implementing Automatic URL Correction

1. Add a new C# class file named `SeoData.cs` to the `App_Code` folder in the `http://seoasp/` project, and type the following code in it. This class contains the IDs and names of a few products and categories, simulating a real product database. (We prefer to avoid using a real database to keep the exercise easier for you to follow. Exercises that use SQL Server database tables are presented later in the book.)

```csharp
using System.Collections.Specialized;

/// <summary>
/// Represents a fictional database with products and categories
/// </summary>
public static class SeoData
{
  // objects that store products and categories data
  public static NameValueCollection Products = new NameValueCollection();
  public static NameValueCollection Categories = new NameValueCollection();

  // static constructor
  static SeoData()
  {
    // add sample products to the collection
    Products.Add("15", "Fortune Cookie");
    Products.Add("31", "Link Juice");
    Products.Add("42", "ASP.NET 2.0 E-Commerce Book");
    Products.Add("45", "Belt Sander");

    // and categories
    Categories.Add("2", "Bookstore");
    Categories.Add("6", "SEO Toolbox");
    Categories.Add("12", "Carpenter's Tools");
  }
}
```

2. Create a new class file named `UrlTools.cs` in your `App_Code` folder, and type this code:

```csharp
using System;
using System.Web;
using System.Configuration;

/// <summary>
/// Class provides support for URL manipulation and redirection
/// </summary>
```

```csharp
public static class UrlTools
{
  // obtain the site domain from the configuration file
  static string siteDomain = ConfigurationManager.AppSettings["SiteDomain"];

  /* ensures the current page is being loaded through its standard URL;
   * 301 redirect to the standard URL if it doesn't */
  public static void CheckUrl()
  {
    HttpContext context = HttpContext.Current;
    HttpRequest request = HttpContext.Current.Request;

    // retrieve query string parameters
    string productId = request.QueryString["ProductID"];
    string categoryId = request.QueryString["CategoryID"];

    // fix category-product URLs
    if (productId != null && categoryId != null)
    {
      CheckCategoryProductUrl(categoryId, productId);
    }
  }

  // checks a category-product URL for compliancy
  // 301 redirects to proper URL, or returns 404 if necessary
  public static void CheckCategoryProductUrl(string categoryId, string productId)
  {
    // the current HttpContext
    HttpContext context = HttpContext.Current;

    // the URL requested by the visitor
    string requestedUrl = context.Request.ServerVariables["HTTP_X_REWRITE_URL"];

    // retrieve product and category names from fictional database
    string categoryName = SeoData.Categories[categoryId];
    string productName = SeoData.Products[productId];

    // if the category or the product doesn't exist in the database, return 404
    if (categoryName == null || productName == null)
    {
      Go404();
    }

    // obtain the standard version of the URL
    string standardUrl = LinkFactory.MakeCategoryProductUrl(categoryName,
categoryId, productName, productId);

    // 301 redirect to the proper URL if necessary
    if (siteDomain + requestedUrl != standardUrl)
    {
      context.Response.Status = "301 Moved Permanently";
      context.Response.AddHeader("Location", standardUrl);
    }
```

```
  }

  // Load the 404 page
  public static void Go404()
  {
    HttpContext.Current.Server.Transfer("~/NotFound.aspx");
  }
}
```

3. Make sure you have the `SiteDomain` value set in `Web.config`:

```
<appSettings>
  <add key="SiteDomain" value="http://seoasp" />
```

4. Open `Global.asax` and call `UrlTools.CheckUrl()` in `Application_BeginRequest()`. This way, `UrlTools.CheckUrl()` gets executed on every user request, and it has a chance to 301 redirect the request to another URL if necessary.

```
void Application_BeginRequest(object sender, EventArgs e)
{
  // ensures a standard URL is used, 301 redirect to it otherwise
  UrlTools.CheckUrl();
}
```

5. Now it's time to put the new code to the test. Note that it's assumed that you have in place one of the URL rewriting solutions presented in Chapter 3, using either ISAPI_Rewrite or UrlRewriter.NET — both will do equally fine. Load `http://seoasp/Product.aspx?CategoryID=6&ProductID=15` in your web browser, and see some magic happen to the URL! Figure 4-10 shows how this request was redirected to its standard, keyword-rich version of the URL.

6. Now try loading the page of a product that doesn't exist in the "database," such as `http://seoasp/Product.aspx?CategoryID=99&ProductID=22`. In this case, as Figure 4-11 shows, you'd get the 404 page you created earlier in this chapter.

One place to verify that a page has been loaded using the standard URL would be the `Page_Load()` event handler of the page. However, we found that it is generally easier to do the URL verification in the `Application_BeginRequest()` handler of `Global.asax`, which is executed on every client request. We use this method as a central place to filter all incoming requests, and decide what to do with them:

```
void Application_BeginRequest(object sender, EventArgs e)
{
  // ensures a standard URL is used, 301 redirect to it otherwise
  UrlTools.CheckUrl();
}
```

The `UrlTools.CheckUrl()` method has the mission to verify that visitor requested the page using the standard URL. If that is not the case, the request is 301 redirected to the standard URL that is supposed to deliver that content. Moreover, if the request is for a product ID or category ID that doesn't exist in our database, the 404 page is returned instead, indicating that the requested content doesn't exist. Let's see how this is implemented.

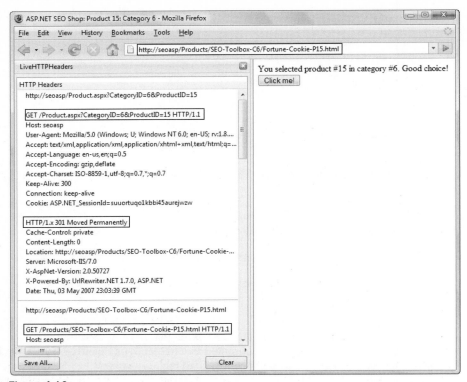

Figure 4-10

Figure 4-11

The `UrlTools.CheckUrl()` method starts by reading the product ID and category ID from the query string:

```
public static void CheckUrl()
{
  HttpContext context = HttpContext.Current;
  HttpRequest request = HttpContext.Current.Request;

  // retrieve query string parameters
  string productId = request.QueryString["ProductID"];
  string categoryId = request.QueryString["CategoryID"];
```

If both these IDs are present, we assume the visitor has requested a category-product page, so we call `CheckCategoryProductUrl()` for further URL checking:

```
  // fix category-product URLs
  if (productId != null && categoryId != null)
  {
    CheckCategoryProductUrl(categoryId, productId);
  }
}
```

Note that if any of the IDs are not present, the function exits without doing any further verification. This behavior is important because we may not want to enforce "standard" URLs for all sections of the web site.

`UrlTools.CheckCategoryProductUrl()` reads the category and product names from our fictional database, which is simulated using the `SeoData` class. In a real-world scenario we'd use a real database, but for the purposes of this exercise it was easier to simply hard-code a few products and categories in `NameValueCollection` objects. We also read the `HTTP_X_REWRITE_URL` server variable, which is used by both ISAPI_Rewrite and UrlRewriter.NET to store the URL that was requested by the visitor. (See Chapter 3 for more details.)

```
public static void CheckCategoryProductUrl(string categoryId, string productId)
{
  // the current HttpContext
  HttpContext context = HttpContext.Current;

  // the URL requested by the visitor
  string requestedUrl = context.Request.ServerVariables["HTTP_X_REWRITE_URL"];

  // retrieve product and category names from fictional database
  string categoryName = SeoData.Categories[categoryId];
  string productName = SeoData.Products[productId];
```

Then we do a simple check to ensure that `categoryName` and `productName` are not null. If any of these is null, we assume they couldn't be found in the database, so we can't create a page to show their details. In this case we call the `Go404()` method, which uses `Server.Transfer()` to load the 404 page we built earlier in this chapter:

```
  // if the category or the product doesn't exist in the database, return 404
  if (categoryName == null || productName == null)
  {
    Go404();
  }
```

If we do have a category name and a product name, we use the link factory built in Chapter 3 to obtain the standard version of the URL, which contains the product and category names and IDs:

```
        // obtain the standard version of the URL
        string standardUrl = LinkFactory.MakeCategoryProductUrl(categoryName,
    int.Parse(categoryId), productName, int.Parse(productId));
```

The `standardUrl` variable will contain a string such as `http://seoasp/Products/SEO-Toolbox-C6/Link-Juice-P31.html`. We compare this value with the URL requested by the visitor. If they don't match, we 301 redirect the request to the URL contained by `standardUrl`:

```
        // 301 redirect to the proper URL if necessary
        if (siteDomain + requestedUrl != properUrl)
        {
            context.Response.Status = "301 Moved Permanently";
            context.Response.AddHeader("Location", standardUrl);
        }
    }
```

Dealing with Multiple Domain Names Properly

Though it's less popular these days, some people desire to have multiple domain names pointing to the same site. For example, let's say we have three domain names:

```
www.example.com
www.example.org
www.example.net
```

The problem is that, especially if we market all three domains, people are free to link to any of these domains. That's a major duplicate content issue. We must pick a "standard" domain and permanently redirect the other domains to that domain.

Let's pick `www.example.com`. This is how to do it with ISAPI_Rewrite:

```
RewriteCond Host: (?!www\.example\.com).*
RewriteRule ^/(.*)$ http://www.example.com/$1 [I,RP]
```

Done! Now everything will get redirected to `www.example.com`. We used `RewriteCond` to place a condition for the rule that follows. In this case, we're interested in verifying that the site has been accessed through `www.example.com`.

This `RewriteCond` directive specifies a condition that is true when the host name is not `www.example.com`. The rewrite rule captures the entire query string of the original URL, as `(.*)`, and passes is to `http://www.example.com`, doing a 301 redirect to the new location. This way, for example, a query to `http://www.example.org?query=string` would be 301 redirected to `http://www.example.com?query=string`.

Using Redirects to Change Domain Names

Sometimes you *have* to change your domain name. Usually this happens in M&A (mergers and acquisitions) cases. Although undesirable, there is a right way to do this, and many wrong ones. Typically both domains need to point to the same web site now that the merger occurred. The *worst* thing one can do is simply point both domains to the same content via DNS. This will result in search engines not knowing which is authoritative. Many links have presumably built up over the years for both domain names, and a search engine will have considerable difficulty ascertaining which to index. The result is a massive duplicate content problem. One could also take down the old domain, or put a page up on the old domain indicating to users that they should visit the new domain. Both of these methods avert duplicate content problems, but do not result in transference of link equity. The proper way to handle such a necessity is to use a 301 redirect to the new domain.

With ISAPI_Rewrite, simply place this in your `httpd.ini` file:

```
RewriteCond Host: old\.example\.com|^www\.old\.example\.com
RewriteRule ^/(.*)$ http://www.new.example.com/$1 [I,RP]
```

This says that if a request for `old.example.com` or `www.old.example.com` comes in, it should be permanently redirected to `www.new.example.com`, keeping all the query string parameters. Note the way we've conditioned the rewrite rule using two `RewriteCond` rules.

Alternatively, you can assert something with another (similar) meaning:

```
RewriteCond Host: (?!www\.new.example\.com).*
RewriteRule ^/(.*)$ http://www.new.example.com/$1 [RP,I]
```

which says, similar to the canonicalization situation, anything that's not the right domain should be redirected.

URL Canonicalization: www.example.com vs. example.com

This is another topic that comes up again and again. Because every search engine (including Google — even after the BigDaddy update) has issues when a web site is accessible under both `www.example.com` and `example.com` domains, we should be responsible webmasters and remove the ambiguity altogether. Otherwise both versions may be indexed and cause duplicate content problems. This is a fairly simple task.

With ISAPI_Rewrite, simply place this in your `httpd.ini` file:

```
RewriteCond Host: ^example\.com
RewriteRule ^/(.*)$ http://www.example.com/$1 [RP,I]
```

This says that if a request for `example.com[path]` comes in, it should be permanently redirected to `www.example.com[path]`.

Alternatively, you can assert something with another (similar meaning):

```
RewriteCond Host: (?!www\.example\.com).*
RewriteRule ^/(.*)$ http://www.example.com/$1 [RP,I]
```

This says that if any request designated to this site comes in with something other than `www.example.com`, it should be changed to that. This is a slightly broader definition, and may or may not be desirable. It will also redirect any other domains that resolve to your site to `www.example.com`.

Please note, it is *not* a good idea to use a site removal tool to remove the example.com pages for a site, even after these changes have been applied! This can result in complete site removal. Matt Cutts of Google says "If you remove one of the www vs. non-www hostnames, it can end up removing your whole domain for six months. Definitely don't do this." (http://www.mattcutts.com/blog/seo-advice-url-canonicalization/). Instead, simply 301 the non-desirable domain to the desirable one, and the problem should slowly be resolved over time.

URL Canonicalization: /Default.aspx vs. /

Unfortunately, the concept of index pages (index.php, Default.aspx, and so on) causes yet another duplicate content problem. If no file name in a directory is provided to a web server, the "index" page is typically provided by default, but without redirection to this page. The problem arises when both URLs are linked, either internally or from other sites. This results in duplicate content because there are two URLs that are used to access the same content. Strictly speaking, neither URL is "more correct," although we naturally favor / over /Default.aspx.

The solution is similar to the one for the www.example.com vs. example.com issue. We must use a 301 redirect to the containing directory whenever we get a request for a file path ending in Default.aspx. The redirection code can simply be implemented using an ISAPI_Rewrite rule, like this:

```
RewriteRule ([^?]*)(Index|Default)\.aspx$ $1 [RP,I]
```

After making this change, trying to load http://seoasp/Default.aspx should redirect you to http://seoasp/.

Other Types of Redirects

Although there are other types of redirects, such as meta refresh and JavaScript redirects, we do not generally recommend their use. Spammers have historically abused them, and for this reason their use is almost *always* suspect. It is recommended that a meta refresh is never used with a delay of less than 10 seconds. A typical meta refresh is illustrated here:

```
<!-- Redirect to SEO Egghead in 10 seconds -->
<meta http-equiv="refresh" content="10;url=http://www.seoegghead.com/">
```

We do not recommend using JavaScript-based redirects at all. If discovered, it will most likely result in some sort of penalty.

Summary

This chapter has illustrated that a fundamental understanding of relevant HTTP status codes is vital to the search engine marketer. Business decisions dictate that pages move, domains change, or that content is removed. Informing the search engine of these decisions using these status codes can avert a very costly "misunderstanding."

5

Duplicate Content

We humans often find it frustrating to listen to people repeat themselves. Likewise, search engines are "frustrated" by web sites that do the same. This problem is called *duplicate content*, which is defined as web content that is either exactly duplicated or substantially similar to content located at different URLs. Duplicate content clearly does not contain anything *original*.

This is important to realize. Originality is an important factor in the human perception of value, and search engines factor such human sentiments into their algorithms. Seeing several pages of duplicated content would not please the user. Accordingly, search engines employ sophisticated algorithms that detect such content and filter it out from search engine results.

Indexing and processing duplicate content also wastes the storage and computation time of a search engine in the first place. Aaron Wall of `http://www.seobook.com/` states that "if pages are too similar, then Google [or other search engines] may assume that they offer little value or are of poor content quality." A web site may not get spidered as often or as comprehensively as a result. And though it is an issue of contention in the search engine marketing community as to whether there is an *explicit* penalty applied by the various search engines, everyone agrees that duplicate content can be harmful.

Knowing this, it would be wise to eliminate as much duplicate content as possible from a web site. This chapter documents the most common causes of duplicate content as a result of web site architecture. It then proposes methods to eliminate it, or remove it from a search engine's view. In this chapter you will:

- ❑ Understand the potential negative effects of duplicate content.
- ❑ Examine the most common types of duplicate content.
- ❑ Learn how to exclude duplicate content using `robots.txt` and `meta` tags.
- ❑ Use ASP.NET code to properly support affiliate links.

A common question asked by search engine marketers is "how much duplicate content is too much?" There is no good answer to that question, as you may have predicted. We advise to simply take the conservative approach of eliminating as much of it as possible.

Causes and Effects of Duplicate Content

You know duplicate content can have a negative effect on web site rankings. But how do you examine whether a particular web site exhibits this problem, and how do you mitigate or avoid it?

To begin, you can divide duplicate content into two main categories:

❑ Duplicate content as a result of site architecture

❑ Duplicate content as a result of content theft

These are discussed separately, because they are essentially completely different problems.

Duplicate Content as a Result of Site Architecture

Some examples of site architecture itself leading to duplicate content are as follows:

❑ Print-friendly pages

❑ Pages with items that are extremely similar, such as a series of differently colored shirts in an e-commerce catalog having similar descriptions

❑ Pages that are part of an improperly configured affiliate program tracking application

❑ Pages with duplicate title or `meta` tag values

❑ Pages that use URL-based session IDs

❑ Pages with substantially similar content that can be accessed via different URLs

❑ Canonicalization problems

To look for duplicate content as a result of site architecture, you can use a "`site:www.example.com`" query to examine the URLs of a web site that a search engine has indexed. All major search engines (Google, Yahoo!, Microsoft Live Search) support this feature. Usually this will reveal quickly if, for example, "print-friendly" pages are being indexed.

Google frequently places content it perceives as duplicate content in the "supplemental index." This is noted at the bottom of a search engine result with the phrase "supplemental result." If your web site has many pages in the supplemental index, it may mean that those pages are considered duplicate content — at least by Google. Investigate several pages of URLs if possible, and look for the aforementioned cases. Look especially at the later pages of results. It is extremely easy to create duplicate content problems without realizing it, so viewing from the vantage point of a search engine may be useful.

Duplicate Content as a Result of Content Theft

Content theft creates an entirely different problem. Just as thieves can steal tangible goods, they can also steal content. This, unsurprisingly, is the reason why it is called content theft. It creates a similar problem for search engines, which strive to filter duplicate content from search results — across different web sites as well — and will sometimes make the wrong assumption as to which instance of the content is the original, authoritative one.

This is an insidious problem in some cases, and can have a disastrous effect on rankings. CopyScape (`http://www.copyscape.com`) is a service that helps you find content thieves by scanning for similar content contained by a given page on other pages. Sitemaps can also offer help by getting new content indexed more quickly and therefore removing the ambiguity as to who is the original author. Sitemaps are discussed at length in Chapter 9.

If you are a victim of content theft, and want to take action, first present the individual using the content illicitly with a cease and desist letter. Use the contact information provided on his web site or in the WHOIS record of the domain name. Failing that, the major search engines have procedures to alert them of stolen content. Here are URLs with the directions for the major search engines:

❑ Google: `http://www.google.com/dmca.html`

❑ Yahoo!: `http://docs.yahoo.com/info/copyright/copyright.html`

❑ MSN: `http://search.msn.com/docs/siteowner.aspx?t=SEARCH_WEBMASTER_CONC_AboutDMCA.htm`

Unfortunately, fighting content theft is ridiculously time-consuming and expensive — especially if lawyers get involved. Doing so for all instances is probably unrealistic; and search engines generally *do* accurately assess who is the original author and display that one preferentially. In Google, the illicit duplicates are typically relegated to the supplemental index. However, it may be necessary to take this action in the unlikely case that the URLs with the stolen content actually rank better than yours.

Excluding Duplicate Content

When you have duplicate content on your site, you can remove it entirely by altering the architecture of a web site. But sometimes a web site *has* to contain duplicate content. The most typical scenario of this is when the business rules that drive the web site require the said duplicate content.

To address this, you can simply exclude it from the view of a search engine. Here are the two ways of excluding pages:

❑ Using the `robots` meta tag

❑ `robots.txt` pattern exclusion

In the following sections, you learn about the `robots` meta tag and about `robots.txt`.

Using the Robots Meta Tag

This is addressed first, not because it's universally the optimal way to exclude content, but rather because it has virtually no limitations as to its application. Using the robots meta tag you can exclude any HTML-based content from a web site on a page-by-page basis, and it is frequently an easier method to use when eliminating duplicate content from a preexisting site for which the source code is available, or when a site contains many complex dynamic URLs.

To exclude a page with meta-exclusion, simply place the following code in the <head> section of the HTML document you want to exclude:

```
<meta name="robots" content="noindex, nofollow" />
```

This indicates that the page should not be indexed (noindex) and none of the links on the page should be followed (nofollow). It is relatively easy to apply some simple programming logic to decide whether or not to include such a meta tag on the pages of your site. It will always be applicable, so long as you have access to the source code of the application, whereas robots.txt exclusion may be difficult or even impossible to apply in certain cases.

To exclude a specific spider, change "robots" to the name of the spider — for example googlebot, msnbot, or slurp. To exclude multiple spiders, you can use multiple meta tags. For example, to exclude googlebot and msnbot:

```
<meta name="googlebot" content="noindex, nofollow" />
<meta name="msnbot" content="noindex, nofollow" />
```

Table 5-1 shows the common user agent names used by the various major search engines. The name of the search engine user agent is not case sensitive; both "googlebot" and "GoogleBot" will do.

Table 5-1

Search Engine	User Agent
Google	Googlebot
Yahoo!	Slurp
MSN Search	Msnbot
Ask	Teoma

In theory, this method is equivalent to the next method that is discussed, robots.txt. The only downside is that the page must be fetched in order to determine that it should not be indexed in the first place. This is likely to slow down indexing. Dan Thies also notes in *The Search Engine Marketing Kit* that "if your site serves 10 duplicate pages for every page of unique content, spiders may still give up indexing ... you can't count on the search engines to fish through your site looking for unique content."

There are two technical limitations are associated with using the meta-exclusion method:

❑ It requires access to the source code of the application. Otherwise, meta tag exclusion becomes impossible because the tag must be placed in the web pages generated by the application.

❑ It only works with HTML files, not with clear text, CSS, or binary/image files.

These limitations can be addressed by using the `robots.txt` file, which is discussed next. However, `robots.txt` also has some limitations as to its application. If you do not have access to the source code of a web application, however, `robots.txt` is your only option.

robots.txt Pattern Exclusion

`robots.txt` is a text file located in the root directory of a web site that adheres to the `robots.txt` standard. Taking the risk of repeating ourselves and generating a bit of "duplicate content," here are three basic things to keep in mind regarding `robots.txt`:

❑ There can be only one `robots.txt` file.

❑ The proper location of `robots.txt` is in the root directory of a web site.

❑ `robots.txt` files located in subdirectories will not be accessed (or honored).

The official resource with the official documentation of `robots.txt` *is* `http://www.robotstxt.org/`. *There you can find a Frequently Asked Questions page, the complete reference, and a list with the names of the robots crawling the web.*

If you peruse your logs, you will see that search engine spiders visit this particular file very frequently. This is because they make an effort not to crawl or index any files that are excluded by `robots.txt` and want to keep a very fresh copy cached. `robots.txt` excludes URLs from a search engine on a very simple pattern-matching basis, and it is frequently an easier method to use when eliminating entire directories from a site, or, more specifically, when you want to exclude many URLs that start with the same characters.

Sometimes for various internal reasons within a (usually large) company, it is not possible to gain access to modify this file in the root directory. In that case, so long as you have access to the source code of the part the application in question, use the meta `robots` tag.

> `robots.txt` is *not* a form of security! It does not prevent access to any files. It *does* stop a search engine from indexing the content, and therefore prevents users from navigating to those particular resources via a search engine results page. However, users could access the pages by navigating directly to them. Also, `robots.txt` itself is a public resource, and anyone who wants to peruse it can do so by pointing their browser to /robots.txt. If anything, using it for "security" would only make those resources even more obvious to potential hackers. To protect content, you should use the traditional ways of authenticating users using secure forms, and authorizing them to visit resources of your site.

A `robots.txt` file includes `User-agent` specifications, which define your exclusion targets, and `Disallow` entries for one or more URLs you want to exclude therein. Lines in `robots.txt` that start with # are comments, and are ignored.

The following `robots.txt` file, placed in the root folder of your site, would not permit any robots (*) to access any files on the site:

```
# Forbid all robots from browsing your site
User-agent: *
Disallow: /
```

The next example disallows any URLs that start with `/directory` from being indexed by Google:

```
# Disallow googlebot from indexing anything that starts with /directory
User-agent: googlebot
Disallow: /directory
```

`googlebot` is Google's user-agent name. It is useful to think of each `Disallow` as matching *prefixes*, not files or URLs. Notably, `/directory.html` (because `/directory` is a prefix of `/directory.html`) would also match that rule, and be excluded. If you want only the contents of the `directory` folder to be excluded, you should specify `/directory/` instead. That last / prevents `/directory.html` from matching. Note also that the leading / is always necessary on exclusions. The following would be invalid:

```
Disallow: directory
```

> **To elaborate, a string specified after `Disallow:` is equivalent to the regular expression `^<your string>.*$` — which means that it matches anything that begins with that string.**

The * we used for `User-agent` doesn't function as a wildcard "glob" operator. Not that it would be useful for anything, but `goo*bot` would not match `googlebot`, and is invalid.

Wildcard "glob" operators are also not *officially* valid in the `Disallow:` directive either, but Google, MSN, and more recently Yahoo!, support this non-standard form of wildcard matching. We generally do not recommend its use, however, both because it is not part of the standard, and because various other search engines do *not* support it.

> **If you must use wildcards in the `Disallow` clause, it is wise to do so only under a specific user-agent clause; for example, `User-agent: googlebot`.**

For information regarding the implementations of wildcard matching from search engine vendors, read:

- ❑ Google: http://www.google.com/support/webmasters/bin/answer.py?answer=35303
- ❑ MSN: http://search.msn.com.sg/docs/siteowner.aspx?t=SEARCH_WEBMASTER_REF_RestrictAccessToSite.htm#b
- ❑ Yahoo!: http://www.ysearchblog.com/archives/000372.html

Using wildcards, the following `robots.txt` file would tell Google not to index any URL containing the substring `print=` anywhere within the URL:

```
User-agent: googlebot
Disallow: /*print=
```

It may seem counterintuitive and rather annoying that there is no `Allow` *directive to complement* `Disallow`. *Certain search engines (Google and Yahoo! included) do indeed permit its use, but nuances of their interpretations may vary, and it is not part of the standard. We strongly recommend not using this directive.*

More robots.txt Examples

One strange-looking edge case is where you don't place any restrictions on the robot explicitly. In the following snippet, the empty `Disallow` directive means "no exclusion" for any robot. It is equivalent to having no `robots.txt` file at all:

```
User-agent: *
Disallow:
```

To exclude multiple URLs, simply enumerate them under a single `User-agent` directive. For example:

```
User-agent: *
Disallow: /directory
Disallow: /file.html
```

This will exclude any file that begins with `/directory`, and any file that begins with `/file.html`.

To use the same rules for multiple search engines, list the `User-agent` directives before the list of `Disallow` entries. For example:

```
User-agent: googlebot
User-agent: msnbot
Disallow: /directory
Disallow: /file.html
```

robots.txt Tips

In theory, according to the `robots.txt` specification, if a `Disallow:` for user agent * exists, as well a `Disallow:` for a specific robot user agent, and that robot accesses a web site, only the more specific rule for that particular robot should apply, and only one `Disallow:` would be excluded. Accordingly, it is necessary to repeat all rules in * under, for example, googlebot's user agent as well to exclude the items listed for `User-agent: *`.

Thus, the following rules would only exclude Z from googlebot, not X, Y, and Z as you may think:

```
User-agent: *
Disallow: X
Disallow: Y

User-agent: googlebot
Disallow: Z
```

If you want X, Y, and Z excluded for googlebot, you should use this:

```
User-agent: *
Disallow: X
Disallow: Y

User-agent: googlebot
Disallow: X
Disallow: Y
Disallow: Z
```

One last example:

```
User-agent: googlebot
Disallow:

User-agent: *
Disallow: /
```

These rules would only allow Google to spider your site. This is because the more specific rule for googlebot overrides the rule for *.

We recommend that webmasters place the exclusions for the default rule, *, last. According to the standard, this should not matter. However, there is some ambiguity as to whether a web spider picks the *first* matching rule, or the *most specific* matching rule. In the former case, if the * rule is placed first, it could conceivably be applied. Listing the * rule last removes that ambiguity.

Generating robots.txt On-the-Fly

Nothing prevents a site developer from programmatically generating the robots.txt file on-the-fly, dynamically. You can include a rewriting rule that maps requests to robots.txt to an ASP.NET script that dynamically generates the necessary content. In this fashion, you can use program logic similar to that used for meta tag exclusion in order to generate a robots.txt file.

The following ISAPI_Rewrite rule delegates the requests for robots.txt to Robots.ashx:

```
RewriteRule ^/robots.txt$ /Robots.ashx
```

The Robots.ashx generic handler file could look like this:

```
<%@ WebHandler Language="C#" Class="Robots" %>
using System.Web;

public class Robots : IHttpHandler
{
  public void ProcessRequest(HttpContext context)
  {
    // get the current HttpResponse object
    HttpResponse response = context.Response;

    // set the proper content type
```

```
    response.ContentType = "text/plain";

    // add dynamic exclusion elements
    response.Write("User-agent: * \n");
    response.Write("Disallow: /Link-Juice-Print-Friendly.html \n");
    response.Write("Disallow: /Fortune-Cookie-Print-Friendly.html \n");

    // include the static exclusion data from robots_static.txt
    context.Response.WriteFile("~/robots_static.txt");

  }

  public bool IsReusable
  {
    get { return false; }
  }
}
```

Note that we've used a generic handler (an `.ashx` file), rather than a Web Form (`.aspx`). As you learned in Chapter 3, generic handlers are useful when we don't require the full functionality provided by Web Forms and the `Page` class. In this case we simply need to generate a plain text file, so it's a perfect scenario to use a generic handler.

`Robots.ashx` starts by setting the `Content-Type`, and generating a couple of `Disallow` entries. In a real-world scenario you'd probably read the `Disallow` data from a database (if a database is not required, you may be better off writing a static `robots.txt` file), but for the purposes of this demonstration we've hard-coded two fictional print-friendly pages:

```
    // set the proper content type
    response.ContentType = "text/plain";

    // add dynamic exclusion elements
    response.Write("User-agent: * \n");
    response.Write("Disallow: /Link-Juice-Print-Friendly.html \n");
    response.Write("Disallow: /Fortune-Cookie-Print-Friendly.html \n");
```

Finally we added to the output the contents of a file named `robots_static.txt`, located in the root of the project:

```
    // include the static exclusion data from robots_static.txt
    context.Response.WriteFile("~/robots_static.txt");
```

Including a static file isn't required, but you'll usually want to hard-code a number of `robots.txt` entries. Let's take this data, for example:

```
User-agent: *
Disallow: /old-documents/
Disallow: /search/
```

If you now load `http://seoasp/robots.txt`, you'd get the output generated dynamically by `Robots.ashx`, which includes the data from `robots_static.txt`. Figure 5-1 shows the results.

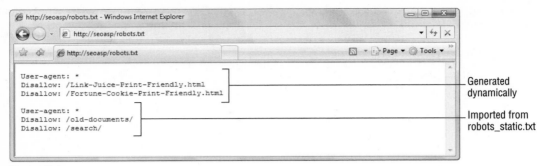

Figure 5-1

Handling robots.txt Limitations

Suppose a site has a number of products at URLs that look like `/Products.aspx?ProductID=<number>`, and a number of print-friendly product pages at the URL `/Products.aspx?ProductID=<number>&Print=1`.

A standard `robots.txt` file cannot conveniently be used to eliminate these print-friendly pages, because the match has to be from the left. There would have to be a `robots.txt` entry for every page, and at that point it degenerates into a case similar to meta tag exclusion. In that case it is simpler to use meta-exclusion. Furthermore, it is reported that there is a limit of 5000 characters for a `robots.txt` file in Google (`http://www.seroundtable.com/archives/003932.html`), so if the list gets too long, it may be problematic.

> *Wildcard matching can be used to accomplish this as mentioned earlier in this chapter, but its use is not standard. The rule would look something like* `Disallow: /Products.aspx*Print=`.

However, in this case there is a standards-based solution. If you reverse the order of the parameters, such that the print-friendly URLs look like `/Products.aspx?Print=1&ProductID=<number>`, you can easily exclude `/Products.aspx?Print=1` in `robots.txt`.

In general, reordering parameters can make `robots.txt` more palatable for dynamic sites. However, in the case of preexisting sites, it can involve changing your URLs, may involve redirects, and that may be undesirable for many reasons, as you know from Chapter 4.

When dealing with an entire directory, on static files, or, in general, cases where many fully qualified file names have the same prefix, it is usually advisable to use `robots.txt` exclusion. Doing so is simpler and reduces stress on your server as well as the robot. In cases where the "left-pattern-matching" logic of a `robots.txt` exclusion will not work, a meta-exclusion will usually work. These methods can complement each other, so feel free to mix and match them as you see fit.

Solutions for Commonly Duplicated Pages

So you've got the tools. Now where can you use them, and when are they appropriate? Sometimes the solution is exclusion, other times there are more fundamental solutions addressing web site architecture.

And though there are an infinite number of causes for duplicate content, there are a number of common culprits worth mentioning. Some of the most frequently observed are the following:

❑ Print-friendly pages

❑ Navigation links and breadcrumb navigation

❑ Affiliate pages

❑ Pages with similar content

❑ Pages with duplicate `meta` tag or `title` values

❑ URL canonicalization problems

❑ Pages with URL-based session IDs

Print-Friendly Pages

One of the most common sources of duplicate content is the "print-friendly" page. A throwback from the day where CSS did not provide a means to provide multiple media for formatting (print, screen, and so on), many programmers simply provided two versions for every page — the standard one and the printable one.

In fact, many programmers still do this today. And though it is not wrong to do so — unless you're a CSS zealot, all print-friendly pages should be excluded using either exclusion method, otherwise a search engine will see two versions of those pages on your site.

Navigation Links and Breadcrumb Navigation

Friendly navigation is clearly desirable for any web site. Unfortunately, it sometimes creates duplicate content. Take the example of a web site that inserts category IDs in URLs of products that are in multiple categories in order to provide breadcrumb navigation. In this way the developer creates many different URLs (one per category, actually) of substantially duplicate content. This section examines breadcrumb navigation now in more detail.

Breadcrumbs are navigational aid elements, usually found on the top of a web page that look something like `home > products > fortune cookies`. They especially help users navigate when they are deeply within a web site. In this case, using the back button is typically frustrating. And in the case that a user arrives from a search engine results page, the back button also certainly doesn't do what you wish it would!

> It's worth noting that breadcrumb navigation is not the only problematic site navigation scheme around. Matrix, faceted, and dynamic drill-down navigation systems are gaining rapidly in popularity. A considerable number of large retailers, such as Wal-Mart, eToys, The Home Depot, and the Discovery Channel Store implement these types of site navigation, and show where the industry is heading.
>
> The duplicate content issues resulting from these complex systems are problematic as well, but this is outside the scope of this book. The same general principles apply.

The SEO consequences of breadcrumb navigation are none when a site product is in only one category. The category can be implied by the database, because there is a 1:1 relationship of product to category.

Therefore, there is no need to pass the category ID in the URL — but even if it is present, there will be only one permutation of product and category. Hence there is no duplicated content.

The problem arises when a product is in more than one category, and a parameter must be passed in order to build the breadcrumb programmatically. Without breadcrumbs, the parameter would be unnecessary, and presumably the user would navigate back to the category page using his or her back button, but now you have a problem. If every product is in an average of three categories, you have three essentially duplicated pages for every product on the site.

> **Rewriting the URLs does nothing to resolve this. For example:**
>
> ```
> /Products/Category-A-C1/Product-A-P10.html
> /Products/Category-B-C2/Product-A-P10.html
> /Products/Category-C-C3/Product-A-P10.html
> ```
>
> **These three URLs are just as problematic as**
>
> ```
> /Product.aspx?CategoryID=1&ProductID=10
> /Product.aspx?CategoryID=2&ProductID=10
> /Product.aspx?CategoryID=3&ProductID=10
> ```
>
> **It's just obscured in the former version.**

The only difference on your pages is the breadcrumb:

```
Home > products > fortune cookies > frosted fortune cookie
Home > products > novelty cookies > frosted fortune cookie
```

This creates a particularly sticky problem. The benefits of friendly site navigation cannot be denied, but it also causes duplicate content issues. This is a topic that we feel is largely ignored by the SEM community. Breadcrumbs are clearly a help for navigation, but can cause problems with regard to duplicate content. In general, using tracking variables in URLs that do not effect substantial changes in the content creates duplicate content.

There are other ways to cope with this issue. Following is a presentation of the ways that you *can* address the duplicate content issues associated with breadcrumbs if you do want to address it.

Using One Primary Category and robots.txt or Meta-Exclusion

This involves setting one category that a product falls into as "primary." It involves adding a field to a database in the application to indicate as such. This is the idea espoused by Dan Thies in his book *The Search Engine Marketing Kit* as well. The upside is that it's bulletproof, in that you will never be penalized by a search engine for having duplicated pages. But there are two downsides:

1. Very often the keywords from your products placed in multiple categories (in the title, perhaps under the breadcrumb, or in the "suggested" products) may yield unexpected rankings for what we call "permutation" keywords. Obviously, with this solution, you only get one of the permutations — the primary one.

Example: Assume a cake is in two categories: "birthday" and "celebration." The resulting titles are "Super Cheesecake: Birthdays" and "Super Cheesecake: Celebration." If the webmaster picks "birthday" as the primary category, a search engine will never see the other page that may rank better for the hypothetical less-competitive keywords "celebration cheesecake," because that page is excluded via `robots.txt` or meta-exclusion.

2. Users may passively "penalize" you by linking the non-primary page. A link to an excluded page has questionable link-equity, arguably none for that page — but perhaps also none to the domain in general.

Changing Up the Content on the Various Permutations

Done right this can also work, but it must be done carefully. If done inadequately, it can, in the worst case, result in a penalty. You could change the description of a hypothetical product on a per-category basis, or add different related products to the page. As you may have guessed, the exact threshold for how much unique content is required is elusive. Use this technique with caution.

Some Thoughts

Which method do we suggest in most cases? The first method — exclusion. If you look closely at the following two links on a web site created by one of the authors of this book:

```
http://www.lawyerseek.com/Practice/In-the-News-C20/Protopic-P38/
http://www.lawyerseek.com/Practice/Pharmaceutical-Injury-C1/Protopic-P38/
```

there are two URLs, but one is excluded in the `robots.txt` file. The former is excluded. The `robots.txt` file at `http://www.lawyerseek.com/` contains the following entry that excludes the following URL:

```
User-agent: *
...
...
Disallow: /Practice/In-The-News-C20/Protopic-P38/
```

Similar Pages

If you have several very similar products that exist on multiple URLs, think about changing your web application to contain the various permutations of the products on one page. Consider the example of a product that comes in several different colors. The resulting product pages would typically contain different pictures but substantially duplicate descriptions. The business logic may dictate that these are different products with different SKUs, but you can still present them on one page with a pull-down menu to select the color/SKU to be added to the shopping cart.

The shopping cart page of an e-commerce site, login pages, and other like pages should also not be indexed, because there is typically no valuable content on such pages. For example, it is easy to see how the following shopping cart URLs could create duplicate content:

```
http://www.example.com/Cart.aspx?AddProductID=1
...
...
http://www.example.com/Cart.aspx?AddProductID=99
```

Pages with Duplicate Meta Tag or Title Values

A common mistake is to set the meta keywords, meta description, or title values on a web site to the same default value programmatically for every page. Aaron Wall of SEOBook states *"If you have complete duplication of any element (page title, meta keywords, meta description) across your site then it is at best a wasted opportunity, but may also hurt your ability to get your site indexed or ranked well in some search engines."* If time and resources cannot be dedicated to creating unique meta tags, they should probably not be created at all, because using the same value for every page is certainly not beneficial. Having identical titles for every page on a web site is also particularly detrimental. Many programmers make this mistake, because it is very easy not to notice it.

URL Canonicalization

Many web sites exhibit subtle but sometimes insidious duplicate problems due to URL canonicalization problems. The two most common of such problems are documented in Chapter 4 in the sections "URL Canonicalization: www.example.com vs. example.com," and "URL Canonicalization: /Default.aspx vs. /."

URL-Based Session IDs

The session management in ASP.NET (and most other server-side web technologies) relies on cookies. The standard way to support visitors who disabled cookie support in their web browsers is to add a session ID in the URL. This feature can be activated in ASP.NET by setting the cookieless="true" attribute to the sessionState element in Web.config. Take this setting, for example:

```
    <sessionState cookieless="true" timeout="20" />
  </system.web>
</configuration>
```

With this setting on, trying to load http://seoasp/Cartoons.aspx would automatically 302 redirect you to a URL like the following:

```
http://seoasp/(S(c3hvob55wirrnwzbeicoo355))/Cartoons.aspx.
```

Figure 5-2 shows the process in action.

> **Read more details about ASP.NET's state implementation from Dino Esposito's article, "Underpinnings of the Session State Implementation in ASP.NET"** (http://msdn2 .microsoft.com/en-us/library/aa479041.aspx).

The problem with URL-based session management is that it causes major problems for search engines, because each time a search engine spiders your web site, it will receive a different session ID and hence a new set of URLs with the same content. Needless to say, this creates an enormous amount of duplicate content.

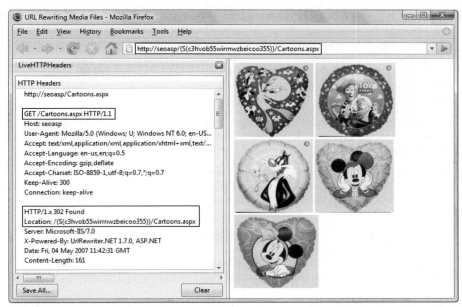

Figure 5-2

> The vast majority of web users have cookies enabled, so in most cases there is no
> real reason to enable URL-based sessions. However, the opposite may be true on
> large e-commerce sites, or in certain demographics where a non-insignificant num-
> ber of users disable cookies in their browsers.

Before deciding that you need URL-based sessions, you must be well aware of the potential negative
effects, which may offset the profits you get from the cookieless visitors:

❑   You can be penalized by search engines for duplicate content, unless you invest in your architec-
     ture and make sure search engines don't see duplicate data.

❑   You can end up with diluted URL equity, if the same content is linked to using different links
     that contain the session ID.

Nevertheless, if it's critical for you to support cookieless visitors, you can. Unfortunately, ASP.NET's URL-
based session handling cannot be programmatically accessed or customized, which makes it useless for
your purposes. It also doesn't integrate well with typical URL rewriting solutions. If you do need to support cookieless sessions, you need to implement your own customized mechanism. We cannot cover the
implementation of such a mechanism in this book — it involves writing a lot of code, which needs to be
customized to the web site's specific needs! However, we'll give you a few hints:

❑   You'll probably want to choose a less aesthetically disturbing way of including session IDs in
     your URLs than that used by default by ASP.NET.

❑ You may only need to support sessions for certain parts of your web site, or only for visitors that have reached a certain state. For example, in an e-commerce web site it is critical to track the visitor when he or she adds items to the shopping cart. If the site is simple enough and doesn't use advanced visitor tracking features, or other session-based features, you can start adding tracking IDs to your visitor's URLs only after he or she adds the first item to the shopping cart. A search engine would never submit a form to add a product to the shopping cart, so it will not reach the shopping cart page.

❑ You can use cloaking techniques such as those discussed in Chapter 11 to add tracking IDs only to your human visitors, and hide them from the web crawlers. However, at the moment of writing this book, this technique implies the risk of being penalized by Google.

❑ Use `robots.txt` or the `meta` exclusion tag to exclude URLs that contain session IDs from the spiders' view. This technique is useful to eliminate duplicate content, but keep in mind that you still need to support a session-less version of the URLs that search engines can index.

Other Navigational Link Parameters

In general, parameters in URLs such as those that indicate that a user came from a particular page can create a large amount of duplicate content. Consider the following imaginary URLs:

```
http://www.example.com/Some-Product.html?from_url=AboutUs.aspx
http://www.example.com/Some-Product.html?from_url=ContactUs.aspx
```

The list could get quite long depending on how many pages link to that product. It's possible to use `robots.txt` or the exclusion `meta` tag to avoid duplicate content problems, but this doesn't reduce the risk of diluting your URL equity.

Rather than using navigational link parameters, it is advisable to use session-based or HTTP_REFERER-based data to track things such as these, even if these solutions may not generate perfectly accurate data. Web analytics tools can provide the same information, although that isn't usually 100% accurate either, depending on the requirements they pose on the client (such JavaScript or cookies support).

Affiliate Pages

Imagine that you have a product, The Ultimate Widget. You set up a great web affiliate program that pays 50% of revenue on the product, and everyone wants to join. Soon, you have thousands of affiliates applying. To indicate to your application which affiliate it was, you add a parameter `?aff=<aff_id>` to your URLs.

In this scenario, your main page for The Ultimate Widget would be located at an URL such as this:

```
http://www.example.com/Products/The-Ultimate-Widget/
```

Your associates would sell the exact same product, which has (naturally) the same product details, through links like these:

```
http://www.example.com/Products/The-Ultimate-Widget/?aff=123
http://www.example.com/Products/The-Ultimate-Widget/?aff=456
```

Unfortunately, assuming all these links were spidered, you now have thousands of pages of duplicate content. This can be a profound problem. As mentioned in the introduction to this chapter, in the worst case, excessive duplicate content can get a site penalized. Also, the incoming link equity will likely be split among several URLs. Special care must be taken to mitigate these problems. Fortunately, there are a few fairly easy solutions.

Using Referrers and Cookies instead of Query String Parameters

Using referrers is effective in that it completely transparently informs your application of where the traffic comes from; simply match the value of `Request.UrlReferrer` against a domain name (or a complete URL if desired), and if there is a match, set a session variable or a cookie accordingly.

The obvious upside is that all links are entirely without parameters, which is potentially great for a link-building campaign. Also, your links will look like natural links to search engines, not like affiliate links.

One major caveat of this method is that certain security software deliberately masks the content of `HTTP_REFERER`, and thus a small amount of affiliate traffic will be unaccounted for. Whether this is acceptable is between you and your affiliates. Also, such a system requires more maintenance if a particular affiliate wants to promote your product on more than one site (you would have to set up associations on a per-referring-domain basis), and by the same token such links could not be used effectively on public forums such as bulletin boards and blog comments.

This method is not demonstrated here because it is typically not a viable solution.

Using Excluded Affiliate URLs

You can also use `robots.txt` or meta-exclusion, as previously discussed, to exclude all URLs that are associated with the affiliate program. For example, you could add the following tag to every affiliate page:

```
<meta name="robots" content="noindex, nofollow">
```

Alternatively, you could place the affiliate script in a subdirectory and exclude it in `robots.txt`:

```
User-agent: *
Disallow: /aff/
```

Redirecting Parameterized Affiliate URLs

It is also possible to use parameterized affiliate URLs, so long as the URLs are redirected to the "main" URL after setting a cookie or session variable for your reference. This section presents two examples, implementing them step-by-step in exercises.

One common theme in these presented solutions is that when a URL containing an affiliate ID is requested, you retain the affiliate ID somewhere else, and then do a 301 redirect to the URL without the affiliate parameters. The examples use the visitor's session to store the affiliate ID, but you may choose to use cookies instead.

> *In Chapter 4 you learned that the 301 status code means "Moved permanently," so the page you redirect to is interpreted as the new permanent location of the requested page. This eliminates any potential duplicate content problems, and cumulates the equity from the affiliate links.*

In the exercise that follows we update `http://seoasp/` application to support affiliate URLs that look like the following, although the general principle applies to other forms of URLs as well:

```
http://seoasp/Products/SEO-Toolbox-C6/Link-Juice-P31.html?Aff=1234.
```

We will redirect such URLs to their version that doesn't contain the affiliate ID.

Redirecting Keyword-Rich Affiliate URLs

1. You need to modify the rule that rewrites keyword-rich product URLs. If using ISAPI_Rewrite, find this piece of code:

```
# Rewrite keyword-rich URLs with a product ID and a category ID
RewriteRule ^/Products/.*-C([0-9]+)/.*-P([0-9]+)\.html$ ↵
/Product.aspx?CategoryID=$1&ProductID=$2 [L]
```

Modify this rule like this:

```
# Rewrite keyword-rich URLs with a product ID and a category ID
RewriteRule ^/Products/.*-C([0-9]+)/.*-P([0-9]+)\.html(\?(.*))?$ ↵
/Product.aspx?CategoryID=$1&ProductID=$2&$4 [L]
```

If using UrlRewriter.NET, the rule should be modified in a similar way, except that the ampersand character (&) should be encoded as `&amp;`, like this:

```
<!-- Rewrite keyword-rich URLs with a product ID and a category ID -->
<rewrite url="^/Products/.*-C([0-9]+)/.*-P([0-9]+).html(\?(.*))?$"
         to="/Product.aspx?CategoryID=$1&amp;ProductID=$2&amp;$4"
         processing="stop" />
```

2. Add a new method named `SaveAffiliate()` to the `UrlTools` class that you created in Chapter 4:

```
/// <summary>
/// Class provides support for URL manipulation and redirection
/// </summary>
public static class UrlTools
{
  // obtain the site domain from the configuration file
  static string siteDomain = ConfigurationManager.AppSettings["SiteDomain"];

  // saves affiliate ID as a persistent cookie
  public static void SaveAffiliate()
  {
    // get the affiliate ID
    HttpContext context = HttpContext.Current;
    string affiliateId = context.Request.QueryString["Aff"];

    // affiliate?
    if (affiliateId != null)
    {
      // create the new cookie
```

```
            HttpCookie cookie = new HttpCookie("AffiliateID", affiliateId);

            // make the cookie valid for 30 days
            cookie.Expires = DateTime.Now.AddDays(30);

            // save the cookie
            context.Response.Cookies.Add(cookie);
        }
    }
```

3. Modify the `Application_BeginRequest()` handler in `Global.asax` to call `UrlTools`
    `.SaveAffiliate()` before calling `UrlTools.CheckUrl()`. This way you have a chance to
    save an eventual affiliate ID before the request is 301 redirected to the standard URL.

```
void Application_BeginRequest(object sender, EventArgs e)
{
    // saves the affiliate id if present
    UrlTools.SaveAffiliate();

    // ensures a standard URL is used, 301 redirect to it otherwise
    UrlTools.CheckUrl();
}
```

4. Modify `Product.aspx` to display affiliate data. First, add a new `Literal` object, like this:

```
<body>
  <form id="form1" runat="server">
    <asp:Literal runat="server" ID="message" />
    <asp:Button ID="myButton" runat="server" Text="Click me!"
OnClick="myButton_Click" />
    <p>
      <asp:Literal runat="server" ID="affiliateDisplay" />
    </p>
  </form>
</body>
```

5. Finally, modify `Page_Load()` to populate the `Literal` control with the affiliate data:

```
<script runat="server">
  protected void Page_Load(object sender, EventArgs e)
  {
    // display affiliate details
    HttpCookie affiliate = Request.Cookies["AffiliateID"];
    affiliateDisplay.Text = "You got here through affiliate: " +
      ((affiliate == null) ? "(no affiliate)" : affiliate.Value);
```

6. Test your new script now. The first test consists of loading a product page without an affiliate
    ID, such as http://seoasp/Products/SEO-Toolbox-C6/Link-Juice-P31.html. Figure 5-3
    shows the result.

7. Now add an affiliate ID. Load http://seoasp/Products/SEO-Toolbox-C6/Link-Juice-P31
    .html?Aff=1234. Expect to be correctly redirected to the main product page, and still get the
    affiliate ID retained. Figure 5-4 shows the expected output, and highlights the 301 redirection.

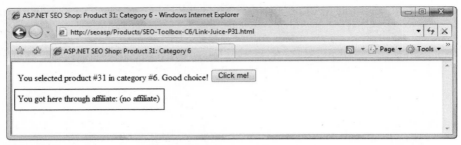

Figure 5-3

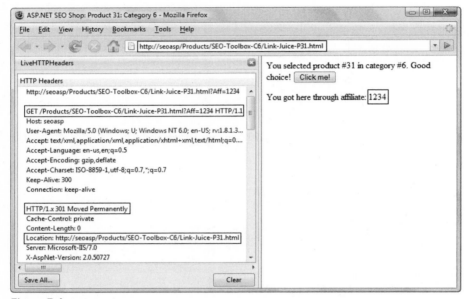

Figure 5-4

As you can see in Figure 5-4, the URL doesn't include any affiliate IDs any more, yet the page retained the affiliate ID. Because the affiliate ID is stored in a persistent cookie that expires in 30 days, the value will be retained even after closing and reopening the browser window. (Note, however, that each web browser stores its own set of cookies, so if a user visits your page using more browsers, it will be regarded as multiple users.)

The implementation starts, again, with a rewriting rule:

```
RewriteRule ^/Products/.*-C([0-9]+)/.*-P([0-9]+)\.html(\?(.*))?$ ↵
/Product.aspx?CategoryID=$1&ProductID=$2&$4 [L]
```

The new bits you've added to the old rule are meant to extract the query string of the original request, and add it to the rewritten URL. The \? bit represents the literal question mark, and (.*) matches everything that follows. The whole expression is made optional using the final question mark, so that query string–free URLs will continue to match and be rewritten successfully.

As a result of the new rule, when the `Aff` parameter is passed to your product page (as in `Link-Juice-P31.html?Aff=1234`), it will be passed at its turn to `Product.aspx`.

Even though the rewritten request points `Product.aspx` as the target, the first real piece of code your application executes is `Application_BeginRequest()` in `Global.asax`. This method first calls `UrlTools.SaveAffiliate()`, which saves an eventual affiliate ID to a cookie, and then `UrlTools.CheckUrl()`, which 301 redirects the request to the standard URL — the one without an affiliate ID:

```
void Application_BeginRequest(object sender, EventArgs e)
{
    // saves the affiliate id if present
    UrlTools.SaveAffiliate();

    // ensures a standard URL is used, 301 redirect to it otherwise
    UrlTools.CheckUrl();
}
```

`UrlTools.SaveAffiliate()` is a simple method that demonstrates how you can save a cookie on your visitor's browser. Basically all you have to do is to create an `HttpCookie` object, and save it to the `Cookies` collection of the `Response` object. When setting an expiration date, the cookie becomes a persistent cookie, which remains even after the user closes up the browser window; otherwise, the cookie would be deleted as soon as the visitor's session closes:

```
// create the new cookie
HttpCookie cookie = new HttpCookie("AffiliateID", affiliateId);

// make the cookie valid for 30 days
cookie.Expires = DateTime.Now.AddDays(30);

// save the cookie
context.Response.Cookies.Add(cookie);
```

Finally there's `Product.aspx`, which reads the cookie information and displays it. If saving cookies is done through the `Response` object, reading them is done through the `Request` object. This makes sense. The code displays `(no affiliate)` if there is no affiliate data in the cookie, or the affiliate ID otherwise:

```
// display affiliate details
HttpCookie affiliate = Request.Cookies["AffiliateID"];
affiliateDisplay.Text = "You got here through affiliate: " +
    ((affiliate == null) ? "(no affiliate)" : affiliate.Value);
```

What about the ternary operator? If you aren't familiar with it, here's a quick explanation. The ternary operator has the form `(condition ? valueA : valueB)`. In case the condition is true, it returns `valueA`, otherwise it returns `valueB`.

In this case, we verify that the affiliate cookie is `null`. If this is true, it means we have no affiliate, so we display `(no affiliate)`.Otherwise, we simply display the affiliate ID.

Summary

We would summarize the entire chapter right here in this paragraph, but that would be duplicate content! Because we don't wish to frustrate our readers, we will keep it short.

Ideally, every URL on a web site would lead to a page that is unique. Unfortunately, it is rarely possible to accomplish this in reality. You should simply eliminate as much duplication as possible. Parameters in URLs that do not effect significant changes in presentation should be avoided. Failing that, as in the problems posed by using breadcrumb navigation, URLs that yield duplicate content should be excluded. The two tools in your arsenal you can use to accomplish this are `robots.txt` exclusion and meta-exclusion.

6

SE-Friendly HTML and JavaScript

In a perfect world, a web site's presentation details would not affect its search engine rankings more so than it affects a human visitor's perception of value — his "rankings." *Relevant content* is what users are after, and the goal of a search engine is to provide it. In this perfect world, web pages that contain the same information would rank similarly regardless of the on-page technologies used in their composition.

Unfortunately, in many cases, quite the opposite is true. Using Flash or AJAX to present information, for example, may render much of your web site invisible to search engines. Likewise, using JavaScript-based links for navigation may bring about the same unfortunate result.

The good news, however, is that applying a deep understanding of these presentation concerns will yield an advantage for you over other web sites that exhibit more naiveté. This chapter explores these concerns. It provides solutions and outlines best practices for web site content presentation.

By the end of this chapter you will acquire knowledge that will enable you to use on-page technologies effectively without detriment to search engine rankings. This chapter teaches you how to:

❑ Implement SE-friendly JavaScript site functionality.

❑ Generate crawlable images and graphical text using two techniques.

❑ Improve the search engine friendliness of your HTML.

❑ Analyze when and how to use AJAX and Flash in your web site.

Overall Architecture

Before diving into gory technical details, it is worth mentioning that there are certain architectural decisions that are categorically problematic for any search engine optimization campaign. If upper management, for example, demands a web site be entirely built in Flash, the search engine marketer will not have much leg room to the end of achieving search engine friendliness.

Likewise, if business logic requires that user agents log in before they can see any content, it is easy to anticipate the problems that will cause for search engine optimization. A spider will *not* log in, and therefore see nothing except the login page.

> *Technically, you could employ cloaking to detect the presence of spiders and deliver the content to them without requiring them to log in. However, this is an especially controversial use of an already controversial technique, cloaking. See Chapter 11 for more details on cloaking.*

Unless there are circumstances that impose contradictory restrictions, we would advise that the following general guidelines be followed:

❑   Do *not* require visitors to log in before they can view your content. A search engine spider cannot fill out forms to create an account or log in!

❑   Present copy as clear text, not images. Use an HTML/CSS-based design — do not use AJAX or Flash pervasively.

❑   Do *not* require visitors to support JavaScript for navigation to be functional.

The rest of this chapter details how to improve the search engine friendliness of a web site by example, through the appropriate use of HTML, JavaScript, and Flash. It explores specific problems, and proposes their solutions.

Search Engine–Friendly JavaScript

Search engines are designed to index content rather than execute application code. Therefore, JavaScript, when used the wrong way, can degrade a web site's search engine friendliness. On the other hand, JavaScript is not *categorically* problematic, and has its appropriate uses.

This section discusses JavaScript's use in the context of the following:

❑   Links

❑   DHTML menus

❑   Popups

❑   Crawlable images and graphical text

JavaScript Links

The first scenario discussed is the use of JavaScript code for navigation. A JavaScript link is any button or text that, when clicked, navigates to another page. A typical JavaScript link looks like this:

```
<a href="#" onClick="location.href='http://www.example.com'; return false;">Some
Text Here</a>
```

The primary objection to using this sort of link is its use of JavaScript where a regular link would suffice. Doing so will typically prevent a search engine spider from following the links, and also prevent users who disable JavaScript from navigating your site. Using them for *all* navigation may prevent a site from being spidered at all. If you must use such links, provide alternative navigation somewhere else on the site.

The same issues would also be apparent in navigation involving other client-side dynamic technologies such as Java applets, AJAX content, and Flash. In general, any navigation not achieved using a standard anchor (<a>) tag will hinder site spidering.

> Some webmasters have reported that spiders, especially Google, seem to be following some obvious-looking JavaScript links in their sites. However, because this is the exception rather than the rule, depending on this is not recommended.

By the same token, using JavaScript as a sort of page exclusion protocol, that is, assuming spiders do not see or crawl links in JavaScript, is also unwise. Even if the JavaScript does achieve the end of obscuring the link from spiders, other sites may link to the URL, which would likely get the page indexed regardless. If you don't want a link to be indexed, you should exclude it using robots.txt or using the meta exclusion tag.

DHTML Menus

Because they're based on JavaScript, DHTML drop-down menus often present problems for search engines as well. It is wise to provide alternative navigation to all elements listed in the menus. You can do this using a set of links at the bottom of the page, a sitemap, or a combination thereof. This way, not only search engines, but also visitors with JavaScript support disabled will be able to navigate the site with ease.

Many drop-down menus are somewhat spider-friendly, whereas others are not at all. The ones that are *not* tend to generate and display HTML on-the-fly using JavaScript. The ones that *are* typically hide and unhide an HTML div element dynamically. The key here is that the HTML and links are actually present, though hidden, in the document. Search engine algorithms may not, however, appreciate the hidden aspect — rendering it an *invisible* on-page factor. It is wise to list the links *visibly* elsewhere in either case.

Popup Windows

The typical method of displaying popups employs JavaScript. And, as you learned, a search engine will likely not spider a page only referred to by JavaScript. So what if you *do* want a popup to be indexed?

The solution is pretty simple. A typical popup link looks like this:

```
<a href="#" onClick="window.open('page.html', 'mywindow', 'width=800,height=600');
return false;">Click here.</a>
```

You could make the popup spiderable by changing the link to this:

```
<a href="page.html" onclick="window.open(this.href, 'mywindow', 'width=800,height
=600'); return false;" target="_blank">Click here.</a>
```

This still presents a popup in a JavaScript-enabled browser. The `onclick` event uses the `window.open` method to open `this.href` — the `href` attribute of that link. Then it returns `false` to prevent the link itself from being honored. On the other hand, the link is still present, so a search engine is able to navigate to it without executing the JavaScript code.

Alternatively, you could simulate a popup by using a regular link that opens a new window via the `target="_blank"` attribute, and have the page itself automatically resize after it displays. Technically, it's not *really* a popup. It's a new window that automatically resizes — but the effect is similar. The link for such a "popup" would look like this:

```
<a href="page.html" target="_blank">Click here</a>
```

You must include JavaScript on the linked page to resize the window. To do so, place the following code in the `onload` attribute of the document's body tag with the appropriate parameters:

```
<body onload="window.resizeTo(800, 600);">
```

Additionally, you can handle the window's `resize` event to keep the window's size constant:

```
<body onresize='setTimeout("window.resizeTo(800, 600);", 100);'>
```

Using `setTimeout` (which in this example causes the window to be resized after 100 milliseconds) ensures the code will work with all browsers. This code obviously works only for users who didn't disable JavaScript in their browsers.

In addition to improving search engine visibility for your popups, you have also accomplished a usability enhancement, because both of these popup varieties will degrade to opening content in a new browser window via the `target="_blank"` attribute if a user's JavaScript functionality is disabled.

These techniques are demonstrated in the upcoming exercise. You'll also explore a usability concern with spiderable popups.

Implementing Popup Navigation

Some sort of navigation should be present to allow the user to get back to the parent page if he or she arrives at the popup through a search engine, or from an external web site. Because popups are not usually created to contain contextual and navigational elements, this presents a problem.

You should at least provide a link back to the home page, and ideally to some more relevant parent page. Otherwise, the user may be completely lost and will proceed to the nearest back button.

It is not always desirable to have a popup spidered by a search engine. Between the navigational concerns, and the fact that popups very often do not contain substantial information, it may be wiser not to. Unless the popup has substantial information, we advise excluding the popups from the spiders' view entirely. See Chapter 5, "Duplicate Content," for information regarding page exclusion.

You can obtain the page from which the user navigated to the popup by reading the_REFERER header value using the `Request.UrlReferrer property`. This information allows you to show navigational elements only if the user has arrived from an external web site, such as a SERP.

This method not 100% reliable, because some firewall applications block the REFERER information. Also, if the referring page is secured via HTTPS, the REFERER information won't be available. In this exercise, when there is no REFERER data, err on the safe side and display the navigational elements.

Let's try out this technique by going through a short exercise.

Implementing Spiderable Popups

1. You should have a Web Form named `Catalog.aspx` in your project, from the previous chapters. Modify it by adding a link to a form named `Popup.aspx`, which we'll create next, like this:

```
<%@ Page Language="C#" %>
<!DOCTYPE html PUBLIC "-//W3C//DTD XHTML 1.0 Transitional//EN"
"http://www.w3.org/TR/xhtml1/DTD/xhtml1-transitional.dtd">

<html xmlns="http://www.w3.org/1999/xhtml">
<head id="Head1" runat="server">
  <title>Spiderable Popups Example</title>
</head>
<body>
  <form id="form1" runat="server">
    <h1>Products on Promotion at SEO Egghead Shop</h1>
    <p>... Content here ...</p>
    <a href="Popup.aspx" target="_blank">Find more about Professional Search Engine
Optimization with ASP.NET: A Developer's Guide to SEO!</a>
  </form>
</body>
</html>
```

2. Load `http://seoasp/Catalog.aspx` to ensure your script loads correctly and displays the new link, as shown in Figure 6-1. Note that this exercise assumes you have built your simple catalog as shown in Chapter 3.

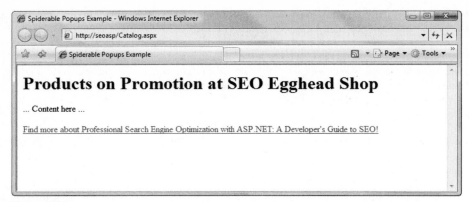

Figure 6-1

3. Create the popup window, Popup.aspx, in your project root, with this code:

```csharp
<%@ Page Language="C#" %>
<!DOCTYPE html PUBLIC "-//W3C//DTD XHTML 1.1//EN"
 "http://www.w3.org/TR/xhtml11/DTD/xhtml11.dtd">

<script runat="server">
  // initialize siteDomain
  private string siteDomain = ConfigurationManager.AppSettings["SiteDomain"];

  // display navigation on page load
  protected void Page_Load(object sender, EventArgs e)
  {
    // initialize displayNav
    bool displayNav = false;

    // if there is no referer (popup was loaded directly), display navigation
    if (Request.UrlReferrer == null)
    {
      displayNav = true;
    }
    // if the REFERER is not from our domain, display navigation
    else
    {
      string refererHost = Request.UrlReferrer.Host;
      string myHost = (new Uri(siteDomain)).Host;
      if (refererHost != myHost) displayNav = true;
    }

    // display the appropriate MultiView page
    if (displayNav)
      navMultiView.ActiveViewIndex = 0;
    else
      navMultiView.ActiveViewIndex = 1;
  }
</script>
```

```html
<html>
  <head>
    <title>Professional Search Engine Optimization with ASP.NET: Table of
Contents</title>
  </head>
  <body onload="window.resizeTo(800, 600);"
        onresize='setTimeout("window.resizeTo(800, 600);", 100);'>
    <h1>Professional Search Engine Optimization with ASP.NET: Table of
Contents</h1>
    <asp:Literal runat="server" ID="navigationLiteral" />

    <asp:MultiView ID="navMultiView" runat="server">
      <asp:View ID="displayNav" runat="server">
        SEOEgghead.com sells high-quality products for search engine marketers and
web developers! <a href="<%= siteDomain %>"> Visit our catalog</a>.
      </asp:View>
      <asp:View ID="noDisplayNav" runat="server">
        This is a popup window loaded from <%= siteDomain %>.
      </asp:View>
    </asp:MultiView>

    <ol>
      <li>You: Programmer and Search Engine Marketer</li>
      <li>A Primer in Basic SEO</li>
      <li>Provocative SE-Friendly URLs</li>
      <li>Content Relocation and HTTP Status Codes</li>
      <li>Duplicate Content</li>
      <li>SE-Friendly HTML and JavaScript</li>
      <li>Web Syndication and Social Bookmarking</li>
      <li>Black Hat SEO</li>
      <li>Sitemaps</li>
      <li>Link Bait</li>
      <li>IP Cloaking, Geo-Targeting, and IP Delivery</li>
      <li>Foreign Language SEO</li>
      <li>Coping with Technical Issues</li>
      <li>Case Study: Building an E-Commerce Catalog</li>
      <li>Site Clinic: So You Have a Web Site?</li>
      <li>Introduction to Regular Expressions</li>
    </ol>
  </body>
</html>
```

4. If you don't already have the following setting in your `Web.config` file, add it now:

```xml
<configuration>
  <appSettings>
    <add key="SiteDomain" value="http://seoasp/" />
  </appSettings>
```

5. This is the moment of truth. Load `http://seoasp/Catalog.aspx` and click the popup link. The navigation bar should look as shown in Figure 6-2. If you get to the popup page through Google, Yahoo!, or MSN, or if you load `http://seoasp/Popup.aspx` directly from the address bar of your browser, the navigation link should appear (see Figure 6-3).

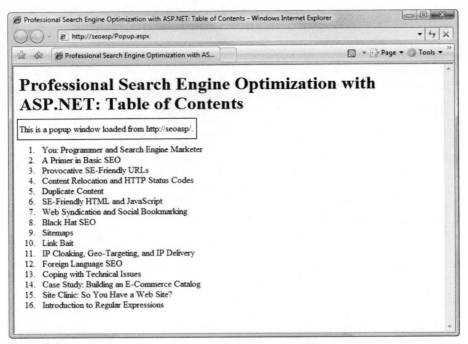

Figure 6-2

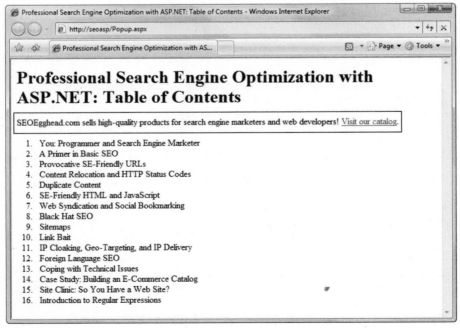

Figure 6-3

6. Now is a great time to test the RefControl plugin for Firefox mentioned in Chapter 2. This plugin allows you to display and modify the REFERER information. If you want to test this plugin, install it and navigate to `http://seoasp/Catalog.aspx`. In the page, click the link that opens the popup window, and note the HTTP REFERER displayed in the status bar. (By default the plugin only shows an icon. To have it display the REFERER data, right-click the plugin icon in the status bar and select Statusbar display ⇨ Referer.)

That was quite a bit of code, but this is a useful technique! You learned how to use the `MultiView` and `View` controls to switch the view between the two possible states of the navigational header. If the popup window is loaded by the visitor directly, or from an external link from a site or search engine, a link to our site domain is provided by the `displayNav View` control:

```
<asp:MultiView ID="navMultiView" runat="server">
  <asp:View ID="displayNav" runat="server">
      SEOEgghead.com sells high-quality products for search engine marketers and
web developers! <a href="<%= siteDomain %>"> Visit our catalog</a>.
  </asp:View>
```

If the popup is loaded from our web site, we display the content from the `noDisplayNav View` control:

```
  <asp:View ID="noDisplayNav" runat="server">
      This is a popup window loaded from <%= siteDomain %>.
  </asp:View>
</asp:MultiView>
```

Notice that both views use the `siteDomain` class member. This is defined as a private member in the implicit `Popup` class that represents the page. Its value is read from the `Web.config` configuration file using the `AppSettings` collection of the `ConfigurationManager` class:

```
<script runat="server">
  // initialize siteDomain
  private string siteDomain = ConfigurationManager.AppSettings["SiteDomain"];
```

The logic used to decide what navigation template to display is quite simple. It's easier to detect the circumstances when the navigation link should be displayed rather than when it shouldn't, so we start by initializing a variable named `displayNav` to `false`. Then we start placing conditions to detect whether this variable should be made `true`, which would cause the navigational link to be displayed.

The first test checks whether or not we have a REFERER value. If there is no REFERER, then the popup window was loaded directly by the visitor, so we should display the navigational links:

```
  // if there is no referer (popup was loaded directly), display navigation
  if (Request.UrlReferrer == null)
  {
    displayNav = true;
  }
```

Note that the REFERER is also null if the source page is located at a secured, HTTPS link.

If there is a REFERER, we check if it's from our domain, or from another domain. In the latter case, we again decide to display the navigational controls:

```
// if the REFERER is not from our domain, display navigation
else
{
  string refererHost = Request.UrlReferrer.Host;
  string myHost = (new Uri(siteDomain)).Host;
  if (refererHost != myHost) displayNav = true;
}
```

In the end, we choose which view to display depending on the value of `displayNav`:

```
// display the appropriate MultiView page
if (displayNav)
  navMultiView.ActiveViewIndex = 0;
else
  navMultiView.ActiveViewIndex = 1;
```

DHTML Popup Windows

As a last alternative, popups can be simulated using DHTML. To accomplish this you can place an invisible `<div>` element at a particular location, then use JavaScript events to hide and unhide it. A robust example is beyond the scope of this book, but the following code is a proof of concept:

```
<span onmouseover="document.getElementById('dhtml_popup_test').style.visibility=
'visible';" onmouseout="document.getElementById('dhtml_popup_test').style.
visibility='hidden';">put your mouse here</span>

<div style="position:absolute; visibility:hidden; border:1px solid black"
id="dhtml_popup_test">This is only visible if your mouse is over the above
text</div>
```

One caveat with this method is that although the text is spiderable, it may be regarded as an invisible on-page factor because it is not visible by default.

Crawlable Images and Graphical Text

This is a topic that frequently puts designers and search engine marketers at war! Designers tend to balk at the thought of not having graphical text at their disposal. But spiders cannot read any text that is embedded in an image, regardless of how clear and obvious it may be to a human reader. Therefore, regular text styled by CSS should be employed whenever possible.

Unfortunately, CSS does not always provide all the flexibility that a designer needs for typesetting. Furthermore, users do not have a uniform set of fonts installed on all computers. This restricts the fonts that can be used reliably in CSS typesetting substantially. Table 6-1 lists the common fonts that are available on typical Windows and Mac installations.

Table 6-1

Font Type	Font Name
Cursive	Comic Sans MS
Monospace	Courier New
Serif	Times New Roman
	Georgia
Sans-serif	Andale Mono
	Arial
	Arial Black
	Impact
	Trebuchet MS
	Verdana

For further reference, check out the more detailed list you can find at `http://www.kdwebpagedesign .com/tut_4.asp`.

So in lieu of depending completely on CSS typesetting, a number of techniques can be used to implement "crawlable images." Using client-side JavaScript, you can walk the document tree of an HTML file and selectively replace text portions with graphical elements after it loads. This is called "text replacement."

The following few pages introduce you to two of the most common implementations of text replacement:

❑ *The "sIFR" replacement method* works by replacing specified text with Flash files. This method is documented at length at `http://www.mikeindustries.com/sifr/`.

❑ *Stewart Rosenberger's text replacement implementation* does the same thing, but replaces the text with images instead. Because the library is written in PHP, we won't provide a step-by-step exercise, but the principle can be easily applied to ASP.NET as well. In Chapter 10 you learn how to generate an image using .NET code. Stewart Rosenberger's text replacement method is described at `http://www.alistapart.com/articles/dynatext`.

Using these techniques, spiders will be able to read the text present in the document (because spiders do not execute the JavaScript code), and human visitors will see either a Flash file or an image containing the text. This keeps *both* humans and robots happy.

The "sIFR" Replacement Method

We must admit, we love sIFR! sIFR is an acronym for "Scalable Inman Flash Replacement." It functions by replacing specified portions of plain text from a web page with a parameterized Flash file on the client side.

sIFR brings these benefits:

❑   sIFR doesn't require users to have the necessary fonts installed, because the fonts are embedded in the Flash file.

❑   If a font is used in multiple pages or headings, it's downloaded by the user's browser only once.

❑   sIFR doesn't hurt search engine rankings, because the plain text is still right there in your web page.

❑   If the user doesn't have Flash or JavaScript installed, the text is simply rendered as normal text.

Before attempting to use sIFR, here's what you need to keep in mind:

❑   For testing purposes, you can use the two flash files that ship with sIFR — `tradegothic.swf` and `vandenkeere.swf`. However, if you want to embed your own fonts into `.swf` files, you'll need Macromedia Flash. At the time of writing, Macromedia Flash 8 Basic costs $349 and Macromedia Flash 8 Professional costs $699. You can download a trial version from `http://www.adobe.com/downloads/` after you register with Adobe; the download size is about 100 MB.

❑   You need to have a license to distribute the fonts you're using for the replacement.

You put sIFR to work in the next exercise, where you modify your product catalog to use a font that isn't supported by default by many web browsers. Look ahead at Figures 6-8 and 6-9 to see the difference between the "before" and "after" versions of the catalog's title.

Using sIFR Properly

If you decide to use sIFR for your projects, we recommend that you also check its documentation at `http://wiki.novemberborn.net/sifr/` and its description at `http://www.mikeindustries.com/sifr/`, because they contain more tips and hints that we could not include in the book. You can find a very useful walkthrough at `http://wiki.novemberborn.net/sifr/How+to+use`. This quote is particularly pertinent: *"sIFR is for headlines, pull quotes, and other small swaths of text. In other words, it is for display type — type which accents the rest of the page. Body copy should remain browser text. Additionally, we recommend not replacing over about 10 blocks of text per page. A few more is fine, but once you get into the 50s or so, you'll notice a processor and speed hit."*

Using sIFR

1.   Start by creating a folder in your project named `sifr`, so the complete path to it will be `/seoasp/sifr/`.

2.   Download sIFR. Navigate to `http://www.mikeindustries.com/sifr/` and find the Download link at the bottom of the page. At the time of writing, the direct link to the latest zip package is `http://www.mikeindustries.com/blog/files/sifr/2.0/sIFR2.0.2.zip`.

3. Unzip the package into your `/seoasp/sifr` folder. The contents of the folder should look in Solution Explorer as shown in Figure 6-4.

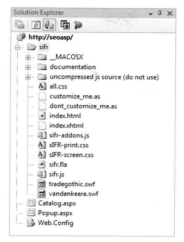

Figure 6-4

4. Open `Catalog.aspx` and add a reference to the `sifr.js` file, and to the two CSS files, as highlighted in the following code snippet:

```
<head id="Head1" runat="server">
  <title>Spiderable Popups Example</title>
  <script src="sifr/sifr.js" type="text/javascript"></script>
  <link rel="stylesheet" href="sifr/sIFR-screen.css" type="text/css" media="screen" />
  <link rel="stylesheet" href="sifr/sIFR-print.css" type="text/css" media="print" />
</head>
```

5. The final step required to see sIFR in action is to select the strings you want replaced. You do this by including JavaScript code that makes the changes when the page loads. Add this code before the closing `</body>` tag in `Catalog.aspx`, as shown in the following code snippet. (Note there are additional ways to do this, as explained in sIFR's documentation.)

```
<! -- sIFR replacement code  -- >
<script type="text/javascript">
// continue only if the sIRF code has been loaded
if(typeof sIFR == "function")
{
  // replace the <h1> text
  sIFR.replaceElement(named({sSelector:"body h1",
                             sFlashSrc:"./sifr/vandenkeere.swf"}));
};
</script>

</body>
</html>
```

6. You're done! If you disable JavaScript and load `http://seoasp/Catalog.aspx`, you get to your catalog page that uses the default heading font, which you can see in Figure 6-5.

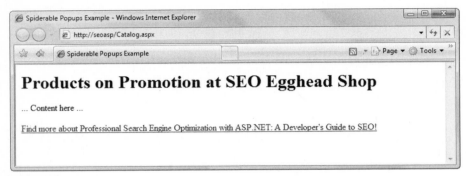

Figure 6-5

7. Loading the very same page with JavaScript and Flash enabled, you get your title drawn with the new font! (See Figure 6-6.)

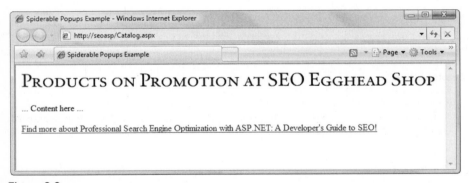

Figure 6-6

After adding this last bit of code, you're done! Your page will now work by default with replaced text. If Flash or JavaScript aren't supported by the user agent, it falls back gracefully to the default page font. As you can see, sIFR is really easy to use! All that you needed to do was to copy sIFR to your project, and then call its functions to have your headings replaced with another font. You referenced the sIFR JavaScript library and its two CSS files in your `Catalog.aspx` script:

```
<head id="Head1" runat="server">
  <title>Spiderable Popups Example</title>
  <script src="sifr/sifr.js" type="text/javascript"></script>
  <link rel="stylesheet" href="sifr/sIFR-screen.css" type="text/css" media="screen" />
  <link rel="stylesheet" href="sifr/sIFR-print.css" type="text/css" media="print" />
</head>
```

After referencing the JavaScript library, you need, of course, to use it. Just referencing `sifr.js` doesn't have any effect by itself — and here the fun part comes. The following code, which you added at the end of `Catalog.aspx`, uses the `sIFR.replaceElement()` function to replace all `<h1>` tags with Flash files that render text:

```
// continue only if the sIRF code has been loaded
if(typeof sIFR == "function")
{
  // replace the <h1> text
  sIFR.replaceElement(named({sSelector:"body h1",
                            sFlashSrc:"./sifr/vandenkeere.swf"}));
};
```

The `(typeof sIFR == "function")` condition verifies that the sIFR library has been loaded successfully, so the script won't attempt to call `sIFR.replaceElement()` in case you forgot to reference the sIFR JavaScript library.

The `replaceElement()` function supports more parameters, but the necessary ones are `sSelector` (which defines which HTML elements should be replaced), and `sFlashSrc` (which references the Flash movie containing the font to be used). However, many more parameters are supported, and can be used when you need to fine-tune the replacement options. Table 6-2 contains the list of parameters that you can use with `replaceElement()`.

Table 6-2

replaceElement() Parameter	Description
sSelector	The CSS element you want to replace. Include whitespace in the string *only* when selecting descendants, such as in `body h1`. You can separate multiple CSS elements using commas.
sFlashSrc	The Flash file that contains the font.
sColor	The text color using hex notation.
sLinkColor	The link color using hex notation.
sHoverColor	The hover link color using hex notation.
sBgColor	The background color using hex notation.
nPaddingTop	Top padding in pixels.
nPaddingRight	Right padding in pixels.
nPaddingBottom	Bottom padding in pixels.
nPaddingLeft	Left padding in pixels.

Continued

Table 6-2 (*continued*)

replaceElement() Parameter	Description
sFlashVars	Parameters to send to the Flash movie. When multiple parameters are used, separate them by &. Supported parameters are textalign, offsetLeft, offsetTop, and underline.
sCase	Set this to upper to transform the text to uppercase, and lower to transform the text to lowercase.
sWmode	Supported values are opaque (the default) and transparent (to enable transparent background).

See the "How to use" documentation at http://wiki.novemberborn.net/sifr/How+to+use for more details about using sIFR.

Note that if you want to use a different font for text replacement, you need to create a Flash movie file that contains that font. To do that, you need to follow a few simple steps that require that you have Macromedia Flash installed on your machine. These steps are:

1. You need to open the sifr.fla file located in your sifr folder with Macromedia Flash (not the Flash Player!). If you don't have Macromedia Flash, you can find the trial download at http://www.adobe.com/downloads/, or at a software catalog web site such as http://www.softpedia.com.

2. The sifr.fla script that you've just loaded allows you to embed fonts into the .swf files that render your graphical text. You'll need to follow the same procedure for each font you want to use. For the purpose of this example choose the Trebuchet MS font (but you can use the font of your choice if you prefer). Double-click the white box in the center of the stage. The "Do not remove this text." text should appear, and the Properties window should be highlighted. Click the font combo box from the Properties window, and choose the font you want to use.

3. Export the new file to an .swf file by going to File ⇨ Export ⇨ Export Movie. When asked for the name, you should name the file depending on the font you've chosen, because that's what the exported file is used for — to store the font.

4. In the options form that shows up after clicking Save, leave the default options, making sure you're exporting to Flash Player 6 format, and click OK.

5. After exporting your file, it's OK to close Macromedia Flash. You don't need to save any changes to sifr.fla.

At the end of this procedure, you'll have an swf file that you can use as a parameter when calling sIFR functions.

Stewart Rosenberger's Text Replacement Method

This method doesn't work with ASP.NET — instead, it works using a PHP script — and we only mention it here because it is another popular technique. If you're interested, you can find a step-by-step example of its implementation in this book's sister, *Professional Search Engine Optimization with PHP: A Developer's Guide to SEO*. Just as with sIFR, this method uses JavaScript to replace page headings with images. However, this time you use image files (not Flash movies), which are created by a PHP script on-the-fly. It is otherwise very similar to sIFR. You can read more about Stewart Rosenberger's text replacement method at http://alistapart.com/articles/dynatext.

Search Engine–Friendly HTML

With some JavaScript-related issues out of the way, there are a number of HTML issues to explore:

- ❑ HTML structural elements
- ❑ Copy prominence and tables
- ❑ Frames
- ❑ Forms

HTML Structural Elements

In general, HTML provides structural elements that may help a search engine understand the overall topicality of documents, as well as where logical divisions and important parts are located, such as <h1> and <h2> tags, <b> tags, and so on. If you don't include these elements in your HTML code, the search engine must make such decisions entirely itself.

Although most hand-coded sites do well in this regard, especially when a search engine marketer is involved, many content management systems are abysmally bad at it. Also, WYSIWYG (What You See Is What You Get) editors typically do not use these tags, and tend to generate HTML with CSS embedded pervasively in style tags. This is not ideal with regard to search engine optimization. For example, this structure:

```
<ol>
  <li>Item 1</li>
  <li>Item 2</li>
  <li>Item 3</li>
</ol>
```

provides more semantic information than this:

```
<img src='bullet.gif' />Item 1<br />
<img src='bullet.gif' />Item 2<br />
<img src='bullet.gif' />Item 3<br />
```

even if they do look entirely identical onscreen using the currently applied styles (CSS).

If you've developed web content using a WYSIWYG editor, it may be wise to hand-edit the generated HTML to optimize the content after the fact. You may also choose to create your HTML directly instead of using such an editor. An additional solution of using a custom markup language is explored later in this chapter.

Copy Prominence and Tables

Copy prominence is the physical depth — that is, the actual position (counted in bytes) in the HTML document where the copy starts within your document. Because search engines may consider the content closest to the top of the HTML document more important, it is wise to avoid placing repetitive or irrelevant content before the primary content on a page.

A common form of content that doesn't need to be at the top of an HTML file is JavaScript code. It is wise to move any JavaScript code located at the top of an HTML document either to the bottom, or to a separate file, because JavaScript has a large footprint and is mostly uninteresting to a spider. You can reference external JavaScript files as follows:

```
<script language="JavaScript" src="my_script.js"></script>
```

When referencing external JavaScript files, don't omit the </script> *tag. If you do that, Internet Explorer won't parse your script.*

The other common manifestation of this problem is that many tables-based sites place their site navigation element on the left. This use of tables tends to push the primary content further down physically, and because of this, may contribute to poorer rankings. If there are many navigational elements above the primary content, it may confuse the search engine as to what is actually the primary content on the page, because the navigational elements are higher physically in the document.

Search engines do try to detect repetitive elements, such as a navigation elements placed physically before the primary content on a page, and at least partially ignore them. Modern search engines also examine the actual displayed location of content rather than just their physical location in a source document. However, avoiding the situation entirely may improve the odds of proper indexing regardless.

There are three solutions for this:

❑   Instead of using a tables-based layout, use a pure CSS-type layout where presentation order is arbitrary. An in-depth discussion of CSS is beyond the scope of this book. For more information, you can consult one of the many books on CSS, such as *Beginning CSS: Cascading Style Sheets for Web Design* (Wiley Publishing, Inc., 2004).

❑   Place the navigation to the right side of the page in a tables-based layout. Figure 6-7 shows an example from http://www.lawyerseek.com.

❑   Apply a technique that designers typically call *the table trick*, which uses an HTML sleight-of-hand to reverse the order of table cells physically in the document without reversing their presentation.

Even if your site uses tables, typically, parts of a document can be rendered using CSS layout on a selective basis. Doing so does not force you to abandon a tables-based layout completely. A good place to look is in repetitive elements (that is, those generated within loops), such as navigational elements and repeated blocks to shrink HTML size, because tables tend to have a large footprint.

Figure 6-7

The Table Trick Explained

The table trick basically boils down to employing a two-by-two table with an empty first cell, using a second cell with a rowspan set to two, and then putting the navigation in the second row "under" the empty first cell.

Take this simple HTML example:

```
<table>
  <tr>
    <td valign="top">Navigation</td>
    <td valign="top">Content</td>
  </tr>
</table>
```

The rendered content would look like Figure 6-8.

Figure 6-8

Now, you could rewrite the HTML code to place the relevant content closer to the beginning in the document, while keeping the visual appearance equivalent, this way:

```
<table>
  <tr>
    <td><! -- empty table cell -- ></td>
    <td rowspan="2" valign="top">Content</td>
  </tr>
  <tr>
    <td valign="top">Navigation</td>
  </tr>
</table>
```

Figure 6-9 shows the result.

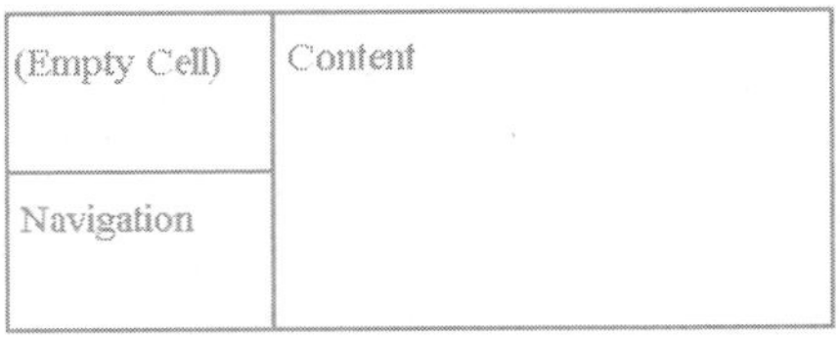

(Empty Cell)	Content
Navigation	

Figure 6-9

This way, the navigation code appears below the content in the physical file, yet it displays on the left when loaded in a browser.

ASP.NET ViewState

As an ASP.NET programmer, you should be familiar with the technology used by ASP.NET to preserve the state of a Web Form between postbacks. When the visitor performs an action that causes a server-side event to occur — such as clicking an <asp:Button> control, selecting a row or a column in a GridView control, and so on — the form is submitted together with a piece of data called ViewState. This is implemented as a hidden element named __VIEWSTATE, which contains the state of every server-side element in the form, and it's passed back and forth between the client and the server to maintain the state of your controls.

ASP.NET's ViewState mechanism is a useful tool indeed, which creates state over HTTP — which itself is a stateless protocol. With HTTP, every client request is handled independently by the server, without knowledge of the previous user activity on the web site. With ASP.NET, you don't need to write any code so that the state of your checkboxes, radio buttons, text boxes, and so on, maintain their state when the form is submitted. Instead, this is handled automatically for you. The only problem is that the ViewState can grow in size significantly if the page contains many controls. For example, if you load `http://www.cristiandarie.ro/BalloonShop/`, which contains two `DataList` controls that display the menus, a `GridView` that displays eight products, and a few other controls, the size of the ViewState data may be around two kilobytes. If you look in the HTML source of the page, you can also see that ViewState looks something like this:

```
<input type="hidden" name="__VIEWSTATE" id="__VIEWSTATE" value="/
wEPDwULLTE0NjI5MjkwNDQPZBYCZg9kFgICAw9kFgoCAw9kFgJmDzwrAAkBAA8WBB4IRGF0YUtleXMWAB4L
XyFJdGVtQ291bnQCCGQWFGYPZBYCZg8VARREZXBhcnRtZW50VW5zZWxlY3RlZGQCAQ9kFgICAQ8PFgoeC05
hdmlnYXRlVXJsBR4uLi9DYXRhbG9nLmFzcHg/RGVwYXJ0bWVudElEPTEeBFRleHQFFEFubml2ZXJzYXJ5IE
JhbGxvb25zHgdUb29sVGlwBT9UaGVVzZSBzd2VldCBiYWxsb29ucyBhcmUgdGhlIHBlcmZlY3QgZ21mdCBmb
3Igc29tZW9uZSB5b3UgbG92ZS4eCENzc0NsYXNzBRREZXBhcnR .........." />
```

> Note that although the ViewState data isn't in human-readable form, it's not encrypted either. The information represents a persisted `System.Web.UI.StateBag` object, which contains name-value pairs representing the state of the controls on the page. You can decipher the ViewState data yourself, or by using one of the many free tools available on the web.

By default, the ViewState is enabled for all server controls. However, if you don't need to persist the state for a specific control, Web User Control, Web Form, or a Master Page, you can disable the ViewState by setting the `EnableViewState` property to `false`. This will speed up the construction of the page, will cause less web traffic, and will make the resulting HTML smaller — but this comes at the cost of losing the persistence functionality.

Disabling the ViewState can be done for the controls whose value is set programmatically on each page load, in the `PageLoad` event handler. In those cases, maintaining state using ViewState isn't necessary. In this book we will not focus on these details further because they relate more to ASP.NET performance optimization than to search engine optimization.

Frames

There have been so many problems with frames since their inception that it bewilders us as to why anyone would use them at all. Search engines have *a lot* of trouble spidering frames-based sites. A search engine cannot index a frames page within the context of its other associated frames. Only individual pages can be indexed. Even when individual pages are successfully indexed, because another frame is often used in tandem for navigation, a user may be sent to a bewildering page that contains no navigation. There is a workaround for that issue (similar to the popup navigation solution), but it creates still other problems. The `noframes` tag also attempts to address the problem, but it is an invisible on-page factor and mercilessly abused by spammers. Any site that uses frames is at such a disadvantage that we must simply recommend not using them at all.

Jacob Nielsen predicted these problems in 1996, and recommended not to use them at the same date. Now, more than ten years later, there is still no reason to use them, and, unlike the also relatively benign problems associated with tables, there is no easy fix. See `http://www.useit.com/alertbox/9612.html`.

Using Forms

A search engine spider will never submit a form, so any content that is behind form navigation will not be visible to a spider. Some ASP.NET developers have the tendency to implement site navigation using server-side buttons or hyperlinks, and writing some redirection code in the event handlers of those controls. This is a bad practice because the spiders are unable to browse such a web site, and simple hyperlinks should be used whenever possible.

> *There are some reports that Google, in particular, does index content behind very simple forms. Forms that consist of one pull-down that directs the user to a particular web page are in this category. However, as with the example of JavaScript links being spidered, we do not recommend depending on this behavior. As a corollary, if such a form points to content that should be excluded, it may be wise to exclude the content with an explicit exclusion mechanism, such as* robots.txt *or the robots* meta *tag!*

There is no magic solution for this problem. However, there is a workaround. As long as your script is configured to accept the parameters from a GET request, you can place the URLs of certain form requests in a sitemap or elsewhere in a site.

So if a form submits its values and creates a dynamic URL like the following:

```
/Search.aspx?CategoryId=1&Color=Red
```

that same link could be placed on a sitemap and a spider could follow it.

Using a Custom Markup Language to Generate SE-Friendly HTML

As mentioned earlier, using a WYSIWYG editor frequently presents a problem with regard to on-page optimization. Frequently, these editors do not generate HTML that uses tags that adequately delineate the structural meaning of elements on a page.

If you are developing a large web site where non-technical personnel contribute content frequently, you could add support for a simple custom markup language. The markup language can ease the management of content for copywriters who are not familiar with HTML. Additionally, it gives the site developer total control over what the HTML looks like after you transform the custom markup language into HTML.

To implement this you use a simple parser. As a bonus, this parser can implement programmatic features and make global changes that are well beyond the scope and possibilities of the CSS realm.

Here is an example snippet of copy using a custom markup language:

```
{HEADING}Using a Custom Markup Language to Generate Optimized HTML{/HEADING}
As we mentioned earlier, using a WYSIWYG editor frequently presents a problem with
regard to on-page optimization.  Frequently, the editors do not generate HTML that
uses tags that adequately delineate the structural meaning of elements on a page.
Since heading tags, such as h1, ul, and strong are indicators of the structure within
a document, not using them will probably {BOLD}{ITALIC}decrease{/ITALIC}{/BOLD} the
rankings of a page, especially when a search engine is relying on on-page factors.
```

Which can be automatically translated to this:

```
<h1 class="custom_markup">Using a Custom Markup Language to Generate Optimized HTML</h1>
As we mentioned earlier, using a WYSIWYG editor frequently presents a problem with
regard to on-page optimization. Frequently, the editors do not generate HTML that uses
tags that adequately delineate the structural meaning of elements on a page. Since
heading tags, such as h1, ul, and strong are indicators of the structure within a
document, not using them will probably <strong><em>decrease</em></strong> the rankings
of a page, especially when a search engine is relying on on-page factors.
```

In this way, you accomplish two goals. You create very clean and optimized HTML. And you do it without making a copywriter run for the hills. In fact, using a markup language like this, which only presents a copywriter with the necessary elements and styles them according to a set of translation rules, may be even easier than using a WYSIWYG tool in our opinion. Whenever needed, the markup language allows the copywriter to break into HTML for particularly complex cases by using an "{HTML}" tag. Let's try a quick example of its use now.

Implementing a Custom Markup Translator

1. If you don't already have the `App_Code` folder in your project, create it by right-clicking the root node in Solution Explorer, and choosing Add ASP.NET Folder ⇨ App_Code. In this folder create a new C# class file named `CustomMarkup.cs`, and then type this code in.

```csharp
using System;
using System.Text.RegularExpressions;
using System.Collections.Generic;

/// <summary>
/// Class that translates custom markup to HTML
/// </summary>
public class CustomMarkup
{
  // store the regular expressions and their string replacements
  private static Dictionary<Regex, string> rs;

  // translates the custom markup from the input string to HTML
  public static string Translate(string markupString)
  {
    // apply each regular expression in the collection
    foreach (Regex x in rs.Keys)
    {
      markupString = x.Replace(markupString, rs[x]);
    }

    // return translated string
    return markupString;
  }

  // static constructor creates the collection of Regex objects
  // and replacement strings used for translation
  static CustomMarkup()
  {
    // create the collection
    rs = new Dictionary<Regex, string>();
```

```
        // translate bold tags
        rs.Add(new Regex(@"\{bold}(.*?)\{/bold}",
          RegexOptions.IgnoreCase), @"<b>$1</b>");

        // translate italic tags
        rs.Add(new Regex(@"\{italic}(.*?)\{/italic}",
          RegexOptions.IgnoreCase), @"<i>$1</i>");

        // translate underline tags
        rs.Add(new Regex(@"\{underline}(.*?)\{/underline}",
          RegexOptions.IgnoreCase), @"<u>$1</u>");

        // translate h1 headings
        rs.Add(new Regex(@"\{heading}(.*?)\{/heading}",
          RegexOptions.IgnoreCase), @"<h1 class=some_class>$1</h1>");

        // translate h2 headings
        rs.Add(new Regex(@"\{subheading}(.*?)\{/subheading}",
          RegexOptions.IgnoreCase), @"<h2 class=some_other_class>$1</h2>");

        // translate hyperlinks
        rs.Add(new Regex(@"\{link:(.*?)}(.*?)\{/link}",
          RegexOptions.IgnoreCase), @"<a href=\'$1\'>$2</a>");

        // translate hyperlinks that open in new window
        rs.Add(new Regex(@"\{elink:(.*?)}(.*?)\{/elink}",
          RegexOptions.IgnoreCase), @"<a href=\'$1\' target=""_blank"">$2</a>");

        // translate unordered list tags
        rs.Add(new Regex(@"\{unordered-list}(.*?)\{/unordered-list}\s*",
          RegexOptions.IgnoreCase), @"<ul>$1</ul>");

        // translate ordered list tags
        rs.Add(new Regex(@"\{ordered-list}(.*?)\{/ordered-list}\s*",
          RegexOptions.IgnoreCase), @"<ol>$1</ol>");

        // translate list elements
        rs.Add(new Regex(@"\\s*{list-element}(.*?)\{/list-element}\s*",
          RegexOptions.IgnoreCase), @"<li>$1</li>");

        // translate picture tags
        rs.Add(new Regex(@"\{picture:(.*?)}",
          RegexOptions.IgnoreCase), @"<img src=""$1"" border=""0"">");

        // remove tabs
        rs.Add(new Regex(@"\t"), "");

        // remove comments
        rs.Add(new Regex(@"\{comment}(.*?)\{/comment}",
          RegexOptions.IgnoreCase), "");
    }
}
```

2. Create a file named `markup.txt` in your `seoasp` folder, and write this text in it:

```
{HEADING}Using a Custom Markup Language to Generate Optimized HTML{/HEADING}
{BOLD}As we mentioned earlier{/BOLD}, using a WYSIWYG editor frequently presents a
problem with regard to on-page optimization.  Frequently, the editors do not generate
HTML that uses tags that adequately delineate the structural meaning of elements on a
page.  Since heading tags, such as h1, ul, and strong are indicators of the structure
within a document, not using them will probably {BOLD}{ITALIC}decrease{/ITALIC}{/BOLD}
the rankings of a page, especially when a search engine is relying on on-page factors.
```

3. Create a Web Form named `TestMarkup.aspx` in your `seoasp` folder, and write this code:

```
<%@ Page Language="C#" %>
<%@ Import Namespace="System.IO" %>
<!DOCTYPE html PUBLIC "-//W3C//DTD XHTML 1.0 Transitional//EN"
"http://www.w3.org/TR/xhtml1/DTD/xhtml1-transitional.dtd">

<script runat="server">
  protected void Page_Load(object sender, EventArgs e)
  {
    // read the contents of markup.txt
    string text = File.ReadAllText(MapPath("markup.txt"));

    // translate the custom markup to HTML, and display it
    messageLiteral.Text = CustomMarkup.Translate(text);
  }
</script>

<html xmlns="http://www.w3.org/1999/xhtml" >
<head runat="server">
  <title>HTML Markup Translator</title>
</head>
<body>
  <form id="form1" runat="server">
    <asp:Literal runat="server" ID="messageLiteral" />
  </form>
</body>
</html>
```

4. Load `http://seoasp/TestMarkup.aspx`, and expect to get the results shown in Figure 6-10.

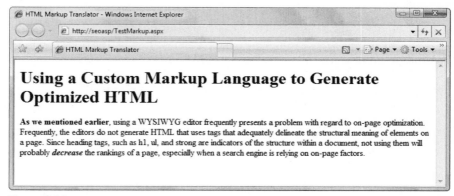

Figure 6-10

179

This was a simple example, which hinted at how useful such a system can be when building a more complex content management system. The little CustomMarkup class knows how to handle these custom markup tags, whose significance is obvious: {bold}, {italic}, {underline}, {heading}, {subheading}, {link}, {elink} (this is a link that opens a new window), {unordered-list}, {ordered-list}, {list-element}, {picture}, and {comment}. The {comment} tags are to be removed from the output HTML. Tab characters in the original text are also removed.

The markup file, markup.txt, doesn't contain any HTML elements, but custom markup elements. With the help of CustomMarkup, you're replacing on-the-fly all the custom markup elements with standard HTML tags.

The CustomMarkup.Translate() method performs a number of regular expression replacements, which transform the custom markup code to HTML. What may not be very obvious is the way these regular expressions are stored for further processing. If you look at the class static constructor, you'll notice that we instantiate a static Dictionary<Regex, string> collection:

```
public class CustomMarkup
{
   // store the regular expressions and their string replacements
   private static Dictionary<Regex, string> rs;

   // static constructor creates the collection of Regex objects
   // and replacement strings used for translation
   static CustomMarkup()
   {
      // create the collection
      rs = new Dictionary<Regex, string>();

      // translate bold tags
      rs.Add(new Regex(@"\{bold}(.*?)\{/bold}",
        RegexOptions.IgnoreCase), @"<b>$1</b>");
   ...
```

If the Dictionary<Regex, string> looks alien to you, then you should know it's part of a new feature in .NET 2.0 named *generics*. This feature allows you to build classes that use types that are unknown at development time. However, they are known at compilation time, so that the compiler still works with strongly typed objects, taking advantage of the implicit performance benefits. Generics are useful when you need to create a class that deals with objects of an unknown type. In our case, we're using the generic Dictionary<TKey, TValue> class, which implements a list whose keys are of the type TKey, and whose values are of the type TValue.

So we store the regular expressions and their string replacement values as a collection whose keys are the regular expressions, and whose values are the replacement strings. The collection is a static object of a class, which means that it's created and stored only once for the application.

```
rs.Add(new Regex(@"\{bold}(.*?)\{/bold}", RegexOptions.IgnoreCase),
      @"<b>$1</b>");
```

Static Members

When you implement functionality that doesn't need to be performed on a particular instance of an object, you can use *static* class members. As opposed to *instance* class members, static members are not part of a particular instance (object) of the class. Instead, they're part of a unique, global object of the class. They're always called upon the class name, rather than an instance name, such as in `HttpUtility.UrlEncode`, `Console.WriteLine`, `Math.Sqrt`, and so on. The language also supports the concept of *static constructors,* which are used to instantiate any static members the class might have. The static constructor is called only once, before the first static member is ever accessed.

Flash and AJAX

Unfortunately, both Flash and AJAX technologies can pose major problems for search engines when used pervasively. Sites that are entirely Flash- or AJAX-based will not be indexed very well, if at all. The rationale is fairly simple. Search engines are designed to index pages, not applications.

> **Sites built entirely with Flash or entirely with AJAX involve a huge paradigm shift. They do not employ pages for the various elements of a site; rather, they are, more or less, an application embedded on a single page.**

Furthermore, even if a search engine could figure out how to interpret a Flash file or AJAX application adequately, parsing and indexing its pertinent content, there would be no way to navigate to that particular part of the application using a URL. Therefore, because the primary goal of a search engine is to provide relevant results to a user, a search engine will be hesitant to rank content in those media well. Lastly, both Flash and AJAX would invite several more innovative and harder-to-detect forms of spam.

The Blended Approach

But before you assume that we vilify Flash and AJAX completely, there is somewhat of a solution. A site designer should only use Flash and AJAX for the areas of the site that require it. This is called *the blended approach.* He or she should design an HTML-based site, and employ Flash and AJAX technologies where they will provide a tangible benefit to the user. He or she should attempt to keep as much of the textual content HTML-based as possible.

Frequently, a mix of HTML and JavaScript (DHTML) can also approximate most of the interactivity of these technologies. For example, clicking a button could hide or unhide an HTML `div` element. This will involve employing the use of smaller Flash or AJAX elements placed inside a traditional HTML layout. In other words, you should use Flash and AJAX as elements on a page, not as the page itself.

Some SEM authorities also recommend providing a non-Flash or AJAX version of content using <noembed> or <noscript>, respectively. Unfortunately, because those tags are invisible (and have been used so pervasively for spam), their efficacy is questionable. Search engines may choose to ignore the content therein completely. They may, however, enhance usability for users with disabilities, so it is not unwise to employ them for that purpose.

This solution also misses the mark for another reason — a typical Flash or AJAX site exists on a single "page," therefore further limiting the utility of the tag, because all content would presumably have to exist on that one page!

Figure 6-11 shows an image of a site that looks like a full Flash application, but was changed to HTML with DHTML and hidden layers. The presented link is `http://www.xactcommunication.com/WristLinx-9/X33XIF-WristLinx-TwoWay-Wristwatch-Radio-35.html`.

Figure 6-11

Summary

On-page technologies are a double-edged sword. New technologies — such as Flash and AJAX — may be boons for usability and have a certain "cool factor," but may make a site entirely invisible to a search engine spider if not used properly. Even seemingly superficial things like the structure of a link may severely impact web site spiderability, and hence search engine friendliness. Lastly, as stated in Chapter 2, invisible on-page factors are not regarded with any confidence by search engines. So despite the fact that tags such as <noembed> and <noscript> were created to address these issues, your success with them will likely be limited.

## 7

Web Feeds and
Social Bookmarking

You've just added some great new content to your web site. *Now what*? Of course, your current visitors will appreciate the content. They may even tell a few friends about it. But there are technologies that you can leverage to facilitate and encourage them to do some free marketing for you.

This chapter explores web feeds and social bookmarking, two technologies that web site visitors can use to access and promote content that they enjoy. Encouraging visitors to do so is a vital part of viral marketing. This chapter discusses various ways to accomplish this, and walks you through three exercises where you:

❑ Create your own RSS feeds.

❑ Syndicate RSS feeds.

❑ Add social bookmarking icons to your pages and feeds.

Web Feeds

The *web feed* is a mechanism used to distribute content over the web in a standardized XML-based format. The typical way for a person to read your content is to visit your web pages, retrieving their content laid out in HTML format. This doesn't work with web feeds, because they typically contain no presentation. Instead, people use specialized programs that retrieve and display the data.

Web feeds are used to disseminate information automatically — to humans as well as other web sites. They are a very effective vehicle for information distribution, and they've become very popular because they make it easy for somebody to read news, or recent blog posts, from his or her favorite sources. Web feeds are also nicely described at http://en.wikipedia.org/wiki/Web_feed.

Feeds encouraged the development of several applications for their consumption. Modern web browsers (including Internet Explorer 7 and Firefox 2.0), desktop applications such as Microsoft Office 2007, and web applications such as Google Reader (http://www.google.com/reader/) allow users to access the feeds they subscribe to from one convenient location. These applications are called aggregators, or feed readers.

Your web site can provide access to some or all of its content through web feeds. They may include links to the actual content as well as other links to elsewhere within your site. Over time, this will garner traffic and links from users who subscribe to your feeds, as well as the various sites that *syndicate* the information.

Web syndication permits other web sites to promote your content. Other webmasters have an incentive to syndicate feeds on their sites as fresh content, because including relevant syndicated content in *moderation* can be a useful resource. It may, however, be wise to abbreviate the amount of information you provide in a feed, because the *full* content appearing on various sites may present duplicate content problems. You may also choose to syndicate other web sites' content.

> *Moderation means that the web site could stand on its own without the syndicated content as well. If it cannot, it is probably a spam site.*

Today, all major blogging platforms provide feeds of some sort. Most other types of content management systems provide them as well. The custom applications that you develop may also benefit from their addition. This chapter demonstrates how to do so.

In order to be usable by everyone, feeds must be provided in a standardized format. RSS and Atom are the most popular choices.

RSS and Atom

Unfortunately, as usual, there are the requisite format wars. There are many competing formats for web syndication. Two of them are discussed here — RSS and Atom.

Both RSS and Atom are XML-based standards. The virtue of XML is that it provides a common framework that applications can use to communicate among multiple architectures and operating system platforms. RSS and Atom feeds can be viewed as plain text files, but it doesn't make much sense to use them like that, because they are meant to be read by a feed reader or specialized software that uses it in the scheme of a larger application. Figure 7-1 shows Jaimie Sirovich's SEO Egghead feed in Cristian's Google Reader list.

RSS has a long and complicated history, with many versions and substantial modifications to the standard. There are two fundamental branches of RSS with two different names. RDF Site Summary (RSS 0.9) was created by Netscape in the late nineties. In response to criticism that it was too complex, a simplified and substantially different version, RSS 0.91, was released. To make things even more interesting, RSS 1.0 is largely a descendant of RSS 0.9, whereas RSS 2.0 is closer to RSS 0.91. RSS 2.0 now stands for *Really Simple Syndication*, and RSS 1.0 still stands for RDF Site Summary. Because this is not a history book on RSS, we will stop here and state that RSS 2.0 is by far the most popular and most adopted at this point. The standard is also now frozen, and no new changes are underway. The standard for RSS 2.0 is located at `http://blogs.law.harvard.edu/tech/rss`.

Figure 7-1

Atom was created because of the standards issues that have plagued RSS over time. It was born in 2003. There are two versions, Atom 0.3 and Atom 1.0. It is far more standardized but also more complicated and less commonly used. It has recently been gaining ground, however. For a more detailed comparison of RSS and Atom, consult `http://www.intertwingly.net/wiki/pie/Rss20AndAtom10Compared`.

We are ambivalent about which standard is employed. RSS 2.0 does have a higher adoption rate, it is simpler by most metrics, and that is the format demonstrated here when you create a web feed. To syndicate feeds you will employ the use of a class written in ASP.NET.

A typical RSS 2.0 feed might look like this:

```
<rss version="2.0">
  <channel>
    <title>example.com breaking news</title>
    <link>http://www.example.org</link>
    <description>A short description of this feed</description>
    <language>en</language>
    <pubDate>Tue, 12 Sep 2006 07:56:23 EDT</pubDate>
    <item>
      <title>Catchy Title</title>
      <link>http://www.example.org/catchy-title.html</link>
      <description>
```

```
        The description can hold any content you wish, including XHTML.
      </description>
      <pubDate>Tue, 12 Sep 2006 07:56:23 EDT</pubDate>
    </item>
    <item>
      <title>Another Catchy Title</title>
      <link>http://www.example.org/another-catchy-title.html</link>
      <description>
        The description can hold any content you wish, including XHTML.
      </description>
      <pubDate>Tue, 12 Sep 2006 07:56:23 EDT</pubDate>
    </item>
  </channel>
</rss>
```

The feed may contain any number of `<item>` elements, each item holding different news or blog entries — or whatever content you want to store.

You can either create feeds for others to access, or you can syndicate feeds that others create. The following sections discuss how to create and consume feeds using an open-source resource named RSS Toolkit.

Creating RSS Feeds

In the following exercise we'll create a feed named "Forthcoming Titles by Cristian Darie," hoping that you'd find both the exercise, and the mentioned titles, interesting.

As mentioned earlier, we'll use an RSS Toolkit that is currently under development at CodePlex.

Using the RSS Toolkit to Generate Feeds

1. Load your `http://seoasp/` project in Visual Web Developer.

2. If you haven't created the App_Code folder already, add it to your project by right-clicking the project root in **Solution Explorer**, and selecting **Add ASP.NET Folder > App_Code**.

3. Navigate to `http://www.codeplex.com/ASPNETRSSToolkit`, and download the binary archive. The file name will be something like `ASPNETRSSToolkit-binary.zip`.

4. Unzip the toolkit archive, and copy the `bin` folder from the archive to your project's `seoasp` folder. Ultimately, you should have a folder named `seoasp/bin`, which contains `RssToolkit.dll` and a few other files.

5. In Visual Web Developer, right-click the root node in Solution Explorer, and select **Refresh Folder**. The new files should appear there.

6. Add a new **Generic Handler** file to the project named `BooksFeed.ashx`, and type this code:

```
<%@ WebHandler Language="C#" Class="BooksFeed" %>
```

```csharp
using System;
using System.Web;
using RssToolkit;

// Class that generates the RSS feed
public class BooksFeed : GenericRssHttpHandlerBase
{
  protected override void PopulateChannel(string channelName, string userName)
  {
    // set channel details; see http://blogs.law.harvard.edu/tech/rss
    Channel["title"] = "Forthcoming Titles by Cristian Darie";
    Channel["link"] = "http://www.cristiandarie.ro/forthcoming/";
    Channel["description"] = "Details about Cristian's forthcoming titles, updated
monthly";
    Channel["ttl"] = "10000"; // how many minutes the content should be cached

    // generic RSS element
    GenericRssElement item;

    // add RSS item
    item = new GenericRssElement();
    item["title"] = "Microsoft ASP.NET AJAX Essentials";
    item["description"] = "Step by step tutorial for creating Web 2.0 applications
using the Microsoft AJAX Library, and the ASP.NET AJAX Extensions.";
    item["link"] = "http://www.cristiandarie.ro/microsoft-ajax-1/";
    Channel.Items.Add(item);

    // add RSS item
    item = new GenericRssElement();
    item["title"] = "Mysterious Book";
    item["description"] = "Mysterious title about the complexity of life
demonstrates that the answer to Life, the Universe and Everything is NOT 42.";
    item["link"] = "http://www.cristiandarie.ro/mystery/";
    Channel.Items.Add(item);

    // add RSS item
    item = new GenericRssElement();
    item["title"] = "A Million Random Digits with 100,000 Normal Deviates";
    item["description"] = "This book is neither forthcoming, nor written by
Cristian Darie, but he surely wishes he had the idea first.";
    item["link"] = "http://www.amazon.com/dp/0833030477/";
    Channel.Items.Add(item);
  }
}
```

7. Execute `BooksFeed.ashx`. If it runs in Internet Explorer 7, you'll see a page such as that in Figure 7-2.

8. Clicking the "Subscribe to this feed" link displays a dialog where you can choose subscription options. In Internet Explorer 7 that dialog looks like Figure 7-3, but it will vary depending on the application used.

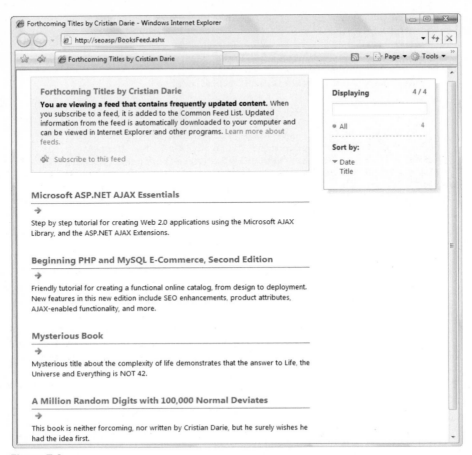

Figure 7-2

Figure 7-3

So what happened? You started by creating a generic handler file, named BooksFeed.ashx. This handler uses the RSS Toolkit to generate our RSS feed. In Chapter 3 you learned that generic handlers implement the IHttpHandler interface, which means they must implement ProcessRequest() and IsReusable. In practice, because we've used the RSS Toolkit, we've relied on it to do some of the low-level implementation for us. More specifically, instead of implementing `IHttpHandler`, we derived our handler class from `GenericRssHttpHandlerBase`:

```
public class BooksFeed : GenericRssHttpHandlerBase
{
```

The `GenericRssHttpHandlerBase` class implements `IHttpHandler`, and takes care of implementing it for us. It also defines a virtual method named `PopulateChannel`, which you must implement in your class.

> The term "virtual method" comes from the OOP terminology. Familiarity with this term and other of the more advanced OOP features aren't absolutely required to finish this book, but still we'd recommend that you study them if you haven't already done so. You can download a tutorial on OOP with C# in PDF format on Cristian Darie's site, at `http://www.cristiandarie.ro/downloads/`.

The RSS Toolkit is flexible and you can extend and customize its features. For example, the `PopulateChannel()` method receives as parameters a channel name and a user name that you can use when generating your feed. The sample feeds that are delivered together with the RSS Toolkit show many possible scenarios in which the toolkit can be used.

In our case, we implemented `PopulateChannel()` by hard-coding our RSS data, starting with the channel title, link, and description. In particular, we've implemented an imaginary RSS feed that would be placed on Cristian Darie's `http://www.cristiandarie.ro` to announce his forthcoming books:

```
protected override void PopulateChannel(string channelName, string userName)
{
    Channel["title"] = "Forthcoming Titles by Cristian Darie";
    Channel["link"] = "http://www.cristiandarie.ro/forthcoming/";
    Channel["description"] = "Details about Cristian's forthcoming titles, updated
monthly";
```

The rest of the code creates the feed items, by specifying the title, description, and link, for each of them:

```
GenericRssElement item;

item = new GenericRssElement();
item["title"] = "Microsoft ASP.NET AJAX Essentials";
item["description"] = "Step by step tutorial for creating Web 2.0 applications
using the Microsoft AJAX Library, and the ASP.NET AJAX Extensions.";
item["link"] = "http://www.cristiandarie.ro/microsoft-ajax-1/";
Channel.Items.Add(item);
```

In spite of ASP.NET's excellent XML built-in features, it's easy to appreciate how easy it is to work with the RSS library. Before moving on, we're showing you the version of the handler that generates the RSS feed by creating its XML contents manually, using an `XmlTextWriter` object. To keep the code shorter, the feed contains only the first of the three items from the previous example.

```
<%@ WebHandler Language="C#" Class="Handler" %>
```

```csharp
using System;
using System.Web;
using System.Text;
using System.Xml;

public class Handler : IHttpHandler
{
  public void ProcessRequest (HttpContext context)
  {
    // get the HttpResponse object for the current request
    HttpResponse response = context.Response;

    // set the content type
    response.ContentType = "text/xml";

    // create XmlTextWriter object
    XmlTextWriter xmlWriter = new XmlTextWriter(response.OutputStream,
Encoding.UTF8);

    // start the RSS feed and generate channel data elements
    xmlWriter.WriteStartDocument();
    xmlWriter.WriteStartElement("rss");
    xmlWriter.WriteAttributeString("version", "2.0");
    xmlWriter.WriteStartElement("channel");
    xmlWriter.WriteElementString("title", "Forthcoming Titles by Cristian Darie");
    xmlWriter.WriteElementString("link",
"http://www.cristiandarie.ro/forthcoming/");
    xmlWriter.WriteElementString("description", "Details about Cristian's
forthcoming titles, updated monthly");
    xmlWriter.WriteElementString("ttl", "10000");

    // generate RSS item
    xmlWriter.WriteStartElement("item");
    xmlWriter.WriteElementString("title", "Microsoft ASP.NET AJAX Essentials");
    xmlWriter.WriteElementString("description", "Step by step tutorial for creating
Web 2.0 applications using the Microsoft AJAX Library, and the ASP.NET AJAX
Extensions.");
    xmlWriter.WriteElementString("link", "http://www.cristiandarie.ro/microsoft-
ajax-1/");
    xmlWriter.WriteEndElement();

    // close feed
    xmlWriter.WriteEndElement();
    xmlWriter.WriteEndElement();
    xmlWriter.WriteEndDocument();
    xmlWriter.Flush();
    xmlWriter.Close();
    response.End();
  }
```

```
  public bool IsReusable
  {
    get
    {
      return false;
    }
  }
}
```

Syndicating RSS Feeds

The RSS Toolkit introduced in the previous exercise doesn't only know how to create RSS feeds — it also knows how to consume them. In the exercise that follows we'll show you some of the capabilities of this library, but keep in mind that the samples delivered with the kit demonstrate even more features.

Reading Feeds Using the RSS Toolkit

1. Open the `seoasp` application in Visual Web Developer. We assume that you have copied the RSS Toolkit files to your `bin` folder as instructed in the previous exercise.

2. Add a new Web Form to your project named `FeedReader.aspx`. Use **Visual C#** for the language, and do not select "Place code in separate file" or "Select master page."

3. Make sure the toolbox is visible (Ctrl + Alt + X), right-click the **Data** tab of the toolbox, and select **Choose Items**. (Now we'll add the `RssDataSource` and `RssHyperlink` objects, from the RSS toolkit, to the toolbox. You can choose another tab than Data if you prefer.)

4. In the Choose Toolbox Items dialog, click **Browse**.

5. Navigate to your `bin` folder, select **RssToolkit.dll** (as shown in Figure 7-4), and click **Open**.

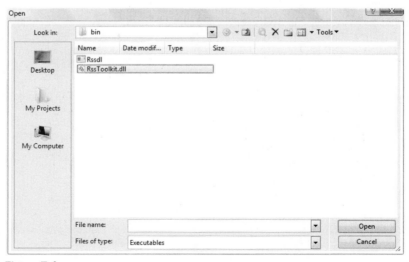

Figure 7-4

6.   Two new elements, **RssDataSource** and **RssHyperlink**, will be selected in the Choose Toolbox Items dialog. Click OK.

7.   The new controls will show up in the Data tab of the toolbox — see Figure 7-5.

Figure 7-5

8.   While `FeedReader.aspx` is open, drag one **RssDataSource** object from the toolbox, to the place after the closing `</div>` element. Then rename the `RssDataSource` object to `booksRssSource`, add a `url` element specifying the URL of the books feed created earlier, and change the page title to Feed Reader Test, as shown in the following code snippet:

```
<%@ Register Assembly="RssToolkit" Namespace="RssToolkit" TagPrefix="cc1" %>
<!DOCTYPE html PUBLIC "-//W3C//DTD XHTML 1.0 Transitional//EN"
"http://www.w3.org/TR/xhtml1/DTD/xhtml1-transitional.dtd">

<script runat="server">

</script>

<html xmlns="http://www.w3.org/1999/xhtml">
<head runat="server">
  <title>Feed Reader Test</title>
</head>
<body>
  <form id="form1" runat="server">
    <div>
    </div>
    <cc1:RssDataSource ID="booksRssSource" url="http://seoasp/BooksFeed.ashx"
runat="server">
```

```
      </cc1:RssDataSource>
    </form>
  </body>
</html>
```

9. Instead of the empty `<div>` element, place the following `DataList` control:

```
<body>
  <form id="form1" runat="server">
    <asp:DataList ID="DataList1" runat="server" DataSourceID="booksRssSource">
      <HeaderTemplate>
        <h2>
          <asp:HyperLink ID="HyperLink1" runat="server"
                          NavigateUrl='<%# booksRssSource.Channel["link"] %>'
                          Text='<%# booksRssSource.Channel["title"] %>' />
        </h2>
      </HeaderTemplate>
      <ItemTemplate>
        <asp:HyperLink runat="server"
                        NavigateUrl='<%# Eval("link") %>'
                        Text='<%# Eval("title") %>' />
      </ItemTemplate>
    </asp:DataList>
    <cc1:RssDataSource ID="booksRssSource" Url="http://seoasp/BooksFeed.ashx"
runat="server">
    </cc1:RssDataSource>
```

10. Execute `FeedReader.aspx`, and expect to get a page similar to that in Figure 7-6.

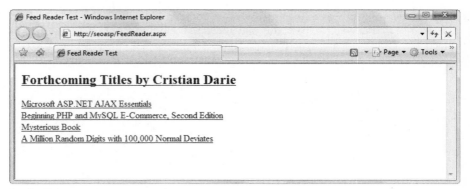

Figure 7-6

This was so simple, wasn't it! The RssDataSource object contained in the RSS Toolkit is great — it reads an RSS feed, and it supplies its data to any ASP.NET object that can consume a data source. In this exercise we've used a simple `DataList`, although any other object, including the `GridView`, `DetailsView`, `Repeater`, and so on, could have been used instead.

Other Sources of Syndicated Content

Various other sources of syndicated content are available, usually in the form of *web services*. These are outside the scope of this book; they are just mentioned for completeness.

Somewhat similar to RSS feeds in that they deliver data to external sources upon request, web services provide more complex communication mechanisms. Communication between clients and web services also occurs in XML-based formats; the most common protocols for web services communication are SOAP and REST.

Many major web-based companies, such as Amazon, eBay, Yahoo!, Google, MSN, and Alexa offer access to their vast amount of content through their web services. You can also provide your own web services to the same end. Numerous books have been written to cover some of these services. For more information on web services, consider *Professional Web APIs with PHP: eBay, Google, Paypal, Amazon, FedEx plus Web Feeds* (Wiley Publishing, Inc., 2006).

Social Bookmarking

Social bookmarking web sites offer users convenient storage of their bookmarks remotely for access from any location. Examples of these sites include del.icio.us, digg, reddit, and so on. These sites usually allow these bookmarks to be private, but many choose to leave them public. And when a particular web page is publicly bookmarked by many users, that is a major positive contributing factor in the ranking algorithm of the search function on a social bookmarking site. Ranking well in these searches presents another *great* source of organic traffic. Furthermore, if a web page is bookmarked by a large number of people, it may result in a front page placement on such a site. This usually results in a landslide of traffic.

Many blogs present links to streamline the process of bookmarking a page. As is typical with facilitating any action desired from a web site user, this may increase the number of bookmarks achieved by a page on your web site. Figure 7-7 shows an example of SEO Egghead with icons for bookmarking a page; highlighted (from left to right) are del.icio.us, digg, Furl, and Reddit.

Figure 7-7

These little icons make it easy for people browsing a web site to do some free marketing for you — in case they like the content at that particular URL and want to bookmark it. To make adding these icons easy, you create a class that will work for any web application. We referenced the icons and list of social bookmarking sites from Sociable, a plugin for WordPress (it's the same plugin used for that purpose on the SEO Egghead blog); kudos to Peter Harkins for putting all those icons together.

You create the social bookmarking library in the following exercise, where you'll add those icons to your catalog page, `Catalog.aspx`.

Note that you wouldn't normally add social bookmarking items on e-commerce catalog pages — except perhaps if it's a very new and exciting product. We've chosen this example to keep the implementation simple for the purposes of the demonstration.

Adding Social Bookmarking Support

1. Create a folder named `social_icons` in your `seoasp` folder.

2. Download the code archive of this book, and copy the `Chapter07/seoasp/social_icons` folder from the archive to your `seoasp` folder.

3. Add a new class file to your `App_Code` folder, named `Social.cs`. In this file we're creating a `struct` named `Social`. An object of this struct represents a social bookmarking site. You'll learn the details after completing the code; for now, type this code in:

```
/// <summary>
/// Structure that represents a social bookmarking service
/// </summary>
public struct Social
{
  // private members
  private string name;
  private string imageFile;
  private string url;

  // properties
  public string Name
  {
    get { return name; }
  }

  public string ImageFile
  {
    get { return imageFile; }
  }

  public string Url
  {
    get { return url; }
    set { url = value; }
  }

  // constructor initializes struct members
  public Social(string name, string imageFile, string url)
  {
```

```
      this.name = name;
      this.imageFile = imageFile;
      this.url = url;
  }
}
```

4. Continue by creating another class file named `SocialCollection.cs`, in the same `App_Code` folder. This class represents a collection of `Social` objects, and implements the `IEnumerable` interface, which is necessary because we want to be able to feed objects of this class to data-bound controls such as `Repeater`, `DataList`, or `GridView`. In this class we make use of a new feature in C# 2.0 named *generics*. You'll learn the details a bit later; for now, type this code:

```csharp
using System;
using System.Collections;
using System.Collections.Generic;

/// <summary>
/// Represents a collection of Social objects
/// </summary>
public class SocialCollection : IEnumerable
{
  // we store the internal collection of Social objects as a dictionary
  private Dictionary<string, Social> socials;

  // initialize the dictionary in the constructor
  public SocialCollection()
  {
    socials = new Dictionary<string, Social>();
  }

  // indexer that allows retrieving elements by name
  public Social this[string name]
  {
    get
    {
      // all keys are lower-case
      name = name.ToLower();

      // return the Social object
      if (socials.ContainsKey(name))
        return socials[name];
      else
        throw new ArgumentException("There is no social site named " + name);
    }
  }

  // create a new Social object and Add(it to the collection
  public void Add(string name, string imageFile, string url)
  {
    // make sure the name is all lower-case
    name = name.ToLower();

    // Add(the Social object to the collection
```

```
        if (!socials.ContainsKey(name))
        {
          // create a new Social object
          Social social = new Social(name, imageFile, url);

          // add the new object to the collection
          socials.Add(name, social);
        }
        else
          throw new ArgumentException("The object already exists: " + name);
      }

      // Add(a Social object to the collection
      public void Add(Social social)
      {
        // Add(the Social object to the collection
        if (!socials.ContainsKey(social.Name.ToLower()))
          socials.Add(social.Name.ToLower(), social);
        else
          throw new ArgumentException("The object already exists: " + social.Name);
      }

      // infractructure code that implements IEnumerable
      IEnumerator IEnumerable.GetEnumerator()
      {
        return GetEnumerator();
      }

      public IEnumerator<Social> GetEnumerator()
      {
        foreach (Social item in socials.Values)
        {
          yield return item;
        }
      }
    }
  }
```

5.   If you don't have it already, create a folder named UserControls in your project. Then add a Web User Control to it, named `SocialIcons.ascx`, and type the following code in. (Yes, you guessed it: we're packaging the icons generator as a user control, so that we can reuse the functionality easily, in multiple pages.)

```
<%@ Control Language="C#" ClassName="SocialIcons" %>

<link href="seoasp.css" type="text/css" rel="stylesheet" />

<asp:Repeater runat="server" ID="socialIconsRepeater">
  <HeaderTemplate>
    <ul id="social">
  </HeaderTemplate>
  <ItemTemplate>
    <li>
      <a rel="nofollow" href="<%# Eval("Url") %>" title="<%# Eval("Name") %>">
```

```
          <img src="social_icons/<%# Eval("ImageFile") %>" alt="<%# Eval("Name") %>" />
        </a>
      </li>
    </ItemTemplate>
    <FooterTemplate>
      </ul>
    </FooterTemplate>
</asp:Repeater>

<script runat="server">
    // the list with social bookmarking services
    private readonly static SocialCollection allSocials;

    // the list with services we need to generate links for
    private string[] socialSiteNames;

    // link and title of the page we're bookmarking
    private string myPageLink, myPageTitle;

    // public properties
    public string MyPageLink
    {
      set { myPageLink = value; }
    }

    public string MyPageTitle
    {
      set { myPageTitle = value; }
    }

    public string SocialSiteNames
    {
      set
      {
        socialSiteNames = value.Split(new char[] { ',' },
          StringSplitOptions.RemoveEmptyEntries);
      }
    }

    protected void Page_Load(object sender, EventArgs e)
    {
      // continue only if the control has been properly initialized
      if (myPageLink == null || myPageTitle == null ||
          socialSiteNames == null || socialSiteNames.Length == 0)
      {
        throw new Exception("The SocialBookmarkIcons control requires you to provide values for
its properties: MyPageLink, MyPageTitle, and SocialSiteNames.");
      }

      // create the collection object
      SocialCollection socials = new SocialCollection();

      // built the collection of Social object
      foreach (string socialName in socialSiteNames)
```

```
        {
            Social newSocial = allSocials[socialName];
            newSocial.Url = newSocial.Url.Replace("{LINK}", HttpUtility.UrlEncode(myPageLink));
            newSocial.Url = newSocial.Url.Replace("{TITLE}", HttpUtility.UrlEncode(myPageTitle));
            socials.Add(newSocial);
        }

        // bind the social icons data to the repeater
        socialIconsRepeater.DataSource = socials;
        socialIconsRepeater.DataBind();
    }

    static SocialIcons()
    {
        // populate the collection of social bookmarking sites
        allSocials = new SocialCollection();
        allSocials.Add("BlinkBits", "blinkbits.png", "http://www.blinkbits.com/bookmarklets/
save.php?v=1&source_url={LINK}&title={TITLE}&body={TITLE}");
        allSocials.Add("BlinkList", "blinklist.png", "http://www.blinklist.com/
index.php?Action=Blink/addblink.php&Description=&Url={LINK}&Title={TITLE}");
        allSocials.Add("Blogmarks", "blogmarks.png", "http://blogmarks.net/
my/new.php?mini=1&simple=1&url={LINK}&title={TITLE}");
        allSocials.Add("co.mments", "co.mments.gif", "http://co.mments.com/
track?url={LINK}&title={TITLE}");
        allSocials.Add("connotea", "connotea.png", "http://www.connotea.org/
addpopup?continue=confirm&uri={LINK}&title={TITLE}");
        allSocials.Add("del.icio.us", "delicious.png", "http://del.icio.us/
post?url={LINK}&title={TITLE}");
        allSocials.Add("De.lirio.us", "delirious.png", "http://de.lirio.us/rubric/
post?uri={LINK}&title={TITLE};when_done=go_back");
        allSocials.Add("Digg", "digg.png", "http://digg.com/
submit?phase=2&url={LINK}&title={TITLE}");
        allSocials.Add("FeedMeLinks", "feedmelinks.png", "http://feedmelinks.com/
categorize?from=toolbar&op=submit&url={LINK}&name={TITLE}");
        allSocials.Add("Furl", "furl.png", "http://www.furl.net/storeIt.jsp?u={LINK}&t={TITLE}");
        allSocials.Add("LinkaGoGo", "linkagogo.png", "http://www.linkagogo.com/
go/AddNoPopup?url={LINK}&title={TITLE}");
        allSocials.Add("Ma.gnolia", "magnolia.png", "http://ma.gnolia.com/
beta/bookmarklet/add?url={LINK}&title={TITLE}&description={TITLE}");
        allSocials.Add("NewsVine", "newsvine.png", "http://www.newsvine.com/
_tools/seed&save?u={LINK}&h={TITLE}");
        allSocials.Add("Netvouz", "netvouz.png", "http://www.netvouz.com/action/
submitBookmark?url={LINK}&title={TITLE}&description={TITLE}");
        allSocials.Add("Reddit", "reddit.png", "http://reddit.com/
submit?url={LINK}&title={TITLE}");
        allSocials.Add("scuttle", "scuttle.png", "http://www.scuttle.org/
bookmarks.php/maxpower?action=add&address={LINK}&title={TITLE}&description={TITLE}");
        allSocials.Add("Shadows", "shadows.png", "http://www.shadows.com/
features/tcr.htm?url={LINK}&title={TITLE}");
        allSocials.Add("Simpy", "simpy.png", "http://www.simpy.com/
simpy/LinkAdd.do?href={LINK}&title={TITLE}");
        allSocials.Add("Smarking", "smarking.png", "http://smarking.com/
editbookmark/?url={LINK}&description={TITLE}");
        allSocials.Add("Spurl", "spurl.png", "http://www.spurl.net/
```

```
spurl.php?url={LINK}&title={TITLE}");
    allSocials.Add("TailRank", "tailrank.png", "http://tailrank.com/
share/?text=&link_href={LINK}&title={TITLE}");
    allSocials.Add("Wists", "wists.png", "http://wists.com/r.php?c=&r={LINK}&title={TITLE}");
    allSocials.Add("YahooMyWeb", "yahoomyweb.png", "http://myweb2.search.yahoo.com/
myresults/bookmarklet?u={LINK}&t={TITLE}");
    }
</script>
```

6. As a last little step, let's add a Style Sheet file to our project, to see how easy is to set up the looks of our social bookmarking icons. The file should be named `seoasp.css`, and it should contain these styles:

```css
#social
{
  padding-top: 5px;
  padding-bottom: 5px;
  border: 1px dashed;
  text-align: center;
}

#social li
{
  padding-left: 5px;
  padding-right: 5px;
  display: inline;
}

#social li a
{
  text-decoration: none;
}

#social li a img
{
  border: 0px;
}
```

7. Your social icons generator is complete now. The final steps consist in creating (or modifying) the `Catalog.aspx` Web Form, in the root of your project, to use the new control as shown in the following code snippet:

```
<%@ Page Language="C#" %>
<%@ Register Src="UserControls/SocialIcons.ascx" TagName="SocialIcons"
TagPrefix="uc1" %>
<!DOCTYPE html PUBLIC "-//W3C//DTD XHTML 1.0 Transitional//EN"
"http://www.w3.org/TR/xhtml1/DTD/xhtml1-transitional.dtd">

<html xmlns="http://www.w3.org/1999/xhtml">
<head runat="server">
  <title>Social Bookmarking Icons Exercise</title>
</head>
<body>
```

```
<form id="form1" runat="server">
  <h1>Products on Promotion at SEO Egghead Shop</h1>
  <p>... Content here ...</p>
  <uc1:SocialIcons ID="socialIcons" runat="server"
        MyPageLink="http://seoasp/Catalog.aspx"
        MyPageTitle="Exciting SEOEgghead Products"
        SocialSiteNames="del.icio.us,digg,furl,reddit,YahooMyWeb" />
</form>
</body>
</html>
```

8. Load `Catalog.aspx`, and you should get the result you see in Figure 7-8.

Figure 7-8

The newly created library knows how to generate links for many social networking web sites: blinkbits, blinklist, blogmarks, co.mments, connotea, del.icio.us, de.lirio.us, digg, feedmelinks, Furl, LinkaGoGo, Ma.gnolia, NewsVine, NetVouz, Reddit, scuttle, Shadows, Simply, Smarking, Spurl, TailRank, Wists, and YahooMyWeb. Wow, this is quite an impressive list, isn't it?

Whenever you add something interesting that other people may want to talk about, you want to facilitate them in doing so. The infrastructure that supports adding social bookmarking icons is formed of a C# struct (`Social`), a C# class (`SocialCollection`), and a Web User Control (`SocialIcons.ascx`):

❑ `Social` is a `struct` (not a `class`) that represents one social bookmarking site.

❑ `SocialCollection` is a class that represents a collection of `Social` objects. It has been designed so that it can be very easily used as a data source for data consumer controls such as `Repeater`, `DataList`, `GridView`, `DetailsView`, and so on.

❑ `SocialIcons` is a simple control that demonstrates how you can use a `Repeater` control to display social bookmarking icons in your site. The control also contains a list of the most common social bookmarking sites, and it can be easily reused in any of your web pages.

As you can see, reusing the functionality provided in this exercise simply implies copying `Social.cs`, `SocialCollection.cs` and `SocialIcons.ascx` in your project, and then using `SocialIcons.ascx` in your Web Forms. Because each of these elements has its own tips and tricks, we'll analyze them individually. We start with `Social`, which is the simplest one. `Social` is a `struct`:

```
/// <summary>
/// Structure that represents a social bookmarking service
/// </summary>
public struct Social
{
```

Structures and Classes

The C# `struct` is lesser-known feature of the language, and yet a very important and useful one. Because many programmers aren't familiar with the term, we'll quickly describe its features here, so you can follow the example.

Structs are very similar to classes: they can contain fields, properties, and methods. Even the syntax of constructing structs is identical to that of creating classes, except the keyword `struct` is used instead of `class`.

The fundamental difference between structs and classes is that structs are *value* types (whose instances are stored on the stack), whereas classes are *reference* types (whose values are stored on the heap). This means that when you create an object of a struct, you have access directly to the `struct`'s data. Objects of reference types, on the other hand, contain pointers to the place in memory where the object is stored. In practice, this affects the way you manipulate these objects. For example, with reference types, when you copy an object (using a simple command such as `a=b;`), the reference is copied, so both objects end up referencing the same object in memory. The content of the object itself isn't duplicated. When you copy a value type, the content is effectively duplicated, and you end up having the same information twice in memory.

Because of these differences, `structs` are particularly useful when you need to store structures of data (and hence the name), whereas classes are preferred for storing functionality.

The `Social` struct contains three properties that describe a social bookmarking site: `Name`, `ImageFile`, and `Url`. The constructor of the struct initializes the values of the private fields that store the properties' data. The properties themselves, except `Url`, are read-only (they only contain `get` accessors), because we don't need to change their values after creating the objects:

```
public struct Social
{
    // private members
    private string name;
    private string imageFile;
    private string url;

    // properties
    public string Name
    {
        get { return name; }
    }
```

```
    public string ImageFile
    {
      get { return imageFile; }
    }

    public string Url
    {
      get { return url; }
      set { url = value; }
    }

    // constructor initializes struct members
    public Social(string name, string imageFile, string url)
    {
      this.name = name;
      this.imageFile = imageFile;
      this.url = url;
    }
  }
```

We hope that you like this neat little structure. However, by itself it can't be so useful. Instead, we're interested in grouping more of these structures, so that in the end we can feed such a group of social web sites to a control that displays them, such as Repeater, DataList, GridView, Tree, and so on.

In order for a class to be readable by these controls, and others, it must implement the IEnumerable interface. So we ended up creating a class named SocialCollection that implements IEnumerable. You'll see that implementing this interface isn't as hard as it sounds:

```
using System;
using System.Collections;
using System.Collections.Generic;

/// <summary>
/// Represents a collection of Social objects
/// </summary>
public class SocialCollection : IEnumerable
{
```

Whenever you need to implement a collection-like class, you need to store the actual collection of objects inside your class. In our case, the SocialCollection class stores internally the list of Social objects as a Dictionary<string, Social> object. If this syntax looks alien to you, then you should know it's part of a new feature in .NET 2.0 named *generics*.

Generics allow us to create (or use) classes that use types that are unknown at development time. However, they are known at compilation time, so that the compiler still works with strongly typed objects, taking advantage of the implicit performance benefits. You can get a feeling of how generics work by analyzing the code of SocialCollection:

```
public class SocialCollection : IEnumerable
{
    // we store the internal collection of Social objects as a dictionary
    private Dictionary<string, Social> socials;
```

Generics are useful when you need to create a class that deals with objects of an unknown type. In our case, we're using the generic `Dictionary<TKey, TValue>` class, which implements a list whose keys are of the type `TKey`, and whose values are of the type `TValue`.

We made the decision to store our `Social` objects in such a structure because it includes the necessary functionality, including the possibility to retrieving the objects by name. For example, we're able to retrieve the `Social` object that contains the data for digg like this, from a `Dictionary<string, Social>` collection, like this:

```
Social digg = socials["digg"];
```

This is nice, isn't it? Using the `Dictionary<string, Social>` type makes it easy to implement this feature easily and efficiently. Other possibilities include using the `Hashtable` object, which also represents a key-value list. In case of `Hashtable`, both the key and the value are `Object` objects, so they can be any object you like. In our case, using `Dictionary<string, Social>` is more efficient because the structure is strongly typed using the data types we need for the keys and for the values.

The definition of `SocialCollection` continues with the class constructor, which simply initializes the `socials` object:

```
// initialize the dictionary in the constructor
public SocialCollection()
{
    socials = new Dictionary<string, Social>();
}
```

Then there comes the indexer. An indexer is a special member of the class that allows retrieving an object based on an index. In our case, where `SocialCollection` represents a collection of `Social` objects, we want the individual objects to be retrievable through an indexer, as highlighted in the following code snippet:

```
// create and populate a SocialCollection object
SocialCollection mySocial = new SocialCollection();
mySocial.Add("digg", ...);
...

// retrieve the Digg Social
Social digg = mySocial["digg"];
```

Because the private member in `SocialCollection` that stores the `Social` objects is a `Dictionary<string, Social>`, which has a built-in indexer, implementing our indexer is a fairly easy task. Note that we only implement the getter of the indexer, meaning that we're making it read-only (adding the setter would be easy, but we don't need it for our purposes). Our indexer implementation also transforms the received key to lowercase, to avoid little spelling mistakes, and it throws an exception if no object with the specified name exists. The significant parts of the indexer are highlighted:

```
// indexer that allows retrieving elements by name
public Social this[string name]
{
    get
```

```
    {
      // all keys are lower-case
      name = name.ToLower();

      // return the Social object
      if (socials.ContainsKey(name))
        return socials[name];
      else
        throw new ArgumentException("There is no social site named " + name);
    }
}
```

Next in `SocialCollection`, we have two `Add()` methods. As you know, having multiple methods using the same name is called *method overloading*, and it works as long as the methods have different parameter types and/or number. In our case, we want to be able to add new `Social` objects to the collection by either specifying the name, image file, and URL of a social bookmarking site, or by providing an already created `Social` object.

The first `Add()` method receives the three mentioned parameters, it creates a `Social` object using those parameters, and adds it to the collection. If an object with the same name exists, an exception is thrown:

```
    // create a new Social object and Add(it to the collection
    public void Add(string name, string imageFile, string url)
    {
      // make sure the name is all lower-case
      name = name.ToLower();

      // Add(the Social object to the collection
      if (!socials.ContainsKey(name))
      {
        // create a new Social object
        Social social = new Social(name, imageFile, url);

        // add the new object to the collection
        socials.Add(name, social);
      }
      else
        throw new ArgumentException("The object already exists: " + name);
    }
```

The second `Add()` method is similar, except it receives a `Social` object as parameter. The same logic is used to add the object to the collection.

```
    // Add(a Social object to the collection
    public void Add(Social social)
    {
      // Add(the Social object to the collection
      if (!socials.ContainsKey(social.Name.ToLower()))
        socials.Add(social.Name.ToLower(), social);
      else
        throw new ArgumentException("The object already exists: " + social.Name);
    }
```

> Note that the key we've used to access `Social` objects from the `Dictionary<string, Social>` collection is the lowercase version of the Social bookmarking site name. So if the `Name` of the site is `Digg`, the key by which its object can be retrieved is `digg`.

The final bit in `SocialCollection` has to do with implementing the `IEnumerable` interface that was mentioned earlier, which lets our class to be used as a data source for data-consuming controls, or as a parameter in `foreach()` statements. Because the underlying object that stores `Social` objects has an enumerator, we provide that rather than coding our own:

```
// infractructure code that implements IEnumerable
IEnumerator IEnumerable.GetEnumerator()
{
  return socials.Values.GetEnumerator();
}
}
```

> If it's not obvious already, what the `SocialCollection` class basically does is to expose the functionality provided by `Dictionary<string, Social>` in a customized way, which is easier to use. It would have also been possible to work directly with `Dictionary<string, Social>` objects, and feed their `Values` collection to data-consuming controls.

Now that `Social` and `SocialCollection` are in place, the final piece of the puzzle is the Web User Control, `SocialIcons.ascx`. This control contains a `Repeater` control, which it binds to a `SocialCollection` object that contains the `Social` elements we want to display. To understand what we're aiming at, take another look at the way we've used the `SocialIcons` control in `Catalog.aspx`:

```
<ucl:SocialIcons ID="socialIcons" runat="server"
        MyPageLink="http://seoasp/Catalog.aspx"
        MyPageTitle="Exciting SEOEgghead Products"
        SocialSiteNames="del.icio.us,digg,furl,reddit,YahooMyWeb" />
```

As you can see, our goal when creating the `SocialIcons` control was to make it as easy to use as possible, reducing the long-term coding effort. To use `SocialIcons` in your form, all you have to do is to provide values for its `MyPageLink`, `MyPageTitle`, and `SocialSiteNames` properties. The former two specify the link and title of the page the icons are being created in, and the latter property is a comma-delimited list of social bookmarking sites.

`SocialIcons.ascx` contains a `Repeater` control that generates the HTML output, and a bit of code that supports the underlying functionality. The control starts with the `<% Control` declaration line, which defines the language that is used for the server-side code, and the class name:

```
<%@ Control Language="C#" ClassName="SocialIcons" %>
```

> If you come from the ASP.NET 1.x world, you should be aware of the architecture changes in ASP.NET 2.0. In particular, Web Forms and Web User Controls are now represented by the same classes that are used for their server-side code scripts. When code-behind files are used, the class code is spread over two files: the `.aspx`, `.ascx`, or `.master` file, and their code-behind file. (Spreading a class over two or more files is possible in .NET 2.0 through a feature named *partial classes* — which explains the keyword partial you can see generated in the code-behind files.)
>
> This theory is important for understanding how the `SocialIcons.ascx` control works. All the controls in `SocialIcons.ascx`, including the `Repeater`, and the fields, properties, and methods written in the `<script>` tag, are all considered to be part of the `SocialIcons` class (whose name is defined by the `ClassName` attribute that you saw earlier), *even though you don't see an explicit class declaration* for the `SocialIcons` class.

Next, you can see a link reference to the `seoasp.css` stylesheet:

```
<link href="seoasp.css" type="text/css" rel="stylesheet" />
```

The `seoasp.css` file is used to beautify the output of the `Repeater` control. However, we don't go into CSS details in this book, so we won't comment on this file further.

Then we can find the `Repeater` control. As you may already know, the `Repeater` is the basic data control in ASP.NET. Basically, all it knows to do is to read a data source, and display its elements in the form specified by the `<ItemTemplate>` element. We also use `<HeaderTemplate>` and `<FooterTemplate>` to generate the header and the footer of the list of icons.

In the `<ItemTemplate>`, you can use `Eval` to extract the data values from the data source. In our case, the data source consists of a collection of `Social` objects, whose `Url`, `ImageFile`, and `Name` properties we read to generate the list of icons. Keep in mind that the contents of the `<ItemTemplate>` are repeated for each `Social` object in the collection.

```
<asp:Repeater runat="server" ID="socialIconsRepeater">
  <HeaderTemplate>
    <ul id="social">
  </HeaderTemplate>
  <ItemTemplate>
    <li>
      <a rel="nofollow" href="<%# Eval("Url") %>" title="<%# Eval("Name") %>">
        <img src="social_icons/<%# Eval("ImageFile") %>" alt="<%# Eval("Name") %>" />
      </a>
    </li>
  </ItemTemplate>
  <FooterTemplate>
    </ul>
  </FooterTemplate>
</asp:Repeater>
```

Just after the repeater, we wrote the server-side code that populates the repeater. The server-side code starts by creating a `SocialCollection` object named `allSocials`:

```
<script runat="server">
  // the list with social bookmarking services
  private readonly static SocialCollection allSocials;
```

This object will store the collection with all the known social bookmarking web sites. Note that there is no `class` definition here. As explained earlier, this code is considered to be part of a class named `SocialIcons`, as defined by the `ClassName` attribute of the control declaration.

Note that `allSocials` is a static object. We made `allSocials` static because we want to store the list with the social bookmarking objects in a global area of the application. This object is initialized only once, in the class static constructor, which only gets executed once in the application lifetime. (Note that there are multiple ways of sharing data in ASP.NET; this is just one technique we've found useful for this scenario.) Taking a look at the constructor of the `SocialIcons` class, you can see that it indeed populates the `allSocials` object with data about social bookmarking sites:

```
static SocialIcons()
{
  // populate the collection of social bookmarking sites
  allSocials = new SocialCollection();
  allSocials.Add("BlinkBits", "blinkbits.png",
"http://www.blinkbits.com/bookmarklets/save.php?v=1&source_url={LINK}&title={TITLE}
&body={TITLE}");
  ...
  ...
}
```

The syntax used to declare the static constructor — and the fact that you don't get a compilation error when using it — confirms that the class you're working on is called `SocialIcons`, even though there is no explicit declaration for it using the typical `class` keyword.

With this theory out of the way, there are only a few elements left to discuss about `SocialIcons.ascx`. Most of the remaining code is the support code for its `MyPageLink`, `MyPageTitle`, and `SocialSiteNames` properties. These are properties backed up by private elements. The only special case is that of `SocialSiteNames`, which is a comma-delimited string containing the site names. In our example, we have set this property to `"del.icio.us,digg,furl,reddit,YahooMyWeb"`. However, as you can see in `SocialIcons.ascx`, the list of names is actually stored internally as a string array:

```
// the list with services we need to generate links for
private string[] socialSiteNames;

// link and title of the page we're bookmarking
private string myPageLink, myPageTitle;

// public properties
public string MyPageLink
{
  set { myPageLink = value; }
}

public string MyPageTitle
```

```
{
  set { myPageTitle = value; }
}


public string SocialSiteNames
{
  set
  {
    socialSiteNames = value.Split(new char[] { ',' },
      StringSplitOptions.RemoveEmptyEntries);
  }
}
```

The core of `SocialIcons.ascx` lies in its `Page_Load()` method, which is executed after the properties that were just discussed had the chance to be set. `Page_Load()` has the role of feeding the `Repeater` control with the data it needs. The method starts by verifying that the necessary properties have been properly set; in case any of them didn't an exception is thrown:

```
protected void Page_Load(object sender, EventArgs e)
{
  // continue only if the control has been properly initialized
  if (myPageLink == null || myPageTitle == null ||
    socialSiteNames == null || socialSiteNames.Length == 0)
  {
    throw new Exception("The SocialBookmarkIcons control requires you to provide
values for its properties: MyPageLink, MyPageTitle, and SocialSiteNames.");
  }
```

Then a new collection of `Social` objects is created. The new collection is created by parsing the list of social web sites that were mentioned through the `SocialSiteNames` property. For each of them, the URL is parsed, and the `{LINK}` and `{TITLE}` placeholders are replaced with the site link and title that were provided using the `MySiteLink` and `MySiteTitle` properties:

```
// create the collection object
SocialCollection socials = new SocialCollection();

// built the collection of Social object
foreach (string socialName in socialSiteNames)
{
  Social newSocial = allSocials[socialName];
  newSocial.Url = newSocial.Url.Replace("{LINK}",
HttpUtility.UrlEncode(myPageLink));
  newSocial.Url = newSocial.Url.Replace("{TITLE}",
HttpUtility.UrlEncode(myPageTitle));
  socials.Add(newSocial);
}
```

After the new `SocialElements` object is created, it's bound to the `Repeater` control, which displays its data for the visitor:

```
// bind the social icons data to the repeater
socialIconsRepeater.DataSource = socials;
socialIconsRepeater.DataBind();
```

Summary

Feeds provide a streamlined method for users to access content, as well as allow other sites to syndicate content. Links that are embedded in the feeds will both provide traffic directly as well as indirectly over time. Users will click the embedded links in the syndicated content. And search engines will see a gradually increasing number of links. This chapter demonstrated a class to easily create an RSS 2.0 feed, as well as a third-party class to read them.

Social bookmarking services offer another sort of organic traffic that should also not be ignored. Streamlining the process of bookmarking on your web site will likely increase the number of bookmarks your site receives, and hence its ranking in the social bookmarking site search function — and perhaps even earn a place on its home page.

8

Black Hat SEO

It may sound quite obvious, but system administrators — those who manage the computers that host your web site, for example, must be acutely aware of computer security concerns. When a particular piece of software is indicated to be vulnerable to hackers, they should find out quickly because it is their priority to do so. Then they should patch or mitigate the security risk on the servers for which they are responsible as soon as possible. Consequently, it may also not surprise you that some of the best system administrators used to be hackers, or are at least very aware of what hacking entails.

Why is this relevant? Although it is *totally unfair* to compare "black hat" search engine marketers to hackers on an ethical plane, the analogy is useful. The "white hat" search engine marketer — that is, a search engine marketer who follows all the rules, must be aware of how a "black hat" operates.

Understanding black hat techniques can help a webmaster protect his or her web sites. Nobody, after all, wants to be caught with his pants down advertising "cheap Viagra." This chapter shows you how to avoid such problems. In this chapter you:

- ❑ Learn about black hat SEO.
- ❑ Learn about the importance of properly escaping input data.
- ❑ Learn how to automatically add the `nofollow` attribute to comment links.
- ❑ Sanitize input data by removing unwanted tags and attributes.
- ❑ Request human input to protect against scripts adding comments automatically.
- ❑ Protect against redirect attacks.

There is quite a bit to go through, so we'd better get started!

What's with All the Hats?

The "hat" terminology, as just alluded to, has been borrowed from the lexicon of hackers. "White hat" search engine marketers play by the rules, following every rule in a search engine's terms of service to the letter. They will never exploit the work of others. "Black hats," on the other hand, to varying degrees, do not follow the rules of a search engine, and may also exploit the work or property of others. In practice, few search engine marketers fit exactly in either "hat" classification. Rather, it is a spectrum, giving rise to a further confusing "gray hat" classification for people on neither side of the fence.

> The black hat versus white hat hacker terminology derives, in turn, from the practice in early western movies of dressing the bad cowboys in black hats, and the good cowboys in white hats. Hollywood has since matured and no longer uses such simplistic symbolism, but its embarrassing memory lives on in the search engine marketing community.

Dan Thies sums it up well in *The Search Engine Marketing Kit*. He states that it *"… boils down to whether you, as an SEO consultant, see yourself as a lawyer or an accountant."*

A lawyer, according to Mr. Thies, must put a client's interests first. Lawyers do the best they can for a client, and view the search engine as an adversary. A "black hat" search engine marketer is a lawyer. He or she will do anything within reason to conquer the adversary — the search engines. The definition of "within reason" varies by the individual's ethical compass. Some of the various methods employed by the "black hat" are discussed in this chapter.

An accountant, on the other hand, has a strict set of rules that are followed by rote. His rules are somewhat arbitrarily defined by a governmental agency. A search engine typically also publishes such rules. And a "white hat" search engine marketer follows them just as an accountant does. He or she is dogmatic about it. A site that does not rank well is assumed to be inadequate. And to fix it, only solutions recommended by a search engine's terms of service are employed.

The distinctions aren't as black and white as the terminology seems to indicate. However, at least being aware of the "black hat" agenda and techniques is helpful to any search engine marketer, regardless of "hat color" for many reasons. Despite the fact that this book primarily addresses the "accountants," there may be times when bending the rules is necessary due to technical or time constraints (though it usually entails risk). At the same time, it is wise to know and understand your opponents' search marketing strategies so they can be analyzed.

> Please be aware that this chapter is by no means a comprehensive manual on "black hat" techniques. We have taken the approach of highlighting those areas that contain pertinent information for a web developer. A printed reference on the topic would become stale rather quickly anyway because the methods change rapidly as the search engines and the cowboys in black hats duke it out on a perpetual basis. And though it is possible to read this chapter cynically, it aims mostly to educate the web developer with what he needs to do to beat the black hat cowboy in a duel. Some resources on "black hat" SEO are SEO Black Hat (`http://www.seoblackhat.com`), and David Naylor's blog (`http://www.davidnaylor.co.uk/`).

Lastly, because many black hat practices exploit other sites' security vulnerabilities, it is useful to know some common vectors, because they typically improve the rankings of another (spam) web site at the potential expense of *your* web site's rankings. For that reason alone, a basic understanding of black hat techniques is important to any search engine marketer.

Bending the Rules

A typical situation when "bending the rules" may be useful is when a site already exists and presents a flaw that cannot be overcome without a complete redesign. Usually a complete redesign, in the context of a functioning web site, is a complex and arduous undertaking. At best, it cannot be done within the time limits prescribed. At worst, it is completely impossible either due to budget or internal politics.

Perhaps the site is designed entirely in Flash (see Chapter 6), or it employs a URL-based session-handler that could throw a spider into a spider-trap of circular, or infinite references. If a total application rewrite is not an option — as is usually the case — *cloaking* may be employed. Cloaking implies delivering different content depending on whether the user agent is a human or a search engine spider. In the former case, an HTML-based version of the site could be presented to the search engine spiders instead of the Flash version. In the latter case, when the user agent is a spider, the site could use cloaking to remove the session ID and other potentially confusing parameters from the URL, hence removing the spider-trap.

A well-known example of cloaking is that employed by the *New York Times*. Essentially, the *New York Times* web site requests users to create (and pay for) an account with them for certain premium content — as shown in Figure 8-1.

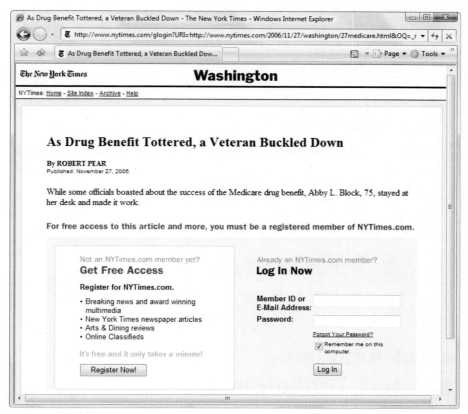

Figure 8-1

However, this restriction isn't imposed on search engines. Indeed, the *New York Times* allows search engines to browse and index its content without an account, which most probably gets `http://www .nytimes.com/` a lot of incoming traffic from search engines. A full write-up is available at `http:// searchenginewatch.com/showPage.html?page=3613561`.

A simple Google `site:` query shows that Google has indexed 7.5 million pages from `nytimes.com` — see Figure 8-2. In this SERP, it's interesting to note that the results don't have the "view cache" link. This is because `nytimes.com` is using a meta `noarchive` tag that prevents search engines from caching the content (and clever users from circumventing the need for subscriptions by using the said cache). Upon close inspection, one discovers that the search engines are indexing the content of many pages from `nytimes.com` to present relevant results in the SERPs, but the content is not actually available to *you*.

This example does highlight quite well the concept that employing techniques that a search engine considers "black hat" can be used for normatively acceptable purposes. It also highlights that Google is willing to bend its rules for certain high-profile web sites.

Google's published policies are *not* ambiguous on the cloaking front — cloaking is considered "black hat" and subject to site penalization. Examples like this one cloud the issue, however. Yahoo! and MSN are less strict and allow cloaking so long as it is not misleading for the user. Cloaking, and the technical and ethical issues it entails, are further explained in Chapter 11.

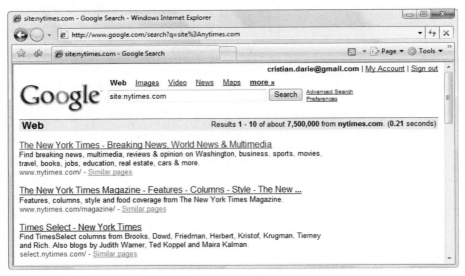

Figure 8-2

Technical Analysis of Black-Hat Techniques

When you view the SERPs for keywords that you would like to acquire, it is often useful to compare your site to the competitions'. If one of your competitors employs a black hat technique, the technique is worthwhile to understand just for that reason alone. Perhaps your competitor has several thousand spam sites pointing at his site, or perhaps his web site is sending optimized content to the search engines via cloaking methods. Some search engine marketers believe in reporting such sites to search engines, whereas some would just like to be aware. That decision is yours.

This chapter details several black hat techniques that are pertinent to every site developer.

Attack Avoidance

Search engine marketers must be aware of several things in black hat SEO from a security perspective. Some black hat search engine marketers exploit faulty or lax software to place links from your site to theirs in order to increase their rankings. This can be either through a bulletin board post, a blog comment, or a generally faulty script. Frequently, black hat techniques employ automated software to seek and exploit such weaknesses.

A black hat marketer may also use some sort of signature in a web application to find many sites using a search engine, such as a version number or tagline. Therefore, it is imperative that any web developer understands this, because being exploited may be to your detriment in rankings, not to mention corporate image. It's clear that nobody wants hundreds of links to spam sites in their forums or comments.

Security notwithstanding, the first step to protect your web site is to keep software that is not under your auspices, that is, third-party software, up to date. For example, not too long ago, many blogging applications did not apply the `rel="nofollow"` attribute to links in comments — because it had not been adopted yet! This weakness had been exploited extensively in the past by black hat SEOs.

One more recent exploit was the HTML insertion flaw in Movable Type, a very popular blogging application, and the problem has been documented at `http://seoblackhat.com/2006/06/10/moveable-type-backlink-exploit/`.

Such problems can be avoided by manually patching the software for vulnerabilities, but updating your software frequently would certainly help, because they are usually corrected on your behalf eventually anyway.

Insertion Attacks

A programmer must escape *all* data processed by his or her web application's code. Escaping means altering the text and other data received from a non-trusted source, such as a comment added by a visitor on your web site, so that it doesn't cause any unwanted side effects when that data is further processed by your application.

Input data validation and escaping is a common security issue. Most experienced web developers know that they must escape or sanitize data sent to a SQL database. Otherwise, carefully constructed input can form a malicious query that exposes and/or vandalizes data. Despite this, many programmers forget to escape SQL input.

Because SQL data escaping isn't directly related to SEO, we will only dwell on it to the extent of its relation to black hat SEO. To illustrate the potential problems of neglecting SQL input data, let's take a hypothetical example. Consider the following C# code that builds a SQL query that searches a table named Products, for products whose name contain a string entered by the visitor:

```
string sql = "SELECT Name, Description FROM Products " +
             "WHERE Name LIKE '%" + query + "%'";
```

Now, if the visitor enters a decent string to search for, such as "seo," the query would behave as expected. On the other hand, what if the query entered by the visitor looks like this:

```
xxxx'; DELETE FROM Products;
```

This would probably do something we don't want. You can find an excellent article on preventing SQL insertion attacks at http://msdn2.microsoft.com/en-us/library/ms998271.aspx. Admittedly, database security is a complex subject that is not to be taken lightly. However, in the next section, you will see how it is closely related to another subject — HTML insertion attacks. Additional reading on the subject can include *SQL Server Security* (McGraw-Hill Osborne Media, 2003), or *SQL Server Security Distilled* (Curlingstone, 2002).

HTML Insertion Attacks

So, although most people are familiar with the concept of "insertion attacks" in the context of SQL, not as many have given much thought to HTML insertion attacks. These are of particular importance in the world of SEO, because they can be (and sometimes are) used by black hat search engine marketers to influence the search engine rankings. You must escape your user-generated HTML, otherwise people can use carefully crafted parameters to make your site advocate and link to terribly unethical web sites. You probably want to make sure you don't advocate any of the above without actually knowing it.

> We cannot stress enough that this is a major problem that is largely ignored. You must fix your vulnerable sites, or someone else will eventually *make* you fix it.

Let's take an example of code before and after the proper escaping practice. First, here's the version that doesn't use a proper escaping technique:

```
// No parameter escaping
string param = Request.QueryString["parameter"];
Response.Write("Your parameter is: " + param);
```

Fortunately, as you'll see, ASP.NET verifies by default if the input data is potentially dangerous, and it throws an error in that case. However, this default validation can be deactivated. Nevertheless, the data should always be correctly escaped, as shown in the following code snippet:

```
// Proper parameter escaping
string param = Request.QueryString["parameter"];
param = HttpUtility.HtmlEncode(param);
Response.Write("Your parameter is: " + param);
```

Microsoft has done a good job documenting potential hacking techniques, and presenting ways to counter them. We've found the article "How To: Prevent Cross-Site Scripting in ASP.NET" particularly helpful. You can read it at `http://msdn2.microsoft.com/en-us/library/ms998274.aspx`.

For web sites with very high security requirements, Microsoft also developed an *Anti-Cross Site Scripting Library*, which works by defining a strict set of allowable characters, and filtering or encoding anything outside this set. You can download this library from `http://msdn2.microsoft.com/en-us/security/aa973814.aspx`.

The following short exercise illustrates the basic escaping technique that should be used when displaying on a web page any data that is not under your control — such as user comments.

Escaping Input Data

1. In your `seoasp` project, create a script named `NoEscaping.aspx` and replace the default code of the template with this:

```
<script runat="server" language="C#">
  protected void Page_Load(object sender, EventArgs e)
  {
    // No parameter escaping
    string param = Request.QueryString["parameter"];
    Response.Write("Your parameter is: " + param);
  }
</script>
```

2. As you can see, the script simply reads the value of `parameter` from the query string and displays it. Let's see how it works. Load `http://seoasp/NoEscaping.aspx?parameter=Hello%20World!`. You should get the result described in Figure 8-3.

3. Let's test our script now by supplying a hyperlink as the parameter. This way we simulate a simple technique a potential hacker or spammer could use to generate pages of our site, with links to his or her spam page. Load `http://seoasp/NoEscaping.aspx?parameter=<a href=http://too.much.spam>spam spam spam</a>`. Surprise, surprise! As you can see in Figure 8-4, ASP.NET validates by default the input data, and blocks such attempts by throwing an exception.

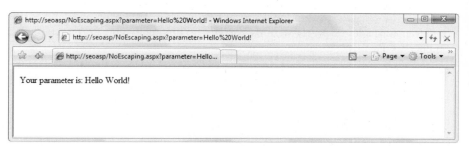

Figure 8-3

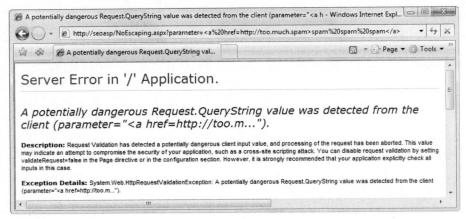

Figure 8-4

4. Everything looks great so far. But what if we actually don't like the automatic request validation feature in ASP.NET? Indeed, there are times when we need to accept legitimate requests that look like hacking attempts, but in fact they are not. In such circumstances, all we have to do is set the `ValidateRequest` property of the page to `false`. To test this feature, create a new script named `NoEscapingNoFiltering.aspx` with this code:

```
<%@ Page Language="C#" ValidateRequest="false" %>

<script runat="server" language="C#">
  protected void Page_Load(object sender, EventArgs e)
  {
    // Don't try this at home
    string param = Request.QueryString["parameter"];
    Response.Write("Your parameter is: " + param);
  }
</script>
```

5. Let's perform the previous test with `NoEscapingNoFiltering.aspx` this time. Load `http://seoasp/NoEscapingNoFiltering.aspx?parameter=<a href=http://too.much.spam> spam spam spam</a>`. Your innocent, and now vulnerable script, nicely takes the parameter and transforms it into an HTML link. You end up linking to `http://too.much.spam`, as shown in Figure 8-5.

Figure 8-5

6. To guard against this kind of attack, you need to properly escape any input data for HTML output. Fortunately, ASP.NET makes this very easy, through the `HttpUtility.HtmlEncode()` method. Create a new script named `Escaping.aspx` with this code:

```
<%@ Page Language="C#" ValidateRequest="false" %>

<script runat="server" language="C#">
  protected void Page_Load(object sender, EventArgs e)
  {
    // Proper parameter escaping
    string param = Request.QueryString["parameter"];
    param = HttpUtility.HtmlEncode(param);

    // Display escaped parameter value
    Response.Write("Your parameter is: " + param);
  }
</script>
```

7. Now provide the same parameter to your new script, `Escaping.aspx`. The link would be `http://seoasp/Escaping.aspx?parameter=<a href=http://too.much.spam>spam spam spam</a>`, and the result is shown in Figure 8-6.

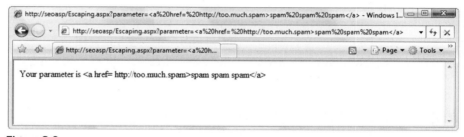

Figure 8-6

The escaping makes a difference, doesn't it! If you look at the source code from this latter page, you'll see that the characters with special significance in HTML pages, such as < and >, have been properly encoded:

```
Your parameter is: &lt;a href=http://too.much.spam&gt;spam spam spam&lt;/a&gt;
```

Of course, you don't want anyone to post anything like that on your web site regardless of whether you escape your input data. However, you're much better off when escaping your data for three main reasons:

❑ Carefully escaped data is much less likely to cause damage when further processed by your scripts in general. Doing so has security implications as well — preventing cross-site scripting attacks.

❑ You aren't providing free links to spammers.

❑ Spammers are less motivated to spend time on your site.

ASP.NET makes it easy to carefully escape your data with its `HttpUtility` class. This class includes several static methods that you need to know about, as listed in Table 8-1.

Table 8-1

ttpUtility Method	Description
HtmlAttributeEncode	HTML-encodes an attribute value.
HtmlDecode	Decodes an HTML-encoded string.
HtmlEncode	Encodes a string for inclusion in an HTML page.
ParseQueryString	Parses a query string into a `NameValueCollection` object.
UrlDecode	Decodes a string that was encoded using `UrlEncode`.
UrlEncode	Encodes a value to be included in the URL. It's particularly useful to encode query string values that contain special characters, such as =, &, spaces, and so on. For example, `UrlEncode("name=Barnes&Noble")` returns `Barnes%26Noble`.
UrlPathEncode	Encodes the path portion of a URL.

You can find an extremely useful table describing the differences between the encoding methods at `http://engineering.meta-comm.com/blogs/misha/content/binary/results.html`.

Avoiding Comment Attacks Using Nofollow

Many black hat spammers will use the comment section of a blog or guestbook, or forums, to post spam messages and links that promote their web sites.

Adding the `rel="nofollow"` attribute to a link will inform the search engine that that particular link is not audited by your site, and should therefore not count as a trusted vote for the popularity of the linked site. And though this doesn't strictly prevent spam, it does remove a lot of the motivation that results in a spammer targeting your site. The link will still work, but it will no longer be as desirable to a spammer because it offers a diminished link equity value.

> In reality, `nofollow` *has far from eliminated comment and guestbook spamming. Unfortunately, it does not eliminate the need for manual auditing and spam filtering. It is just a deterrent.*

You can use the same technique when including links to sites that you don't want to "vote." Here's an example:

```
<a rel="nofollow" href="http://too.much.spam">Bad site!</a>
```

It is also important to realize that too many links without `rel="nofollow"` may hurt your rankings if they are linking to "bad neighborhoods" as well as damage your reputation and credibility. All major search engines currently support the `nofollow` feature.

Automated scripts may still target your site, only because, frequently, the spamming is done in bulk, and the spammer has not investigated your site specifically. In practice, however, using nofollow *is likely to cut down on spam. Either way, if* nofollow *is employed, the damage is mitigated as it can only damage visitor perception, not search engine rankings, because the links will not be seen as votes to a bad neighborhood by a search engine. Collectively, because most web sites will begin using this feature, it will yield inferior results, and spammers will use such techniques less frequently.*

In the exercise that follows you create a simple class, named NoFollow, which employs a series of regular expressions that alter all links in a text buffer by adding the rel="nofollow" attribute, but only to links that are not in a predefined "white list."

Creating and Using a Nofollow Library

1. If you haven't already done so by following the previous chapters, create the App_Code folder to your seoasp application. You can have Visual Web Developer create it for you by right-clicking the root node of the project in Solution Explorer and selecting Add ASP.NET Folder ⇨ App_Code. Then add a new class file to this folder, named NoFollow.cs, and add this code to it:

```
using System;
using System.Text.RegularExpressions;

/// <summary>
/// NoFollow contains the functionality to add rel=nofollow to unstusted links
/// </summary>
public static class NoFollow
{
  // the white list of domains (in lower case)
  private static string[] whitelist =
     { "seoasp", "www.seoegghead.com", "www.cristiandarie.ro" };

  // finds all the links in the input string and processes them using fixLink
  public static string FixLinks(string input)
  {
    // define the match evaluator
    MatchEvaluator fixThisLink = new MatchEvaluator(NoFollow.fixLink);

    // fix the links in the input string
    string fixedInput = Regex.Replace(input,
                                      "(<a.*?>)",
                                      fixThisLink,
                                      RegexOptions.IgnoreCase);

    // return the "fixed" input string
    return fixedInput;
  }

  // receives a Regex match that contains a link such as
  // <a href="http://too.much.spam/"> and adds ref=nofollow if needed
  private static string fixLink(Match linkMatch)
  {
    // retrieve the link from the received Match
    string singleLink = linkMatch.Value;

    // if the link already has rel=nofollow, return it back as it is
```

```
      if (Regex.IsMatch(singleLink,
                     @"rel\s*?=\s*?['""]?.*?nofollow.*?['""]?",
                     RegexOptions.IgnoreCase))
  {
    return singleLink;
  }

    // use a named group to extract the URL from the link
    Match m = Regex.Match(singleLink,
                     @"href\s*?=\s*?['""]?(?<url>[^'""]*)['""]?",
                     RegexOptions.IgnoreCase);
    string url = m.Groups["url"].Value;

    // if URL doesn't contain http://, assume it's a local link
    if (!url.Contains("http://"))
  {
    return singleLink;
  }

    // extract the host name (such as www.cristiandarie.ro) from the URL
    Uri uri = new Uri(url);
    string host = uri.Host.ToLower();

    // if the host is in the whitelist, don't alter it
    if (Array.IndexOf(whitelist, host) >= 0)
  {
    return singleLink;
  }

    // if the URL already has a rel attribute, change its value to nofollow
    string newLink = Regex.Replace(singleLink,
           @"(?<a>rel\s*=\s*(?<b>['""]?))((?<c>[^'""\s]*|[^'""]*))(?<d>['""]?)?",
           "${a}nofollow${d}",
           RegexOptions.IgnoreCase);

    // if the string had a rel attribute that we changed, return the new link
    if (newLink != singleLink)
  {
    return newLink;
  }

    // if we reached this point, we need to add rel=nofollow to our link
    newLink = Regex.Replace(singleLink, "<a", @"<a rel=""nofollow""",
                         RegexOptions.IgnoreCase);
    return newLink;
  }
}
```

2. Create a Web Form in your project named `Comments.aspx`, with this code:

```
<%@ Page Language="C#" %>
<!DOCTYPE html PUBLIC "-//W3C//DTD XHTML 1.0 Transitional//EN"
```

```
"http://www.w3.org/TR/xhtml1/DTD/xhtml1-transitional.dtd">
<html xmlns="http://www.w3.org/1999/xhtml">
<head runat="server">
  <title>Professional Search Engine Optimization with ASP.NET</title>
</head>
<body>
  <h1>Adding rel=nofollow</h1>
  <%
  string s1 = @"<p>Hello! Take a look at <a href=""http://too.much.spam"">cool ↵
link</a>!</p>";
  string s2 = @"<p>This is link from a <a href=""http://seoasp/Default.aspx""> ↵
whitelisted domain</a>.</p>";

  Response.Write(NoFollow.FixLinks(s1));
  Response.Write(NoFollow.FixLinks(s2));
  %>
</body>
</html>
```

3. Load `http://seoasp/Comments.aspx`, and expect to get the result shown in Figure 8-7.

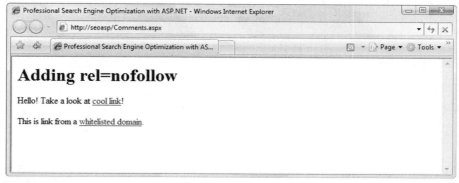

Figure 8-7

4. Excellent, the links show up correctly on the web page. To verify this worked as expected, view the HTML source. If you're using Internet Explorer, right-click the page and choose View Source. The HTML source should reveal you have generated `nofollow` just for the first link — see Figure 8-8.

Note that we've formatted the HTML code in Figure 8-8 manually in the file for better clarity. Web browsers read the HTML code in the same way regardless of how it's formatted.

The script gracefully handles modifying the `rel` attribute if it already exists. Your white list should include the host of the current site, or other sites that you're happy to link to. This allows fully qualified internal links to work as they should. It also does not touch any link that does not start with `http://` because those links, by definition, are from the current site.

223

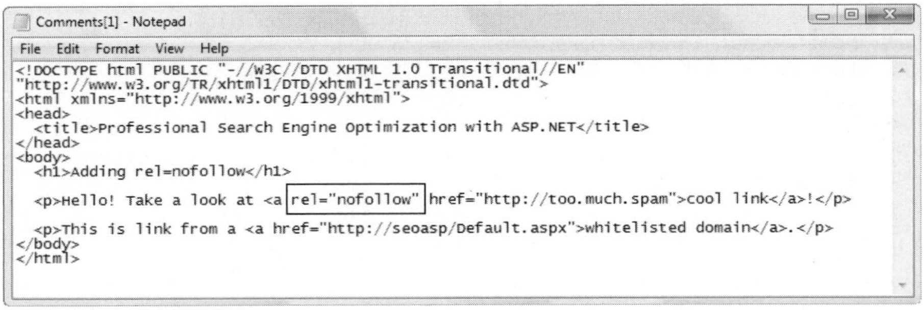

Figure 8-8

Using the `NoFollow` class is very simple. Instead of displaying content that may contain a link as-is, you should filter it through the `NoFollow.FixLinks()` method, as you did in `Comments.aspx`:

```
<%
string s1 = @"<p>Hello! Take a look at <a href=""http://too.much.spam"">cool ↵
link</a>!</p>";
string s2 = @"<p>This is link from a <a href=""http://seoasp/Default.aspx""> ↵
whitelisted domain</a>.</p>";

Response.Write(NoFollow.FixLinks(s1));
Response.Write(NoFollow.FixLinks(s2));
%>
```

For this to work properly, you need to define the "white list," which is the list of allowed hosts. For the purposes of this exercise we've defined it as an array inside the `NoFollow` class:

```
public static class NoFollow
{
    // the white list of domains (in lower case)
    private static string[] whitelist =
        { "seoasp", "www.seoegghead.com", "www.cristiandarie.ro" };
```

Here the list of white-listed domains contains only the local domain, www.seoegghead.com, and www.cristiandarie.ro. To avoid extra processing, we've assumed the hosts are all written in lowercase in this list.

The logic of the code in the `NoFollow` class is pretty clear, until you get into the details of the regular expressions involved, which are more complex than those from the previous chapters. For example, this is the first time where we've used the `MatchEvaluator` class. This class is used when you need to use `Regex.Replace` to perform a regular expressions–based replacement, but when for each match you need to implement more complex logic to calculate the text it should be replaced with. `MatchEvaluator` lets you define a method that is called for each match, and the return value of that method is used for the match replacement.

If this sounds a bit complicated, let's see how it works in practice. The highlighted line in the following code snippet defines a match evaluator using the `NoFollow.fixLink` method:

```
// finds all the links in the input string and processes them using fixLink
public static string FixLinks(string input)
```

```
{
    // define the match evaluator
    MatchEvaluator fixThisLink = new MatchEvaluator(NoFollow.fixLink);
```

Then we use `Regex.Replace` to find all the `<a href>` links in the input string, and replace them with their "fixed value." Because calculating the replacement for each link involves more complex logic, we use the match evaluator:

```
    // fix the links in the input string
    string fixedInput = Regex.Replace(input,
                            "(<a.*?>)",
                            fixThisLink,
                            RegexOptions.IgnoreCase);

    // return the "fixed" input string
    return fixedInput;
}
```

What this piece of code basically does is to find all the matches in the input string for the `(<a.*?>)` expression, and send each of those matches to the `fixThisLink` evaluator to get the replacement value.

The `fixThisLink` evaluator calls the `NoFollow.fixLink` method, providing the match as a parameter, as a `Match` object. If we now look at the definition of `fixLink`, we can see that it indeed takes a `Match` object as a parameter:

```
    // receives a Regex match that contains a link such as
    // <a href="http://too.much.spam/"> and adds ref=nofollow if needed
    private static string fixLink(Match linkMatch)
    {
        // retrieve the link from the received Match
        string singleLink = linkMatch.Value;
```

We leave understanding the remaining code in `fixLink()` to you as an exercise. It basically follows a relatively simple logical sequence to decide whether it should add `rel="nofollow"` to the link received as a parameter.

If you haven't already, you should read Chapter 3 for a practical introduction to regular expressions. Appendix A is an even more friendly and thorough introduction to regular expressions.

Sanitizing User Input

A similar problem exists with regard to any user-provided content, such as blog comments, guest books, and forum posts. In that case as well, you must take care to remove any potentially malicious content. There are two approaches to achieving this.

You can entirely disable HTML by escaping it as you did in the exercise with `HtmlEncode()`. Here's an example:

```
Response.Write(HttpUtility.HtmlEncode(any_user_data));
```

instead of

```
Response.Write(any_user_data);
```

Sometimes, however, it is desirable to permit a limited dialect of HTML tags. To that end it is necessary to sanitize the input by removing only potentially malicious tags and attributes (or, because achieving security is easier as such — allow only tags and attributes that *cannot* be used maliciously).

Some applications take the approach of using a proprietary markup language instead of HTML. A similar topic was discussed in Chapter 6 in the section "Using a Custom Markup Language to Generate SE-Friendly HTML," but to a different end — enhancing on-page HTML optimization. It can also be used to ensure that content is sanitized. In this case, you would execute `HttpUtility.HtmlEncode()` *to encode the HTML tags, and use a translation function and a limited set of proprietary tags such as* {link} *and* {/link}, {image} *and* {/image}, *to permit only certain functionality. This is the approach of many forum web applications such as vBulletin and phpBB. And indeed for specific applications where users are constantly engaged in dialog and willing to learn the proprietary markup language, this makes sense. However, for such things as a comment or guest book, HTML provides a common denominator that most users know, and allowing a restrictive dialect is probably more prudent with regard to usability. That is the solution discussed here.*

As usual, in order to keep your code tidy, group the HTML sanitizing functionality into a separate file. Go through the following quick exercise, where you create and use this new little library. The code is discussed afterwards.

Sanitizing User Input

1. Create a new class file named `Sanitize.cs` in your `App_Code` folder, and write this code:

```
using System;
using System.Text.RegularExpressions;

/// <summary>
/// Sanitize contains functionality to remove unaccepted tags or attributes
/// </summary>
public static class Sanitize
{
  // list of accepted/harmless tags (in lower case)
  private static string[] allowedTags =
    { "p", "h1", "b", "i", "a", "ul", "li", "pre", "hr", "blockquote", "img" };

  // list of attributes that need to be sanitized
  private static string badAttributes =
    "onerror|onmousemove|onmouseout|onmouseover|" +
    "onkeypress|onkeydown|onkeyup|javascript:";

  // sanitizes the HTML code in $inputHTML
  public static string FixTags(string inputHtml)
  {
    // define the match evaluator
    MatchEvaluator fixThisLink = new MatchEvaluator(Sanitize.fixTag);

    // process each tags in the input string
    string fixedHtml = Regex.Replace(inputHtml,
                                "(<.*?>)",
                                fixThisLink,
                                RegexOptions.IgnoreCase);
```

```
      // return the "fixed" input string
      return fixedHtml;
    }

    // remove tag if is not in the list of allowed tags
    private static string fixTag(Match tagMatch)
    {
      string tag = tagMatch.Value;

      // extrag the tag name, such as "a" or "h1"
      Match m = Regex.Match(tag,
                            @"</?(?<tagName>[^\s/]*)[>\s/]",
                            RegexOptions.IgnoreCase);
      string tagName = m.Groups["tagName"].Value.ToLower();

      // if the tag isn't in the list of allowed tags, it should be removed
      if (Array.IndexOf(allowedTags, tagName) < 0)
      {
        return "";
      }

      // remove bad attributes from the tag
      string fixedTag = Regex.Replace(tag,
                        "(" + Sanitize.badAttributes + @")(\s*)(?==)",
                        "SANITIZED", RegexOptions.IgnoreCase);

      // return the altered tag
      return fixedTag;
    }
  }
```

2. Modify `Comments.aspx` by adding a third comment that contains an unaccepted `onerror` attribute:

```
<%@ Page Language="C#" %>
<!DOCTYPE html PUBLIC "-//W3C//DTD XHTML 1.0 Transitional//EN"
"http://www.w3.org/TR/xhtml1/DTD/xhtml1-transitional.dtd">

<html xmlns="http://www.w3.org/1999/xhtml">
<head runat="server">
  <title>Professional Search Engine Optimization with ASP.NET</title>
</head>
<body>
  <h1>Adding rel=nofollow and sanitizing bad tags and attributes</h1>
  <%
    string s1 = @"<p>Hello! Take a look at <a href=""http://too.much.spam"">cool↵
link</a>!</p>";
    string s2 = @"<p>This is link from a <a href=""http://seoasp/Default.aspx"">↵
whitelisted domain</a>.</p>";
    string s3 = @"<p>Sanitizing <img src=""INVALID-IMAGE""" +
                @"onerror='location.href=""http://too.much.spam/""'>!</p>";

    Response.Write(NoFollow.FixLinks(s1));
    Response.Write(NoFollow.FixLinks(s2));
```

```
         Response.Write(s3);
      %>
   </body>
</html>
```

3.   Note you haven't sanitized the s3 string yet. Take a look at what happens without the sanitizing function applied. Loading http://seoasp/Comments.aspx should redirect you automatically to http://too.much.spam/, as shown in Figure 8-9. This address doesn't exist, obviously, but the exercise proved how easy it is to implement such redirects if the data isn't escaped.

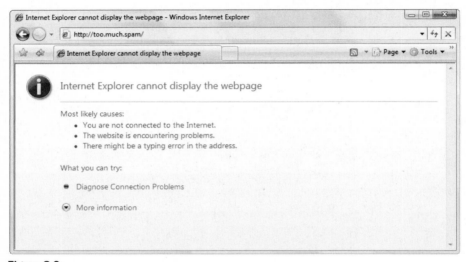

Figure 8-9

4.   Now, let's use the sanitizing function by updating Comments.aspx. Find this line:

```
Response.Write(s3);
```

and replace it with this line:

```
Response.Write(Sanitize.FixTags(s3));
```

5.   Now load http://seoasp/Comments.aspx once again. Fortunately, this time you will not be redirected to the spam site, as it happened earlier. You should get the output shown in Figure 8-10.

6.   It's also worth looking at the source code of the page. In Figure 8-11 you can see that your script changed the onerror attribute to SANITIZED. (Once again, we've reformatted the HTML source manually a little bit to make it more readable.)

To sanitize user input, you simply call the Sanitize.FixTags() method on the user-provided input. It will strip any tags that are not in the variable allowedTags list, as well as common attributes that can be cleverly used to execute JavaScript.

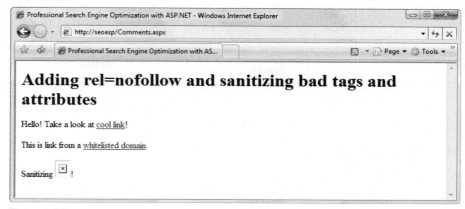

Figure 8-10

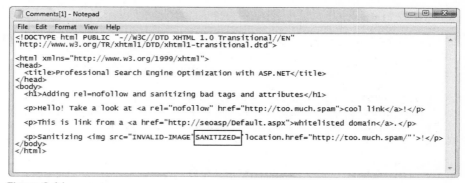

Figure 8-11

Without sanitizing the input HTML, the cleverly constructed code shown in the exercise automatically redirects to `http://too.much.spam`. The event `onerror` is executed upon an error. Because the image `INVALID-IMAGE` does not exist (which causes an error), it executes the `onerror` event, `location.href='http://www.spamsite.com'`, causing the redirection.

After the code is sanitized, `onerror` is replaced with `SANITIZED`, and nothing occurs.

> *The* `sanitizeHTML` *function does not typically return valid HTML. In practice, this does not matter, because this function is really designed as a stopgap method to prevent spam. The modified HTML code will not likely cause any problems in browsers or search engines, either. Eventually, the content would be deleted or edited by the site owner anyway.*

Having such "black hat" content within a web site can damage both the human as well as the search engine's perception of reputation. Embedding JavaScript-based redirects can raise red flags in search engine algorithms and may result in penalties and web site bans. It is therefore of the utmost importance to address and mitigate these concerns.

Note that the `nofollow` functionality was not used in this latest example, but you could combine `nofollow` with `sanitize` to obtain a better result, like this:

```
Response.Write(NoFollow.FixLinks(Sanitize.FixTags(s3)));
```

Lastly, your implementations — both `noFollowLinks()` and `sanitizeHTML()` — will not exhaustively block *every* attack, or allow the flexibility some programmers require. They do, however, make a spammer's life much more difficult, and he or she will likely proceed to an easier target.

Requesting Human Input

One common problem webmasters and developers need to consider are the automatic spam robots, which submit comments on unprotected blogs or other web sites that support comments.

The typical solution to this problem is to use what is called a "CAPTCHA" image that requires the visitor to read a graphical version of text with some sort of obfuscation. A typical human can read the image, but an automated script cannot. This approach, however, unfortunately presents usability problems, because blind users can no longer access the functionality therein.

Because .NET's GDI+ functionality is programmer-friendly, it's fairly easy to create such CAPTCHA images. You can find articles with full source code at http://www.codeproject.com/useritems/CaptchaControl.asp and http://www.15seconds.com/issue/040202.htm.

An improvement on this scheme is an alternative recording of the same information. This is used to overcome the usability issues presented by CAPTCHA. As a more simple but effective example, in the following exercise you create a small library that asks simple math questions. We'll name it `SimpleCAPTCHA`.

Creating and Using SimpleCAPTCHA

1. Create a new script named `AddComment.aspx` in your project, and add the following code:

```
<%@ Page Language="C#" %>
<!DOCTYPE html PUBLIC "-//W3C//DTD XHTML 1.0 Transitional//EN"
"http://www.w3.org/TR/xhtml1/DTD/xhtml1-transitional.dtd">

<script runat="server">
  // submit comment when visitor clicks the Submit button
  protected void submitButton_Click(object sender, EventArgs e)
  {
    // continue only if there is the visitor typed a comment
    if (commentTextBox.Text.Trim() == "")
    {
      feedbackLabel.Text = "Please write a comment.";
    }
    else
    {
      feedbackLabel.Text = "Thank you for your comment!";
      commentTextBox.Text = "";
```

```
       // ... code that adds the comment to the database ...
    }
  }
</script>

<html xmlns="http://www.w3.org/1999/xhtml">
<head runat="server">
  <title>Professional Search Engine Optimization with ASP.NET</title>
</head>
<body>
  <form runat="server">
    <h1>Captcha Testing</h1>
    <p>
      Enter a comment:
      <br />
      <asp:TextBox ID="commentTextBox" Width="400" Rows="5"
                   TextMode="MultiLine" runat="server" />
    </p>
    <p>
      <asp:Button ID="submitButton" runat="server"
                  Text="Submit Comment" OnClick="submitButton_Click" />
    </p>
    <p>
      <asp:Label ForeColor="Red" ID="feedbackLabel" runat="server" />
    </p>
  </form>
</body>
</html>
```

2. Execute the AddComment.aspx page, write a comment, and click **Submit Comment**. You should receive a confirmation that everything worked alright, and that the comment has been submitted.

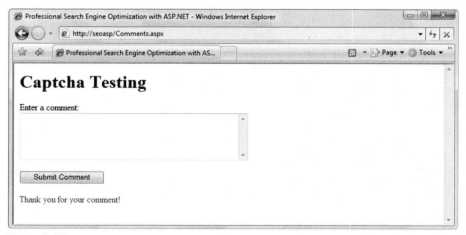

Figure 8-12

3. To implement the CAPTCHA functionality in a way that is easy to reuse, we'll create it as a Web User Control. This way, we'll be able to reuse it in any number of Web Forms by just including the control where it is needed. Let's first create a new folder to place our control. Right-click the project root in **Solution Explorer**, select **New Folder**, and create a new folder named **UserControls**.

4. Right-click the **UserControls** folder, select **Add New Item**, and select the **Web User Control** template. Name your new Web User Control file **SimpleCaptcha.ascx**, and select the **Place code in separate file** check box. Because this control contains quite a bit of code, we want it stored separately into a code-behind file. Click **Add** to have Visual Web Developer create the control and its code-behind file.

5. Type the following code in `SimpleCaptcha.ascx`.

```
<%@ Control Language="C#" AutoEventWireup="true" CodeFile="SimpleCaptcha.ascx.cs"
Inherits="UserControls_SimpleCaptcha" %>
<p>
  <asp:Label ID="captchaLabel" runat="server" />
  <asp:TextBox ID="captchaAnswerTextBox" runat="server" />
  <asp:HiddenField ID="correctAnswerHidden" runat="server" />
</p>
```

6. Let's edit the code-behind file now. Switch to `SimpleCaptcha.ascx.cs` by either clicking the **View Code** button in Solution Explorer, or by double-clicking the file in Solution Explorer. Then complete the existing code like this:

```
using System;
using System.Web;
using System.Web.Security;
using System.Web.Configuration;

public partial class UserControls_SimpleCaptcha : System.Web.UI.UserControl
{
  // define array with known numbers
  private static string[] numbers =
    { "Zero", "One", "Two", "Three", "Four", "Five", "Six",
      "Seven", "Eight", "Nine", "Ten", "Eleven", "Twelve",
      "Thirteen", "Fourteen", "Fifteen", "Sixteen", "Seventeen",
      "Eighteen", "Nineteen", "Twenty" };

  // define possible question formats
  private static string[] questions =
    { "What is {0} plus {1}?",
      "What is the sum of {0} and {1}?",
      "What is {0} added to {1}?",
      "What is {0} + {1}?" };

  // display the captcha question when the page is loaded
  protected void Page_Load(object sender, EventArgs e)
  {
    // Don't regenerate the question on postbacks
    if (!IsPostBack)
    {
      displayQuestion();
```

```
        }
    }

    // return true if the supplied answer is correct, or false otherwise
    public bool CheckAnswer()
    {
        // retrieve answer and the hash of the correct answer
        string answer = captchaAnswerTextBox.Text;
        string correctAnswerHash = correctAnswerHidden.Value;

        // calculate the hash of the answer
        answer = answer.Trim() + HttpContext.Current.Request.UserHostAddress;
        string answerHash =
          FormsAuthentication.HashPasswordForStoringInConfigFile(answer, "md5");

        // display new question
        displayQuestion();

        // indicate if the answer was correct
        return (answerHash == correctAnswerHash);
    }

    private void displayQuestion()
    {
        // generate random numbers and question
        Random random = new Random();
        int number_1 = random.Next(numbers.Length);
        int number_2 = random.Next(numbers.Length);
        int question_no = random.Next(questions.Length);

        // build the question
        string question = String.Format(questions[question_no],
                                    numbers[number_1], numbers[number_2]);

        // calculate the answer, add the visitor's IP, and calculate the hash
        string answer = (number_1 + number_2).ToString();
        answer += HttpContext.Current.Request.UserHostAddress;
        string answerHash =
          FormsAuthentication.HashPasswordForStoringInConfigFile(answer, "md5");

        // save the hash of the correct answer and populate the form
        correctAnswerHidden.Value = answerHash;
        captchaLabel.Text = question;
        captchaAnswerTextBox.Text = "";
    }
}
```

7. Let's now add the `SimpleCaptcha.ascx` control to our `AddComment.aspx` page. Add the highlighted lines of code to `AddComment.aspx`:

```
<%@ Page Language="C#" %>
<%@ Register Src="UserControls/SimpleCaptcha.ascx" TagName="SimpleCaptcha"
TagPrefix="uc1" %>
```

```
<!DOCTYPE html PUBLIC "-//W3C//DTD XHTML 1.0 Transitional//EN"
"http://www.w3.org/TR/xhtml1/DTD/xhtml1-transitional.dtd">

<script runat="server">
  // submit comment when visitor clicks the Submit button
  protected void submitButton_Click(object sender, EventArgs e)
  {
    // continue only if there is the visitor typed a comment
    if (commentTextBox.Text.Trim() == "")
    {
      feedbackLabel.Text = "Please write a comment.";
    }
    else if (!simpleCaptcha.CheckAnswer())
    {
      feedbackLabel.Text = "Wrong answer!";
    }
    else
    {
      feedbackLabel.Text = "Thank you for your comment!";
      commentTextBox.Text = "";
      // ... code that adds the comment to the database ...
    }
  }
</script>

<html xmlns="http://www.w3.org/1999/xhtml">
<head runat="server">
  <title>Professional Search Engine Optimization with ASP.NET</title>
</head>
<body>
  <form runat="server">
    <h1>Captcha Testing</h1>
    <p>
      Enter a comment:
      <br />
      <asp:TextBox ID="commentTextBox" Width="400" Rows="5"
                   TextMode="MultiLine" runat="server" />
    </p>
    <p>
      <uc1:SimpleCaptcha ID="simpleCaptcha" runat="server" />
    </p>
    <p>
      <asp:Button ID="submitButton" runat="server"
                  Text="Submit Comment" OnClick="submitButton_Click" />
    </p>
    <p>
      <asp:Label ForeColor="Red" ID="feedbackLabel" runat="server" />
    </p>
  </form>
</body>
</html>
```

8. Though this is not necessarily relevant for the CAPTCHA code, it's worth switching
AddComment.ascx in Design view, to see how Visual Web Developer integrates the newly
added Web User Control in your Web Form. Although your Web User Control is located in

separate files (`SimpleCaptcha.ascx` and `SimpleCaptha.ascx.cs`), you can still see its output in the designer window of `AddComment.aspx`, as shown in Figure 8-13.

Because this isn't a general ASP.NET development book we didn't pay much attention to the Visual Web Developer designer. However, always keep in mind that you can have it generate some of the code for you. For example, not only can you drag and drop controls from the ToolBox, but you can also add Web User Controls to a form by dragging them from Solution Explorer.

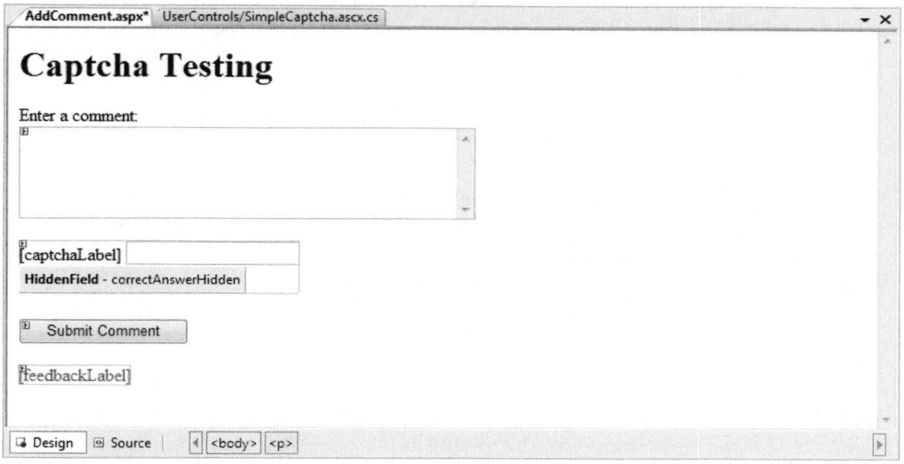

Figure 8-13

9. Load `AddComment.aspx` again, type some text in the comment box, and click **Submit Comment**. If you supply the wrong answer to the CAPTCHA question, the comment will not be submitted. Either way, the CAPTCHA message is updated to display a different question (see Figure 8-14).

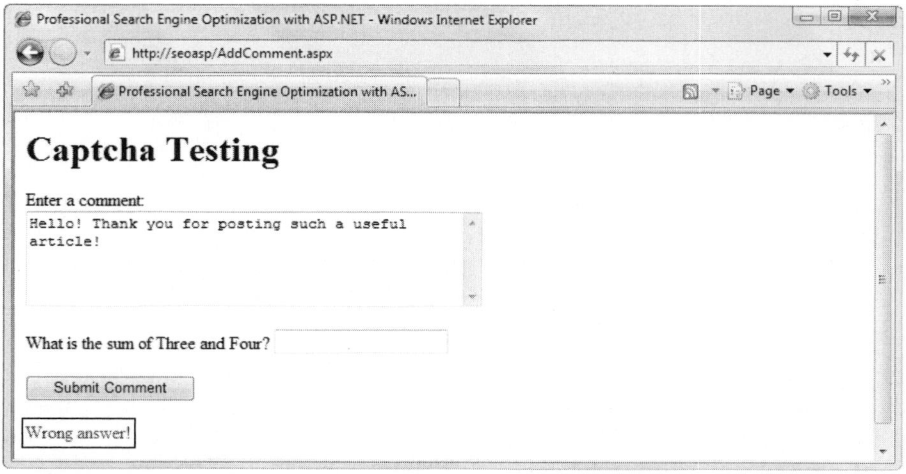

Figure 8-14

Using the simple CAPTCHA library, it's quite easy to implement a simple "human" check before you accept a comment submission.

> *Our little CAPTCHA control is still not bulletproof. It can be improved by implementing a more complex mechanism such as the use of obfuscated images. However, the script does its job nicely and it's appropriate to be used on small web sites.*

To include the CAPTCHA question in a page, you simply need to include the `SimpleCaptcha.ascx` Web User Control in a form, and call its `CheckAnswer()` method when the user submits a comment. When including Web User Controls into a form, you first need to declare them at the beginning of the form, as we did in `AddComment.aspx`:

```
<%@ Register Src="UserControls/SimpleCaptcha.ascx" TagName="SimpleCaptcha"
TagPrefix="uc1" %>
```

This is the standard way of including a Web User Control in ASP.NET. Apart from specifying the path to the `.ascx` file, the definition also mentions a `TagName` and a `TagPrefix`. To include objects of this type into the form, you refer to the control as `TagPrefix:TagName`. As with the other control, you also need to add the `runat="server"` attribute, and give an ID for the object:

```
<uc1:SimpleCaptcha ID="simpleCaptcha" runat="server" />
```

After having the `simpleCaptcha` object in place, you can call its methods just as you do with any other object in ASP.NET. In particular, in the `SimpleCaptcha` class we've defined the `CheckAnswer()` method, which returns true if the text entered by the visitor in the box is the correct answer:

```
if (!simpleCaptcha.CheckAnswer())
{
  feedbackLabel.Text = "Wrong answer!";
}
```

Now that you know how to use the `SimpleCaptcha` control, let's see how it works inside. If you look inside `SimpleCaptcha.ascx`, you can see it contains three controls: a label, a text box, and a hidden field:

```
<p>
  <asp:Label ID="captchaLabel" runat="server" />
  <asp:TextBox ID="captchaAnswerTextBox" runat="server" />
  <asp:HiddenField ID="correctAnswerHidden" runat="server" />
</p>
```

The purpose of the label and of the text box is obvious: we use the label to display the CAPTCHA question, and the text box to allow the visitor to enter the answer. The hidden field is used to store the hash value of the correct answer. Yes, this is correct: when the visitor reads a page that includes our CAPTCHA control, he or she will have access to the correct answer — but in a hashed form. This looks something like 9A013872D8B2EBD2CEC51B17313348E2.

As a little measure to increase the security of this method, the IP of the visitor is also appended to the correct answer of the CAPTCHA question before hashing. When verifying the correctness of the submitted answer, the IP is added to that answer, and the hash value of the resulted string is compared to the hash value that has been calculated using the known correct answer. The visitor's IP is added to the mix to make it harder for a potential hacker script to submit forms using a known correct answer/hash pair.

> ### What Is Hashing?
>
> Hashing is a means by which you obtain a unique calculated value that represents an object. Different objects should always have different hash values. The two most popular hashing algorithms are MD5 (Message Digest 5 — `http://en.wikipedia.org/wiki/MD5`) and SHA (Secure Hash Algorithm — `http://en.wikipedia.org/wiki/SHA-1`).
>
> The hash value of a piece of data is calculated by applying a mathematical function (the hash algorithm) to that object's data. The property of these hashing algorithms that makes it very useful when security is involved is that you can't easily obtain the original data from its hashed version (the algorithm is effectively one-way).
>
> Take the example at hand: the hashed value of "662" is "be3159ad04564bfb90db9e32851ebf9c," but you couldn't obtain the original "662" value if someone told you the hash value. This property makes hashing particularly useful when storing user passwords into a database. When the user tries to authenticate, the typed password is hashed, and the resulting hash value is compared to the hash value of the original (correct) password, which was stored when the user initially created his or her password. If the two values are identical, the entered password is correct. You do not need to store the actual passwords to authenticate users.

Note that .NET has support for more hashing and encryption algorithms, and the functionality is powerful and configurable using the classes in the `System.Security.Cryptography` namespace. However, we've used the `FormsAuthentication.HashPasswordForStoringInConfigFile()` method to perform the hashing. This method has been created to make it easier for developers to create hash values for passwords to be stored in the `Web.config` file, when implementing a Forms Authentication scheme. However, as you can see, the method can become quite handy in other scenarios as well.

We've used the MD5 (Message Digest 5) hashing algorithm, which is the most widely used hashing algorithm. Another popular hashing algorithm, which is generally agreed to be more secure (although a bit slower) is SHA (Secure Hash Algorithm). You can use this instead by supplying `sha1` as a parameter to `HashPasswordForStoringInConfigFile`, instead of `md5`.

301 Redirect Attacks

A legitimate site will often employ a script that redirects URLs, as part of an internal linking scheme, using URLs like this:

```
http://www.example.com/Redirect.aspx?url=http://another.example.com
```

In this case, `Redirect.aspx` would redirect to the URL specified by the `url` parameter. This is not a practice that we recommend, however. The problem comes when a 301 redirect is used. The fact that such a redirection link can be altered to point to any other URL is manifest from the URL itself. And a 301 redirect will be interpreted as a vote. Black hat SEOs will link to such a URL from many spam sites so as to acquire a vote.

You may want to revisit Chapter 4 for more details on the HTTP status codes and redirection.

For example, someone from `http://too.much.spam/` may post links, on their site or others, to URLs such as `http://www.example.com/Redirect.aspx?url=http://too.much.spam/`. If these links do 301 redirects to `http://too.much.spam/`, a search engine would interpret that the content at `http://www.example.com` was moved to `http://too.much.spam/`, effectively giving credit to the latter site.

> This practice can also be applied to humans, and, in that case, is called "phishing." The attacker tries to suggest, to human visitors and to search engines, that your site (`http://www.example.com/`) is in some way is associated with `http://too.much.spam/`. Popular web sites should be particularly careful, because the potential (illicit) benefits that can be achieved through phishing are significant.
>
> An example involving a previous Google "phishing" vulnerability is cited here:
>
> `http://ha.ckers.org/blog/20060807/google-spam-redirects/`

If you use such a redirection script in your site, there are three possible solutions to prevent 301 attacks:

- ❑ Use a 302 redirect instead of 301
- ❑ Use `robots.txt` to exclude `Redirect.aspx`
- ❑ Use a database-driven solution, so that `http://www.example.com` redirects only known links

Any of these solutions will suffice. The last is usually unnecessary for most sites, but it's mentioned here because, theoretically, leaving a script like that can be used by a social engineer to assert that your site advocates any other site to a non-sophisticated layman — phishing.

Using a 302 Redirect

As discussed in Chapter 4, 302 redirects do not transfer any link equity, and therefore have little value from a spammer's perspective. However, they may potentially have a use to "phishers," as mentioned later.

```
string newUrl = Request.QueryString["url"];
Response.Redirect(newUrl, true);
```

Using robots.txt to Exclude Redirect.aspx

This technique can be used in addition to using a 302 redirect. It, however, does not prevent "phishing," either. Read Chapter 5, if you haven't already, for more details on the `robots.txt` file.

```
User-agent: *
Disallow: /Redirect.aspx
```

Using a Database-Driven Solution

You could store the URL (either embedded in the script itself, or in a database), instead of embedding it visibly in the URL:

```
// define URL lookup table
string[] urlLookup = { "www.example.com/1",
```

```
                    "www.example.com/2",
                    "www.example.com/3" };

// get the redirect ID
int urlId = int.Parse(Request.QueryString["urlID"]);

// redirect
Response.Redirect(urlLookup[urlId], true);
```

Your URLs in this case would look like `http://www.example.com/Redirect.aspx?redirect_id=[number]`, and eliminate problems.

With this solution, you're also free to use 301 redirects, which can be beneficial because 301 redirects count as votes. (However, never use 301 redirects when the URL can be freely modified.)

If you already have a web site that redirects to the URL specified as query string parameter, you could also simply verify that it's a known URL before performing the redirect. In the following code snippet we do a 301 redirect:

```
// define URL lookup table
string[] urlLookup = { "www.example.com/1",
                       "www.example.com/2",
                       "www.example.com/3" };

// get the redirect ID
string url = Request.QueryString["url"].ToLower();

// redirect
if (Array.IndexOf(urlLookup, url) >= 0)
{
  Response.Status = "301 Moved Permanently";
  Response.AddHeader("Location", url);
}
```

Content Theft

This concept is detailed in Chapter 9, where the use of sitemaps is discussed. A black hat SEO may employ the use of scripts to lift part or even all of another site's content — using an RSS feed perhaps, or screen scraping. Many take various pieces of content from many sites and glue them together, leading to what Chris Boggs, director of online marketing of Cs Group terms as "Frankenstein content." The spammers who take a site's content verbatim are more of a concern, however, and using sitemaps may prevent, or at least reduce, the necessity of a cease and desist order.

If you know the IP address of a script on a web server scraping the content, you can also block requests from that IP. For the blocking technique we recommend using 302s rather than simply delivering the alternate content. You can intercept the requests and redirect them using either an ISAPI filter such as ISAPI_Rewrite, or in the `Application_BeginRequest` event in `Global.asax`.

```
void Application_BeginRequest(object sender, EventArgs e)
{
  // where to redirect bad visitors to
```

```
string badUrl = "~/AccessDenied.aspx";
string badIp = "127.0.0.1";

// get visitor data
string reqIp = Request.UserHostAddress;
string reqFile = Request.AppRelativeCurrentExecutionFilePath;

// 302 redirect if necessary
if (reqIp == badIp && reqFile != badUrl)
{
   Response.Redirect(badUrl, true);
}
}
```

We used `Response.Redirect()` to implement the 302 redirection. Note that the second parameter of this method is an optional parameter that has been introduced in .NET 2.0, and it specifies whether the page execution should stop immediately. To transfer the request to another file without using a redirect and modifying the requested URL, you can use `Server.Transfer()` instead of `Response.Redirect()`.

On Buying Links

As a result of the new focus on link-building to acquire relevant links, instead of the historical focus on on-page factors (discussed in Chapter 2), an entire industry of link-buying has sprung up. This is expected, because it is a natural reaction by the search engine marketing industry to facilitate their jobs. It is Matt Cutts' (of Google) opinion that purchased links should include a `rel="nofollow"` attribute. However, in practice this has proven to be Matt Cutts' wishful thinking, because this policy has never been widely adopted for obvious reasons.

We consider buying links completely ethical, so long as the links are semantically related. Realistically, content providers can reject placing your link on their site if it is not relevant, and if they consider it as relevant, there is no reason to include the `rel="nofollow"` attribute. In our opinion Matt Cutts' argument doesn't approximate an analogy of traditional marketing. Therefore, buying links, when done properly, is not a black hat technique. When done aggressively and improperly, it may, however, be perceived as spamming by a search engine.

Digital Point Co-op, Link Vault

Both Digital Point Co-op (`http://www.digitalpoint.com/tools/ad-network/`) and Link Vault (`http://www.link-vault.com`) are advertising networks that operate on the premise that they are promoting sites on other semantically related sites. In reality, however, their real purpose is questioned by many. We will form no clear conclusion here, but using such techniques may be against the guidelines of search engines and can result in penalties when used in excess.

Link Vault is probably safe when used in small doses, but the other networks like Digital Point Co-op, which advertise their existence with an invisible one-pixel image in the ad copy (for tracking) are extremely dangerous in our opinion. And though it hasn't provably gotten anyone into major trouble yet, it may in the future. If we can write a regular expression with ease that detects Digital Point links, can anyone reasonably conclude that Google cannot detect it? Google can clearly proceed to at least *devalue* those links.

Summary

This chapter summarized the black hat techniques that are requisite background material for every search engine marketer. We do not advocate the use of any of these techniques. Understanding them, however, may provide insight as to how a competitor is ranking. It may also serve as an education, in that it will prevent the inadvertent use of such questionable tactics in the future. Lastly, it prevents you from being the victim of certain black hat techniques that can be detrimental to your web site.

9

Sitemaps

A sitemap provides an easy way for both humans and search engines to reference pages of your web site from one central location. Usually, the sitemap enumerates all, or at least the important, pages of a site. This is beneficial for humans in that it can be a navigational aide, and for search engines, because it may help a web site get spidered more quickly and comprehensively.

In this chapter you learn about:

❑   The two types of sitemaps: traditional sitemaps and search engine sitemaps.

❑   The Google XML sitemaps standard.

❑   The Yahoo! plaintext sitemaps standard.

❑   The new sitemaps.org standard — implemented by all search engines.

You'll implement ASP.NET code that generates both Google and Yahoo! search engine sitemaps programmatically. But first, this chapter starts at the beginning and talks about traditional sitemaps.

Traditional Sitemaps

A traditional sitemap is simply an HTML web page that contains links to the various pages of your web site. Typically the page breaks down the pages into groupings for easy reading. This kind of sitemap is generally designed to assist humans in navigating, but search engine marketers realized early on that it had a beneficial side effect of helping spiders to crawl a site.

Historically, search engines did not crawl very deeply into a web site, and it helped to link pages located deeper in the site hierarchy (that is, one must traverse many pages to arrive there) from a sitemap page. Today, that particular problem is *mostly* squashed (search engines now do a much better job at crawling more deeply), but a sitemap may still assist in getting such pages spidered faster. It may also improve their rankings somewhat by providing an additional internal link.

Traditional sitemaps, as well as search engine sitemaps (discussed next), are especially useful to cite pages that are not linked anywhere else in a web site's navigation. Indeed, the Google sitemap help page says that *"sitemaps are particularly beneficial when users can't reach all areas of a website through a browseable interface."*

Creating a traditional sitemap is done as any other web page is. It can be created by hand, or generated dynamically using ASP.NET. The sitemap page should be linked to in the navigation or footer of every web page in your web site — or at least on the home page. For larger sites, it may make sense to create a multiple-page sitemap, partitioned into sections somehow, because we recommend not having too many links on a page. Please refer to Chapter 6, "SE-Friendly HTML and JavaScript," for recommendations regarding internal linking and pagination.

> *We used that unfortunate vague qualifier again — "too many." As usual, there really is no concrete definition for "too many," and it varies by search engine, but search engine marketers usually cite an upper limit of 50 to 100 links per page.*

Search Engine Sitemaps

Search engine sitemaps are not for human consumption. Rather, they are specifically designed to facilitate search engines to spider a web site. Especially if a site has added or modified content deep within its navigation, it may take many weeks before a search spider takes note of the changes without any assistance. Likewise, if a web page is referenced nowhere in a web site's navigational structure, it will not get spidered without any assistance, either.

> **We do question how well such an orphaned page would rank, and we would recommend using a traditional sitemap in any case because it *does* provide an internal link, whereas a search engine sitemap does not.**

Search engine sitemaps provide this assistance. Google and Yahoo! both have implementations in that vein. MSN search does not offer one at the time of writing. However, the end of this chapter points to a new unified standard that all search engines will eventually adhere to.

Search engine sitemaps do *not* replace the traditional spidering of a site, so a site will continue to get spidered normally. But if their systems notice changes via these sitemaps, a spider will visit the included URLs more quickly.

You can see how a traditional sitemap accomplishes some of the same things that a search engine sitemap does. Because the traditional sitemap is linked prominently on the web site, it is frequently spidered. Thus, by linking deep content on a traditional sitemap page, you can accomplish most of the same goals, but it is still advantageous to create a search engine sitemap.

For example, you can inform Google how often a page is likely to change, or that a change occurred with a later timestamp on a web page. You can also "ping" Google to inform it of changes within the actual sitemap.

> *By the same token, if the timestamps are out of date, providing a sitemap can actually be detrimental. If you do choose to provide timestamps, you must dutifully update it when changes occur!*

We recommend using both traditional and search engine sitemaps.

> Let's also note one lesser-known benefit of using sitemaps — mitigation of the damage as a result of content theft and scraper sites. Unfortunately, on the web there are unsavory characters who, without permission, lift content from your web site and place it on theirs.
>
> These sites are called *most* affectionately "scraper sites," but when it happens to you, they're called much less affectionate terms. One of the most difficult challenges search engines face is assigning the original author of content that is duplicated in several places. As discussed in Chapter 5, search engines aim to filter duplicate content from their indices. When you get filtered as a result of scrapers stealing your content, it can be particularly difficult to resolve. If a well-ranked scraper site (they do exist) gets spidered with your content before you do, *your web site content* may be deemed the duplicate! Because search engine sitemaps will get your new web pages spidered more quickly, they may help in avoiding some of these content-theft snafus.

The Yahoo! sitemap protocol is less popular than the Google protocol, but this chapter demonstrates code that allows both to be created with the same ASP.NET code. Thus, it is worthwhile to support both formats, because it will require minimal effort. Because the Yahoo! sitemap protocol uses only a subset of the information that the Google sitemap protocol does, if provided, that information will simply be ignored when the Yahoo! list is created.

Google and Yahoo! both also support reading news feeds in the formats of RSS and Atom. These formats may suffice for blogs and certain content management systems; often, they are provided by such applications by default. The problem with these implementations is that they usually only enumerate the newest content, and this is only really suitable for a blog. If you are doing search engine optimization for a blog, feel free to skip this chapter and use the feed functionality provided by your blog application instead. Also, theoretically it would be possible to create an RSS or Atom feed with all URLs as a sitemap for a site that is not a blog, but this is probably not what Yahoo! or Google expects, and we would not recommend it.

Using Google Sitemaps

Google has a very elaborate standard for providing a sitemap. It allows a webmaster to provide information in several formats, but the preferred format is an XML-based standard specified by Google. Google claims that using Google Sitemaps will result in "a smarter crawl because you can tell [them] when a page was last modified or how frequently a page changes." For more information regarding Google Sitemaps, visit http://www.google.com/webmasters/sitemaps/. There is also a Google-run Sitemaps blog at http://sitemaps.blogspot.com/.

However, according to Google, "using this protocol does not guarantee that your web pages will be included in search indexes," and "… using this protocol will not influence the way your pages are ranked by Google." Creating a sitemap for your site entails the following:

1. Creating a Google account, if you don't have one: https://www.google.com/accounts/NewAccount.

2. Creating a sitemap file.

3. Adding the sitemap to your account.

4. Verifying the site. This implies making a certain change to your site, so that Google will know you're a person authorized to modify the site. Doing so involves the addition of a randomly named file or meta-tag to your web site. To maintain Google sitemap functionality, these must not be removed once added.

Please see `http://www.google.com/support/webmasters/bin/answer.py?answer=34592&topic=8482` for more details about this procedure.

The Google Sitemaps service also allows you to see if there are any issues with the crawling of a site; these include errors returned by your server (404, 500, and so on), errors as a result of networking, and so on. It also gives you a list of URLs as restricted by `robots.txt` *and various statistics useful for analysis.*

As soon as you've finished the registration process, you can create the sitemap file named `sitemap.xml`, in the root of your web site, and then submit this file using the Google Sitemaps page. `sitemap.xml` could look like this:

```
<?xml version="1.0" encoding="UTF-8"?>
<urlset xmlns="http://www.google.com/schemas/sitemap/0.84">
 <url>
  <loc>http://www.cristiandarie.ro/</loc>
  <lastmod>2006-09-17</lastmod>
  <changefreq>weekly</changefreq>
  <priority>0.5</priority>
 </url>
 <url>
  <loc>http://www.cristiandarie.ro/books/</loc>
  <lastmod>2006-09-17</lastmod>
  <changefreq>weekly</changefreq>
  <priority>0.8</priority>
 </url>
 <url>
  <loc>http://www.cristiandarie.ro/forthcoming/</loc>
  <lastmod>2006-09-17</lastmod>
  <changefreq>weekly</changefreq>
  <priority>0.2</priority>
 </url>
</urlset>
```

The file contains a `<url>` element for each URL that you need to include. The children of this element have these meanings:

❑   `<loc>` specifies the URL.

❑   `<lastmod>` specifies the last modification date for the URL. The date is written in ISO 8601 format, which is YYYY-MM-DD. The standard also supports a number of alternative notations, and also supports the inclusion of the time. ISO 8601 is very nicely described at `http://www.iso.org/iso/en/prods-services/popstds/datesandtime.html`.

❑   `<changefreq>` tells Google how often the page changes. The possible values are `always` (for pages that change with each request), `hourly`, `daily`, `weekly`, `monthly`, `yearly`, and `never`.

❑   `<priority>` lets you tell Google how you evaluate the importance of individual pages of your web site as compared to the others. The value is a number between 0.0 and 1.0. Please note that the `<priority>` element only has significance over the relative importance of pages *within* a web site, and it *does not* affect the overall ranking of a web site!

Using Yahoo! Sitemaps

Yahoo!'s sitemap protocol is considerably simpler than Google's API. It too supports several formats including news feeds, but the format discussed here is the flat URL list plaintext file. It does not utilize XML, nor does it ask for any information other than a list of URLs delimited by linefeeds. Yahoo! requires that a file named `urllist.txt` appear in the root directory of a web site, and that you register a Yahoo! account with them.

The site must then be added at `http://submit.search.yahoo.com/free/request`. Arguably, Yahoo! accomplishes some of what Google does with its simpler approach — though it does not accept information regarding last modified dates, estimates of update frequency, or the relative importance of the pages. Yahoo! also cannot be pinged regarding sitemap updates.

The Yahoo! sitemaps equivalent of the previously shown Google sitemap would be a file named `urllist` `.txt` in the root directory of a web site with the following contents:

```
http://www.cristiandarie.ro/
http://www.cristiandarie.ro/books/
http://www.cristiandarie.ro/forthcoming/
```

Like Google, using Yahoo!'s sitemap protocol will not influence a web site's rankings, but it may get a site spidered more quickly.

Informing Google about Updates

In general, Google does a pretty good job at reading your sitemap at intervals and taking note of any updates; however, you can tell Google that your sitemap has changed by making a request to this URL:

```
http://www.google.com/webmasters/sitemaps/ping?sitemap=http://seoasp/sitemap.xml
```

If you load this URL with a web browser you'll simply be informed that your sitemap has been added to the queue, and that you should register your sitemap through `http://www.google.com/webmasters/` `sitemaps` if you haven't already (see Figure 9-1).

Creating such a request programmatically is simple. Program logic can be implemented to ping this URL when changes occur to your Google sitemap, such as whenever a product or content page is modified.

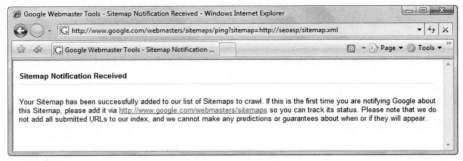

Figure 9-1

The Sitemaps.org Standard Protocol

Currently there is a new standardized initiative for a search engine sitemaps protocol that works with all search engine vendors. The standard and information is available at `http://www.sitemaps.org/`. It adheres mostly to the Google standard except that its XML namespace is different:

```
<urlset xmlns="http://www.google.com/schemas/sitemap/0.84">
```

becomes:

```
<urlset xmlns="http://www.sitemaps.org/schemas/sitemap/0.9">
```

Also, using this sitemaps protocol does not require creating any account with the particular search engine vendors. Rather, you must simply "ping" a URL in the following format with the location of the sitemap at least once (and optionally more when there are updates):

```
<searchengine_URL>/ping?sitemap=sitemap_url
```

At this time, the only search vendor adhering to this standard is Google — recognizing requests such as:

```
http://www.google.com/webmasters/sitemaps/ping?sitemap=www.example.com/sitemap.xml
```

MSN hasn't implemented this functionality yet, but Yahoo! supports sitemap notification using this (non-standard) request:

```
http://search.yahooapis.com/SiteExplorerService/V1/updateNotification?appid=[YOUR_Y
AHOO_APPLICATION_ID]&url=http://www.example.com/sitemap.xml
```

> **To get a Yahoo Application ID visit** `http://api.search.yahoo.com/webservices/register_application`.

You may instead place the sitemap URL in your `robots.txt` file like so:

```
Sitemap: http://www.example.com/sitemap.xml
```

For more current information on this subject, please visit the book's updates page maintained by Cristian Darie at `http://www.cristiandarie.ro/seo-asp/`.

Generating Sitemaps Programmatically

It would be useful to have a library that can create Yahoo! and Google sitemaps programmatically using the same information. The exercise that follows demonstrates such a library.

You'll create a class named `Sitemap`, which can store a number of links from your site, and generate the associated Yahoo! and Google sitemap files for you.

Generating Sitemaps

1. We'll start this exercise by making sure you have the necessary components from the previous chapters. First of all, you need the `SiteDomain` setting defined in `Web.config`:

```
<configuration>
...
  <appSettings>
    <add key="SiteDomain" value="http://seoasp" />
...
```

2. You need the `LinkFactory.cs` and `SeoData.cs` files in your `App_Code` folder. The former is required to generate the sitemap URLs based on product and category data, and the latter serves as our fictional database of products and categories. In a real-world scenario, `SeoData.cs` would be replaced by the products and categories database of your application. (Feel free to take the necessary files from the code download of this chapter, if needed.)

3. We'll write a generic handler file named `Sitemap.ashx` that will generate the Google and Yahoo! sitemap data. Let's rewrite requests to `sitemap.xml` and `urllist.txt` to this generic handler. If you're using `ISAPI_Rewrite`, add these rules to `httpd.ini`:

```
# Rewrite requests for sitemap.xml (Google sitemap)
RewriteRule ^/sitemap.xml$ /Sitemap.ashx?Target=google [L]

# Rewrite requests for urllist.txt (Yahoo! sitemap)
RewriteRule ^/urllist.txt$ /Sitemap.ashx?Target=yahoo [L]
```

In case you're using UrlRewriter.NET, the rules are:

```
<!-- Rewrite requests for sitemap.xml (Google sitemap) -->
<rewrite url="^/sitemap.xml$" to="/Sitemap.ashx?Target=google" processing="stop" />

<!-- Rewrite requests for urllist.txt (Yahoo! sitemap) -->
<rewrite url="^/urllist.txt$" to="/Sitemap.ashx?Target=yahoo" processing="stop" />
```

4. By reading the two rewrite rules you've just written, it's easy to intuit that `Sitemap .ashx?Target=google` will need to return an XML structure containing the Google sitemap, and `Sitemap.ashx?Target=yahoo` will need to return a text with your list of URLs. Let's write the code that does that. Add a generic handler file named `Sitemap.ashx`, in the root of your project, and type this code in:

```csharp
<%@ WebHandler Language="C#" Class="Sitemap" %>

using System;
using System.Web;
using System.Xml;
using System.Configuration;
using System.Collections.Generic;

public class Sitemap : IHttpHandler
{
  // structure that represents a sitemap item
  struct SitemapItem
  {
    // public fields representing the sitemap item properties
    public string Url, LastMod, ChangeFreq, Priority;

    // constructor initializes the fields
    public SitemapItem(string url, string lastMod, string changeFreq, string
priority)
    {
      this.Url = url;
      this.LastMod = lastMod;
      this.ChangeFreq = changeFreq;
      this.Priority = priority;
    }
  }

  // the entry-point method called when the handler is loaded
  public void ProcessRequest(HttpContext context)
  {
    // retrieve the value of the Target parameter
    string target = context.Request.QueryString["Target"];

    // if there is no target, quit
    if (target == null) return;

    // generate the requested sitemap
    if (target.ToLower() == "google")
    {
      GenerateGoogleSitemap();
    }
    else if (target.ToLower() == "yahoo")
    {
      GenerateYahooSitemap();
    }
  }

  // generates the Google sitemap of the site
```

```csharp
  private void GenerateGoogleSitemap()
  {
    // obtain the current HttpResponse object
    HttpResponse response = HttpContext.Current.Response;

    // set the content type
    response.ContentType = "text/xml";

    // use an XmlWriter to generate the Google sitemap
    XmlWriter xmlWriter = XmlWriter.Create(response.OutputStream);

    // write the start element
    xmlWriter.WriteStartElement("urlset",
"http://www.google.com/schemas/sitemap/0.84");

    // obtain the list of sitemap items
    List<SitemapItem> sitemapItems = GetSitemapItems();

    // generate the sitemap items
    foreach (SitemapItem sitemapItem in sitemapItems)
    {
      // generate the <url> element and its contents
      xmlWriter.WriteStartElement("url");
      xmlWriter.WriteElementString("loc", sitemapItem.Url);
      xmlWriter.WriteElementString("lastmod", sitemapItem.LastMod);
      xmlWriter.WriteElementString("changefreq", sitemapItem.ChangeFreq);
      xmlWriter.WriteElementString("priority", sitemapItem.Priority);
      xmlWriter.WriteEndElement();
    }

    // close the document
    xmlWriter.WriteEndElement();
    xmlWriter.Flush();
  }

  // generates the Yahoo sitemap of the site
  private void GenerateYahooSitemap()
  {
    // obtain the current HttpResponse object
    HttpResponse response = HttpContext.Current.Response;

    // set the content type
    response.ContentType = "text/plain";

    // obtain the list of sitemap items
    List<SitemapItem> sitemapItems = GetSitemapItems();

    // generate the sitemap items
    foreach (SitemapItem sitemapItem in sitemapItems)
    {
      response.Write(sitemapItem.Url + "\n");
    }
  }
```

```
// builds the list of items that need to be included in the sitemap
private List<SitemapItem> GetSitemapItems()
{
  // declare list of sitemap items
  List<SitemapItem> sitemapItems = new List<SitemapItem>();

  // create the list of URLs to include in the sitemap
  sitemapItems.Add(new SitemapItem(
    ConfigurationManager.AppSettings["SiteDomain"] + "/Catalog.html",
    "2007/05/05", "daily", "0.3"));

  sitemapItems.Add(new SitemapItem(
    LinkFactory.MakeCategoryProductUrl(SeoData.Categories["12"], 12,
    SeoData.Products["45"], 45), "2007/05/05", "weekly", "0.6"));

  sitemapItems.Add(new SitemapItem(
    LinkFactory.MakeCategoryProductUrl(SeoData.Categories["2"], 2,
    SeoData.Products["42"], 42), "2007/05/05", "weekly", "0.6"));

  sitemapItems.Add(new SitemapItem(
    LinkFactory.MakeCategoryProductUrl(SeoData.Categories["6"], 6,
    SeoData.Products["15"], 15), "2007/05/05", "weekly", "0.6"));

  sitemapItems.Add(new SitemapItem(
    LinkFactory.MakeCategoryProductUrl(SeoData.Categories["6"], 6,
    SeoData.Products["31"], 31), "2007/05/05", "weekly", "0.6"));

  // return the list of Sitemap objects
  return sitemapItems;
}

public bool IsReusable
{
  get
  {
    return false;
  }
}
}
```

5.   Load `http://seoasp/sitemap.xml`. You should get a Google sitemap with the products from `SeoData` class, as shown in Figure 9-2.

6.   Load http://seoasp/urllist.txt. You should get a Yahoo! sitemap, as shown in Figure 9-3.

So the `Sitemap.ashx` generic handler knows how to create both Yahoo! and Google sitemap formats. How does it do it? The `Sitemap` class starts by defining a `struct` named `SitemapItem` (the concept of `struct` was explained in Chapter 7). Objects of this `struct` represent sitemap items, whose details are stored in the four public fields (`Url`, `LastMod`, `ChangeFreq`, `Priority`). The struct also has a constructor that initializes these fields.

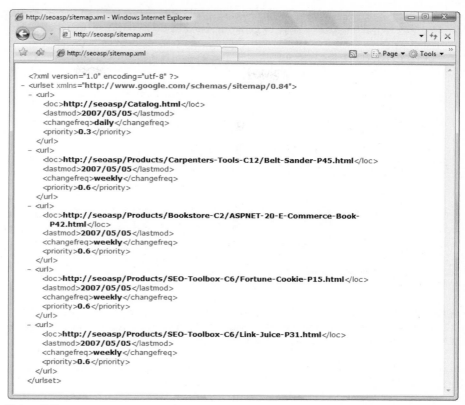

Figure 9-2

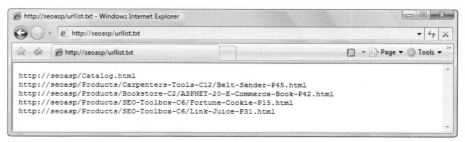

Figure 9-3

Note that the generally recommended practice is to store the data in private fields, and expose it through public properties. In the case of structs this rule is a bit more flexible, and we preferred not to follow it to keep the code shorter and easier to read.

As you know from your previous exposure to generic handlers, when the `.ashx` file is requested, its `ProcessRequest()` method is executed to generate the output. In our case, this method reads the `Target` parameter from the query string, and depending on its value it calls the appropriate method that generates the requested sitemap:

```
// generate the requested sitemap
if (target.ToLower() == "google")
{
    GenerateGoogleSitemap();
}
else if (target.ToLower() == "yahoo")
{
    GenerateYahooSitemap();
}
```

`GenerateGoogleSitemap()` and `GenerateYahooSitemap()` read through the list of sitemap items returned by `GetSitemapItems()`, and build the output based on the list elements. The code for the Google sitemap is sensibly larger because that sitemap contains more details for each URL, and it comes in URL format. To generate the output XML document easily we used the `XmlWriter` class, which takes care of many implementation details for us. We won't go into details because the code is pretty much self-explanatory.

> The `XmlReader` and `XmlWriter` classes are ideal for simple XML document manipulation. They're less complex and easier to work with than the `Xml` class, and using them is much less prone to errors and more convenient than manipulating the XML document yourself.

`GetSitemapItems()` returns a `List<SitemapItem>` object, making use of the *generics* feature, which is new in .NET 2.0. This was described briefly in Chapter 6. In this case, understanding it is even simpler: you can regard `List<SitemapItem>` as a data type with an "unusual" name, which represents a collection of `SitemapItem` objects.

> If you work with ASP.NET 1.1, you need to either create your own collection of `SitemapItem` objects, or use one of the built-in collection classes that store `Objects`, such as `ArrayList`. For example, the code would continue to run perfectly fine if you replace all instances of `List<Sitemap>` with `ArrayList` instead of `List<Sitemap>`, although doing so is a bit less efficient.

When creating the list of items we make use of `LinkFactory.MakeCategoryProductUrl()` to obtain the product URLs. This represents one more instance when the link factory proves to be very helpful. The product and category names are read from the `SeoData` class, which is meant to replace a database.

In Chapter 14, in the e-commerce case study, we'll use a more realistic scenario, where the product and category data will be read from the database, rather than a hard-coded class.

Summary

In this chapter you learned about the two forms of sitemaps — traditional and search engine based. Search engine sitemaps, read only by search engines, help a web site get spidered more quickly and comprehensively. Traditional sitemaps are designed for human consumption, but they are beneficial to the same end as well.

There is no conflict in creating both forms of sitemaps. A properly designed traditional sitemap also benefits human usability in ways a search engine sitemap cannot. We recommend creating both in the interest of usability as well as speedy and comprehensive indexing.

10

Link Bait

Link bait is any content or feature within a web site that is designed to bait viewers to place links to it from other web sites. Matt Cutts defines link bait as "something interesting enough to catch people's attention." Typically, users on bulletin boards, newsgroups, social bookmarking sites, or blogs will place a link to a web site in some copy that further entices a fellow member or visitor to click. It is an extremely powerful form of marketing because it is viral in nature, and links like these are exactly what a search engine algorithm wants to see — that is, votes for a particular web site.

Some readers might notice some similarities between this first paragraph and the Wikipedia page on Link Bait. That is because Jaimie Sirovich originally created the wiki page on Link Bait himself.

Soliciting links via link-exchanging is less effective than it once was to the end of improving rankings, as discussed in Chapter 2. Link bait creation is one of the newer popularized concepts in link building. In the article at `http://www.seomoz.org/blogdetail.php?ID=703`, Rand Fishkin of SEOmoz states "… I'd guess that if Matt (from Google) or Tim (from Yahoo!) had their druthers, this would be the type of tactic they'd prefer were used to achieve rankings." It is frequently, with a lot of luck and some skill, an economical and ethical way to get links to a web site; it is considered to be a white hat search engine optimization technique universally.

This chapter introduces the link bait concept, then shows an example of what we term "interactive link bait," which is an *application* that garners links naturally and virally.

As discussed in Chapter 2, building links is a crucial part of any search engine optimization campaign. In general, a site that earns links over time will be seen as valuable by a search engine. Link bait, in reality, is not a new concept. People have been linking to things that they like since the inception of the World Wide Web. It is just a concise term that describes an extremely effective technique — "provide something useful or interesting in order to entice people to link to your web site."

Hooking Links

Link bait is a hit-or-miss technique. Do not expect success with every attempt. However, one clever idea, when implemented, may yield thousands of links. Andy Hagans of BizNicheMedia launched a contest in January 2006, which perhaps is link bait itself, which offers $1,000.00 for what they assess as the best link baiting idea (`http://www.biznichemedia.com/2006/01/biznichemedia_1.html`). Good ideas are seemingly made of gold.

Link bait will be generated as a matter of course on any web site with quality content. However, learning to recognize content as such is useful in itself. Social bookmarking sites such as the famed `http://del.icio.us` and `http://www.digg.com` can help to promote content. Including hooks to such services may provide an easy "call to action" for users to promote you. This is a popular technique especially used to promote blogs. This topic was discussed at length in Chapter 7.

> *Careful consideration should be given before trying to get some of your content displayed on popular sites such as Digg or Slashdot. If your content makes it to the front page, it can cause your server to grind to a halt due to inbound traffic. Make sure your application and server are well prepared and tested using extensive stress testing.*

There are myriad ways to "hook" a link. There are many examples, but there are a few basic categories of hooks that they tend to fall into. They are:

- Informational hooks
- News story hooks
- Humor/fun hooks
- "Evil" hooks

Informational Hooks

These are resources that people will tend to link to by virtue of the fact that they provide useful information. For example, posting a "how-to" article for how to set up a web server is an informational hook. A user will read the article one day, it will help him, and then the user will post a link to it somewhere indicating that it was helpful. As time progresses, this may happen several times, and many links will accumulate.

News Story Hooks

The early bird catches the worm — and perhaps the links, too. Being the first web site to report a pertinent news story will typically get your web site cited as a source via links as the news spreads. Posting an op-ed with a different and refreshing opinion on news may also get some attention. Debate always encourages dialogue, and it is viral in nature.

Humor/Fun Hooks

People love to laugh, and humorous content is very viral in nature. A good joke is always going to spread. Alexa often highlights this when a blog with a funny post appears in the "Movers and Shakers" section with an increase in traffic of quadruple-digit percents. Traffic increases like that are almost always accompanied by links as a lasting effect. Fun games also work, because people send those around as well.

Evil Hooks

Saying something unpopular or mean will likely get links and attention, but it may be the wrong type of attention. Be careful with this technique.

Traditional Examples of Link Bait

One typical baiting scheme is a prank — or something otherwise extremely funny and/or controversial. Typically, if a certain amount of momentum is created, that is, a few users see it and post it, the rest becomes automatic, as hundreds or thousands of users spread the link about the Internet. One fine example is Zug's "Viagra Prank." Viagra, one of the most queried key phrases in the search engine landscape, is also extremely competitive.

In Zug's "Viagra Prank," `http://www.zug.com/pranks/viagra/`, the author writes about a man who attempts to order Viagra from a Viagra spam site, and reflects on his experience. It's actually rather funny. So funny, in fact, that we've decided to place it in this book. After reading this book, you may choose to tell your friend and place it on your blog. And the cycle continues. That particular page has been in Google's top 10 for "viagra" for many months (at the time of writing), because there are many hundreds of high-quality links linking to it.

Another example of link bait is Burger King's "Subservient Chicken," a funny game where you can tell a man dressed up as a chicken what to do; and a more narcissistic example is a blog entry on the SEO Egghead blog, `http://www.seoegghead.com/blog/seo/mattcuttsarama-a-summary-of-useful-stuff-matt-cutts-has-said-p112.html`). Other traditionally successful examples of link bait include contests, funny pictures, and cartoons.

Unfortunately, some of these link bait examples are not well-suited to straight-edge sites. A particular scheme may look funny and hook links on a personal web site, but may simply look too unprofessional in the context of a commercial site. One form of link bait that can be adapted to any kind of site — even the more conservative ones — is the interactive *web tool*. These tools provide free, useful functionality to users, but usually require at least some programming on the part of the web developer.

Lastly, do not forget that extremely valuable or insightful content is the original link bait. High-quality content is important for many other reasons. Matt Cutts affirms this when he states "if everything you ever say is controversial, it can be entertaining, but it's harder to maintain credibility over the long haul." We could not agree more. And for some sites, being controversial is simply not an option.

Interactive Link Bait: Put on Your Programming Hardhat!

Interactive link bait is an interactive application that attracts links. It's typically useful, or at least cute. Common examples of electronic link bait are RustyBrick's *Future Page Rank Predictor* (`http://www.rustybrick.com/pagerank-prediction.php`), which purports to be a tool to foretell your page rank on the next update (but also notes that it's entirely fictitious), and Text-Link-Ads' Link Calculator (`http://www.text-link-ads.com/link_calculator.php`).

The latter is an example of a useful tool. A tool to approximate the value of a link on a page should attract many relevant links from the search engine marketing community. And, in our opinion, it does usually manage to calculate reasonable estimations.

The former is an example of a cute tool. PageRank, more recently, is widely regarded as less important than it used to be. However, in a time when the green bar in the toolbar meant everything to search engine marketers, the idea of predicting PageRank was extremely appealing, and, despite the fact that the tool itself stated it was fictitious, many people used and linked to it. According to Yahoo!, as of June 2006, the page has more than 3,000 links (Yahoo! reports backlinks the most accurately of all search engines; see: http://www.seroundtable.com/archives/002473.html).

Other traditional examples of interactive link bait include calorie counters, mortgage calculators, and currency converters.

Case Study: Fortune Cookies

Because the sample e-commerce catalog will sell cookies, this example will be a cute graphical fortune cookie tool that tells a site visitor his or her fortune. This tool may be included by other web sites, so that they too can provide their visitors with fortunes. It can include a logo for branding, and it contains a link to your store in order to hook your links and encourage more users to use the tool. The fortunes are stored in a list and returned randomly. A few sample fortunes are in the sample database script. The fortune cookie image looks like Figure 10-1.

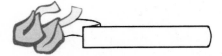

Figure 10-1

A page is placed on your site to showcase the tool, and you link to that page from your site menu with the anchor text "free fortune cookies." This effects some click-throughs. You show users how to add the fortune cookie to their sites on the page, and the HTML to do so, in turn, is linked to your free fortune cookie page. You also may place a link to another part of your site below that says "Get your free cookies at Cookie Ogre's Warehouse." The following is a quick exercise that demonstrates the technique.

Building the Fortune Cookie

1. Open the seoasp project in Visual Web Developer, and create a folder named images in the root folder. Then copy the fortune_cookie.gif file from the book's code download to the images folder.

2. Create a new **Generic Handler** named FortuneCookie.ashx in the seoasp project, with this code:

```
<%@ WebHandler Language="C#" Class="FortuneCookie" %>

using System;
```

```
using System.Web;
using System.Drawing;
using System.Drawing.Imaging;

// generates a random fortune cookie image
public class FortuneCookie : IHttpHandler
{
  public void ProcessRequest(HttpContext context)
  {
    // Define the possible fortune messages
    string[] fortunes = {"Jaimie Sirovich will become your\r\nfavorite author.",
      "You will recommend this book to\r\nall your friends.",
      "Tomorrow you will make \r\nyour first million.",
      "You will read Microsoft \r\nAJAX Library Essentials"};

    // Get a random fortune message
    Random randomGenerator = new Random();
    string fortuneMessage = fortunes[randomGenerator.Next(fortunes.Length)];

    // Load the empty fortune cookie image
    string imageLocation = context.Server.MapPath("/Images/fortune_cookie.gif");
    Bitmap emptyCookieBitmap = new Bitmap(imageLocation);

    // Create the new fortune cookie image
    Bitmap fortuneCookieBitmap =
      new Bitmap(emptyCookieBitmap.Width, emptyCookieBitmap.Height);

    // Create a Graphics object, and use it to draw the cookie to the new image
    Graphics gr = Graphics.FromImage(fortuneCookieBitmap);
    gr.DrawImage(emptyCookieBitmap, 0, 0);

    // Draw the fortune text on the new cookie image
    Font messageFont = new Font("Comic Sans MS", 10, FontStyle.Bold);
    gr.DrawString(fortuneMessage, messageFont, Brushes.Black, 130, 48);

    // Output the image and clear the Graphics object
    context.Response.Clear();
    context.Response.ContentType = "image/jpeg";
    fortuneCookieBitmap.Save(context.Response.OutputStream, ImageFormat.Jpeg);
    gr.Dispose();
  }

  public bool IsReusable
  {
    get
    {
      return true;
    }
  }
}
```

3. Load `FortuneCookie.ashx` in your web browser. The result should look like Figure 10-2.

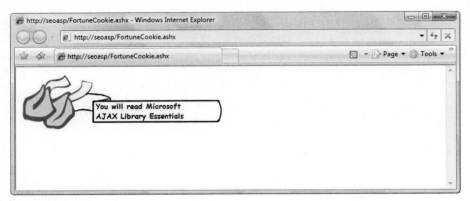

Figure 10-2

4. To be used as link bait, the fortune cookie needs to be easily placed in other pages. Assume that one of your visitors has a page named `LinkBait.html`, and that he or she wants to add your fortune cookie to that page. Create a new HTML page named `LinkBait.html` in your `seoasp` folder, and type the following code. The highlighted piece of code is what you need to give your visitors so that they can use your fortune cookie:

```
<!DOCTYPE html PUBLIC "-//W3C//DTD XHTML 1.1//EN"
  "http://www.w3.org/TR/xhtml11/DTD/xhtml11.dtd">
<html>
  <head>
    <title>Professional Search Engine Optimization with ASP.NET: LinkBait
Example</title>
  </head>
  <body>
    <h1>Professional Search Engine Optimization with ASP.NET: LinkBait Example</h1>

<a href="http://seoasp/">
  <img src="http://seoasp/FortuneCookie.ashx" border="0">
</a>
<br />Get your free
<a href="http://seoasp/">cookies at Cookie Ogre's Warehouse</a>.

  </body>
</html>
```

5. After adding the highlighted code, your visitor can load `http://seoasp/LinkBait.html` to admire his or her new fortune cookie, as shown in Figure 10-3.

The basic idea is very simple. You need to tell your visitors that if they paste the following code into their HTML pages, they get a free fortune cookie:

```
<a href="http://seoasp/">
  <img src="http://seoasp/FortuneCookie.ashx" border="0">
</a>
<br />Get your free
<a href="http://seoasp/">cookies at Cookie Ogre's Warehouse</a>.
```

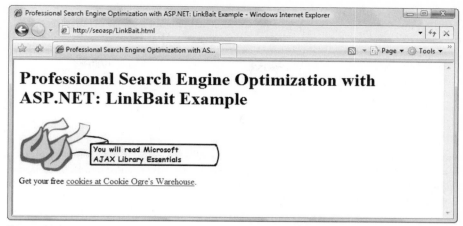

Figure 10-3

What's interesting about this code is that it not only delivers the fortune cookie, but it also includes a link to your web site (and the tool, so others may get fortunes). A small amount of users may remove the link, but a significant amount will leave the link around the image. You're providing your visitor with a free service, in exchange for some publicity.

The code of the fortune cookie generator itself is simple. It's implemented as a generic handler — this was introduced in Chapter 3. It simply takes a random text from an array, and displays it over the cookie image contained in `fortune_cookie.gif`. If you had more entries, it would make more sense to use a database, but for simplicity's sake you store the possible fortune phrases into an array:

```
// Define the possible fortune messages
string[] fortunes = {"Jaimie Sirovich will become your\r\nfavorite author.",
   "You will recommend this book to\r\nall your friends.",
   "Tomorrow you will make \r\nyour first million.",
   "You will read Build Your Own \r\nASP.NET 2.0 Web Site"};
```

To obtain a random string from the array, we use the `Random` class. The `Next()` method of this class returns a random integer number. The overload that receives a single parameter returns an nonnegative integer less than the value of the parameter.

```
// Get a random fortune message
Random randomGenerator = new Random();
string fortuneMessage = fortunes[randomGenerator.Next(fortunes.Length)];
```

After getting the fortune message, we're loading the fortune cookie image from the disk into a `Bitmap` object:

```
// Load the empty fortune cookie image
string imageLocation = Server.MapPath("/Images/fortune_cookie.gif");
Bitmap emptyCookieBitmap = new Bitmap(imageLocation);
```

Because the bitmap loaded from the disk cannot be modified directly, we're creating another `Bitmap` object, named `fortuneCookieBitmap`, with the same dimensions as the original image:

```
// Create the new fortune cookie image
Bitmap fortuneCookieBitmap =
  new Bitmap(emptyCookieBitmap.Width, emptyCookieBitmap.Height);

// Create a Graphics object, and use it to draw the cookie to the new image
Graphics gr = Graphics.FromImage(fortuneCookieBitmap);
gr.DrawImage(emptyCookieBitmap, 0, 0);
```

At this moment the new `Bitmap` object contains the cookie image, and we need to draw the fortune text on it. Fortunately, this is a very simple task, which involves creating a `Font` object that contains the details of the font we're using, and then using the `DrawString()` method of the `Graphics` object to draw the text using the specified font on the image:

```
// Draw the fortune text on the new cookie image
Font messageFont = new Font("Comic Sans MS", 10, FontStyle.Bold);
gr.DrawString(fortuneMessage, messageFont, Brushes.Black, 130, 48);
```

Finally, after we have a bitmap with the fortune cookie image and text, we want to output it. Once again, this task proves to be very simple. At the end we also dispose of the `Graphics` object, which is a good programming practice because it clears the resources used by this object faster than .NET's garbage collector would do:

```
// Output the image and clear the Graphics object
this.Context.Response.Clear();
this.Response.ContentType = "image/jpeg";
fortuneCookieBitmap.Save(this.Response.OutputStream, ImageFormat.Jpeg);
gr.Dispose();
```

It's worth noting that we've only touched superficially .NET's graphics capabilities. For example, it is very easy to activate antialiasing or fine-tune the encoding quality of the outputted image by setting only a few parameters. We'll leave to you as homework investigating these possibilities.

Also keep in mind that this was just one hypothetical example of link bait. Because we cannot possibly assist readers with all of their ideas for link bait, we will suggest that if you do have a great idea, but cannot implement it yourself, that you can use a service like eLance (http://www.elance.com/), which can assist you in finding a freelance programmer. For simple projects this can be very effective.

Summary

Link bait is not a new concept; it is just a concise term that describes an effective search engine marketing technique. Although some search engine marketers shun the term as just another word for viral marketing, we think the term and concept is quite useful. Deliberately creating link bait can provide a large return on investment, and even learning to recognize link bait when it is created as a matter of course is useful, because it can prompt a search engine marketer to provide hooks to services such as social bookmarking services to aid in the propagation of the bait.

11

Cloaking, Geo-Targeting, and IP Delivery

Cloaking is defined as the practice of providing different content to a search engine spider than is provided to a human user. It is an extremely controversial technique in the realm of search engine optimization. And like most things controversial, cloaking can be used both constructively and destructively. It is discussed in depth in this chapter, along with a discussion of the controversy surrounding its use. Geo-targeting is a similar practice, but it provides different content to both spiders and users on the basis of their respective geographical regions — and its use is far less controversial. Both practices are typically implemented using a technology called IP delivery.

In this chapter, you:

❑ Learn the fundamentals of cloaking, geo-targeting, and IP delivery.

❑ Implement IP-delivery–based cloaking and geo-targeting in step-by-step exercises.

About Cloaking, Geo-Targeting, and IP Delivery

Before writing any code, make sure you understand several important definitions:

❑ **Cloaking** refers to the practice of delivering different content to a search engine than to human visitors browsing a web site. In practice, cloaking is usually implemented through IP delivery. See http://en.wikipedia.org/wiki/Cloaking for more details.

❑ **Geo-targeting** is similar to cloaking in that it provides different content depending on the type of visitor — but this time by their physical location on Earth. Search engine spiders are not treated any differently than human visitors. This technique is useful when you want to show different content to a user from France than to a user from the United States, for example.

❑ Both cloaking and geo-targeting are covered in this same chapter because they're usually implemented in practice using the same technique — IP delivery.

❑ **IP delivery** is the practice of using the IP, the network address of the connecting computer, whether robot or human, and sending different content based on that. A database is used to assist with the process. In the case of cloaking, the database stores the IP addresses of the various spiders that may hit your site. The cloaking script implementation scans the list to see if the current IP is a spider, and the programmer can use this information to effect changes in presentation or logic. In the case of geo-targeting, the database stores various ranges of IP addresses, and indicates where these ranges of IPs are in the world. A geo-targeting script scans the list to see in which country the current IP is located, and the programmer can use this value to effect changes in presentation or logic.

❑ Usually, implementations of IP-delivery–based cloaking also look at the User-Agent header of the request. The user agent header is a header sent by both browsers and spiders. It, however, is not regarded as authoritative, because both users and spiders may not tell the truth about who they really are. In the former case, spiders indicate that they are humans in order to detect spamming employing cloaking as a means to provide optimized spam content to the spiders, while providing different content to the users. In the latter case, users (usually competitors) may actually set the user agent in their browser to that of a spider to see if a site is cloaking on the basis of user agent. It provides a convenient method for people to see if your site employs cloaking by *spoofing* their user agent. This is why many implementations of cloaking do not use it as a determining factor.

To change your user agent in your browser, see http://johnbokma.com/mexit/2004/04/24/ changinguseragent.html *(in Firefox) or* http://winguides.com/registry/display .php/799/ *(for Internet Explorer).*

More on Geo-Targeting

Geo-targeting is related to foreign search engine optimization in that it allows a site to tailor content to various regions. Foreign language SEO is discussed in more detail in the following chapter.

For example, Google uses geo-targeting to redirect users of www.google.com to country-specific domains, which is an implied approval of IP delivery as an ethical practice. This is a stark contrast to Google's current stated stance on cloaking.

Geo-targeting is regarded as ethical by all search engines. Matt Cutts of Google states (http://www .mattcutts.com/blog/boston-pubcon-2006-day-1/#comment-22227) that *"IP delivery [for geo-targeting] is fine, but don't do anything special for Googlebot. Just treat it like a typical user visiting the site."* However, because Google may use the actual physical location of *your web server* in the ranking algorithms, it may be wise to use this technique to redirect your users to a server located in their region, instead of simply changing the content. That is one example that is featured in this chapter.

One obvious caveat with regard to geo-targeting is that it can be misled by VPNs and strange network configurations in general that span multiple countries. This may be a concern, but it's likely to affect only a small minority of users.

A Few Words on JavaScript Redirect Cloaking

JavaScript cloaking is the (usually deceptive) use of redirecting a user to a different page with JavaScript. Because spiders do not execute JavaScript, this used to be an effective method to feed spam to search engines. Most notoriously, BMW of Germany was briefly removed from the German Google search engine index. Matt Cutts states in his blog (`http://www.mattcutts.com/blog/ramping-up-on-international-webspam/`) that "*... our webspam team continued ramping up our anti-spam efforts by removing bmw.de from our index ...*" And, although search engines do not generally execute JavaScript, they do look for this technique.

Using JavaScript to implement cloaking is not advisable in our opinion, because it is really only useful for spamming — in contrast to IP-delivery–based cloaking. It also requires a totally new page to be implemented, whereas IP-delivery–based cloaking can effect small changes in presentation, as you'll see in the examples.

The most trivial implementation of Java redirect cloaking is one that simply changes the location of a page via JavaScript. The following is an example of JavaScript redirect cloaking code:

```
<script language='javascript'>
<!--
document.location = 'http://www.example.com/new_location.html';
-->
</script>
```

In practice, different methods are used to obscure this code from a search engine's view to make it more difficult to detect. Because this method is almost always used for spamming, it is not discussed further.

The Ethical Debate on Cloaking

Very few areas of search engine optimization evoke as much debate as cloaking. Dan Thies states that "*cloaking is a very risky technique.*" He also states that "*... the intent of cloaking is to deceive search engines.*" This is a statement with which we do not entirely agree. In the opinion of many, there are legitimate uses of cloaking. In practice, Yahoo! and MSN are relatively ambivalent regarding cloaking for non-deceptive purposes.

Google, at the time of writing this text, states unequivocally in its terms of service that cloaking is not within its guidelines regardless of intent. In its webmaster guidelines at `http://www.google.com/support/webmasters/bin/answer.py?answer=40052` Google says that "*... cloaking ... may result in removal from our index.*"

Dan Thies states that "we do not consider IP cloaking to be an acceptable technique for professionals to associate themselves with." We take a milder view, especially in light of recent developments.

Recently, Google has also shown some ambivalence in actual enforcement of this principle. In particular, the *New York Times* cloaks content. In short, it shows a search engine spider the entirety of a news article, but only shows the abstract to a regular user. Human users must pay to be able to see the same content a search engine can read. The *New York Times* uses IP-delivery–based cloaking to do this.

The New York Times clearly uses IP-delivery–based cloaking, and does not pay attention to the user agent. If that were not the case, users could spoof their user agent and get a free subscription. We tried it. It doesn't work!

Meanwhile, Matt Cutts of Google states *"Googlebot and other search engine bots can only crawl the free portions that non-subscribed users can access. So, make sure that the free section includes meaty content that offers value."* Danny Sullivan, editor of SearchEngineWatch, stated with regard to the *New York Times*:

"Do I think the NYT is spamming Google? No. Do I think they are cloaking? Yes. Do I think they should be banned because Google itself warns against cloaking? No. I've long written that Google guidelines on that are outdated. To be honest, it's a pretty boring issue to revisit, very 2004. The NYT is just the latest in a string of big companies showing that cloaking in and of itself isn't necessarily bad."

We don't necessarily agree with this statement. Clicking a link in a SERP that gets you to a subscription page *is deceiving* to users. Results of a search engine query are supposed to contain data relevant to what the user has searched for. We leave the assessment to you.

Cloaking may be becoming more normatively acceptable recently, but it should still be avoided as the first choice for solving a problem. Solutions that do not involve cloaking should be applied instead. Some of this was previously discussed in Chapter 8. Cloaking is often suggested as a solution to preexisting sites that use Flash or AJAX, and it is also the only way to implement indexed subscription-based content, as in the *New York Times* example.

Examples of legitimate uses of cloaking — in our opinion — are demonstrated in this chapter.

Cloaking Dangers

Clearly, despite the fact that certain uses of cloaking are becoming accepted, it is still a risk, and it is likely that if you are caught by a search engine for using cloaking for a purpose that it deems as spam, your site will be banned. Therefore, if you are not an extremely popular site whose ban would elicit a public response, and you're not willing to take a risk, cloaking should be avoided — at least for Google. Minor changes are probably safe, especially for Yahoo! and MSN, as implemented in the exercise that follows, where you replace a figure with text.

It is, however, very difficult to define the meaning of "minor change," and a ban may still occur in the worst case. As aforementioned, `http://bmw.de` was reincluded in the index in a matter of days; however, in practice, for a smaller business, it would likely be much more devastating and take more time to get reincluded after such a ban. The cloaking toolkit provided in this chapter allows you to cloak for some search engines and not others. We cannot comment further, because it is a very complex set of decisions. Use your own judgment.

Using the Meta Noarchive Tag

One problem that arises with cloaking is that the cache feature provided by most major search engines would display the cloaked version to human visitors, instead of version they are intended to see. Needless to say, this is probably not what you want for several reasons — among them, that it conveniently indicates to your competitors that you are cloaking.

To prevent this, the following meta tag should be added to the `<head>` section of all cloaked documents:

```
<meta name="robots" content="noarchive" />
```

If you are cloaking only for a specific spider, you can use a tag (or multiple tags) like the following. (This can also be applied for `noindex`, `nofollow`, as shown in Chapter 5.)

```
<meta name="googlebot" content="noarchive" />
```

This prevents the cache from being stored or displayed to users. The *New York Times* also notably uses this tag to prevent people from reading its content through the search engines' cache.

Implementing Cloaking

In this upcoming exercise you're implementing a simple cloaking library, in the form of a class named `Cloak`, which uses a supporting class named `CloakDb`, many stored procedures, and a couple of data tables.

To test your cloaking library, you'll create a script named `CloakTest.aspx`, which will have the output shown in Figure 11-1 if read by a human user, and the output shown in Figure 11-2 when read by a search engine.

Figure 11-1

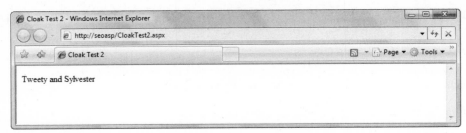

Figure 11-2

Showing different output depending on the type of the visitor (spider or human) is simple, provided that you know how to detect the type of the visitor — and that is where the challenge lies. We do this by matching the user agent and the IP of the visitor against a list of known user agents and IPs used by the search engine spiders. Using this data we obtain a value of the SpiderMatch enum, which reflects the details of the spider match. This enumeration has four values:

- ❑ SpiderMatch.NoMatch is used to specify that neither the user agent nor the IP of the visitor matches that of a spider
- ❑ SpiderMatch.MatchUA is used when the user agent is that of a spider
- ❑ SpiderMatch.MatchIP is used when the IP is that of a spider
- ❑ SpiderMatch.MatchUAandIP is used when both the user agent and the IP are those of a spider

The cloaking data, which contains the user agents and IPs used by search engines, is retrieved from Dan Kramer's iplists.com. Kudos to Dan to providing such a useful set of data for everyone to use! If you're curious to sneak peek into such a list now, load http://www.iplists.com/nw/google.txt into your web browser. You'll get a page such as that in Figure 11-3.

The first line of the page contains the name of the search engine spider. The following records contain the user agent names used by that search engine when crawling web sites. Finally, there's the list of IPs, or IP prefixes, of the crawlers. Similar pages are provided by iplists.com for the other major search engines as well, at the following addresses:

- ❑ Google: http://www.iplists.com/nw/google.txt
- ❑ Yahoo!: http://www.iplists.com/nw/inktomi.txt
- ❑ Microsoft Live Search (MSN): http://www.iplists.com/nw/msn.txt
- ❑ Ask: http://www.iplists.com/nw/askjeeves.txt
- ❑ Altavista: http://www.iplists.com/nw/altavista.txt
- ❑ Lycos: http://www.iplists.com/nw/lycos.txt
- ❑ Wisenut: http://www.iplists.com/nw/wisenut.txt

In our solution, we'll store the data from all these sources in a table named CloakData, and versioning information in a table named CloakUpdate. This latter table is useful so that we can update our CloakData table with fresh data only when iplists.com releases new versions of its IP and user agent lists. We'll get back to this a little later.

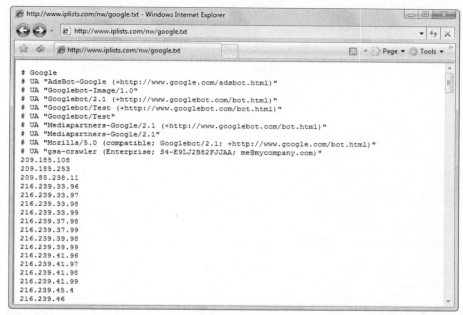

```
# Google
# UA "AdsBot-Google (+http://www.google.com/adsbot.html)"
# UA "Googlebot-Image/1.0"
# UA "Googlebot/2.1 (+http://www.googlebot.com/bot.html)"
# UA "Googlebot/Test (+http://www.googlebot.com/bot.html)"
# UA "Googlebot/Test"
# UA "Mediapartners-Google/2.1 (+http://www.googlebot.com/bot.html)"
# UA "Mediapartners-Google/2.1"
# UA "Mozilla/5.0 (compatible; Googlebot/2.1; +http://www.google.com/bot.html)"
# UA "gsa-crawler (Enterprise; S4-E9LJ2B82FJJAA; me@mycompany.com)"
209.185.108
209.185.253
209.85.238.11
216.239.33.96
216.239.33.97
216.239.33.98
216.239.33.99
216.239.37.98
216.239.37.99
216.239.39.98
216.239.39.99
216.239.41.96
216.239.41.97
216.239.41.98
216.239.41.99
216.239.45.4
216.239.46
```

Figure 11-3

This class that you'll use from your ASP.NET scripts for cloaking purposes is `Cloak`. This class has seven public methods:

- ❏ `IsSpider()` returns a level of confidence, using the constants as enumerated earlier, that the current visitor is a spider.

- ❏ `IsSpider(string spiderName)` verifies if the visitor is a spider of the search engine mentioned as a parameter, returning a level of confidence as with the previous method.

- ❏ `IsSpiderIP(string ip)` returns `true` if the IP provided as a parameter is that of a spider, or `false` otherwise.

- ❏ `IsSpiderIP(string ip, string spiderName)` returns `true` if the IP provided as the first parameter is that of the spider mentioned as the second parameter, or `false` otherwise.

- ❏ `IsSpiderUA(string ua)` returns `true` if the user agent name provided as parameter is that of a search engine, or `false` otherwise.

- ❏ `IsSpiderUA(string ua, string spiderName)` returns `true` if the user agent name provided as the first parameter is used by the search engine specified through the second parameter, or `false` otherwise.

- ❏ `UpdateAll()` updates the database with fresh data from `iplists.com`, but not more often than once a week, and only when `iplists.com` releases a new version of its files. This mechanism uses a separate database table to record the date and version of the last update, and calls the script at `http://www.iplists.com/nw/version.php` to check the version of the `iplists.com` files.

If you have such functionality at hand, it becomes very simple to display different content based on the type of visitor, like this:

```
if (Cloak.IsSpider())
{
  // send output for search engines
}
else
{
  // send output for human visitors
}
```

All the methods in `Cloak` need data from the `CloakData` or `CloakUpdate` tables. To maintain clarity in our solution, improve code reuse and maintenance, we didn't implement the data access logic in the `Cloak` class, preferring to have that class store only the high-level logic necessary for implementing the necessary features. Instead, we'll create another class named `CloakDb` that deals with database access. `CloakDB` contains methods such as `AddSpiderRecord()`, `DeleteSpider()`, `CheckIP()`, and others; you can guess their functionality, but we'll discuss the details after the exercise.

One last thing to warn you about is that we'll use stored procedures for keeping the SQL code that manipulates the database. This is a common practice in the ASP.NET world, and unless you have specific reasons for doing otherwise, we recommend that you keep your SQL code in stored procedures rather than including it in your C# files. In the long term, this practice brings great benefits in terms of code and security maintenance and performance.

To give you a visual aid in following the exercise you're about to do, see Figure 11-4, which is a simplified diagram containing most of the elements you'll create. A number of methods are omitted for clarity, but the diagram should be descriptive enough to help give you an idea of what you are about to implement.

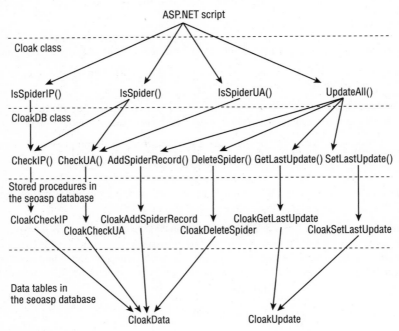

Figure 11-4

Let's write some code, then! We'll discuss the details after you've finished creating the working example on your machine. We're implementing our solution in a bottom-to-top fashion: we start by preparing the database, then we'll continue by creating the supporting classes, and will finish by creating a simple ASP.NET script that tests the cloaking functionality.

Implementing and Testing the Cloaking Library

1. We start by preparing the database structures that will store the cloaking data. Start the SQL Server Management Studio Express, and connect to your local SQL Server instance using SQL Server authentication, using the user **seouser**, with the password **seomaster**, as shown in Figure 11-5. (You created the seoasp database and the seouser user in Chapter 1.)

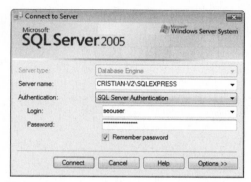

Figure 11-5

2. Click the **New Query** button, and a new query window should appear. If you configured your seouser login correctly in Chapter 1, the seoasp database should be selected for you, as you can see in Figure 11-6.

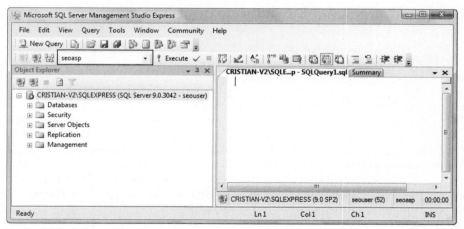

Figure 11-6

3. Type the following SQL code in the query editor, to create the `CloakData` and `CloakUpdate` tables:

```
CREATE TABLE CloakData (
  ID INT IDENTITY(1,1) PRIMARY KEY NOT NULL,
  SpiderName VARCHAR(255) NOT NULL DEFAULT '',
  RecordType CHAR(2) NOT NULL DEFAULT 'UA' CHECK(RecordType IN ('UA','IP')) ,
  Value VARCHAR(255) NOT NULL
);

CREATE INDEX CloakValueIndex ON CloakData(Value);

CREATE TABLE CloakUpdate (
  Version VARCHAR(255) NOT NULL PRIMARY KEY,
  UpdatedOn DATETIME NOT NULL
);
```

4. Press F5 to execute the query. The result should look like Figure 11-7.

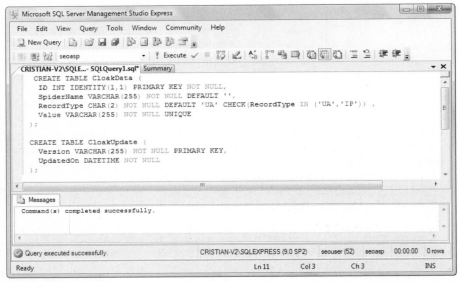

Figure 11-7

5. Either create a new query window or clear the contents of your current one, type the code for the following stored procedures, and then execute the script by clicking the **Execute** icon or by pressing F5. Alternatively, instead of creating all the procedures in one step, you can create them one at a time, to make it easier to find any eventual typing mistakes. In this case, you don't need the GO commands that separate the procedures anymore.

Note that you can't create a stored procedure twice. If you've already created a procedure and then want to modify its code, you need to use ALTER PROCEDURE instead of CREATE PROCEDURE. Both commands have the same syntax.

```sql
CREATE PROCEDURE CloakCheckIP
  (@IPValue VARCHAR(255),
    @SpiderName VARCHAR(255) = '')
AS
SELECT COUNT(*) FROM CloakData
WHERE RecordType = 'IP'
AND (Value = @IPValue OR Value LIKE @IPValue + '.%')
AND (@SpiderName = '' OR SpiderName = @SpiderName)

GO


CREATE PROCEDURE CloakCheckUA
  (@UAValue VARCHAR(255),
    @SpiderName VARCHAR(255) = '')
AS
SELECT COUNT(*) FROM CloakData
WHERE RecordType = 'UA'
AND Value = @UAValue
AND (@SpiderName = '' OR SpiderName = @SpiderName)

GO


CREATE PROCEDURE CloakSetLastUpdate
  (@NewVersion VARCHAR(255),
    @UpdatedOn DATETIME)
AS
TRUNCATE TABLE CloakUpdate;
INSERT INTO CloakUpdate(Version, UpdatedOn)
VALUES (@NewVersion, @UpdatedOn)

GO


CREATE PROCEDURE CloakGetLastUpdate
AS
SELECT Version, UpdatedOn FROM CloakUpdate

GO


CREATE PROCEDURE CloakDeleteSpider
  (@SpiderName VARCHAR(255))
AS
DELETE FROM CloakData
WHERE SpiderName = @SpiderName

GO


CREATE PROCEDURE CloakAddSpiderRecord
  (@SpiderName VARCHAR(255),
    @RecordType CHAR(2),
    @Value VARCHAR(255))
AS
INSERT INTO CloakData (SpiderName, RecordType, Value)
VALUES (@SpiderName, @RecordType, @Value);
```

6. To keep our solution tidy, we'll save the connection string in the project's configuration file, rather than in our C# code. This makes it possible to easily modify the database connection string without needing to recompile the application, and it offers a centralized place where you can store your application settings. Open `Web.config` by double-clicking its entry in Solution Explorer, and add the following connection string:

```
<configuration xmlns="http://schemas.microsoft.com/.NetConfiguration/v2.0">
<appSettings/>
  <connectionStrings>
    <add name="CloakDatabase" connectionString="Server=(local)\SqlExpress; ↵
User=seouser;Password=seomaster;Database=seoasp" />
  </connectionStrings>
```

7. Now it's time to write some C# code. Create a class file named `CloakDb.cs` in your `App_Code` folder:

```csharp
using System;
using System.Data;
using System.Data.SqlClient;
using System.Configuration;

/// <summary>
/// Class represents the interface to the CloakData database
/// </summary>
public static class CloakDb
{
  // returns the date and the version of the last update
  public static bool GetLastUpdate(ref string version, ref DateTime updatedOn)
  {
    // create a SqlCommand object with a connection to the cloak database
    SqlCommand command = CloakDb.createCommand("CloakDatabase");

    // set the name of the stored procedure to execute
    command.CommandText = "CloakGetLastUpdate";

    // create a new DataTable object
    DataTable results = new DataTable();

    // execute the stored procecure and load the results into the DataTable
    command.Connection.Open();
    try { results.Load(command.ExecuteReader()); }
    finally { command.Connection.Close(); }

    // return false if no update record was found
    if (results.Rows.Count == 0)
    {
      return false;
    }
    else
    {
      version = results.Rows[0]["Version"].ToString();
      updatedOn = (DateTime)results.Rows[0]["UpdatedOn"];
      return true;
    }
```

```csharp
      }

      // saves the time and date of the last database update
      public static void SetLastUpdate(string version, DateTime updatedOn)
      {
        // create a SqlCommand object with a connection to the cloak database
        SqlCommand command = CloakDb.createCommand("CloakDatabase");

        // set the name of the stored procedure to execute
        command.CommandText = "CloakSetLastUpdate";

        // add stored procedure parameter
        SqlParameter p = new SqlParameter("@NewVersion", version);
        command.Parameters.Add(p);

        // add stored procedure parameter
        p = new SqlParameter("@UpdatedOn", updatedOn);
        command.Parameters.Add(p);

        // execute the stored procecure and load the results into the DataTable
        command.Connection.Open();
        try { command.ExecuteNonQuery(); }
        finally { command.Connection.Close(); }
      }

    // saves the time and date of the last database update
    public static void AddSpiderRecord(string spiderName, string recordType, string
value)
      {
        // create a SqlCommand object with a connection to the cloak database
        SqlCommand command = CloakDb.createCommand("CloakDatabase");

        // set the name of the stored procedure to execute
        command.CommandText = "CloakAddSpiderRecord";

        // @SpiderName
        SqlParameter p = new SqlParameter("@SpiderName", spiderName);
        command.Parameters.Add(p);

        // @RecordType
        p = new SqlParameter("@RecordType", recordType);
        command.Parameters.Add(p);

        // add stored procedure parameter
        p = new SqlParameter("@Value", value);
        command.Parameters.Add(p);

        // execute the stored procecure and load the results into the DataTable
        command.Connection.Open();
        try { command.ExecuteNonQuery(); }
        finally { command.Connection.Close(); }
      }

    // deletes the records of a spider from the database
```

```
public static void DeleteSpider(string spiderName)
{
  // create a SqlCommand object with a connection to the cloak database
  SqlCommand command = CloakDb.createCommand("CloakDatabase");

  // set the name of the stored procedure to execute
  command.CommandText = "CloakDeleteSpider";

  // @SpiderName
  SqlParameter p = new SqlParameter("@SpiderName", spiderName);
  command.Parameters.Add(p);

  // execute the stored procecure and load the results into the DataTable
  command.Connection.Open();
  try { command.ExecuteNonQuery(); }
  finally { command.Connection.Close(); }
}

// verify if the supplied User Agent is that of the specified spider
// (if spiderName is an empty string, all spiders are checked)
public static bool CheckUA(string uaValue, string spiderName)
{
  // create a SqlCommand object with a connection to the cloak database
  SqlCommand command = CloakDb.createCommand("CloakDatabase");

  // set the name of the stored procedure to execute
  command.CommandText = "CloakCheckUA";

  // @UAValue
  SqlParameter p = new SqlParameter("@UAValue", uaValue);
  command.Parameters.Add(p);

  // @SpiderName
  p = new SqlParameter("@SpiderName", spiderName);
  command.Parameters.Add(p);

  // execute the stored procedure
  command.Connection.Open();
  int numberOfMatches;
  try { numberOfMatches = (int)command.ExecuteScalar(); }
  finally { command.Connection.Close(); }

  // return true if there was a match
  return (numberOfMatches > 0);
}

// verify if the supplied IP is that of the specified spider
// (if spiderName is an empty string, all spiders are checked)
public static bool CheckIP(string ipValue, string spiderName)
{
  // create a SqlCommand object with a connection to the cloak database
  SqlCommand command = CloakDb.createCommand("CloakDatabase");
```

```
        // set the name of the stored procedure to execute
        command.CommandText = "CloakCheckIP";

        // @UAValue
        SqlParameter p = new SqlParameter("@IPValue", ipValue);
        command.Parameters.Add(p);

        // @SpiderName
        p = new SqlParameter("@SpiderName", spiderName);
        command.Parameters.Add(p);

        // execute the stored procedure
        command.Connection.Open();
        int numberOfMatches;
        try { numberOfMatches = (int)command.ExecuteScalar(); }
        finally { command.Connection.Close(); }

        // return true if there was a match
        return (numberOfMatches > 0);
    }

    // creates and prepares a new SqlCommand object on a new connection
    private static SqlCommand createCommand(string connectionName)
    {
        // obtain the database connection string
        string connectionString =
ConfigurationManager.ConnectionStrings[connectionName].ConnectionString;

        // obtain a database specific connection object
        SqlConnection conn = new SqlConnection(connectionString);

        // create a database specific command object
        SqlCommand comm = conn.CreateCommand();

        // set the command type to stored procedure
        comm.CommandType = CommandType.StoredProcedure;

        // return the initialized command object
        return comm;
    }
}
```

8. Create another class named `Cloak`, in a new file named `Cloak.cs` in your `App_Code` folder, with this code:

```
using System;
using System.Net;
using System.IO;
using System.Text.RegularExpressions;
using System.Web;

/// <summary>
/// Enumeration with the possible levels of spider match confidence
```

```csharp
    /// </summary>
    public enum SpiderMatch
    {
      NoMatch, // neither the user agent or IP matches that of a spider
      MatchUA, // the user agent is that of a spider
      MatchIP, // the IP is that of a spider
      MatchUAandIP // both the user agent and the IP are those of a spider
    }

    /// <summary>
    /// Cloak offers functionality for cloaking support
    /// </summary>
    public static class Cloak
    {
      // returns the confidence level of the current visitor being a spider
      // (0 = no match, 2 = user agent matched, 3 = ip matched, 5 = ua + ip)
      public static SpiderMatch IsSpider()
      {
        return IsSpider("");
      }

      public static SpiderMatch IsSpider(string spiderName)
      {
        // default confidence level to 0
        SpiderMatch confidence = 0;

        // visitor's user agent
        string visitorUA = HttpContext.Current.Request["HTTP_USER_AGENT"];
        string visitorIP = HttpContext.Current.Request["REMOTE_ADDR"];

        // verify user agent and IP matches
        bool uaMatches = CloakDb.CheckUA(visitorUA, spiderName);
        bool ipMatches = CloakDb.CheckIP(visitorIP, spiderName);

        // obtain confidence level
        if (uaMatches && ipMatches) confidence = SpiderMatch.MatchUAandIP;
        else if (uaMatches) confidence = SpiderMatch.MatchUA;
        else if (ipMatches) confidence = SpiderMatch.MatchIP;
        else confidence = SpiderMatch.NoMatch;

        // return level of confidence that visitor is a spider
        return confidence;
      }

      // verify if the supplied IP is that of a spider
      public static bool IsSpiderIP(string ip)
      {
        return CloakDb.CheckIP(ip, "");
      }

      // verify if the supplied IP is that of the specified spider
      public static bool IsSpiderIP(string ip, string spiderName)
      {
        return CloakDb.CheckIP(ip, spiderName);
```

```
  }

  // verify if the supplied UserAgent is that of a spider
  public static bool IsSpiderUA(string ua)
  {
    return CloakDb.CheckUA(ua, "");
  }

  // verify if the supplied user agent is that of the specified spider
  public static bool IsSpiderUA(string ua, string spiderName)
  {
    return CloakDb.CheckUA(ua, spiderName);
  }

  // updates cloak data; returns true if an update has been performed
  public static bool UpdateAll()
  {
    // read the version and the update date from the database
    string dbVersion = "";
    DateTime dbUpdatedOn = new DateTime();
    CloakDb.GetLastUpdate(ref dbVersion, ref dbUpdatedOn);

    // abort if the database was updated sooner than 7 days ago
    if (DateTime.Now - new TimeSpan(7, 0, 0, 0) < dbUpdatedOn) return false;

    // read the latest cloak version published by iplists
    WebRequest request = HttpWebRequest.Create(
      "http://www.iplists.com/nw/version.php");
    Stream responseStream = request.GetResponse().GetResponseStream();
    StreamReader reader = new StreamReader(responseStream);
    string latestVersion = reader.ReadLine();

    // abort if we alredy have the last version of the database
    if (dbVersion == latestVersion) return false;

    // update the database version and date
    CloakDb.SetLastUpdate(latestVersion, DateTime.Now);

    // update the database
    updateSpiderData("google", "http://www.iplists.com/nw/google.txt");
    updateSpiderData("yahoo", "http://www.iplists.com/nw/inktomi.txt");
    updateSpiderData("msn", "http://www.iplists.com/nw/msn.txt");
    updateSpiderData("ask", "http://www.iplists.com/nw/askjeeves.txt");
    updateSpiderData("altavista", "http://www.iplists.com/nw/altavista.txt");
    updateSpiderData("lycos", "http://www.iplists.com/nw/lycos.txt");
    updateSpiderData("wisenut", "http://www.iplists.com/nw/wisenut.txt");

    // return true to signal that we've updated the data
    return true;
  }

  private static void updateSpiderData(string spiderName, string spiderUrl)
  {
    // create the request object
```

```
        WebRequest request = HttpWebRequest.Create(spiderUrl);
        // create a stream to read data from the URL
        Stream responseStream = request.GetResponse().GetResponseStream();

        // load the list of IPs into a string
        StreamReader reader = new StreamReader(responseStream);
        string inputString = reader.ReadToEnd();
        reader.Close();

        // delete the database data we have for the spider
        CloakDb.DeleteSpider(spiderName);

        // use a regular expression to extract the user agents
        MatchCollection matches;
        matches = Regex.Matches(inputString,
          @"^# UA ""(?<url>.*)""$",
          RegexOptions.ExplicitCapture | RegexOptions.Multiline);

        // add each matched user agent to the database
        foreach (Match m in matches)
        {
          string ua = m.Groups["url"].ToString();
          CloakDb.AddSpiderRecord(spiderName, "UA", ua);
        }

        // regular expression that extract the spider IPs
        matches = Regex.Matches(inputString,
          "^(?<ip>[0-9.]+)$", RegexOptions.Multiline);

        // add the matched IPs to the database
        foreach (Match m in matches)
        {
          string ip = m.Groups["ip"].ToString();
          CloakDb.AddSpiderRecord(spiderName, "IP", ip);
        }
      }
    }
}
```

9. Create a file named `CloakTest.aspx` in the root of your project, and modify the generated template code as follows:

```
<%@ Page Language="C#" %>

<!DOCTYPE html PUBLIC "-//W3C//DTD XHTML 1.0 Transitional//EN"
"http://www.w3.org/TR/xhtml1/DTD/xhtml1-transitional.dtd">

<script runat="server">
  protected void Page_Load(object sender, EventArgs e)
  {
    // update the cloak database if necessary
    bool wasUpdated = Cloak.UpdateAll();
```

```
      // verify if the current client is a spider
      SpiderMatch confidence = Cloak.IsSpider();

      // show the results
      message.Text = wasUpdated ?
        "The cloaking database was updated. " :
        "The cloaking database was not updated. ";

      message.Text += (confidence == SpiderMatch.NoMatch) ?
        "You are not a spider." :
        "You are a spider (confidence: " + confidence + ").";
  }
</script>

<html xmlns="http://www.w3.org/1999/xhtml" >
<head runat="server">
  <title>Cloak Test</title>
</head>
<body>
  <form id="form1" runat="server">
    <asp:Literal runat="server" id="message" />
  </form>
</body>
</html>
```

10. Load `CloakTest.aspx`. If everything works as planned, the page will simply output "The cloaking database was updated. You are not a spider" as shown in Figure 11-8. On any subsequent requests (before a week elapses), the message should read "The cloaking database was **not** updated. You are not a spider."

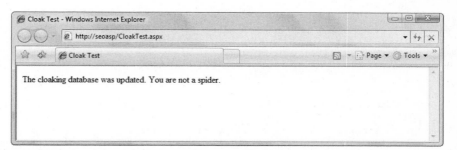

Figure 11-8

11. Your `CloakData` table from the `seoasp` database was populated with search engine data when you called `Cloak.UpdateAll()`. To view the contents of this table, you can use either Visual Web Developer or SQL Server Management Studio. Using the latter, expand the Databases ➪ seoasp ➪ Tables node in Object Explorer, right-click the seouser.CloakData table entry, and select Open Table. If everything worked alright, you should see the list of IPs and user agents in your table, as shown in Figure 11-9.

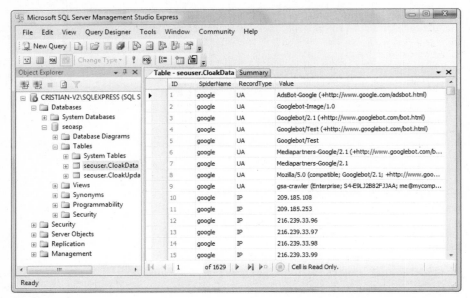

Figure 11-9

12. Now, for a more realistic example of the use of your cloaking library, create a new file in your `seoasp` project, named `CloakTest2.aspx` (or modify `CloakTest.aspx`), and type this code in it:

```
<%@ Page Language="C#" %>
<!DOCTYPE html PUBLIC "-//W3C//DTD XHTML 1.0 Transitional//EN"
"http://www.w3.org/TR/xhtml1/DTD/xhtml1-transitional.dtd">

<script runat="server">
  protected void Page_Load(object sender, EventArgs e)
  {
    // obtain the confidence level
    SpiderMatch isSpider = Cloak.IsSpider();

    // display customized output for search engines
    if (isSpider != SpiderMatch.NoMatch)
    {
      message.Text = "Tweety and Sylvester";
      image.Visible = false;
    }
    else
      image.ImageUrl = "http://seoasp/Images/tweety.jpg";
  }
</script>

<html xmlns="http://www.w3.org/1999/xhtml" >
<head id="Head1" runat="server">
  <title>Cloak Test 2</title>
</head>
```

```
<body>
  <form id="form1" runat="server">
    <asp:Literal runat="server" id="message" />
    <asp:Image runat="server" id="image" />
  </form>
</body>
```

13. Create a folder named Images in your seoasp folder, and copy the tweety.jpg image from the code download of the book to this folder.

14. Load http://seoasp/CloakTest2.aspx. Because you're not a search engine, you will be shown the picture of Tweety and Sylvester, as shown in Figure 11-1.

15. The simplest way to test what happens if you're a search engine is to add your local IP to the simple_cloak table. Use SQL Server Express Manager to connect to your seoasp database, and execute the following query:

```
INSERT INTO CloakData (SpiderName, RecordType, Value)
VALUES ('localtest', 'IP', '127.0.0.1')
```

16. Load http://seoasp/CloakTest2.aspx again. This time the script will think you're a search engine, and will output the text "Tweety and Sylvester" instead of the picture, as shown in Figure 11-2.

Everything seems to be working great, so what happened? Implementing cloaking is basically a three-step process.

First, you needed to prepare the cloaking database and the cloaking classes. The CloakData table stores data about search engine IPs and user agents, and the CloakUpdate table stores data about the last database update. You use this latter table to store the time and version of your last update.

Second, you need to decide what kind of output to display to search engines, and what output to send for the other kinds of clients. Note that in our case we displayed some text instead of a picture, but this shouldn't be taken as a generally recommended practice. How and whether you implement cloaking, if at all, strictly depends on the needs of your web site.

Finally, after you've decided what to show to your search engines, you simply need to use the Cloak class to detect when your visitor is a search engine. The Cloak.IsSpider() methods return a value of the SpiderMatch enum, which reflects the details of the spider match. The enum has four possible values:

- ❏ SpiderMatch.NoMatch is used to specify that neither the user agent nor IP matches that of a spider

- ❏ SpiderMatch.MatchUA is used when the user agent is that of a spider

- ❏ SpiderMatch.MatchIP is used when the IP is that of a spider

- ❏ SpiderMatch.MatchUAandIP is used when both the user agent and the IP are those of a spider

In our demo we assumed the visitor was a search engine when the confidence was different than SpiderMatch.NoMatch, but in production you should assert that the confidence be SpiderMatch .MatchIP or SpiderMatch.MatchUAandIP because the user agent value is easily manipulated, whereas the IP is not.

Before moving on to see some examples where cloaking can help, let's quickly analyze the code that you've written, and the database structures you've created in this exercise. You started by creating the `CloakData` table, which stores data regarding the spider user agent names and IPs.

The `ID` column is an `IDENTITY` column, with an identity seed of 1 and an identity increment of 1, specified as `IDENTITY(1, 1)`. This means that when creating the first record in the table the automatically generated ID will be 1, and on each new record a new ID will be generated by increasing the last generated value by 1. It's also worth noting the `RecordType` column, which uses a `CHECK` constraint to ensure that it can only contain two values: `UA` (for user agent entries) and `IP` (for IP entries).

```
CREATE TABLE CloakData (
   ID INT IDENTITY(1,1) PRIMARY KEY NOT NULL,
   SpiderName VARCHAR(255) NOT NULL DEFAULT '',
   RecordType CHAR(2) NOT NULL DEFAULT 'UA' CHECK(RecordType IN ('UA','IP')) ,
   Value VARCHAR(255) NOT NULL
);
```

The `Value` column stores the IP or the user agent, and `SpiderName` contains the name of the search engine. Sample values from the `CloakData` table can be seen in Figure 11-9. Because most of the queries on `CloakData` are based on the `Value` field, we then added an index on this field:

```
CREATE INDEX CloakValueIndex ON CloakData(Value);
```

If you're a database expert, you may have noticed that the structure of `CloakData` *could be improved. For example, the spider names, which are currently repeated in the* `SpiderName` *column, could be taken to a separate table. But for the purposes of our cloaking library, we consider that it's most beneficial to keep our table structure similar to that downloaded from* `iplists.com`.

The other table you've created is `CloakUpdate`, which contains two fields: `Version` and `UpdatedOn`. This table will be populated with a single record, where `Version` is the spider data version downloaded from `iplists.com`, and `UpdatedOn` is the date and time of the latest database update:

```
CREATE TABLE CloakUpdate (
   Version VARCHAR(255) NOT NULL PRIMARY KEY,
   UpdatedOn DATETIME NOT NULL
);
```

Our code will use this data to avoid downloading the data from `iplists.com` more than once per week, or when we already have the latest version.

After creating the data tables, you've written a few stored procedures that work with these tables. We consider the code in most of these procedures is simple enough and doesn't deserve closer attention. We'll only look at `CloakCheckIP`, which has a couple of twists. This procedure receives as parameter an IP value, and the name of a spider. It must return the number of records in `CloakData` that match the supplied IP and spider name. Here is again the code of that stored procedure, with the conditions that perform the match highlighted:

```
CREATE PROCEDURE CloakCheckIP
   (@IPValue VARCHAR(255),
    @SpiderName VARCHAR(255) = '')
AS
```

```
SELECT COUNT(*) FROM CloakData
WHERE RecordType = 'IP'
AND (Value = @IPValue OR Value LIKE @IPValue + '.%')
AND (@SpiderName = '' OR SpiderName = @SpiderName)
```

Let's analyze the conditions in the WHERE clause, one at a time. The meaning of the condition WHERE RecordType = 'IP' is obvious, however the following ones need to be explained. Regarding the IP value, the cloak database contains both complete IPs, such as 216.239.33.96, but also IP prefixes, such as 72.30.9. In the latter case, any IP that has that prefix, such as 72.30.9.55, is probably a spider.

To check that the IP received as parameter matches one of the IP prefixes stored in the database, we use the LIKE operator, and the % wildcard. This wildcard matches any string of characters, so we can successfully use it to check if a string is the prefix of another string. The following condition could be used to match both complete IPs and IP prefixes: Value LIKE @IPValue + '%'.

Here however, our condition looks a bit more complicated than that because we wanted to guard against a potential problem, albeit one that is unlikely to happen too often. The preceding condition would make 72.30.9 be a match for IPs like 72.30.9x.yyy, which is incorrect. Although when compared as strings the former IP is indeed a prefix of the latter, when compared as IPs, the third number of the IP should be identical. To avoid such problems, for a database IP to be considered a match for the supplied IP, it should be either identical to the supplied IP, or be a prefix by appending a dot: Value = @IPValue OR Value LIKE @IPValue + '.%'.

The database stored procedures are accessed by the methods of the CloakDb class. Each method in the CloakDb class has a corresponding stored procedure (and vice versa), except createCommand(), which is a helper method for the other methods of the class. createCommand() creates a database connection object using the connection data read from Web.config, then creates a command object, configures it to work with stored procedures, and finally returns this object. Here is again the code of this method for your convenience, with the significant parts highlighted:

```
// creates and prepares a new SqlCommand object on a new connection
private static SqlCommand createCommand(string connectionName)
{
  // obtain the database connection string
  string connectionString =
ConfigurationManager.ConnectionStrings[connectionName].ConnectionString;

  // obtain a database specific connection object
  SqlConnection conn = new SqlConnection(connectionString);

  // create a database specific command object
  SqlCommand comm = conn.CreateCommand();

  // set the command type to stored procedure
  comm.CommandType = CommandType.StoredProcedure;

  // return the initialized command object
  return comm;
}
```

ADO.NET

This is the first time in this book when you work with ADO.NET. Though we can't provide a tutorial for this technology, we're explaining the general principles here so that you can follow the exercise. ADO.NET contains more groups of classes that can be used to interact with various kinds of databases. The names of these classes are prefixed with the data provider they work with.

When interacting with SQL Server, you use those classes whose name start with `Sql`, and are located in the `System.Data.SqlClient` namespace, such as `SqlConnection`, `SqlCommand`, `SqlParameter`, and so on. Other supported prefixes include `Oracle`, `OleDb`, and `Odbc`. Most existing database systems support the OLE DB and/or ODBC interfaces, but whenever a native interface is supported, such as that for SQL Server or Oracle, that should be used instead.

It's worth knowing that ADO.NET 2.0 even introduced a number of generic classes, whose prefix is `Db`, and that can be used to dynamically use the correct data provider depending on the query string specified without losing any performance, but we didn't go into these details to keep our code to the point. You can find practical examples on how to use these generic classes on Cristian's ASP.NET 2.0 E-Commerce book, or other ASP.NET 2.0 or ADO.NET 2.0 books.

In our exercise we've used these ADO.NET 2.0 classes:

❑   `SqlConnection` represents a connection to the database.

❑   `SqlCommand` is used to execute a SQL query or a stored procedure using an existing connection.

❑   `SqlParameter` represents a parameter you can attach to a `SqlCommand` whose `CommandText` property is set to a stored procedure or a parameterized query that needs that parameter.

In the `createCommand()` method we create a `SqlConnection` object and an associated `SqlCommand` object, and we configure the `SqlCommand` object to work with stored procedures by setting its `CommandType` property to `CommandType.StoredProcedure`. This way, when we later set its `CommandText` property, it will know that the string of that property represents the name of a stored procedure that needs to be executed, instead of the code of a SQL query, which is the default.

Any database operation, including that of executing stored procedures or queries, implies three steps: opening the database connection, executing one or more commands that use that connection, and finally closing the connection. It's recommended to open the connection just before you want to execute the command and closing it immediately afterwards, for performance reasons: open connections consume resources on the database server.

The `SqlCommand` object has four methods whose names start with `Execute` that can be used to execute your queries or stored procedures:

❑   `ExecuteNonQuery()` is used to execute a query that doesn't return any records, such as an `INSERT`, `UPDATE`, or `DELETE` operation. It returns the number of rows affected, so that you can find how many rows your query inserted, updated, or deleted.

❑ ExecuteScalar() is used to execute a SELECT query or a stored procedure that returns a single value. We use this method to execute the CloakCheckUA and CloakCheckIP stored procedures, which return the number of records that contain a match for the specified user agent or IP. If the stored procedure or query executed with ExecuteScalar() return a set of data, then the first column of the first row is taken as the return value.

❑ ExecuteReader() is used to execute a SELECT query or a stored procedure that returns a result set formed of more rows and/or more columns. It returns a SqlDataReader object, which is a forward-only, read-only cursor that parses the results. In our examples, we load the SqlDataReader into a DataTable object, which reads its data and persists it for further manipulation.

The methods in CloakDb use the SqlCommand object returned by createCommand() to execute the stored procedures. The code, albeit a little bit lengthy, is pretty straightforward. It's particularly interesting to note the try-finally block we've used to execute the command. In .NET, you can use try-catch-finally blocks to catch exceptions raised when errors happen. When the catch block isn't present, the exception isn't caught, but the finally block is always executed. We use this system to ensure the database connection always gets closed as soon as possible, even when an error occurs when executing the stored procedure.

```
try { command.ExecuteNonQuery(); }
finally { command.Connection.Close(); }
```

The Cloak.cs file contains the SpiderMatch enum and the Cloak class. You already know that SpiderMatch is an enumeration that contains the spider-matching possibilities. Here is the code again:

```
public enum SpiderMatch
{
  NoMatch, // neither the user agent or IP matches that of a spider
  MatchUA, // the user agent is that of a spider
  MatchIP, // the IP is that of a spider
  MatchUAandIP // both the user agent and the IP are those of a spider
}
```

The Cloak class is the most interesting of all, mostly because it's meant to be used from scripts that require cloaking functionality. The public methods of this class were described before the exercise. Their code is quite self-explanatory.

The only method that deserves more attention is UpdateAll(), which updates the spider data using the information from iplists.com. In order not to abuse the resources of iplists.com, this method doesn't perform updates more frequently than once a week:

```
// updates cloak data; returns true if an update has been performed
public static bool UpdateAll()
{
  // read the version and the update date from the database
  string dbVersion = "";
```

```
DateTime dbUpdatedOn = new DateTime();
CloakDb.GetLastUpdate(ref dbVersion, ref dbUpdatedOn);

// abort if the database was updated sooner than 7 days ago
if (DateTime.Now - new TimeSpan(7, 0, 0, 0) < dbUpdatedOn) return false;
```

The method also reads the IP lists version number from `http://www.iplists.com/nw/version.php`. In case the version number recorded in the database is the same as the version number provided by `iplists.com`, we stop the update:

```
// read the latest cloak version published by iplists
WebRequest request = HttpWebRequest.Create(
  "http://www.iplists.com/nw/version.php");
Stream responseStream = request.GetResponse().GetResponseStream();
StreamReader reader = new StreamReader(responseStream);
string latestVersion = reader.ReadLine();

// abort if we alredy have the last version of the database
if (dbVersion == latestVersion) return false;
```

Note that this code isn't bulletproof. If you intend to use it in production, it may be worth adding more advanced error handling and reporting techniques. It's also worthwhile to point out that reading web data using the `WebRequest` class, as shown here, might fail if executed behind a proxy server, in which case the `WebProxy` class should be used to pass credentials and such to the proxy server.

`UpdateAll()` uses a private helper method named `updateSpiderData()` to load the data of a spider into our database. This method uses regular expressions to parse the input text and extract each IP record. The code isn't trivial, but it's also not overly complex either, so we'll leave understanding it for you as an exercise.

Cloaking Case Studies

Following are a few typical scenarios where cloaking could be used:

❑ Rendering text images as text

❑ Redirecting excluded content to a non-excluded equivalent

❑ Feeding subscription-based content only to the spider (*New York Times* example)

❑ Using cloaking to disable URL-based session handling for spiders

Rendering Images as Text

Unfortunately, as discussed in Chapter 6, the use of graphics containing text is detrimental to search engine optimization. The reasoning is simple — search engines cannot read the graphics contained by text. So one obvious ethical use of cloaking would be to detect if a user agent is a spider, and replace the images with the text included by the said image. Using the cloaking classes presented in this chapter, it would be implemented as follows:

```
if (Cloak.IsSpider() == SpiderMatch.MatchIP)
{
```

```
  // display text for spiders
}
else
{
  // display image for human visitors
}
```

We will note, however, that sIFR (presented in Chapter 6) is likely a better solution to this problem for text headings, because it does not entail the same risk.

Redirecting Excluded Content

As discussed in Chapter 5, if you have, for example, a product in three categories, it will usually result in two almost identical pages with three different URLs. This is a fundamental duplicate content problem. In Chapter 3 we suggested the concept of a "primary category," and then proceeded to exclude the non-primary pages using robots.txt or meta-exclusion. The cloaking variation is to simply 301 redirect all non-primary pages to the primary page if the user agent is a spider.

Feeding Subscription-Based Content Only to Spiders

This is the *New York Times* example. In this case, the code would detect if a user agent is a spider, then echo either a substring of the content if the user agent is human, or the entire content if it is a spider. Using the cloaking toolkit in this chapter, it would be implemented as follows:

```
if (Cloak.IsSpider() == SpiderMatch.MatchUAandIP)
{
  // display full content
}
else
{
  // display partial content
}
```

Implementing Geo-Targeting

Geo-targeting isn't very different than cloaking — so you'll probably feel a little deja-vu as you read this section. When implementing geo-targeting, we must find the geographical location of the user depending on its IP address, and feed it with content that is customized depending the location. To associate IPs with geographical locations, we'll use the free geo-target database provided by MaxMind (http://www.maxmind.com/).

After creating the database table — GeoTargetData — you'll create a class named GeoTarget that includes the necessary geo-targeting features, supported by another class named GeoTargetDb, and a stored procedure.

The whole solution is simpler than the cloaking one because this time we're not implementing an updating mechanism. Because the geo-targeting database isn't likely to change as frequently as search engine spider data (and the liabilities associated with being incorrect are lesser), in this case you won't implement an automatic update feature. Instead, the exercise assumes that you'll populate your database with geo-targeting data once, and then update it periodically yourself. Also, we don't check the visitor's user agent, because that isn't a factor anymore.

The GeoTarget class contains three methods to be used by an application:

❑ GetRegionCode() returns the country code of the current visitor.

❑ GetRegionCode(string ip) returns the country code of that IP.

❑ IsRegion(string regionCode) receives a region code, and returns a Boolean value that specifies if the current visitor is from that region.

❑ IsRegion(string regionCode, string ip) returns a Boolean value that specifies if ip is from the country with the code specified by regionCode.

At the end of the exercise you'll test your geo-targeting library by displaying a geo-targeted welcome message to your visitor. A person from the United States would get the greeting that's shown in Figure 11-10, and a person from Romania would be shown the message that appears in Figure 11-11.

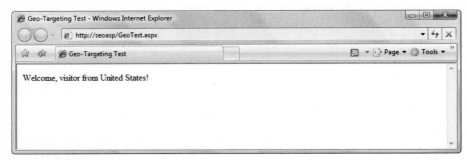

Figure 11-10

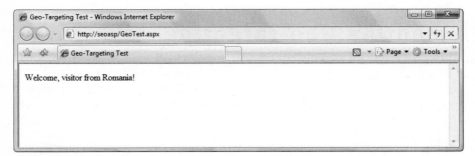

Figure 11-11

Put this to work in the following exercise.

Implementing Geo-Targeting

1. Connect to your `seoasp` database, as you did in the previous exercise, and execute the following SQL command. It will create the `GeoTargetData` table:

```
CREATE TABLE GeoTargetData (
  StartIpText VARCHAR(15) NOT NULL,
  EndIpText VARCHAR(15) NOT NULL,
  StartIpNumeric BIGINT NOT NULL,
  EndIpNumeric BIGINT NOT NULL,
  CountryCode CHAR(2) NOT NULL,
  CountryName VARCHAR(50) NOT NULL,
  PRIMARY KEY(StartIpText, EndIpText));

CREATE INDEX NumericIpIndex ON GeoTargetData(StartIpNumeric, EndIpNumeric);

CREATE INDEX CountryCodeIndex ON GeoTargetData(CountryCode);
```

2. To be able to create and execute the next stored procedure, `GeoTargetImport`, the user needs `BULK OPERATIONS` privileges. To grant this privilege to the `seouser` account, use SQL Server Management Studio to log in as administrator into your SQL Server instance. If you're the one who installed SQL Server, logging in using Windows Authentication should do. Then open a new query window, make sure the current database is `master`, and execute this statement:

```
GRANT ADMINISTER BULK OPERATIONS TO seouser;
```

3. Continue by creating the following stored procedures:

```
CREATE PROCEDURE GeoTargetImport
AS
-- Clear the GeoTargetData table
DELETE FROM GeoTargetData
-- Load new data into GeoTargetData
BULK INSERT GeoTargetData
FROM 'C:\seoasp\GeoTargetData\GeoIPCountryWhois.csv'
WITH (FORMATFILE='C:\seoasp\GeoTargetData\GeoIPCountryWhois.fmt');

CREATE PROCEDURE GeoTargetGetRegion
  (@IP VARCHAR(15))
AS
SELECT CountryCode
FROM GeoTargetData
WHERE StartIpNumeric <= @IP AND EndIpNumeric >= @IP;
```

4. Create a folder named `GeoTargetData` in your `seoasp` folder. Then download http://www.maxmind.com/download/geoip/database/GeoIPCountryCSV.zip, and unzip the file in the `GeoTargetData` folder you just created. You should end up with a file named `GeoIPCountryWhois.csv` in your `GeoTargetData` folder.

Note that we're not including the `GeoIPCountryWhois.csv` file in the book's code download. You need to download and unzip that file for yourself even when using the code download.

5. In your `GeoTargetData` folder, create a file named `GeoIPCountryWhois.fmt`, and type this content in it. This is a file that specifies the format in which the data of `GeoIPCountryWhois.csv` is stored.

```
9.0
6
1       SQLCHAR     0       15      "\",\""     1       StartIPText         ""
2       SQLCHAR     0       15      "\",\""     2       EndIPText           ""
3       SQLCHAR     0       15      "\",\""     3       StartIPNumeric      ""
4       SQLCHAR     0       15      "\",\""     4       EndIPNumeric        ""
5       SQLCHAR     0       15      "\",\""     5       CountryCode         ""
6       SQLCHAR     0       50      "\"\n\""    6       CountryName         ""
```

6. Add the following connection string to `Web.config`:

```
<connectionStrings>
  <add name="CloakDatabase"
connectionString="Server=(local)\SqlExpress;User=seouser;Password=seomaster;Database=
seoasp" />
  <add name="GeoTargetDatabase"
connectionString="Server=(local)\SqlExpress;User=seouser;Password=seomaster;Database=
seoasp" />
</connectionStrings>
```

7. Start SQL Server Management Studio Express again, this time logging in using seouser/seomaster. Then open a new query window, and execute your new stored procedure. This way you test that it works fine, and you also populate your database with geotargeting data. Because the command populates your database with about 65,000 records, it will take a couple of seconds (or so) to execute.

```
exec GeoTargetImport
```

To test that the data was imported correctly, you can open the `GeoTargetData` table in SQL Server Management Studio. You should see records as shown in Figure 11-12.

8. In your `seoasp` project, add a class file named `GeoTargetDb` to the `App_Code` folder, with this code:

```
using System;
using System.Web;
using System.Data;
using System.Data.SqlClient;
using System.Configuration;

/// <summary>
/// Summary description for GeoTargetDb
/// </summary>
public class GeoTargetDb
{
  public static string GetRegion(long longIp)
  {
    // create a SqlCommand object with a connection to the cloak database
    SqlCommand command = createCommand("GeoTargetDatabase");

    // set the name of the stored procedure to execute
    command.CommandText = "GeoTargetGetRegion";
```

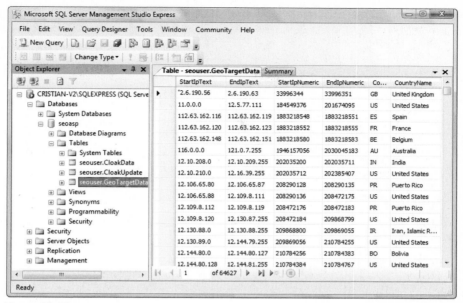

Figure 11-12

```csharp
      // @IP
      SqlParameter p = new SqlParameter("@IP", longIp);
      command.Parameters.Add(p);

      // execute the stored procedure
      command.Connection.Open();
      string countryCode;

      try { countryCode = command.ExecuteScalar().ToString(); }
      catch { countryCode = ""; }
      finally { command.Connection.Close(); }

      // return the country code
      return countryCode;
    }

  // Creates and prepares a new SqlCommand object on a new connection
  private static SqlCommand createCommand(string connectionName)
  {
    // obtain the database connection string
    string connectionString =
ConfigurationManager.ConnectionStrings[connectionName].ConnectionString;

    // obtain a database specific connection object
    SqlConnection conn = new SqlConnection(connectionString);

    // create a database specific command object
    SqlCommand comm = conn.CreateCommand();

    // set the command type to stored procedure
    comm.CommandType = CommandType.StoredProcedure;
```

```
      // return the initialized command object
      return comm;
   }
}
```

9. Also in `App_Code`, create `GeoTarget.cs` with this code:

```
using System;
using System.Web;

/// <summary>
/// Summary description for GeoTarget
/// </summary>
public class GeoTarget
{
  // returns the region code of the current visitor
  public static string GetRegionCode()
  {
    string visitorIp = HttpContext.Current.Request["REMOTE_ADDR"];
    return GetRegionCode(visitorIp);
  }

  // returns the region code of the IP
  public static string GetRegionCode(string ip)
  {
    string[] ipp = ip.Split(new char[] { '.' });

    long longIp = 16777216 * long.Parse(ipp[0]) + 65536 * long.Parse(ipp[1]) +
                  256 * long.Parse(ipp[2]) + long.Parse(ipp[3]);

    return GeoTargetDb.GetRegion(longIp);
  }

  // verifies if the current visitor is from the specified region
  public static bool IsRegionCode(string regionCode)
  {
    return (GetRegionCode() == regionCode);
  }

  // verifies if the provided IP is from the specified region
  public static bool IsRegionCode(string regionCode, string ip)
  {
    return (GetRegionCode(ip) == regionCode);
  }
}
```

10. To test these classes, create a Web Form named `GeoTest.aspx` in the root of your project, and edit it like this:

```
<%@ Page Language="C#" %>
<!DOCTYPE html PUBLIC "-//W3C//DTD XHTML 1.0 Transitional//EN"
"http://www.w3.org/TR/xhtml1/DTD/xhtml1-transitional.dtd">

<script runat="server">
```

```
protected void Page_Load(object sender, EventArgs e)
{
  // display geo-targeted welcome message
  if (GeoTarget.IsRegionCode("RO"))
  {
    message.Text = "Welcome, visitor from Romania!";
  }
  else if (GeoTarget.IsRegionCode("US"))
  {
    message.Text = "Welcome, visitor from United States!";
  }
  else if (GeoTarget.GetRegionCode() ==  String.Empty)
  {
    message.Text = "Welcome, visitor! We couldn't find your country code!";
  }
  else
  {
    message.Text = "Welcome, visitor! Your country code is: " +
GeoTarget.GetRegionCode();
  }
}
</script>

<html xmlns="http://www.w3.org/1999/xhtml" >
<head id="Head1" runat="server">
  <title>Geo-Targeting Test</title>
</head>
<body>
  <form id="form1" runat="server">
    <asp:Literal runat="server" id="message" />
  </form>
</body>
</html>
```

11. Now, if Jaimie from the United States loaded this script, he would get the output shown in Figure 11-10. If Cristian loaded the same script, he would get the output that was shown in Figure 11-11.

Note that when loading the script from your local machine, your IP is 127.0.0.1, which doesn't belong to any country — so the message you'd get is "Welcome, visitor! We couldn't find your country code!" To test your region, you need to supply your network IP address as the second parameter of GeoTarget.IsRegionCode(), *or as the first parameter to* GeoTarget.GetRegionCode().

In this exercise you presented different output depending on the country the visitor is from. Another popular use of geo-targeting involves redirecting visitors to localized web sites depending on their region. This example is analogous to the example of Google's practice of redirecting visitors from foreign countries from www.google.com to their respective local version of Google.

Here is an example of implementing this feature, using your simple geo-targeting library. To redirect French users to http://fr.example.com, you'd need to do something like this:

```
If (GeoTarget.IsRegion("FR"))
{
  Response.Redirect("Location: http://fr.example.com");
}
```

297

Summary

We hope you've had fun going through the exercises in this chapter! Although cloaking is a potential minefield in search engine optimization, we have shown some of its relevant uses. Geo-targeting, on the other hand, is a unanimously accepted practice that you can use to offer a more pleasant browsing experience to your international visitors. Both, in turn, rely on IP-delivery technology to function.

12

Foreign Language SEO

Incidentally, the authors of this book are from two different countries. Jaimie is from the United States and speaks English, along with some Hebrew and Spanish. Cristian is from Romania and speaks Romanian, English, and some French. Why does this matter? There are concerns — both from a language angle, as well as some interesting technical caveats when one decides to target foreign users with search engine marketing. This chapter reviews some of the most pertinent factors in foreign language search engine optimization.

> *As far as this book is concerned, "foreign" refers to anything other than the United States because this book is published in the United States. We consider the UK to be foreign as well; and UK English is a different language dialect, at least academically.*

The Internet is a globalized economy. Web sites can be hosted and contain anything that the author would like. Users are free to peruse pages or order items from any country. Regardless, for the most part, a user residing in the United States would like to see widgets from the United States. And a user in Romania would like to see widgets from Romania. It is also likely that a user in England would prefer to see products from England, not the United States — regardless of the language being substantially the same. There are some exceptions, but in general, to enhance user experience, a search engine may treat web sites from the same region in the same language as the user preferentially.

Foreign Language Optimization Tips

Needless to say, Internet marketing presents many opportunities; and nothing stops a search engine marketer from targeting customers from other countries and/or languages. However, he or she should be aware of a few things, and use all applicable cues to indicate properly to the search engine which language and region a site is focused on.

First of all, if you aim at a foreign market, it is essential to employ a competent copywriting service to author or translate your content to a particular foreign language. He or she should know how to translate for the *specific* market you are targeting. American Spanish, for example, is somewhat different than Argentine Spanish. Even proper translation may be riddled with problems. Foreign language search behavior often differs by dialect, and using the common terminology is key.

Indicating Language and Region

A webmaster should use the `lang` attribute in a meta tag, or inside an enclosing `span` or `div` tag in HTML. Search engines may be able to detect language reasonably accurately, but this tag also provides additional geographical information. The language codes `es-mx`, `es-us`, and `es-es` represent Spanish from Mexico, the United States, and Spain, respectively. This is helpful, because a language dialect and region cannot be detected easily, if at all, just by examining the actual copy. Here's an example:

```
Use '<span lang="es-us">CONTENT</span>' to indicate language in a particular text
region.
```

or:

```
Use '<meta lang="es-us"> in the header ("<head>") section of the page to indicate
language of the entire page.
```

Table 12-1 lists a few examples of languages and region modifiers.

Table 12-1

Language	Dialects
English	en-AU (Australia), en-CA (Canada), en-GB (UK), en-US (United States), en-HK (Hong Kong)
German	de-AT (Austria), de-BE (Belgium), de-CH (Switzerland), de-DE (Germany)
French	fr-CA (Canada), fr-CH (Switzerland), fr-FR (France), fr-MC (Monaco),
Spanish	es-AR (Argentina), es-CU (Cuba), es-ES (Spain), es-MX (Mexico), es-US (United States)
Japanese	ja (Japan)

You can find a complete list at `http://www.i18nguy.com/unicode/language-identifiers.html`.

Server Location and Domain Name

Search engines sometimes also use the actual geographic location of a web server as a cue in target market identification, and hence determining rankings in that region. Therefore, it is desirable to locate your web server in the same geographic region as is targeted. It is also desirable to use the country-code domain applicable to your target country, but that is not necessary if a `.com` or `.net` domain is used.

The original domain suffixes — `.com`, `.net`, and so on — are not strictly U.S. domains and are somewhat region-agnostic. For that reason, especially if the site is in English targeting UK individuals, it becomes very important to use other cues to indicate what region the site targets. Using something other than a `.com` or `.net` should be avoided for a differing region; that is, a `.co.uk` should probably not be used for a Japanese site, despite the obvious language cues, and it certainly should not be used for an American site, which would normally lack such cues.

A server's physical location can be derived by IP using a database of IP range locations. You used such a database in the geo-targeting example from Chapter 11. In the case of a UK site hosted on a `.com` domain, it is important to check that the server is located in the UK, not just that the company has a presence in the UK. You can check the location of a netblock using the tool at `http://www.dnsstuff.com/tools/ipall.ch?domain=xxx.xxx.xxx.xxx`. Many hosting companies in the UK actually locate their servers elsewhere in Europe due to high overhead in the UK.

> *Subdomains can be used on a `.com` or a `.net` domain name as a means to locate hosting elsewhere. So instead of `http://www.example.com/uk`, `http://uk.example.com` could be used, and a separate server with a UK IP address could be employed. This is the only way to accomplish this, because subfolders on a web server must be delivered by the same IP address/network.*

Include the Address of the Foreign Location if Possible

This is an obvious factor that search engines are known to use for local search. Ideally, a web site would have the address in the footer of every page.

Dealing with Accented Letters (Diacritics)

Many languages, including Spanish and most other European languages, have accented letters. In practice, especially on American keyboards, which lack the keys necessary to generate these characters, users do not use the accented characters (that is, é vs. e). Yet some search engines, including Google, do distinguish, and they represent different words in an index, effectively.

Figure 12-1 shows a Google search on Mexico. You can access this page through `http://www.google.com/search?q=Mexico`. Figure 12-2 shows a search for México, through `http://www.google.com/search?q=M%C3%A9xico`. As you can see, the results are very different.

Google Trends also makes it clear that the two keywords have entirely different quantities of traffic, with the unaccented version winning by a landslide. This is probably because Mexico itself is also an American word, but it is clear that not all Spanish speakers use the accented spelling as well. Figure 12-3 shows the Google Trends comparison between Mexico and México, which you can reach yourself at `http://www.google.com/trends?q=Mexico%2C+M%C3%A9xico`.

URLs are particularly appropriate because it actually looks more professional to remove the accented characters, because they are encoded in the URL and look confusing — that is, `/Mexico.html` versus `/M%C3%A9xico.html`.

It may also be possible to use the unaccented characters in a misspelling in a heading, because that is normatively acceptable in some languages. The following function normalizes accented characters in Western European languages to their non-accented equivalents. It can be applied anywhere in code, including to URL functions and code at the presentation level.

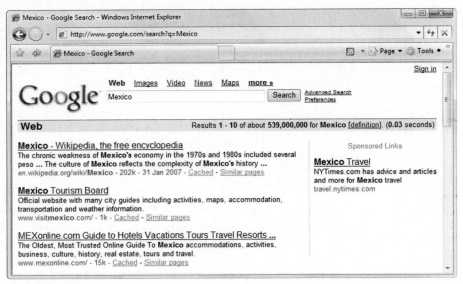

Figure 12-1

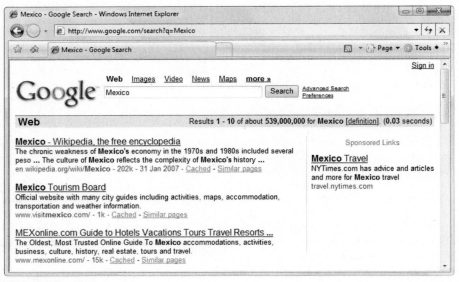

Figure 12-2

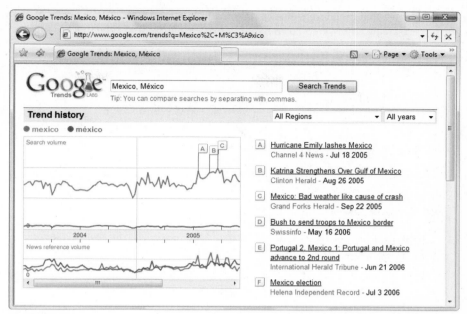

Figure 12-3

Following is a function that replaces accented characters with their non-accented equivalents. This function is a modified version of the one originally written by Michael Kaplan at `http://blogs.msdn.com/ michkap/archive/2005/02/19/376617.aspx`. The function receives as parameter a string, and returns the version of that string where the accents have been removed.

> *Make sure to seriously test such a function in your environment though. There is no definitive solution for issues that deal with character encoding, and the effect is different depending on the languages you're dealing with.*

```
private string removeDiacritics(string s)
{
  string normalizedString = s.Normalize(NormalizationForm.FormD);
  StringBuilder stringBuilder = new StringBuilder();

  foreach (char c in normalizedString)
    if (CharUnicodeInfo.GetUnicodeCategory(c) != UnicodeCategory.NonSpacingMark)
      stringBuilder.Append(c);

  return stringBuilder.ToString();
}
```

To quickly test-drive this function, we've created the following ASP.NET Web Form. If you want to add it to your project, create a new Web Form named `Foreign.aspx`, and type this code in it:

```
<%@ Page Language="C#" %>
<%@ Import Namespace="System.Globalization" %>

<!DOCTYPE html PUBLIC "-//W3C//DTD XHTML 1.0 Transitional//EN"
"http://www.w3.org/TR/xhtml1/DTD/xhtml1-transitional.dtd">

<script runat="server">
  protected void Page_Load(object sender, EventArgs e)
  {
    string myString = "México & Mexico";

    // HTML Encode
    originalLabel.Text = HttpUtility.HtmlEncode(myString);

    // HTML Encode again, to display the HTML code in the web browser
    htmlEncodedLabel.Text = HttpUtility.HtmlEncode(originalLabel.Text);

    // URL Encode
    urlEncodedLabel.Text = HttpUtility.UrlEncode(myString);

    // Remove character accents
    noDiacriticsLabel.Text = removeDiacritics(myString);
  }

  // function for removing diacritics inspired by Michael Kaplan's article at
  // http://blogs.msdn.com/michkap/archive/2005/02/19/376617.aspx
  private string removeDiacritics(string s)
  {
    string normalizedString = s.Normalize(NormalizationForm.FormD);
    StringBuilder stringBuilder = new StringBuilder();

    foreach (char c in normalizedString)
      if (CharUnicodeInfo.GetUnicodeCategory(c) != UnicodeCategory.NonSpacingMark)
        stringBuilder.Append(c);

    return stringBuilder.ToString();
  }
</script>

<html xmlns="http://www.w3.org/1999/xhtml">
<head id="Head1" runat="server">
  <title>ASP.NET Encoding Test</title>
</head>
<body>
  <form id="form1" runat="server">
    <p>
      Original string: <asp:Label ID="originalLabel" runat="server" />
    </p>
```

```
    <p>
      URL Encoded: <asp:Label ID="urlEncodedLabel" runat="server" />
    </p>
    <p>
      HTML Encoded: <asp:Label ID="htmlEncodedLabel" runat="server" />
    </p>
    <p>
      No diacritics: <asp:Label ID="noDiacriticsLabel" runat="server" />
    </p>
  </form>
</body>
</html>
```

Loading the file in your web browser should load a page like that shown in Figure 12-4.

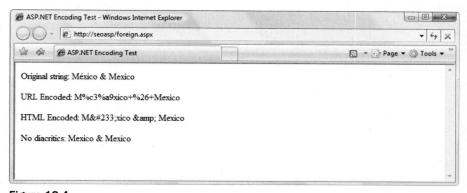

Figure 12-4

This little exercise not only shows how to simply alter the accented characters, but is also a simple demonstration for the `UrlEncode()` and `HtmlEncode()` methods of the `HttpUtility` class.

Foreign Language Spamming

Google in particular has begun to focus more of its efforts on combating the foreign language spamming that has been going on, mostly with impunity. Matt Cutts stated in his blog at `http://www.mattcutts .com/blog/seo-mistakes-spam-in-other-languages/` that "I expect Google to pay a lot more attention to spam in other languages, whether it be German, French, Italian, Spanish, Chinese, or any other language. For example, I have no patience for keyword-stuffed doorway pages that do JavaScript redirects, no matter what the language."

We expect all search engines to follow. Spanish, in particular, is the next front for search engine marketing, as well as Chinese; it would be wise, therefore, to avoid any spamming techniques in any language, tempting though it may be. It may work now, but it will definitely be less successful in the future.

Summary

Ironically, one of the effects of globalization is the need for better localization efforts. The search engine optimization strategies when dealing with foreign language web sites aren't much different than with dealing with .coms. Still, there are a few specific issues to keep in mind, and this chapter introduced you to the most important of them.

13

Coping with
Technical Issues

This chapter deals with a few common technical issues that relate to SEO efforts:

- ❏ Unreliable hosting or DNS
- ❏ Changing hosting providers
- ❏ Cross-linking
- ❏ Split testing
- ❏ Broken links (and how to detect them)

Unreliable Web Hosting or DNS

It is common sense that if a web site is down it cannot get spidered, but we'll state it regardless: *When a site is down, it cannot get spidered.* And when your domain's designated DNS is down, your site cannot get spidered either — even if your web server is actually up. Reliable hosting *and* DNS, then, is critical to your web site's well-being. A web site that is down will irritate users and result directly in fewer users visiting your web site. It may also reflect badly on your business, and users may not be back. Likewise, if a search engine spider visits your web site and it does not respond after quite a few unsuccessful attempts, it may result in your web site getting dropped from the index. For this reason we recommend cutting costs elsewhere.

This underscores the need to find reliable hosting. In a field that is ultra-competitive, many web hosting providers choose to provide large amounts of bandwidth and features while compromising service and support. Two dollars per month for hosting will likely get you just that — two dollars worth of web hosting. A lot can be gleaned from the list compiled by NetCraft of "Hosting Providers' Network Performance." You can find this information at `http://uptime.netcraft.com/perf/reports/Hosters`. There is also an abundance of specific information, including praises and gripes at WebHostingTalk — `http://www.webhostingtalk.com`.

Most of the time, users opt to use a web hosting provider's DNS. This may be wise, because they may need to alter DNS records in order to move you to another server with another IP if the server your web site is located on fails. However, domain providers (Network Solutions, GoDaddy, and so on) have more recently begun to offer free managed DNS services as well. If you use managed DNS, the hosting provider will not be able to change your domain's records to reflect the new IP, and your site will be down as a result. For this reason, we do not recommend using managed DNS unless your provider is aware of it, and knows to notify you, so that you can change the records yourself to reflect the new IP.

Changing Hosting Providers

Should the need exist to change hosting providers, the process must be completed in the proper order. Not doing so may result in a time window where your site is unreachable; and this is clearly not desirable, from both a general *and* SEO perspective. The focus of this elaborate process is to prevent both users and search engines from perceiving that the site is gone — or in the case of virtual hosting, possibly seeing the wrong site.

Virtual hosting means that more than one web site is hosted on one IP. This is commonplace, because the world would run out of IPs very quickly if every web site had its own IP. The problem arises when you cancel service at your old web hosting provider and a spider still thinks your site is located at the old IP. In this case, it may see the wrong site or get a 404 error; and as you suspect, this is not desirable.

The proper approach involves having your site hosted at both hosting providers for a little while. When your site is 100% functional at the new hosting provider, DNS records should then be updated. If you are using a managed DNS service, simply change the "A" records to reflect the new web server's IP address. This change should be reflected almost instantly, and you can cancel the web hosting service at the old provider shortly thereafter. If you are using your old web hosting provider's DNS, you should change to the new hosting provider's DNS. This change may take up to 48 hours to be fully reflected throughout the Internet. Once 48 hours have passed, you can cancel your service at the old hosting provider.

You do not have to follow these procedures exactly; the basic underlying concept is that there is a window of time where both users and spiders may still think your site is located at the old hosting provider's IP address. For this reason, you should only cancel after you are certain that that window of time has elapsed.

One helpful hint to ease the process of moving your domain to a new web hosting provider is to edit your `hosts` file to reflect the new IP on your local machine. This causes your operating system to use the value provided in the file instead of using a DNS to get an IP address for the specified domains. This functionality was also used to set up the `http://seoasp/` domain. On Windows machines, the file is located in `C:\WINDOWS\system32\drivers\etc\hosts`. Add the following lines, where "xxx.xxx.xxx.xxx" is your web site's new IP address:

```
xxx.xxx.xxx.xxx www.yourdomain.com
xxx.xxx.xxx.xxx yourdomain.com
```

This will let you access your web site at the new provider as if the DNS changes were already reflected. Simply remove the lines after you are done setting up the site on the new web hosting provider's server to verify the changes have actually propagated.

If you have concerns about this procedure, or you need help, you may want to contact your new hosting provider and ask for assistance. Explain your concerns, and hopefully they will be able to accommodate you and put your mind at ease. If they are willing to work with you, it is a good indication that they are a good hosting provider.

Cross-Linking

A typical spammer's accoutrement consists of several thousand cross-linked web sites. These sites collectively drive ad revenue from the aggregate of many usually obscure, but nevertheless queried search terms. Many sites containing many key phrases have to be created to make his spam enterprise worthwhile. Originally, many spammers hosted all of the sites from one web hosting company, and, hence, the same or similar IP addresses. Search engines caught on, and may have applied filters that devalue links exchanged between the web sites within similar IP ranges. This made it much harder to spam, because a spammer would need to host things at different ISPs to continue his enterprise.

Similarly, it has been speculated that Google in particular, because it is a registrar that does not actually sell domain names, looks at the records associated with domains. Yahoo! is also a registrar, so it may follow suit; but it actually sells domains, so the intent is less clear.

In both cases, even if you are not a spammer, and you want to cross-link, it may be advisable to obscure the relationship. Many larger web hosting companies have diverse ranges of IPs, and can satisfy your explicit request for a different range. The information that is provided to a domain registrar is up to you, but if the name and address do vary, the information must also be valid regardless. Otherwise you risk losing the domain according to ICANN policies. There is also an option for private registration, which prevents Google or Yahoo! from using an automated process to find relationships, at least. To check the registration information for a domain, use a WHOIS tool such as the one at http://www.seoegghead .com/tools/whois-search.php. Figure 13-1 shows the tool displaying the data for www.yahoo.com.

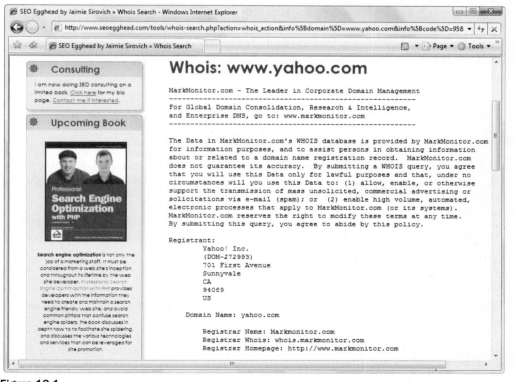

Figure 13-1

MSN Search has a useful feature that allows you to see all virtual hosts on one IP by the syntax of IP:xxx.xxx.xxx.xxx. Multiple statements can be separated by OR to request a list of a range of IPs. This lets you see who else is hosting in a range. Spam tends to travel in packs. Search engine algorithms are also aware of this. The fact that the operator exists may be a tacit admission by Microsoft that it does examine the sites in an IP range for some reason. See Figure 13-2 for an example, where we examined the sites located at 66.39.117.78.

Figure 13-2

SEO-Aware Split Testing

Often, marketers want to create several variations on content for a particular URL in the interest of observing which one converts the best. It is typically an ongoing optimization process, and many different variations may be served over time to that end. This is called *split testing*.

The problem with split testing is that, if it isn't implemented correctly, it may result in complex problems. When implementing changes on a page, there are actually three important effects to analyze:

1. The variation of the performance of the page in search results.
2. The variation in the page CTR.
3. The variation in the conversion rate for visitors that land on your page (the primary purpose of split testing).

You don't necessarily want to sacrifice CTR or rankings for higher conversion rates. But if you do split testing, it's good to be aware of these possible consequences.

This complicates matters, because it introduces other factors into the performance equation. For example, if a page converts *twice* as well, but doesn't rank at all, it may be a net loss for a web site that is driven by organic search. Therefore, you must consider search engine optimization principles when making any changes for split testing.

Ideally, all changes would be purely aesthetic. In most cases doing so would not affect the rankings or CTR of the page — which would make it easier to analyze your results. If the changes are more profound, such as changing the on-page content, the page search engine rankings can be influenced, and this must also be taken into consideration as a performance factor.

One method employed to collect data for split testing is to randomly show page A or page B and track conversion rates for each. Unfortunately, when done incorrectly, this practice can confuse search engines or raise red flags. This is the other problem with split testing. At worst, implementing this will be perceived as spamming and/or cloaking.

There are three different approaches to implement split testing:

1.   Redirect requests for a page to other pages with variations randomly.

2.   Use internal program logic to display the variations randomly.

3.   Implement temporal split testing.

The first two methods are similar in that they randomly display variations of a page. However, redirects are not ideal in this situation because they may confuse search engines, and they should be avoided. Therefore, we recommend using internal program logic. This is consistent with Matt Cutts' recommendation in his video at `http://video.google.com/videoplay?docid=1156145545372854697`.

That implies some light programming. For example, if you have five versions of a web page, `page[1..5].html`, you can use `Response.WriteFile()` to display its variations, like this:

```
protected void Page_Load(object sender, EventArgs e)
{
  // define the number of available pages
  int pageCount = 5;

  // obtain a random page number
  Random randomGenerator = new Random();
  int pageNumber = randomGenerator.Next(pageCount) + 1;

  // display
  switch (pageNumber)
  {
    case 1:
      Response.WriteFile("page1.html");
      break;

    case 2:
      Response.WriteFile("page2.html");
      break;

    case 3:
      Response.WriteFile("page3.html");
      break;
```

```
    case 4:
      Response.WriteFile("page4.html");
      break;

    case 5:
      Response.WriteFile("page5.html");
      break;
  }
}
```

In this example, a random number is generated to decide what page to display. An alternate implementation can be done using server-side includes in the `.aspx` page, using the `<!--#include file="[page_name]"-->` syntax. If the pages you want to load contain ASP.NET server-side code that needs to be executed, they need to be loaded using `Server.Transfer()`, which passes the request processing to another page without changing the URL.

The problem, regardless, is that if the pages are significantly different and served randomly, it might actually be perceived as cloaking. Matt Cutts hinted at that in the aforementioned video.

Cloaking may be used to show only one version to a particular search engine. This eliminates the problem whereby a certain version ranks better in search engines than others. It also eliminates the possibility that it will be perceived as spam *academically* (so long as you're not detected!). Yes, cloaking is being used to prevent the perception of cloaking! However, we recommend doing this with a caution that Google frowns upon it.

Either way, if you're detected, you might be sent to the corner. For more information on cloaking, read Chapter 11.

The last method, "temporal split testing," is also safe, and extremely easy to implement. Simply collect data for one time span for A (perhaps a week), and again for B. However, doing so may be less accurate and requires more time to make determinations.

So, in summary:

1. Don't ignore the organic, possibly detrimental, effects of split testing.

2. Use internal program logic or temporal-based split testing. Do not use redirects.

3. You can use cloaking to show only one version to search engines, but Google frowns upon this approach.

Detecting Broken Links

Broken links are telltale sign of a poorly designed site. The Google Webmaster Guidelines advise webmasters to "Check for broken links and correct HTML." There are a number of online tools that you can use for checking links, such as the one at `http://www.webmaster-toolkit.com/link-checker.shtml`.

However, in many cases you'll want to create your own tools for internal verification. To give you some starting advice, we'll show you how to detect a broken link, and how to follow the redirection path of a link. Once you understand how to accomplish these tasks, you'll be able to create a customized library for your own solution.

Luckily enough, making web requests and reading status codes is pretty simple with the .NET Framework: the System.Net namespace contains all the functionality you need. Typically you start by creating an HttpWebRequest instance, by providing it with the URL you want to check or read. Then you create an HttpWebResponse instance, which effectively accesses the URL and obtains the required data. Because accessing the URL can generate an exception if the URL doesn't exist, we'll wrap the necessary code in a try/catch block.

If you want to test this yourself, save the following script as CheckLink.aspx:

```
<%@ Page Language="C#" %>
<%@ Import Namespace="System.Net" %>

<!DOCTYPE html PUBLIC "-//W3C//DTD XHTML 1.0 Transitional//EN"
"http://www.w3.org/TR/xhtml1/DTD/xhtml1-transitional.dtd">

<script runat="server">
  protected void Page_Load(object sender, EventArgs e)
  {
    // the URL to start from
    string url = "http://www.seoegghead.com/does_not_exist.html";
    myOutput.Text = "URL: " + url;

    // create the request object
    HttpWebRequest request = (HttpWebRequest)HttpWebRequest.Create(url);

    // retrieve the contents
    try
    {
      // read the URL
      HttpWebResponse linkResponse = (HttpWebResponse)request.GetResponse();

      // retrieve the status code of the destination
      int statusCode = (int)linkResponse.StatusCode;
      string statusDescription = linkResponse.StatusDescription;

      // display output
      myOutput.Text += "<br />Status code: " + statusCode;
      myOutput.Text += "<br />Status description: " + statusDescription;
    }
    catch (WebException ex)
    {
      myOutput.Text += "<br />Error: " + ex.Message;
    }
  }
</script>

<html xmlns="http://www.w3.org/1999/xhtml">
<head runat="server">
  <title>Link Checker Test</title>
</head>
<body>
```

```
      <form id="form1" runat="server">
        <div>
          <asp:Literal runat="server" ID="myOutput" />
        </div>
      </form>
  </body>
  </html>
```

Note that the code has been mainly optimized for reading clarity, but it's not necessarily **customized for** performance or extensibility. Doing so would be simple, but it needs to be done in the **context of a more** complex scenario than that at hand.

Running the script would generate the output shown in Figure 13-3.

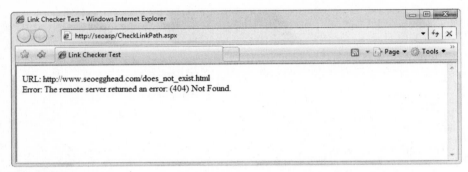

Figure 13-3

The script is simple enough. It starts by defining the destination URL in a string variable, **and it outputs** it on the screen by populating the myOutput Literal object. (Once again, don't take this **as good pro-**gramming practice in a real-world scenario.)

```
// the URL to start from
string url = "http://www.seoegghead.com/does_not_exist.html";
myOutput.Text = "URL: " + url;
```

We continue by creating the HttpWebRequest object. Creating the object is easy, using the HttpWebRequest.Create() static method. There's just one trick: the method returns a **generic** WebRequest object, which you need to explicitly cast to HttpWebRequest:

```
// create the request object
HttpWebRequest request = (HttpWebRequest)HttpWebRequest.Create(url);
```

The next step is to effectively access the destination URL. Because this process can generate **an** exception — which can happen if the destination URL returns a 404 — we're wrapping all **the code in a** try/catch block. Then we read the URL using the GetResponse() method of the HttpWebRequest class. Once again, an explicit cast is needed — this time to HttpWebResponse.

```
// retrieve the contents
try
{
```

```
// read the URL
HttpWebResponse linkResponse = (HttpWebResponse)request.GetResponse();
```

Assuming that no exception is thrown by this method call, we move on to display a few details regarding the request. Note that if the original URL returns a redirection status code, `GetResponse()` will automatically follow the redirects, and will retrieve the data of the final destination URL:

```
        // retrieve the status code of the destination
        int statusCode = (int)linkResponse.StatusCode;
        string statusDescription = linkResponse.StatusDescription;

        // display output
        myOutput.Text += "<br />Status code: " + statusCode;
        myOutput.Text += "<br />Status description: " + statusDescription;
    }
```

If the initial request generated an exception, we catch it and display the exception's details. This is the piece of code that displays the error line in Figure 13-3:

```
    catch (WebException ex)
    {
        myOutput.Text += "<br />Error: " + ex.Message;
    }
}
```

What you should know is that the `HttpWebResponse` object is quite powerful and it can give you a lot of details related to the request, without you needing to parse the headers yourself. For example, in the script you just wrote, you can read `linkResponse.ContentLength` to obtain the `Content-Length` header value. Of particular importance is its `Headers` property, which is a collection that you can use to retrieve header data that isn't accessible through other properties of the object. In the next example we'll read `linkResponse.Headers["Location"]` to obtain the value of the `Location` header.

One possible inconvenience with the `CheckLink.aspx` script is that you aren't shown any existing redirects that may happen before the final content is received. Fortunately, the `HttpWebRequest` object has a property named `AllowAutoRedirect`, which determines if redirects should be followed automatically. The default value is `true`, but if you set it to `false`, you can manually follow the redirection chain yourself.

To see this in practice, save the following piece of code as a new Web Form named `CheckLinkPath.aspx`:

```
<%@ Page Language="C#" %>
<%@ Import Namespace="System.Net" %>
<%@ Import Namespace="System.Text" %>
<%@ Import Namespace="System.IO" %>
<!DOCTYPE html PUBLIC "-//W3C//DTD XHTML 1.0 Transitional//EN"
"http://www.w3.org/TR/xhtml1/DTD/xhtml1-transitional.dtd">

<script runat="server">
  protected void Page_Load(object sender, EventArgs e)
  {
    // the URL to start from
    string url = "http://www.cristiandarie.ro/seophp.aspx";
```

```
// request object
HttpWebRequest request;

// start by assuming that the provided URL is the final URL
bool reachedDestination = true;

// don't make more than this number of requests
int maxRequests = 10;

// display data about one request at each iteration
do
{
  // initialize the destination location to null
  string location = null;

  // try to read data from the URL
  try
  {
    // make a HTTP request, without allowing autoredirects
    request = (HttpWebRequest)HttpWebRequest.Create(url);
    request.AllowAutoRedirect = false;

    // display the URL we're trying to reach
    myOutput.Text += "URL: " + url;

    // retrieve the contents
    HttpWebResponse linkResponse = (HttpWebResponse)request.GetResponse();

    // retrieve the location
    location = linkResponse.Headers["Location"];

    // display data about the URL
    string output = "";
    output += "<p>Server: " + linkResponse.Server;
    output += "<br />Content type: " + linkResponse.ContentType;
    output += "<br />Content length: " + linkResponse.ContentLength;
    output += "<br />Status code: " + (int)linkResponse.StatusCode;
    output += "<br />Status description: " + linkResponse.StatusDescription;
    if (location != null)
      output += "<br />Destination: " + location + "</p>";
    myOutput.Text += output;
  }
  catch (Exception ex)
  {
    myOutput.Text += "<br />Error: " + ex.Message;
  }

  // decide if another iteration is necessary
  if (location != null)
  {
    url = location;
    reachedDestination = false;
  }
  else
```

```
              reachedDestination = true;

            // count down to maximum number of requests
            maxRequests--;
          }
          // continue the loop until we reach the destination or reach the maximum
          // allowed number of requests
          while (!reachedDestination && maxRequests > 0);
        }
</script>

<html xmlns="http://www.w3.org/1999/xhtml">
<head id="Head1" runat="server">
  <title>Link Checker Test</title>
</head>
<body>
  <form id="form1" runat="server">
    <div>
      <asp:Literal runat="server" ID="myOutput" />
    </div>
  </form>
</body>
</html>
```

The code isn't much more complex than that of CheckLink.aspx, but a few extra variables were needed to implement following the redirection chain, and to ensure that we stop if we haven't reached a final page after a number of redirects — this is useful to avoid potential infinite loops.

At each iteration, we make sure to read the Location header. By definition, this header is used to specify a redirection destination. Executing the code as shown would generate the results that you can see in Figure 13-4.

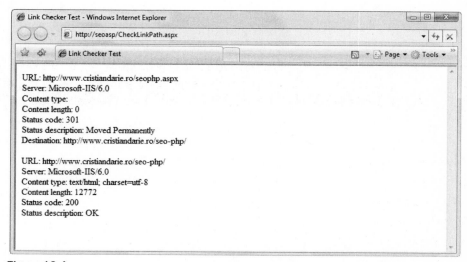

Figure 13-4

As you can see, the initial request to `http://www.cristiandarie.ro/seophp.aspx` resulted in a 301 redirect to `http://www.cristiandarie.ro/seo-php/`, which is the destination URL, with a final status code of 200.

Summary

This chapter talked about a few common technical problems that you may encounter when maintaining your web sites. You've learned about the detrimental effects of unreliable web hosting providers (and how to safely switch!), as well as the dangers of having cross-linked web sites in the same C class. You've explored safe approaches to split testing. At the end of the chapter you had your share of geek-fun, building the `LinkChecker` library. This chapter has finished covering all necessary background material. In the next chapter you build a search-engine–optimized cookie catalog. We hope you are hungry!

14

Case Study: Building an E-Commerce Store

You've come a long way in learning how to properly construct a web site with regard to search engine optimization. Now it is time to demonstrate and tie together what you have learned. In this chapter we'll work together to build an e-commerce store called "Cookie Ogre's Warehouse." This store sells all sorts of SEO-flavored cookies and pastries.

You'll notice that the site you're building in this chapter is very basic, and highlights only the most important SEO-related principles taught in this book. The simplicity is necessary for the purposes of this demonstration, because a complex implementation could easily be extended throughout an entire book itself. Features such as catalog searching and administration, shopping cart and check-out, product recommendations, and more, are demonstrated step-by-step in Cristian's e-commerce books.

In this chapter you:

❑   Develop a set of requirements for a simple product catalog

❑   Implement the product catalog using search engine friendly methods

Establishing the Requirements

As with any other development project, you design your site based on a set of requirements. For Cookie Ogre's Warehouse, we've come up with this short list:

❑   The catalog contains products that are grouped into categories.

❑   A product can belong to any number of categories, and a category can contain many products.

❑ The properties of a product are name, price, description, the primary category that it is part of, and an associated search engine brand.

❑ The properties of a category are: name.

❑ The properties of a brand are: name.

❑ The home page of the catalog contains links to the category pages. The page title should contain the site name.

❑ A category page displays the category name, the site name, a link to the home page, and links to the pages of the products in that category. The page title should contain the site name and the category name.

❑ Category pages should have a maximum number of products it can display, and use a paging feature to allow the visitors to browse the products on multiple pages.

❑ A product page must display the product name, price, and a link to the home page, a link to its primary category, the product's description, and the associated brand name and picture.

❑ Because a product can be reached through more category links, all the links except the one associated with its primary category must be excluded through `robots.txt`.

❑ The product details page should contain an Add to Cart button that performs minimal server-side functionality. The purpose is to test that URL rewriting doesn't affect the ability to perform server postbacks.

❑ All catalog pages must be accessible through keyword-rich URLs.

❑ The site should have customized 404 and 500 pages.

❑ If a catalog page is accessed through a URL other than the proper version, it should be automatically 301 redirected to the proper version.

❑ If a catalog page URL contains the ID of a category or a product that doesn't exist, the 404 page should be delivered.

❑ If a processing error happens inside the application, the 500 page should be delivered, and an email containing the error details should be automatically sent to the web site administrator.

❑ Requests for and `Default.aspx` and `Catalog.aspx`, which is the catalog's home page, should be automatically 301 redirected to `/`. Requests for `/` should be served by `Catalog.aspx` through URL rewriting.

❑ Canadian users should see the product price in CAD currency. All the other visitors should see the price in USD.

Implementing the Product Catalog

Starting from the basic list of requirements depicted earlier, you've come to implement three catalog pages, whose functionality is sustained by numerous helper scripts. The first catalog page is delivered by `Catalog.aspx`, and it looks as shown in Figure 14-1.

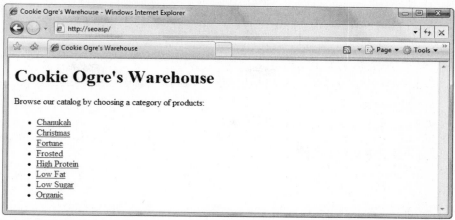

Figure 14-1

Trying to load `http://seoasp/Default.aspx`, or `http://seoasp/Catalog.aspx`, would 301 redirect you to `http://seoasp/`. Clicking one of the category links gets you to `Category.aspx`, which displays the details of the category, including links to its products. The script is accessed — obviously — through a keyword-rich URL, so the user will never know it's a page named `Category.aspx` that does all the work. The page lets you browse through multiple pages of products in the category. In Figure 14-2, the web site was configured to display two products on every page, but in a real-world web site that has many products, you'd use a larger value.

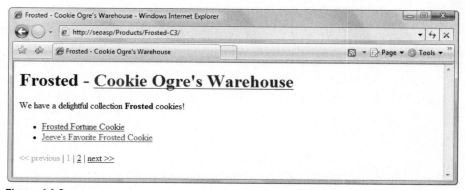

Figure 14-2

Clicking a product link in the category page loads the details page of that product, which looks like that shown in Figure 14-3. Notice the link to the primary category of the product at the bottom of the page, and the Add to Cart button which we've added to ensure that postbacks are handled correctly. Clicking that button simply displays "The product was added to your shopping cart!" next to the button.

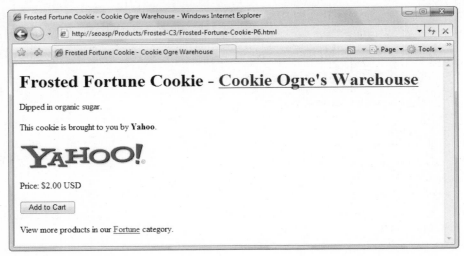

Figure 14-3

Now you see what we're up to. Follow the steps of the exercise to implement it, and we'll discuss the implementation details afterwards.

The installation instructions build the application from scratch. If you have been working through earlier chapters of the book, you will already have some of the files in your seoasp *application.*

Developing Cookie Ogre's Warehouse

1. In order to display different prices for Canadian users, you need geo-targeting functionality, which was covered in Chapter 11. Because the exercise is quite long, the steps are not repeated here. Please follow the geo-targeting exercise in Chapter 11 to create and populate the GeoTargetData table, and create the GeoTarget and GeoTargetDb classes.

2. Inside your seoasp project folder, create a folder named Media. This folder needs to contain four image files named 1.jpg, 2.jpg, 3.jpg, and 4.jpg, which contain the search engine company logos — Google, Yahoo!, Microsoft, and Ask. Take files from the code download of this chapter, and copy them to your Media folder.

3. Now create the necessary database structures. Connect to your SQL Server database using SQL Server Management Studio. If you created and configured the seoasp database as instructed in Chapter 1, you should be able to login as **seouser** with the password **seomaster**. Open a new query window, make sure the **seoasp** database is selected, and type the following SQL code to create and populate the Brands table:

```
CREATE TABLE Brands (
  ID INT NOT NULL PRIMARY KEY,
  Name VARCHAR(50) NOT NULL
);

INSERT INTO Brands (ID, Name) VALUES (1, 'Google');
INSERT INTO Brands (ID, Name) VALUES (2, 'Yahoo');
```

```
INSERT INTO Brands (ID, Name) VALUES (3, 'Microsoft');
INSERT INTO Brands (ID, Name) VALUES (4, 'Ask');
```

4. Continue by executing these SQL commands, which create and populate the `Categories` data table:

```
CREATE TABLE Categories (
  ID INT NOT NULL PRIMARY KEY,
  Name VARCHAR(50) NOT NULL
);

INSERT INTO Categories (ID, Name) VALUES (1, 'Chanukah');
INSERT INTO Categories (ID, Name) VALUES (2, 'Christmas');
INSERT INTO Categories (ID, Name) VALUES (3, 'Frosted');
INSERT INTO Categories (ID, Name) VALUES (4, 'Low Sugar');
INSERT INTO Categories (ID, Name) VALUES (5, 'Low Fat');
INSERT INTO Categories (ID, Name) VALUES (6, 'High Protein');
INSERT INTO Categories (ID, Name) VALUES (7, 'Fortune');
INSERT INTO Categories (ID, Name) VALUES (8, 'Organic');
```

5. Next you're creating and populating the `ProductCategories` table, which contains associations between products and categories. Each record is formed of a product ID and a category ID:

```
CREATE TABLE ProductCategories (
  ProductID INT NOT NULL,
  CategoryID INT NOT NULL,
  PRIMARY KEY (ProductID, CategoryID)
);

INSERT INTO ProductCategories (ProductID, CategoryID) VALUES (1, 3);
INSERT INTO ProductCategories (ProductID, CategoryID) VALUES (2, 4);
INSERT INTO ProductCategories (ProductID, CategoryID) VALUES (2, 5);
INSERT INTO ProductCategories (ProductID, CategoryID) VALUES (3, 6);
INSERT INTO ProductCategories (ProductID, CategoryID) VALUES (4, 2);
INSERT INTO ProductCategories (ProductID, CategoryID) VALUES (4, 3);
INSERT INTO ProductCategories (ProductID, CategoryID) VALUES (5, 1);
INSERT INTO ProductCategories (ProductID, CategoryID) VALUES (6, 7);
INSERT INTO ProductCategories (ProductID, CategoryID) VALUES (6, 8);
INSERT INTO ProductCategories (ProductID, CategoryID) VALUES (6, 3);
```

6. The last table you're creating is `Products`. This contains data about each product sold by the Cookie Ogre's Warehouse:

```
CREATE TABLE Products (
  ID INT NOT NULL PRIMARY KEY,
  BrandID INT NOT NULL,
  Name VARCHAR(255) NOT NULL,
  Price Money NOT NULL,
  Description VARCHAR(2000) NOT NULL,
  PrimaryCategoryID INT NOT NULL
);

INSERT INTO Products VALUES (1, 1, 'Matt Cutts'' Spam Flavored Cookie', 2.00,
'This delicious cookie tastes exactly like spam.', 3);
```

```
INSERT INTO Products VALUES (2, 2, 'Jeremy Zawodny''s Snickerdoodles', 3.00,
'These cookies are the Zawodny Family secret recipe, passed down throughout the
generations. They are low fat and low sugar.', 4);

INSERT INTO Products VALUES (3, 3, 'Bill Gates'' Cookie', 999999.99, 'These cookies
taste like... a million bucks. Note: before consuming, these cookies must be
activated by Microsoft.', 6);

INSERT INTO Products VALUES (4, 4, 'Jeeve''s Favorite Frosted Cookie', 2.00,
'Shaped like a butler, sugar coated. Now in Christmas holiday colors.', 3);

INSERT INTO Products VALUES (5, 1, 'Google Menorah Cookies', 3.00, 'Snatched from
one of the famed snack bars at Google while all of the employees were home. ', 1);

INSERT INTO Products VALUES (6, 2, 'Frosted Fortune Cookie', 2.00, 'Dipped in
organic sugar.', 7);
```

7. Execute the following SQL code, which creates the `GetCategories`, `GetCategory`, `GetProduct`, and `GetBrand` stored procedures:

```
-- Get all categories
CREATE PROCEDURE GetCategories
AS
SELECT ID, Name
FROM Categories
ORDER BY Name

GO

-- Get one category
CREATE PROCEDURE GetCategory
  (@CategoryID INT)
AS
SELECT ID, Name
FROM Categories
WHERE ID = @CategoryID

GO

-- Get one product
CREATE PROCEDURE GetProduct(@ProductID INT)
AS
SELECT ID, BrandID, Name, Price, Description, PrimaryCategoryID
FROM Products
WHERE Products.ID = @ProductID

GO

-- Get one brand
CREATE PROCEDURE GetBrand(@BrandID INT)
AS
SELECT ID, Name
FROM Brands
WHERE Brands.ID = @BrandID
```

8. Execute the following code, which creates the `GetProductsInCategory` stored procedure. The code is a little bit more complex because it needs to support paging. The procedure returns the list of products in the specified category page, and returns the total number of products in that category through the `@HowManyProducts` output parameter, which is required when implementing the pager in category pages.

```
-- Get a page of products from the specified category
CREATE PROCEDURE GetProductsInCategory
   (@CategoryID INT,
    @PageNumber INT,
    @ProductsPerPage INT,
    @HowManyProducts INT OUTPUT)
AS

-- declare a new TABLE variable
DECLARE @Products TABLE
(RowNumber INT IDENTITY(1,1),
 ID INT,
 BrandID INT NOT NULL,
 Name VARCHAR(255) NOT NULL,
 Price Money NOT NULL,
 Description VARCHAR(2000) NOT NULL,
 PrimaryCategoryID INT NOT NULL)

-- populate the table variable with the complete list of products
INSERT INTO @Products
SELECT Products.ID, BrandID, Name, Price, Description, PrimaryCategoryID
FROM Products INNER JOIN ProductCategories
  ON Products.ID = ProductCategories.ProductID
WHERE ProductCategories.CategoryID = @CategoryID
ORDER BY Products.Name

-- return the total number of products using an OUTPUT variable
SELECT @HowManyProducts = COUNT(ID) FROM @Products

-- extract the requested page of products
SELECT ID, BrandID, Name, Price, Description, PrimaryCategoryID
FROM @Products
WHERE RowNumber > (@PageNumber - 1) * @ProductsPerPage
  AND RowNumber <= @PageNumber * @ProductsPerPage
```

9. Execute the following code, which creates the `GetSecondaryProductCategories` stored procedure. This is required when generating the `robots.txt` exclusion data, which needs to include all product pages that are located in other categories than the primary one. This is necessary to avoid duplicate content problems.

```
CREATE PROCEDURE GetSecondaryProductCategories
AS
SELECT Products.ID as ProductID,
       Products.Name as ProductName,
       ProductCategories.CategoryID AS SecondaryCategoryID,
       Categories.Name AS SecondaryCategoryName
FROM Products INNER JOIN ProductCategories
  ON (ProductCategories.ProductID = Products.ID)
```

```
INNER JOIN Categories
  ON (ProductCategories.CategoryID = Categories.ID)
WHERE Products.PrimaryCategoryID <> ProductCategories.CategoryID
```

10. Now you need to add the following settings to your `Web.config` file. You should already have some of them from the geo-targeting exercise. **Be sure to set the email account data properly if you intend to use the error logging feature.**

```xml
<configuration>
...
...
  <appSettings>
    <!-- Site domain -->
    <add key="SiteDomain" value="http://seoasp" />

    <!-- Email information for sending automatic error reports -->
    <add key="EmailServer" value="email.example.com" />
    <add key="ErrorEmailFrom" value="from@example.com" />
    <add key="ErrorEmailTo" value="errors@example.com" />
    <add key="ErrorEmailSmtpUserName" value="smtp_user_name" />
    <add key="ErrorEmailSmtpPassword" value="smtp_password" />

    <!-- The number of products used for paging -->
    <add key="ProductsPerPage" value="1" />
  </appSettings>

  <connectionStrings>
    <add name="GeoTargetDatabase" connectionString="Server=(local)\SqlExpress; ↵
User=seouser;Password=seomaster;Database=seoasp" />
    <add name="ProductsDatabase" connectionString="Server=(local)\SqlExpress; ↵
User=seouser;Password=seomaster;Database=seoasp" />
  </connectionStrings>
```

11. If you intend to use `ISAPI_Rewrite` for URL rewriting, install the Lite version of the product that you can download from `http://www.isapirewrite.com`, and type the following in its `httpd.ini` configuration file (located by default in `Program Files\Helicon\ISAPI_Rewrite`):

```
[ISAPI_Rewrite]

# Redirect to correct domain if incorrect to avoid canonicalization problems
RewriteCond Host: (?!seoasp).*
RewriteRule ^/(.*)$ http://seoasp/$1 [RP,I]

# Redirect requests to the home page
RewriteRule ^/(Default\.aspx|Catalog\.aspx)$ http://seoasp/ [RP]

# Rewrite the home page
RewriteRule ^/?$ /Catalog.aspx [L]

# Rewrite keyword-rich URLs for paged category pages
RewriteRule ^/Products/.*-C([0-9]+)/Page-([0-9]+)/?$ /Category.aspx?CategoryID=↵
$1&Page=$2 [L]
```

```
# Rewrite keyword-rich URLs for category pages
RewriteRule ^/Products/.*-C([0-9]+)/?$ /Category.aspx?CategoryID=$1&Page=1 [L]

# Rewrite keyword-rich URLs with a product ID and a category ID
RewriteRule ^/Products/.*-C([0-9]+)/.*-P([0-9]+)\.html$ /Product.aspx?↵
CategoryID=$1&ProductID=$2 [L]

# Rewrite media files
RewriteRule ^/.*-M(.+)$ /Media/$1 [L]

# Rewrite robots.txt
RewriteRule ^/robots.txt$ /Robots.ashx
```

12. If you use `ISAPI_Rewrite`, skip this step. **Don't implement rewriting using both ISAPI_Rewrite and UrlRewriter.NET!** If you use UrlRewriter.NET for URL rewriting, copy `Intelligencia.UrlRewriter.dll` and `Intelligencia.UrlRewriter.xml` from the `\bin\Release` folder of the product page (that you download from `http://www.url-rewriter.net`) to your application's `Bin` folder. Then add the following elements to your `Web.config` file, making sure the `<configSections>` element is the *first* child element of `<configuration>`:

```
<configuration>
  <configSections>
    <section name="rewriter" requirePermission="false"
type="Intelligencia.UrlRewriter.Configuration.RewriterConfigurationSectionHandler, ↵
Intelligencia.UrlRewriter" />
  </configSections>

  <system.webServer>
    <modules runAllManagedModulesForAllRequests="true">
    <add name="UrlRewriter" type="Intelligencia.UrlRewriter.RewriterHttpModule" />
    </modules>

    <validation validateIntegratedModeConfiguration="false" />
  </system.webServer>

  <rewriter>
    <!-- Redirect to correct domain to avoid canonicalization problems -->
    <!-- This rule works with UrlRewriter.Net 2.0:
    <unless header="HTTP_HOST" match="seoasp">
      <rewrite url=" ^/(.*)$" to="http://seoasp/$1" processing="stop" />
    </unless>-->

    <!-- Redirect requests to the home page. Update if necessary. -->
    <redirect url="/(Default\.aspx|Catalog\.aspx)" to="http://seoasp/"
permanent="true" />

    <!-- Rewrite the home page -->
    <rewrite url="^/$" to="/Catalog.aspx" processing="stop" />

    <!-- Rewrite media files -->
    <rewrite url="^/.*-M(.+)$" to="/Media/$1" processing="stop" />

    <!--Rewrite Robots file-->
```

```
        <rewrite url="^/robots.txt$" to="/Robots.ashx" processing="stop" />

        <!-- Group rewrite rules that deal with product URLs -->
        <if url="^/Products/.*">

          <!-- Rewrite keyword-rich URLs for paged category pages -->
          <rewrite url="^/Products/.*-C([0-9]+)/Page-([0-9]+)/?$"
                   to="/Category.aspx?CategoryID=$1&amp;Page=$2"
                   processing="stop" />

          <!-- Rewrite keyword-rich URLs for category pages -->
          <rewrite url="^/Products/.*-C([0-9]+)/$"
                   to="/Category.aspx?CategoryID=$1&amp;Page=1"
                   processing="stop" />

          <!-- Rewrite keyword-rich URLs with a product ID and a category ID -->
          <rewrite url="^/Products/.*-C([0-9]+)/.*-P([0-9]+)\.html$"
                   to="/Product.aspx?CategoryID=$1&amp;ProductID=$2"
                   processing="stop" />

        </if>
      </rewriter>
```

```
    <system.web>
      <httpModules>
        <add type="Intelligencia.UrlRewriter.RewriterHttpModule, Intelligencia. ↵
UrlRewriter" name="UrlRewriter" />
      </httpModules>
    <!-- ... -->
    </system.web>
```

13. In your application's `App_Code` folder, create a class file named `LinkFactory.cs`, and add the following code. This file contains helper functions that create links to product pages, category pages, and media files.

```csharp
using System;
using System.Web;
using System.Configuration;
using System.Text.RegularExpressions;

/// <summary>
/// LinkFactory creates absolute links to locations in our site
/// </summary>
public static class LinkFactory
{
  // regular expression that removes characters that aren't a-z, 0-9, dash,
underscore or space
  private static Regex purifyUrlRegex = new Regex("[^-a-zA-Z0-9_ ]",
RegexOptions.Compiled);

  // regular expression that changes dashes, underscores and spaces to dashes
  private static Regex dashesRegex = new Regex("[-_ ]+", RegexOptions.Compiled);

  // build a link to the first page of products in a category
```

```csharp
  public static string MakeCategoryUrl(string categoryName, string categoryId)
  {
    return MakeCategoryUrl(categoryName, categoryId, 1);
  }

  // builds a link to a category subpage
  public static string MakeCategoryUrl(string categoryName, string categoryId,
int page)
  {
    // prepare the category name for inclusion in URL
    categoryName = prepareUrlText(categoryName);

    // read the site domain from configuration file
    string siteDomain = ConfigurationManager.AppSettings["SiteDomain"];

    // build the keyword-rich URL
    string url = String.Format("{0}/Products/{1}-C{2}/",
      siteDomain, categoryName, categoryId);
    if (page != 1)
      url += String.Format("Page-{0}/", page);

    // return the URL
    return HttpUtility.UrlPathEncode(url);
  }

  // builds a link to a product page
  public static string MakeCategoryProductUrl(
    string categoryName, string categoryId, string productName, string productId)
  {
    // prepare the product name and category name for inclusion in URL
    categoryName = prepareUrlText(categoryName);
    productName = prepareUrlText(productName);

    // read the site domain from configuration file
    string siteDomain = ConfigurationManager.AppSettings["SiteDomain"];

    // build the keyword-rich URL
    string url = String.Format("{0}/Products/{1}-C{2}/{3}-P{4}.html",
      siteDomain, categoryName, categoryId, productName, productId);

    // return the URL
    return HttpUtility.UrlPathEncode(url);
  }

  // builds a link to a media file
  public static string MakeMediaUrl(string name, string extension, string id)
  {
    // prepare the medium name for inclusion in URL
    name = prepareUrlText(name);

    // read the site domain from configuration file
    string siteDomain = ConfigurationManager.AppSettings["SiteDomain"];

    // build the keyword-rich URL
```

```
    string url = String.Format("{0}/{1}-M{2}.{3}", siteDomain, name, id,
extension);

    // return the URL
    return HttpUtility.UrlPathEncode(url);
  }

  // prepares a string to be included in an URL
  private static string prepareUrlText(string urlText)
  {
    // remove all characters that aren't a-z, 0-9, dash, underscore or space
    urlText = purifyUrlRegex.Replace(urlText, "");

    // remove all leading and trailing spaces
    urlText = urlText.Trim();

    // change all dashes, underscores and spaces to dashes
    urlText = dashesRegex.Replace(urlText, "-");

    // return the modified string
    return urlText;
  }
}
```

14. Add another class file to the `App_Code` folder, named `UrlTools.cs`. This class is responsible for making 301 redirects to the standard version of a URL if the visitor isn't already there, and feeding the 404 page if a nonexistent product or category is requested.

```
using System;
using System.Web;
using System.Data;
using System.Configuration;

/// <summary>
/// Class provides support for URL manipulation and redirection
/// </summary>
public static class UrlTools
{
  // obtain the site domain from the configuration file
  public readonly static string SiteDomain =
ConfigurationManager.AppSettings["SiteDomain"];

  /* ensures the current page is being loaded through its standard URL;
   * 301 redirect to the standard URL if it doesn't */
  public static void CheckUrl()
  {
    HttpContext context = HttpContext.Current;
    HttpRequest request = HttpContext.Current.Request;

    // retrieve query string parameters
    string productId = request.QueryString["ProductID"];
    string categoryId = request.QueryString["CategoryID"];
    string page = request.QueryString["Page"];
```

```csharp
      // check category-product URLs
      if (categoryId != null && productId != null)
      {
        CheckCategoryProductUrl(categoryId, productId);
      }
      // check category URLs
      else if (categoryId != null && page != null)
      {
        CheckCategoryUrl(categoryId, page);
      }
    }

    // checks a category URL for compliancy
    // 301 redirects to proper URL, or returns 404 if necessary
    public static void CheckCategoryUrl(string categoryId, string page)
    {
      // the current HttpContext
      HttpContext context = HttpContext.Current;

      // the URL requested by the visitor
      string requestedUrl = context.Request.ServerVariables["HTTP_X_REWRITE_URL"];

      // retrieve category data
      DataRow categoryRow = CatalogDb.GetCategory(categoryId);

      // if the category or the product doesn't exist in the database, return 404
      if (categoryRow == null)
      {
        NotFound();
      }

      // get category name
      string categoryName = categoryRow["Name"].ToString();

      // obtain the standard version of the URL
      string standardUrl = LinkFactory.MakeCategoryUrl(categoryName, categoryId,
int.Parse(page));

      // 301 redirect to the proper URL if necessary
      if (SiteDomain + requestedUrl != standardUrl)
      {
        context.Response.Status = "301 Moved Permanently";
        context.Response.AddHeader("Location", standardUrl);
      }
    }

    // checks a category-product URL for compliancy
    // 301 redirects to proper URL, or returns 404 if necessary
    public static void CheckCategoryProductUrl(string categoryId, string productId)
    {
      // the current HttpContext
      HttpContext context = HttpContext.Current;

      // the URL requested by the visitor
```

```
        string requestedUrl = context.Request.ServerVariables["HTTP_X_REWRITE_URL"];

        // retrieve product and category data
        DataRow categoryRow = CatalogDb.GetCategory(categoryId);
        DataRow productRow = CatalogDb.GetProduct(productId);

        // if the category or the product doesn't exist in the database, return 404
        if (categoryRow == null || productRow == null)
        {
          NotFound();
        }

        // get product and category names
        string categoryName = categoryRow["Name"].ToString();
        string productName = productRow["Name"].ToString();

        // obtain the standard version of the URL
        string standardUrl = LinkFactory.MakeCategoryProductUrl(categoryName,
categoryId, productName, productId);

        // 301 redirect to the proper URL if necessary
        if (SiteDomain + requestedUrl != standardUrl)
        {
          context.Response.Status = "301 Moved Permanently";
          context.Response.AddHeader("Location", standardUrl);
        }
    }

    // Load the 404 page
    public static void NotFound()
    {
      HttpContext.Current.Server.Transfer("~/NotFound.aspx");
    }
}
```

15.   Also in `App_Code`, create a class file named `CatalogDb.cs`, and type the following code. This file contains a class named `CatalogDb`, which includes Catalog database access methods, such as those for reading product and category data. The methods return a `DataTable` object when they need to return more data records, or a `DataRow` object when they need to return a single data record.

```
using System;
using System.Web;
using System.Data;
using System.Data.SqlClient;
using System.Configuration;

/// <summary>
/// Summary description for GeoTargetDb
/// </summary>
public class CatalogDb
{
  // retrieves the details of o brand
  public static DataRow GetBrand(string brandId)
```

```
{
  // create a SqlCommand object with a connection to the cloak database
  SqlCommand command = createCommand("ProductsDatabase");

  // set the name of the stored procedure to execute
  command.CommandText = "GetBrand";

  // @BrandID
  SqlParameter p = new SqlParameter("@BrandID", brandId);
  command.Parameters.Add(p);

  // create a new DataTable object
  DataTable results = new DataTable();

  // execute the stored procecure and load the results into the DataTable
  command.Connection.Open();
  try { results.Load(command.ExecuteReader()); }
  finally { command.Connection.Close(); }

  // return a DataRow containing the category details
  return (results.Rows.Count > 0) ? results.Rows[0] : null;
}

// retrieves all categories
public static DataTable GetCategories()
{
  // create a SqlCommand object with a connection to the cloak database
  SqlCommand command = createCommand("ProductsDatabase");

  // set the name of the stored procedure to execute
  command.CommandText = "GetCategories";

  // create a new DataTable object
  DataTable results = new DataTable();

  // execute the stored procecure and load the results into the DataTable
  command.Connection.Open();
  try { results.Load(command.ExecuteReader()); }
  finally { command.Connection.Close(); }

  // return the results
  return results;
}

// retrieves the details of a category
public static DataRow GetCategory(string categoryId)
{
  // create a SqlCommand object with a connection to the cloak database
  SqlCommand command = createCommand("ProductsDatabase");

  // set the name of the stored procedure to execute
  command.CommandText = "GetCategory";

  // @CategoryID
```

```
        SqlParameter p = new SqlParameter("@CategoryID", categoryId);
        command.Parameters.Add(p);

        // create a new DataTable object
        DataTable results = new DataTable();

        // execute the stored procecure and load the results into the DataTable
        command.Connection.Open();
        try { results.Load(command.ExecuteReader()); }
        finally { command.Connection.Close(); }

        // return a DataRow containing the category details
        return (results.Rows.Count > 0) ? results.Rows[0] : null;
    }

    // retrieves a page of products from a category
    public static DataTable GetProductsInCategory(string categoryId, int pageNumber,
out int howManyPages)
    {
        // create a SqlCommand object with a connection to the cloak database
        SqlCommand command = createCommand("ProductsDatabase");

        // set the name of the stored procedure to execute
        command.CommandText = "GetProductsInCategory";

        // @CategoryID
        SqlParameter p = new SqlParameter("@CategoryID", categoryId);
        command.Parameters.Add(p);

        // @PageNumber
        p = new SqlParameter("@PageNumber", pageNumber);
        command.Parameters.Add(p);

        // @PageNumber
        p = new SqlParameter("@ProductsPerPage",
          ConfigurationManager.AppSettings["ProductsPerPage"]);
        command.Parameters.Add(p);

        // @HowManyPages
        p = new SqlParameter("@HowManyProducts", SqlDbType.Int);
        p.Direction = ParameterDirection.Output;
        command.Parameters.Add(p);

        // create a new DataTable object
        DataTable results = new DataTable();

        // execute the stored procecure and load the results into the DataTable
        command.Connection.Open();
        try { results.Load(command.ExecuteReader()); }
        finally { command.Connection.Close(); }

        // return the number of product pages as an out parameter
        int howManyProducts =
Int32.Parse(command.Parameters["@HowManyProducts"].Value.ToString());
```

```
        howManyPages = (int)Math.Ceiling((double)howManyProducts /
                double.Parse(ConfigurationManager.AppSettings["ProductsPerPage"]));

    // return the results
    return results;
}

// retrieves the details of one product
public static DataRow GetProduct(string productId)
{
    // create a SqlCommand object with a connection to the cloak database
    SqlCommand command = createCommand("ProductsDatabase");

    // set the name of the stored procedure to execute
    command.CommandText = "GetProduct";

    // @CategoryID
    SqlParameter p = new SqlParameter("@ProductID", productId);
    command.Parameters.Add(p);

    // create a new DataTable object
    DataTable results = new DataTable();

    // execute the stored procecure and load the results into the DataTable
    command.Connection.Open();
    try { results.Load(command.ExecuteReader()); }
    finally { command.Connection.Close(); }

    // return a DataRow containing the product details
    return (results.Rows.Count > 0) ? results.Rows[0] : null;
}

// retrieves the products with secondary categories for robots.txt exclusion
public static DataTable GetSecondaryProductCategories()
{
    // create a SqlCommand object with a connection to the cloak database
    SqlCommand command = createCommand("ProductsDatabase");

    // set the name of the stored procedure to execute
    command.CommandText = "GetSecondaryProductCategories";

    // create a new DataTable object
    DataTable results = new DataTable();

    // execute the stored procecure and load the results into the DataTable
    command.Connection.Open();
    try { results.Load(command.ExecuteReader()); }
    finally { command.Connection.Close(); }

    // return the results
    return results;
}

// creates and prepares a new SqlCommand object on a new connection
```

```
    private static SqlCommand createCommand(string connectionName)
    {
      // obtain the database connection string
      string connectionString =
ConfigurationManager.ConnectionStrings[connectionName].ConnectionString;

      // obtain a database specific connection object
      SqlConnection conn = new SqlConnection(connectionString);

      // create a database specific command object
      SqlCommand comm = conn.CreateCommand();

      // set the command type to stored procedure
      comm.CommandType = CommandType.StoredProcedure;

      // return the initialized command object
      return comm;
    }
}
```

16. It's time to create `Catalog.aspx` in your `seoasp` folder, with the following code. This file generates the first page of the catalog, displaying all the existing categories of the catalog:

```
<%@ Page Language="C#" EnableViewState="false" %>
<!DOCTYPE html PUBLIC "-//W3C//DTD XHTML 1.0 Transitional//EN"
"http://www.w3.org/TR/xhtml1/DTD/xhtml1-transitional.dtd">

<script runat="server">
  protected void Page_Load(object sender, EventArgs e)
  {
    // load the list of categories
    categoriesRepeater.DataSource = CatalogDb.GetCategories();
    categoriesRepeater.DataBind();
  }
</script>

<html xmlns="http://www.w3.org/1999/xhtml">
<head runat="server">
  <title>Cookie Ogre's Warehouse</title>
</head>
<body>
  <form id="form1" runat="server">
    <h1>Cookie Ogre's Warehouse</h1>

    <!-- Repeater control displays the products list -->
    <asp:Repeater ID="categoriesRepeater" runat="server">
      <HeaderTemplate>
        Browse our catalog by choosing a category of products:
        <ul>
      </HeaderTemplate>
      <ItemTemplate>
        <li>
          <a href="<%# LinkFactory.MakeCategoryUrl(Eval("Name").ToString(),
Eval("ID").ToString()) %>">
```

```
                    <%# Eval("Name") %>
                </a>
            </li>
        </ItemTemplate>
        <FooterTemplate>
            </ul>
        </FooterTemplate>
    </asp:Repeater>
  </form>
</body>
</html>
```

17. Now create `Category.aspx` in your `seoasp` folder. This script displays category details:

```
<%@ Page Language="C#" EnableViewState="false" %>
<%@ Import Namespace="System.Data" %>

<!DOCTYPE html PUBLIC "-//W3C//DTD XHTML 1.0 Transitional//EN"
"http://www.w3.org/TR/xhtml1/DTD/xhtml1-transitional.dtd">

<script runat="server">
  // product attributes are stored as private fields
  private string categoryId;
  private string categoryName;
  private int page;
  private int howManyPages;

  // fill the form with data
  protected void Page_Load(object sender, EventArgs e)
  {
    // get category ID
    categoryId = Request.QueryString["CategoryID"];

    // obtain category name
    DataRow categoryRow = CatalogDb.GetCategory(categoryId);
    categoryName = categoryRow["Name"].ToString();

    // what page?
    string pageString = Request.QueryString["Page"];
    page = (pageString == null) ? 1 : int.Parse(pageString);

    // display the category products and get the number of pages
    productsRepeater.DataSource = CatalogDb.GetProductsInCategory(categoryId, page,
out howManyPages);
    productsRepeater.DataBind();

    // of the total number of pages is lower than the requested page, send 404
    if (page > howManyPages)
    {
      UrlTools.NotFound();
    }

    // create an ArrayList with the page numbers
    ArrayList pageNumbers = new ArrayList();
```

```
            for (int i = 1; i <= howManyPages; i++) pageNumbers.Add(i);

        // bind the pager repeater to the page numbers array
        pagerRepeater.DataSource = pageNumbers;
        pagerRepeater.DataBind();
    }
</script>

<html xmlns="http://www.w3.org/1999/xhtml">
<head runat="server">
  <title><%= categoryName %> - Cookie Ogre's Warehouse</title>
</head>
<body>
  <form id="form1" runat="server">
    <h1>
      <%= categoryName %> -
      <a href="<%= UrlTools.SiteDomain %>">Cookie Ogre's Warehouse</a>
    </h1>
    <p>
      We have a delightful collection <b><%= categoryName %></b> cookies!
    </p>

    <!-- Repeater control displays the products list -->
    <asp:Repeater ID="productsRepeater" runat="server">
      <HeaderTemplate>
        <ul>
      </HeaderTemplate>
      <ItemTemplate>
        <li>
        <a href="<%# LinkFactory.MakeCategoryProductUrl(categoryName, categoryId,
Eval("Name").ToString(), Eval("ID").ToString()) %>">
          <%# Eval("Name") %>
        </a>
        </li>
      </ItemTemplate>
      <FooterTemplate>
        </ul>
      </FooterTemplate>
    </asp:Repeater>

    <!-- Repeater control displays pager links -->
    <asp:Repeater ID="pagerRepeater" runat="server">
      <HeaderTemplate>
        <asp:HyperLink ID="h2" runat="server" Text="<< previous"
          NavigateUrl='<%# LinkFactory.MakeCategoryUrl(categoryName, categoryId,
page - 1) %>'
          Enabled='<%# page > 1 %>' /> |
      </HeaderTemplate>
      <ItemTemplate>
        <asp:HyperLink ID="h3" runat="server" Text='<%# Container.DataItem %>'
          NavigateUrl='<%# LinkFactory.MakeCategoryUrl(categoryName, categoryId,
(int)Container.DataItem) %>'
          Enabled='<%# page != (int)Container.DataItem %>' /> |
      </ItemTemplate>
```

```
        <FooterTemplate>
          <asp:HyperLink ID="h2" runat="server" Text="next >>"
            NavigateUrl='<%# LinkFactory.MakeCategoryUrl(categoryName, categoryId,
page + 1) %>'
            Enabled='<%# page < howManyPages %>' />
        </FooterTemplate>
      </asp:Repeater>
    </form>
  </body>
</html>
```

18.   Finally, create `Product.aspx` in your `seoasp` folder. This is the page that individual products appear on:

```
<%@ Page Language="C#" EnableViewState="False" %>
<%@ Import Namespace="System.Data" %>

<!DOCTYPE html PUBLIC "-//W3C//DTD XHTML 1.0 Transitional//EN"
"http://www.w3.org/TR/xhtml1/DTD/xhtml1-transitional.dtd">

<script runat="server">
  // product attributes are stored as private fields
  private string productId, productName, productDescription;
  private decimal productPrice;
  private string brandId, brandName;
  private string primaryCategoryId, primaryCategoryName;

  // fill the form with product data
  protected void Page_Load(object sender, EventArgs e)
  {
    // get product ID
    productId = Request.QueryString["ProductID"];

    // obtain product details or send 404 if product doesn't exist
    DataRow productRow = CatalogDb.GetProduct(productId);
    if (productRow == null)
    {
      UrlTools.NotFound();
      return;
    }
    else
    {
      // read product details from the DataRow
      productName = productRow["Name"].ToString();
      productPrice = decimal.Parse(productRow["Price"].ToString());
      productDescription = productRow["Description"].ToString();
      primaryCategoryId = productRow["PrimaryCategoryID"].ToString();
      brandId = productRow["BrandID"].ToString();

      // obtain the brand name
      brandName = CatalogDb.GetBrand(brandId)["Name"].ToString();

      // obtain the primary category name
      primaryCategoryName =
CatalogDb.GetCategory(primaryCategoryId)["Name"].ToString();
```

```
            // required to support PostBack events in the page
            Context.RewritePath("/?");
        }
    }

    protected void addToCartButton_Click(object sender, EventArgs e)
    {
        cartLabel.Text = "The product was added to your shopping cart!";
    }
</script>

<html xmlns="http://www.w3.org/1999/xhtml">
<head id="Head1" runat="server">
    <title><%= productName %> - Cookie Ogre Warehouse</title>
</head>
<body>
    <form id="form1" runat="server">
        <!-- Display title, which includes link to the home page -->
        <h1>
            <%= productName %> -
            <a href="<%= UrlTools.SiteDomain %>">Cookie Ogre's Warehouse</a>
        </h1>

        <!-- Display the product description -->
        <p><%= productDescription %></p>

        <!-- Display the brand name and logo -->
        <p>This cookie is brought to you by <b><%= brandName %></b>.</p>
        <p><img src="<%= LinkFactory.MakeMediaUrl(brandName, "jpg", brandId) %>"/></p>

        <!-- Display the product price -->
        <p>Price:
            <%= GeoTarget.IsRegionCode("CA") ?
                    String.Format("{0:c} CAD", productPrice * (decimal)1.17) :
                    String.Format("{0:c} USD", productPrice)  %>
        </p>

        <!-- Add to cart button and label -->
        <p>
            <asp:Button ID="addToCartButton" runat="server" Text="Add to Cart"
OnClick="addToCartButton_Click" />
            <asp:Label ID="cartLabel" runat="server" />
        </p>

        <!-- Link to the primary category of the product -->
        View more products in our
        <a href="<%= LinkFactory.MakeCategoryUrl(primaryCategoryName,
primaryCategoryId) %>">
            <%= primaryCategoryName %></a>
        category.
    </form>
</body>
</html>
```

19. To enable URL auto-correction, add the following code to your `Global.asax` file. Create this file by right-clicking the project root in Solution Explorer, selecting **Add New Item...** from the context menu, and choosing the **Global Application Class** template.

```
<%@ Application Language="C#" %>
<%@ Import Namespace="System.Net" %>
<%@ Import Namespace="System.Net.Mail" %>
<%@ Import Namespace="System.Configuration" %>

<script RunAt="server">
  void Application_BeginRequest(object sender, EventArgs e)
  {
    // ensures a standard URL is used, 301 redirect to it otherwise
    UrlTools.CheckUrl();
  }
...
</script>
```

20. To enable error logging, add the `Application_Error()` method to `Global.asax`. This will automatically send an email containing the details of the error in case a problem happens with the application (with other words, when an unhandled exception is raised). Note that you need to set correct email account data in `Web.config` in order for this to work. This step is optional.

```
// email the error details when an unhandled exception is raised
void Application_Error(Object sender, EventArgs e)
{
  // get the exception details
  Exception ex = Server.GetLastError();
  if (ex.InnerException != null) ex = ex.InnerException;

  // get the current date and time
  string dateTime = DateTime.Now.ToLongDateString() + ", at "
                  + DateTime.Now.ToShortTimeString();

  // build the error message
  string errorMessage = "Exception generated on " + dateTime;
  System.Web.HttpContext context = System.Web.HttpContext.Current;
  errorMessage += "\n\n Page location: " + context.Request.RawUrl;
  errorMessage += "\n\n Message: " + ex.Message;
  errorMessage += "\n\n Source: " + ex.Source;
  errorMessage += "\n\n Method: " + ex.TargetSite;
  errorMessage += "\n\n Stack Trace: \n\n" + ex.StackTrace;

  // email the error details
  string mailServer = ConfigurationManager.AppSettings["EmailServer"];
  string from = ConfigurationManager.AppSettings["ErrorEmailFrom"];
  string to = ConfigurationManager.AppSettings["ErrorEmailTo"];
  string smtpUser = ConfigurationManager.AppSettings["SmtpHostUserName"];
  string smtpPassword = ConfigurationManager.AppSettings["SmtpHostPassword"];

  string subject = "Example.com error report";
  try
  {
    SmtpClient mailClient = new SmtpClient(mailServer);
```

```
      MailMessage mailMessage = new MailMessage(from, to, subject, errorMessage);
      mailClient.Credentials = new NetworkCredential(smtpUser, smtpPassword);
      mailClient.Send(mailMessage);
    }
    catch (Exception myex) {  }
  }
```

21. The final step is to exclude the product links that aren't on the primary category. Obtaining this data isn't extremely complicated, but it does involve a longer-than-usual SQL query. Also, although you didn't implement shopping cart and search features, assume that you do and deliberately exclude their pages using `robots.txt`, to avoid duplicate content problems. Create the following `Robots.ashx` generic handler in your `seoasp` folder, and type the following code. This file is already mapped to handle `robots.txt`.

```
<%@ WebHandler Language="C#" Class="Robots" %>
using System.Web;
using System.Data;

public class Robots : IHttpHandler
{
  public void ProcessRequest(HttpContext context)
  {
    // get the current HttpResponse object
    HttpResponse response = context.Response;

    // set the proper content type and send the Disallow line
    response.ContentType = "text/plain";
    response.Write("User-agent: * \n");

    // declare necessary variables
    string productId, productName, categoryId, categoryName, url;

    // retrieve the product categories that need to be excluded
    DataTable toExcludeTable = CatalogDb.GetSecondaryProductCategories();

    // parse the list of products and categories and exclude their links
    foreach (DataRow row in toExcludeTable.Rows)
    {
      // get data from the data row
      productId = row["ProductID"].ToString();
      productName = row["ProductName"].ToString();
      categoryId = row["SecondaryCategoryID"].ToString();
      categoryName = row["SecondaryCategoryName"].ToString();

      // use the link factory to obtain the URL
      url = LinkFactory.MakeCategoryProductUrl(categoryName, categoryId,
                                              productName, productId);

      // remove the domain name from the URL
      url = url.Replace(UrlTools.SiteDomain, "");

      // send url to the output to exclude it
      response.Write(string.Format("Disallow: {0} \n", url));
    }
```

```
      // include the static exclusion data from robots_static.txt
      context.Response.WriteFile("~/robots_static.txt");
  }

  public bool IsReusable
  {
    get { return false; }
  }
}
```

22. Add any static parts of your `robots.txt` in a file named `robots_static.txt`, in the root of your project:

```
Disallow: /Cart/
Disallow: /Search/
```

23. Add a Web Form named `NotFound.aspx` to your project. This file will display the 404 not found page of your web site.

```
<%@ Page Language="C#" %>
<!DOCTYPE html PUBLIC "-//W3C//DTD XHTML 1.0 Transitional//EN"
"http://www.w3.org/TR/xhtml1/DTD/xhtml1-transitional.dtd">

<script runat="server">
  protected void Page_Load(object sender, EventArgs e)
  {
    // set the 404 status code
    Response.StatusCode = 404;
  }
</script>

<html xmlns="http://www.w3.org/1999/xhtml" >
<head id="Head1" runat="server">
  <title>Cookie Ogre Warehouse Page Not Found</title>
</head>
<body>
  <form id="form1" runat="server">
    <h1>Cookie Ogre Warehouse</h1>
    <p>The page you requested doesn't exist on our web site. Please visit our
<a href="<%= UrlTools.SiteDomain %>">home page</a>.</p>
  </form>
</body>
</html>
```

24. Add a Web Form named `ServerError.aspx` to your project. This file will display the 500 Internal Server Error page of your web site.

```
<%@ Page Language="C#" %>
<!DOCTYPE html PUBLIC "-//W3C//DTD XHTML 1.0 Transitional//EN"
"http://www.w3.org/TR/xhtml1/DTD/xhtml1-transitional.dtd">

<script runat="server">
  protected void Page_Load(object sender, EventArgs e)
  {
```

```
      // set the 500 status code
      Response.Status = "500 Internal Server Error";
   }
</script>

<html xmlns="http://www.w3.org/1999/xhtml" >
<head>
   <title>Cookie Ogre Warehouse Server Error</title>
</head>
<body>
   <h1>Sorry!</h1>
   <p>We're currently experiencing technical difficulties, and can't display the
page you requested.
   Please accept our apologies, and visit us at <a href="<%= UrlTools.SiteDomain
%>"><%= UrlTools.SiteDomain %></a> soon.</p>
</body>
</html>
```

25. Set the 404 pages of your IIS or your web hosting account to `NotFound.aspx`. Then set up the 404 and 500 pages in your `Web.config` as shown in the following code snippet. This ensures that any 404 pages that aren't handled by your application will be properly handled by `NotFound.aspx`, and that 500 pages will be handled by `ServerError.aspx`.

```
      <customErrors mode="On" defaultRedirect="~/ServerError.aspx">
         <error statusCode="404" redirect="~/NotFound.aspx" />
         <error statusCode="500" redirect="~/ServerError.aspx" />
      </customErrors>
   </system.web>
</configuration>
```

26. That's it! Load `http://seoasp/` and expect to see the page shown in Figure 14-1. Play around with your site a little bit to ensure it works. Also verify that loading `http://seoasp/robots.txt` yields the results shown in Figure 14-4.

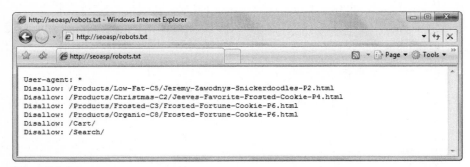

Figure 14-4

Next, analyze how you made this work, and what design decisions you have made to implement the set of requirements. Most of the technical details were explained earlier in this book, so we'll now focus only on explaining the big picture.

To understand such an application, even a simple one, you need to start with the database. Let's see how the database works and how the data is organized. Your database is comprised of four data tables:

❑   `Brands` — Contains search engine company names.

❑   `Categories` — Contains the categories in which your products are grouped.

❑   `Products` — Contains data about the products in your catalog.

❑   `ProductCategories` — Contains associations between products and categories. This table is required because a product can be contained by more than one category, so that multiple associations can be created for each product, and for each category. (If each of your products belonged to a single category, you could have referenced that category through a separate column in the `Products` table, instead of creating the `ProductCategories` table — just like you're now using the `PrimaryCategoryID` column in `Products`.)

To visualize the relationship between these tables, see the diagram in Figure 14-5.

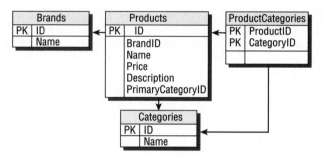

Figure 14-5

> Note the database structure isn't fully optimized for real-world usage. You should add *foreign keys* to your tables to enforce the relationships. Each table should be also tuned for the kind of operations it will support. Adding indexes to the `Name` columns, for example, would increase the performance for queries that use those columns in the WHERE clause.

The data in these tables is read by stored procedures, which in turn are read by the methods of the `CatalogDb` class using ADO.NET. Please read Chapter 11 for a very quick intro into stored procedures and ADO.NET. A couple of stored procedures, `GetProductsInCategory` and `GetSecondaryProductCategories`, which are a bit more complicated and deserve closer attention, are detailed next.

`GetProductsInCategory` retrieves a page of products from a specified category. As you know, the category pages are configured to display a maximum number of products (set via the `ProductsPerPage` setting in `Web.config`), and use the pager to allow visitors to browse the pages of products. `GetProductsInCategory` receives three parameters that it uses to send back the required page of products (CategoryID, PageNumber, and ProductsPerPage). There's also an output parameter, HowManyProducts, through which the stored procedure sends back the total number of products in the category. This information is necessary for creating the pager.

```
-- Get a page of products from the specified category
CREATE PROCEDURE GetProductsInCategory
  (@CategoryID INT,
   @PageNumber INT,
   @ProductsPerPage INT,
   @HowManyProducts INT OUTPUT)
AS
```

The task of reading a specific page of products is more difficult than it may seem at first sight, because — unless you're using SQL Server 2005 — there's no easy way to assign a row number for each record in a set of records. And without the row number, it's hard to ask, for example, for the 6th to 10th products in the list — which would be required if you'd be reading the second page of products, for a page that displays five products per page.

If you use SQL Server 2005, you have access to a function named ROW_NUMBER(), which generates the index for each record. For Cookie Ogre's Warehouse we chose a method that works equally well with all versions of SQL Server, although it's not as elegant as using ROW_NUMBER(). This technique involves using a TABLE variable that contains the columns of the data you're querying, plus one additional field named RowNumber:

```
-- declare a new TABLE variable
DECLARE @Products TABLE
(RowNumber INT IDENTITY(1,1),
 ID INT,
 BrandID INT NOT NULL,
 Name VARCHAR(255) NOT NULL,
 Price Money NOT NULL,
 Description VARCHAR(2000) NOT NULL,
 PrimaryCategoryID INT NOT NULL)
```

The trick is that the RowNumber field is an IDENTITY(1,1) field, so when filling this table with product data, RowNumber will automatically be populated with the row number. Adding records to a TABLE variable is done as with regular tables. We use SELECT INTO to read all the products that belong to the category we're interested in, and we add them to the @Products variable:

```
-- populate the table variable with the complete list of products
INSERT INTO @Products
SELECT Products.ID, BrandID, Name, Price, Description, PrimaryCategoryID
FROM Products INNER JOIN ProductCategories
  ON Products.ID = ProductCategories.ProductID
WHERE ProductCategories.CategoryID = @CategoryID
ORDER BY Products.Name
```

Note the SELECT query should be sorted by some criteria, so that future queries will read the products in the same order. Unless ORDER BY is used, although that's unlikely, SQL Server can return the same results sorted differently when the query is executed multiple times. After @Products is populated with the products of the category, @HowManyProducts is populated with the records count — which represents the number of products in the category. This is an output variable, which the ASP.NET code will read for building the pager with links to the product pages.

```
-- return the total number of products using an OUTPUT variable
SELECT @HowManyProducts = COUNT(ID) FROM @Products
```

Finally, some simple logic is used to determine which records of @Products are those in the page of products specified by @PageNumber.

```
-- extract the requested page of products
SELECT ID, BrandID, Name, Price, Description, PrimaryCategoryID
FROM @Products
WHERE RowNumber > (@PageNumber - 1) * @ProductsPerPage
  AND RowNumber <= @PageNumber * @ProductsPerPage
```

Note that you can also implement the paging feature using ASP.NET code. This solution implies reading the entire list of items from the database, and using C# code to read the extract and display the items you're interested in. This is usually very easy to implement, especially in ASP.NET 2.0, which even includes features for code-free paging and data binding. However, this technique implies sending large data sets from the database to the ASP.NET application on each request. Needless to say, site performance can be affected seriously if your store has thousands of products or more. Letting SQL Server deal with large amounts of data — which is its purpose, after all — is usually the way to go when performance is a concern.

The other stored procedure we're having a closer look at is GetSecondaryProductCategories. This procedure uses two INNER JOINs to retrieve a list with the product and category IDs and names, for all non-primary product categories. A product always has a single primary category (specified by its PrimaryCategoryID column). All the other product-category links need to be excluded using robots.txt, and the data returned by this procedure return the data required to build the robots.txt entries.

```
CREATE PROCEDURE GetSecondaryProductCategories
AS
SELECT Products.ID as ProductID,
       Products.Name as ProductName,
       ProductCategories.CategoryID AS SecondaryCategoryID,
       Categories.Name AS SecondaryCategoryName
FROM Products INNER JOIN ProductCategories
  ON (ProductCategories.ProductID = Products.ID)
INNER JOIN Categories
  ON (ProductCategories.CategoryID = Categories.ID)
WHERE Products.PrimaryCategoryID <> ProductCategories.CategoryID
```

The diagram in Figure 14-5 should help follow the relationships between the tables. Note that in a real site, where you also implement catalog administration features, you'll need to make sure that the primary category ID specified by the PrimaryCategoryID field is a real category that the product is associated with in the ProductCategories table. Otherwise, all the links to that product page would be excluded from the spider's view — which is obviously not something that you want.

The C# functions we use to execute stored procedures are located in the `CatalogDb` class. There you can find methods that return data about your categories, products, and brands. The methods that need to return more records do so by returning `DataTable` objects; the others return `DataRow` objects.

The methods in `CatalogDb` are called by all catalog components that require data about products, categories, or brands. For example, `UrlTools` requires this data in order to check if the product asked for exists, and if it's requested through its standard URL. The Web Forms — `Catalog.aspx`, `Category.aspx`, and `Product.aspx` — need the data to show it to the visitor.

Some of the data read from the database is stored as private fields in the classes that represent the Web Forms, and their values can be directly accessed and inserted into the output like this:

```
<head id="Head1" runat="server">
  <title><%= productName %> - Cookie Ogre Warehouse</title>
</head>
```

The same technique can be used to read public properties or fields, such as the `public readonly` field `SiteDomain` of the `UrlTools` class.

```
<h1>
  <%= productName %> -
  <a href="<%= UrlTools.SiteDomain %>">Cookie Ogre's Warehouse</a>
</h1>
```

To display lists of categories, products, and the categories pager, the `Repeater` control is used. This is a basic data-bound control that knows how to read a collection of data and display that data using templates. The contents of `<HeaderTemplate>` are sent to the output only once, when the repeater is rendered. The content of `<ItemTemplate>` is generated multiple times — once for each item of data from the data source. So if the repeater's data source is a `DataTable` object with ten data rows, the content of `<ItemTemplate>` is displayed ten times. Finally, `<EndTemplate>` is used to display any content you want generated only once at the end of your repeater object. (Two other template types are supported by `Repeater`: `<AlternatingItemTemplate>` and `<SeparatorTemplate>`.)

To understand how this works in practice, let's analyze the `Repeater` in `Catalog.aspx`. In order for the `Repeater` to show up and do anything useful (and any other data-bound control, for that matter), you need to bind it to a data source. The `Repeater` in `Catalog.aspx` is bound to the `DataTable` object returned by `CatalogDb.GetCategories`:

```
protected void Page_Load(object sender, EventArgs e)
{
  // load the list of categories
  categoriesRepeater.DataSource = CatalogDb.GetCategories();
  categoriesRepeater.DataBind();
}
```

Now let's look at its templates. The header template displays some header text, and the beginning `<ul>` tag for our products list:

```
<!-- Repeater control displays the products list -->
<asp:Repeater ID="categoriesRepeater" runat="server">
```

```
<HeaderTemplate>
  Browse our catalog by choosing a category of products:
  <ul>
</HeaderTemplate>
```

The item template, however, does most of the work. It includes the `<li>` and `</li>` tags required for displaying the list items, and the `Eval()` function is used to read field data from the data source, and `LinkFactory.MakeCategoryUrl()` is used to generate the category links:

```
<ItemTemplate>
  <li>
    <a href="<%# LinkFactory.MakeCategoryUrl(Eval("Name").ToString(),
Eval("ID").ToString()) %>">
      <%# Eval("Name") %>
    </a>
  </li>
</ItemTemplate>
```

Finally, the footer template generates the closing `</ul>` tag:

```
<FooterTemplate>
  </ul>
</FooterTemplate>
</asp:Repeater>
```

Hyperlinks in template items can be also generated (obviously) using the `Hyperlink` control. This is demonstrated in `pagerRepeater`, the repeater used to display the pager links in category pages. The data source of that repeater is simply an `ArrayList` object that we populate with the page numbers. This way, the `<ItemTemplate>` of the repeater is displayed for each page number, and the repeater's header and footer templates are used to generate the `<< previous` and `next >>` links.

`Product.aspx` was used as a test case for checking postback functionality. As you learned in Chapter 3, URL rewriting breaks the function of postback events. Read the details in Chapter 3, but for a quick reminder, postbacks happen when the form is submitted to the server for handling an event that has happened on the client side (such as a button click). The problem is that the `action` attribute of the form is hard-coded to the rewritten version of the URL — such as `Catalog.aspx?CategoryID=5`, instead of the URL that generated the event, such as `/Products/Low-Fat-C5/`. Chapter 3 discussed potential solutions to this problem. For Cookie Ogre's Warehouse we chose to use `Context.RewritePath` to rewrite the current path to `/?`. The effect of this is that the action attribute of the form will be rendered as `action=""`, in which case the browser will automatically submit the form to the current page.

```
// required to support PostBack events in the page
Context.RewritePath("/?");
```

Note that this approach is potentially dangerous, because rewriting the path in different parts of the page life cycle can break certain functionality. When server-side events need to be supported site-wide, different approaches are recommended.

Summary

We hope you've had fun developing Cookie Ogre's Warehouse! Even though the implemented functionality is very simplistic, it did demonstrate how to tie together the bits and pieces of code you met in the previous chapters of the book. At this point your journey into the world of technical search engine optimization is almost complete. In the next chapter you'll meet a checklist of details to look after when improving the search engine friendliness of an existing site.

15

Site Clinic: So You Have a Web Site?

Although we recommend otherwise, many web sites are initially built without any regard for search engines. Consequently, they often have a myriad of architectural problems. These problems comprise the primary focus of this book. Unfortunately, it is impossible to exhaustively and generally cover the solutions to all web site architectural problems in one short chapter. But thankfully, there is quite a bit of common ground involved.

Likewise, there are many feature enhancements that web sites may benefit from. Some only apply to blogs or forums, whereas others apply generally to all sites. Here, too, there is quite a bit of common ground involved. Furthermore, many such enhancements are easy to implement, and may even offer instant results.

This chapter aims to be a useful list of common fixes and enhancements that many web sites would benefit from. This list comprises two general kinds of fixes or enhancements:

❑ Items 1 through 9 in the checklist can be performed without disturbing site architecture. These items are worthwhile for most web sites and should be tasked without concern for detrimental effects.

❑ Items 10 through 15 come with caveats when implemented and should therefore be completed with caution — or not at all.

This chapter is not intended to be used alone. Rather, it is a sort of "alternative navigation" scheme that one with a preexisting web site can use to quickly surf *some* of the core content of this book. Appropriate references to the various chapters in this book are included with a brief description. Eventually, we hope that you read the book from cover to cover. But until then, dive in to some information that you can use right away!

1. Creating Sitemaps

There are two types of sitemaps — traditional and search engine sitemaps. Both are relatively easy to add to a web site. A traditional sitemap is created as any other HTML web page, whereas a search engine sitemap is formatted specifically according to a search engine's specifications. Creating either will typically increase the rate at which your content gets indexed, as well as get deeper or otherwise unreferenced content indexed. The former is important, not only because it gets you indexed faster in the first place, but it may mitigate content theft. A well-organized traditional sitemap is also useful for the human user.

Both types of sitemaps are covered in detail in Chapter 9, "Sitemaps."

2. Creating News Feeds

News feeds are a great way to streamline the process of content distribution. You can create news feeds so that others can conveniently read or syndicate a web site's content. Or you can programmatically use news feeds to publish information provided by others.

Read more on this topic, and learn how to optimize your web site for social search in Chapter 7, "Web Feeds and Social Bookmarking."

3. Fixing Duplication in Titles and Meta Tags

Using the same titles or meta tags on many pages of a web site can be detrimental to rankings. This may be, in part, because a search engine does not want such redundant-looking results to be displayed in its SERPs, because a user's perceived relevance is consequentially lowered. Furthermore, a generic-looking title will usually not prompt a user to click. This is usually a minor fix to an oversight made by a programmer.

More such commonly encountered SEO-related problems are mentioned in Chapter 2, "A Primer in Basic SEO." Duplicate content is discussed at length in Chapter 5, "Duplicate Content."

4. Getting Listed in Reputable Directories

Getting back links from reputable directories can provide a boost in the rankings — or at least get a new web site indexed to start. Best of the Web (`http://botw.org`), DMOZ (`http://dmoz.org`), Joe Ant (`http://joeant.com`), and Yahoo Directory (`http://dir.yahoo.com`) are the web site directories we recommend.

DMOZ is free, but also notoriously difficult to get into. Though we will not espouse our opinion as to why, we invite you to use Google to search for "get into DMOZ" and interpret the results.

5. Soliciting and Exchanging Relevant Links

Sending a few friendly emails to get a link from a neighbor may result in a few high-quality links. Exchanging links in *moderation* with various related *relevant* web sites may also help with search engine rankings. "Moderation," as usual, is difficult to define. However, a good metric is whether you believe that the link could realistically appear on its own regardless. If not, or it's on a "directory" page referenced at the bottom of the page with a sea of other random links, probably not!

6. Buying Links

Because relevant links are a major factor in search engine rankings, they have an equity — a "link equity." Predictably, individuals and businesses are now in the business of selling links. There is some disagreement, however, as to whether this is against the terms of service of the various search engines.

> *This topic is discussed in Chapter 8, "Black Hat SEO," although we do* not *consider buying relevant links a black hat practice. Several reputable companies are in the business of selling or brokering links.*

We strongly recommend only buying relevant links. This is not only because it is definitely against the terms of service of many search engines to buy irrelevant links, but also because such irrelevant links do not work as well in the first place. Some reputable link brokers are listed here:

❑ Text Link Ads (`http://www.text-link-ads.com`)

❑ Text Link Brokers (`http://www.textlinkbrokers.com`)

❑ LinkAdage (`http://www.linkadage.com/`)

Text Link Ads also estimates the value of a link on a given web site. The tool is located at `http://www.text-link-ads.com/link_calculator.php`.

> *Chapter 2, "A Primer in Basic SEO," discusses the essentials of link building and related concepts at length.*

7. Creating Link Bait

Although link bait can be difficult and hit-or-miss as far as results, it can frequently be an extremely economical way to build links. Link bait can vary from useful information and humor to intricate site tools and browser toolbars. For example, the link value calculator cited in section 6 is a great example of link bait.

> *Link bait is discussed in Chapter 10, "Link Bait."*

8. Adding Social Bookmarking Functionality

Social bookmarking web sites allow users to bookmark and tag content with keywords and commentary. The aggregate of this information is used both to cite popular content within certain time frames and niches, as well as by query. Popular content may be featured on the home page of such a site or ranked well for relevant keywords. Adding icons and buttons to web pages that facilitate the process of bookmarking will likely increase the number of users who bookmark your content.

Social bookmarking is discussed in Chapter 7, "Web Feeds and Social Bookmarking."

9. Starting a Blog and/or Forum

Blogs and forums both may attract traffic and links in droves if approached correctly. Bloggers readily exchange links amongst themselves, and a blog may also afford a company a more casual place to post less mundane, fun content. Whereas a humorous comment would not fit in a corporate site proper, it may be more appropriate for a blog. Blogs work quite well in harmony with social bookmarking functionality.

Forums, once they gain momentum, also attract many links. The trick to a forum is building such momentum. Once started, much of the content is generated by the users. If a web site does not already have many thousands of unique visitors per day, though, a forum is most likely not going to be a success.

10. Dealing with a Pure Flash or AJAX Site

Flash sites present many problems from a search engine optimization perspective. There is really no way to approach this problem, except to design a site that replaces or supplements the Flash design that is *not* Flash-based. There are other less onerous "solutions," but they are less than ideal.

Flash sites are discussed in Chapter 6, "SE-Friendly HTML and JavaScript."

11. Preventing Black Hat Victimization

Black hat SEOs are always on the lookout for places to inject links, JavaScript redirects, and spam content. Properly sanitizing and/or escaping foreign data can prevent or mitigate such attacks. Where links are appropriate to post, if they are unaudited, they should be "nofollowed." Known, problematic anonymous proxies should be blocked. Vulnerabilities to such attacks are typically found in comments, guestbooks, and forums.

This material is covered in detail in Chapter 8, "Black Hat SEO."

12. Examining Your URLs for Problems

URLs with too many parameters or redirects can confuse a search engine. You should construct URLs with both users and search engines in mind.

> URLs are discussed in Chapter 3, "Provocative SE-Friendly URLs." Redirects are discussed in Chapter 4, "Content Relocation and HTTP Status Codes." In Chapter 13, "Coping with Technical Issues," you learn how to build your own library that verifies the links within your web site are functional.

13. Looking for Duplicate Content

Having many pages with the same or similar content in excess can result in poorer rankings. And though it is a matter of contention as to whether an explicit *penalty* exists for having duplicate content, it is undesirable for many reasons. Duplicate content is, however, not a simple problem with a single cause. Rather, it is a complex problem with myriad causes.

> Duplicate content is the subject of aptly named Chapter 5, "Duplicate Content."

14. Eliminating Session IDs

Use of URL-based session management may allow users with cookies turned off to use a web site that requires session-related information, but it may also wreak havoc for the web site in search engines. For this reason URL-based sessions should either be completely turned off, or cloaking should be employed to turn off the URL-based session management if the user-agent is a spider.

> Session IDs and their associated problems are discussed at length in Chapters 3 and 11, respectively.

15. Tweaking On-Page Factors

On-page factors may have diminished in effect over the years, but it is still advantageous to author HTML that employs elements that mean something semantically. Especially if you author HTML using a WYSIWYG editor, or use a content management system with a WYSIWYG editor, this may not be occurring. Other problems may involve having a large navigation element physically before the content, as well as large unnecessary `ViewState` data, which may not be only detrimental to SEO, but it also hurts performance.

> Chapter 6 discusses the aforementioned topics as well as many other HTML and JavaScript-related issues at length.

Summary

Wow, so much to do! And this chapter is only a guide covering *some* of the important points for those who already have a preexisting web site. There is much more information throughout this book than the 15 sections touched upon here. But covering these bases should go a long way in getting you started. So grab that can of Red Bull and dive in!

Simple Regular Expressions

This appendix examines some basic aspects of constructing regular expressions. One reason for working through the simple regular expressions presented in this chapter is to illuminate the regular expressions used in Chapter 3 and further extend your knowledge of regular expressions.

The following exercises use OpenOffice.org Writer — a free document editor that makes it easy to apply regular expressions to text, and verify that they do what you expected. You can download this tool from `http://www.openoffice.org`.

> **This appendix has been "borrowed" from *Beginning Regular Expressions* (Wiley Publishing, Inc., 2005) by Andrew Watt. We recommend this book for further (and more comprehensive) reference into the world of regular expressions.**

The examples used are necessarily simple, but by using regular expressions to match fairly simple text patterns, you should become increasingly familiar and comfortable with the use of foundational regular expression constructs that can be used to form part of more complex regular expressions. Other chapters explore additional regular expression constructs and address progressively more complex problems.

One of the issues this chapter explores in some detail is the situation where you want to match occurrences of characters other than those characters simply occurring once.

This chapter looks at the following:

- ❑ How to match single characters
- ❑ How to match optional characters
- ❑ How to match characters that can occur an unbounded number of times, whether the characters of interest are optional or required
- ❑ How to match characters that can occur a specified number of times

First, let's look at the simplest situation: matching single characters.

Matching Single Characters

The simplest regular expression involves matching a single character. If you want to match a single, specified alphabetic character or numeric digit, you simply use a pattern that consists of that character or digit. So, for example, to match the uppercase letter L, you would use the following pattern:

```
L
```

The pattern matches any occurrence of the uppercase L. You have not qualified the pattern in any way to limit matching, so expect it to match any occurrence of uppercase L. Of course, if matching is being carried out in a case-insensitive manner (which is discussed in Chapter 4), both uppercase L and lowercase l will be matched.

Matching a Single Character

You can apply this pattern to the sample document UpperL.txt, which is shown here:

```
Excel had XLM macros. They were replaced by Visual Basic for Applications in later
versions of the spreadsheet software.

CMLIII

Leoni could swim like a fish.

Legal difficulties plagued the Clinton administration. Lewinski was the source of
some of the former president's difficulties.
```

1. Open OpenOffice.org Writer, and open the file UpperL.txt.

2. Use the Ctrl+F keyboard shortcut to open the Find and Replace dialog box, and check the Regular Expressions check box and the Match Case check box in the Options section.

3. Enter the regular expression pattern L in the Search For text box at the top of the Find and Replace dialog box, and click the Find All button.

If all has gone well, each occurrence of an uppercase L should be highlighted.

Figure A-1 shows the matching of the pattern L in OpenOffice.org Writer against the sample document UpperL.txt. Notice that there are five matches contained in the sequences of characters XLM, CMLIII, Leoni, Legal, and Lewinski.

The default behavior of OpenOffice.org Writer is to carry out a case-insensitive match. As you can see in Figure A-1, I have checked the Match Case check box so that only the same case as specified in the regular expression is matched.

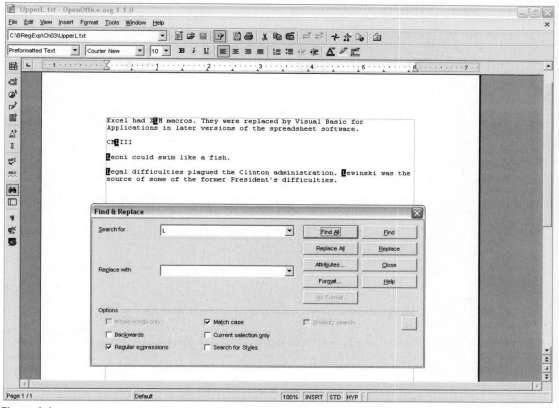

Figure A-1

For each character in the document, OpenOffice.org Writer checks whether that character is an upper-case L. If it is, the regular expression pattern is matched. In OpenOffice.org Writer, a match is indicated by highlighting of the character(s) — in this case, a single character — for each match, assuming that the Find All button has been clicked.

How can you match a single character using JavaScript?

Matching a Single Character in JavaScript

You want to find all occurrences of uppercase L. You can express the simple task that you want to use regular expressions to do as follows:

Match any occurrence of uppercase L.

You can see, using JavaScript as a sample technology, how most regular expression engines will match the pattern L using the XHTML file UpperL.html, shown here:

```
<html>
<head>
<title>Check for Upper Case L</title>
<script language="javascript" type="text/javascript">
```

```
var myRegExp = /L/;

function Validate(entry){
return myRegExp.test(entry);
} // end function Validate()

function ShowPrompt(){
var entry = prompt("This script tests for matches for the regular expression
pattern: " + myRegExp + ".\nType in a string and click on the OK button.", "Type
your text here.");
if (Validate(entry)){
alert("There is a match!\nThe regular expression pattern is: " + myRegExp + ".\n
The string that you entered was: '" + entry + "'.");
} // end if
else{
 alert("There is no match in the string you entered.\n" + "The regular expression
pattern is " + myRegExp + "\n" + "You entered the string: '" + entry + "'." );
} // end else

} // end function ShowPrompt()

</script>
</head>
<body>
<form name="myForm">
<br />
<button type="Button" onclick="ShowPrompt()">Click here to enter text.</button>
</form>
</body>
</html>
```

1. Navigate in Windows Explorer to the directory that contains the file UpperL.html and double-click the file. It should open in your default browser.

2. Click the button labeled Click Here to Enter Text. A prompt window is shown, as you can see in Figure A-2.

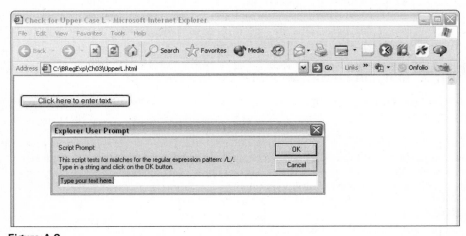

Figure A-2

3. Type a character or a string in the text box that contains the default text *Type your text here,* and the JavaScript code will test whether or not there is a match for the regular expression pattern, in this case L. Click the OK button.

4. Inspect the alert box that is displayed to assess whether or not a match is present in the string that you entered. Figure A-3 shows the message when a successful match is made. Figure A-4 shows the message displayed when the string that you enter does not match the regular expression pattern.

Figure A-3

Figure A-4

The simple web page contains JavaScript code.

The JavaScript variable myRegExp is assigned the literal regular expression pattern L, using the following declaration and assignment statement:

```
var myRegExp = /L/;
```

In JavaScript, the forward slash is used to delimit a regular expression pattern in a way similar to how paired quotes are used to delimit a string. There is an alternate syntax, which is not discussed here.

When you click the button labeled Click Here to Enter Text, the ShowPrompt() function is called.

The entry variable is used to collect the string you enter in the prompt box:

```
var entry = prompt("This script tests for matches for the regular expression
pattern: " + myRegExp + ".\nType in a string and click on the OK button.", "Type
your text here.");
```

The output created depends on whether or not the text you entered contains a match for the regular expression pattern. Once the text has been entered and the OK button clicked, an if statement is executed, which checks whether or not the text you entered (and which is stored in the entry variable) contains a match for the regular expression pattern stored in the variable myRegExp:

```
if (Validate(entry)){
```

361

The `if` statement causes the `Validate` function to be called:

```
function Validate(entry){
return myRegExp.test(entry);
} // end function Validate()
```

The `test()` method of the `myRegExp` variable is used to determine whether or not a match is present.

If the `if` statement

```
if (Validate(entry))
```

returns the Boolean value `true`, the following code is executed

```
alert("There is a match!\nThe regular expression pattern is: " + myRegExp + ".\n
The string that you entered was: '" + entry + "'.");
```

and uses the `myRegExp` and `entry` variables to display the regular expression pattern and the string that you entered, together with explanatory text.

If there is no match, the following code is executed, because it is contained in the `else` clause of the `if` statement:

```
alert("There is no match in the string you entered.\n" + "The regular expression
pattern is " + myRegExp + "\n" + "You entered the string: '" + entry + "'." );
```

Again, the `myRegExp` and `entry` variables are used to give feedback to the user about what is to be matched and the string that he or she entered.

Of course, in practice, you typically want to match a sequence of characters rather than a single character.

Matching Sequences of Characters That Each Occur Once

When the regular expression pattern `L` was matched, you made use of the default behavior of the regular expression engine, meaning that when there is no indication of how often a character (or sequence of characters) is allowed to occur, the regular expression engine assumes that the character(s) in the pattern occur exactly once, except when you include a quantifier in the regular expression pattern that specifies an occurrence other than exactly once. This behavior also allows the matching of sequences of the same character.

To match two characters that are the same character and occur twice without any intervening characters (including whitespace), you can simply use a pattern with the desired character written twice in the pattern.

Matching Doubled Characters

As an example, look at how you can match sequences of characters where a character occurs exactly twice — for example, the doubled `r` that can occur in words such as `arrow` and `narrative`.

A problem definition for the desired match can be expressed as follows:

Match any occurrence of the lowercase character r immediately followed by another lowercase r.

An example file, `DoubledR.txt`, is shown here:

```
The arrow flew through the air at great speed.

This is a narrative of great interest to many readers.

Apples and oranges are both types of fruit.

Asses and donkeys are both four-legged mammals.

Several million barrels of oil are produced daily.
```

The following pattern will match all occurrences of `rr` in the sample file:

```
rr
```

1. Open OpenOffice.org Writer, and open the sample file `DoubledR.txt`.
2. Use the keyboard shortcut Ctrl+F to open the Find and Replace dialog box.
3. Check the Regular Expressions check box and the Match Case check box.
4. Enter the pattern `rr` in the Search For text box and click the Find All button.

Figure A-5 shows `DoubledR.txt` opened in OpenOffice.org Writer, as previously described. Notice that all occurrences of `rr` are matched, but single occurrences of `r` are not matched.

The pattern `rr` indicates to the regular expression engine that an attempt should be made to match the lowercase alphabetic character `r`; then, if that first match is successful, an attempt should be made to match the next character. The entire match is successful if the second character is also a lowercase `r`.

If the attempt to match the first character fails, the next character is tested to see if it is a lowercase `r`. If it is not a lowercase `r`, the match fails, and a new attempt is made to match the following character against the first `r` of the regular expression pattern.

You can also try this out in the Komodo Regular Expression Toolkit, as shown in Figure A-6, which matches successive lowercase ms. You can download the latest trial version of the Komodo IDE, which includes the Regular Expression Toolkit, from `http://activestate.com/Products/Komodo`. Komodo version 2.5 is used in this chapter. Clear the regular expression and the test text from the Komodo Toolkit. Enter **mammals** in the area for the string to be matched, and type **m** in the area for the regular expression. At that point, the initial m of `mammals` is matched. Then type a second **m** in the area for the regular expression, and the highlight indicating a match moves to the mm in the middle of `mammals`, as you can see in Figure A-6.

Appendix A: Simple Regular Expressions

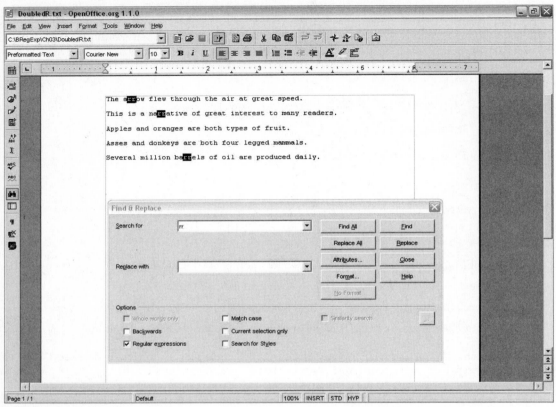

Figure A-5

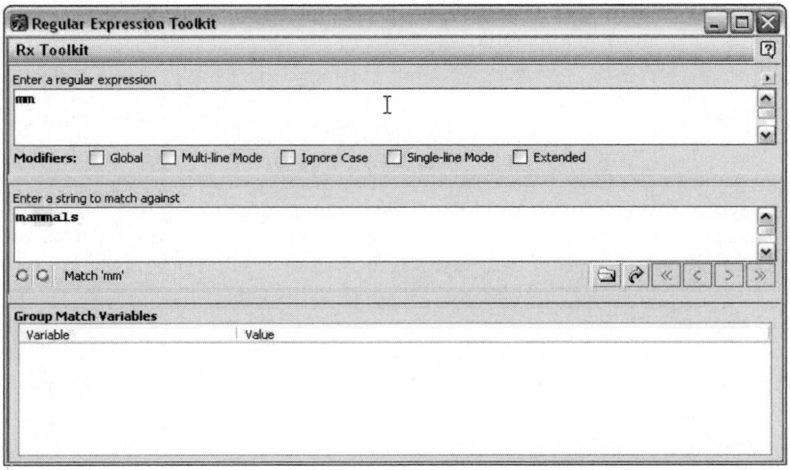

Figure A-6

These two examples have shown how you can match doubled characters using one of the syntax options that are available. Later in this chapter, you look at an alternative syntax that can match an exact number of successive occurrences of a desired character, which can be exactly two or can be a larger number. The alternative syntax uses curly braces and, in addition to allowing matches of an exact number of occurrences, allows variable numbers of occurrences to be matched.

Introducing Metacharacters

To match three characters, you can simply write the character three times in a row to form a pattern. For example, to match part numbers that take the form ABC123 (in other words, three alphabetic characters followed by three numeric digits, which will match the alphabetic characters AAA), simply use the following pattern:

```
AAA
```

To match the other part of such part numbers, you need to introduce the concept of a *metacharacter*. The patterns you have seen so far include characters that stand, literally, for the same character. A metacharacter can be a single character or a pair of characters (the first is typically a backslash) that has a meaning other than the literal characters it contains.

There are several ways in which you can match the 123 part of a part number of the form ABC123. One is to write the following:

```
\d\d\d
```

Each \d is a metacharacter that stands for a numeric digit 0 through 9, inclusive. The \d metacharacter does *not* stand for a backslash followed by a lowercase d.

Notice that the \d metacharacter differs significantly in meaning from the literal characters we have used in patterns so far. The character L in a pattern could match only an uppercase L, but the metacharacter \d can match *any* of the numeric digits 0, 1, 2, 3, 4, 5, 6, 7, 8, or 9.

A metacharacter often matches a *class* of characters. In this case, the metacharacter \d matches the class of characters that are numeric digits.

When you have the pattern \d\d\d, you know that it matches three successive numeric digits, but it will match 012, 234, 345, 999, and hundreds of other numbers.

Matching Triple Numeric Digits

Suppose that you want to match a sequence of three numeric digits. In plain English, you might say that you want to match a three-digit number. A slightly more formal way to express what you want to do is this: Match a numeric digit. If the first character is a numeric digit, attempt to match the next character as a numeric digit. If both the characters are numeric digits, attempt to match a third successive numeric digit.

The metacharacter \d matches a single numeric digit; therefore, as described a little earlier, you could use the pattern

```
\d\d\d
```

to match three successive numeric digits.

If all three matches are successful, a match for the regular expression pattern has been found.

The test file, ABC123.txt, is shown here:

```
ABC123

A234BC

A23BCD4

Part Number DRC22

Part Number XFA221

Part Number RRG417
```

For the moment, let's aim to match only the numeric digits using the pattern \d\d\d shown earlier.

For this example, we will use JavaScript, for reasons that will be explained in a moment.

1. Navigate to the directory that contains the files ABC123.txt and ThreeDigits.html. Open ThreeDigits.html in a web browser.

2. Click the button labeled Click Here to Enter Text.

3. When the prompt box opens, enter a string to test. Enter a string copied from ABC123.txt.

4. Click the OK button and inspect the alert box to see if the string that you entered contained a match for the pattern \d\d\d.

Figure A-7 shows the result after entering the string Part Number RRG417.

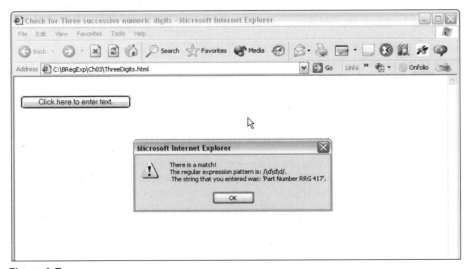

Figure A-7

Try each of the strings from ABC123.txt. You can also create your own test string. Notice that the pattern \d\d\d will match any sequence of three successive numeric digits, but single numeric digits or pairs of numeric digits are not matched.

The regular expression engine looks for a numeric digit. If the first character that it tests is not a numeric digit, it moves one character through the test string and then tests whether that character matches a numeric digit. If not, it moves one character further and tests again.

If a match is found for the first occurrence of \d, the regular expression engine tests if the next character is also a numeric digit. If that matches, a third character is tested to determine if it matches the \d metacharacter for a numeric digit. If three successive characters are each a numeric digit, there is a match for the regular expression pattern \d\d\d.

You can see this matching process in action by using the Komodo Regular Expression Toolkit. Open the Komodo Regular Expression Toolkit, and clear any existing regular expression and test string. Enter the test string **A234BC**; then, in the area for the regular expression pattern, enter the pattern **\d**. You will see that the first numeric digit, 2, is highlighted as a match. Add a second **\d** to the regular expression area, and you will see that 23 is highlighted as a match. Finally, add a third **\d** to give a final regular expression pattern \d\d\d, and you will see that 234 is highlighted as a match. See Figure A-8.

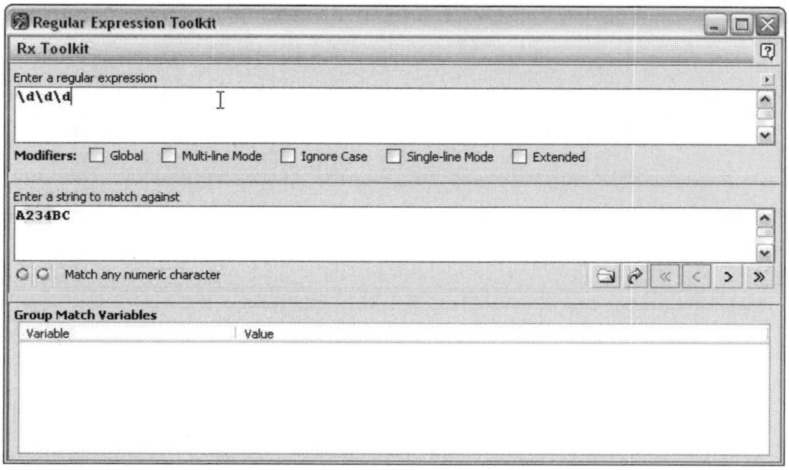

Figure A-8

You can try this with other test text from ABC123.txt. I suggest that you also try this out with your own test text that includes numeric digits and see which test strings match. You may find that you need to add a space character after the test string for matching to work correctly in the Komodo Regular Expression Toolkit.

Why did we use JavaScript for the preceding example? Because we can't use OpenOffice.org Writer to test matches for the \d metacharacter.

Appendix A: Simple Regular Expressions

Matching numeric digits can pose difficulties. Figure A-9 shows the result of an attempted match in `ABC123.txt` when using OpenOffice.org Writer with the pattern `\d\d\d`.

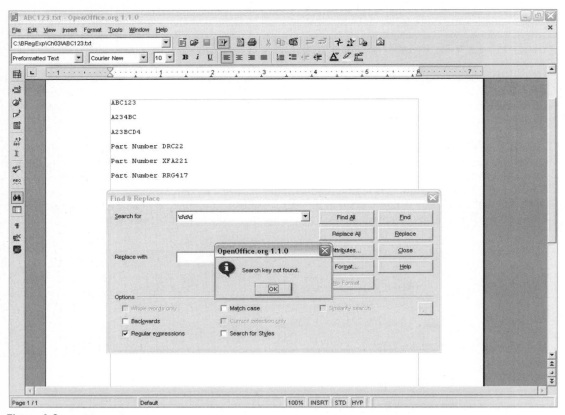

Figure A-9

As you can see in Figure A-9, no match is found in OpenOffice.org Writer. Numeric digits in OpenOffice.org Writer use nonstandard syntax in that OpenOffice.org Writer lacks support for the `\d` metacharacter.

One solution to this type of problem in OpenOffice.org Writer is to use character classes, which are described in detail in Chapter 5. For now, it is sufficient to note that the regular expression pattern

```
[0-9][0-9][0-9]
```

gives the same results as the pattern `\d\d\d`, because the meaning of `[0-9][0-9][0-9]` is the same as `\d\d\d`. The use of that character class to match three successive numeric digits in the file `ABC123.txt` is shown in Figure A-10.

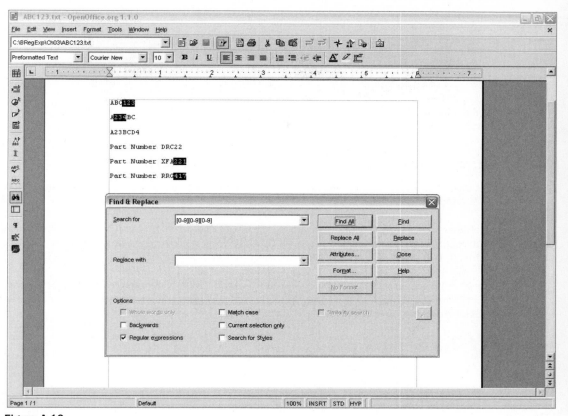

Figure A-10

Another syntax in OpenOffice.org Writer, which uses POSIX metacharacters, is described in Chapter 12.

The findstr utility also lacks the \d metacharacter, so if you want to use it to find matches, you must use the preceding character class shown in the command line, as follows:

```
findstr /N [0-9][0-9][0-9] ABC123.txt
```

You will find matches on four lines, as shown in Figure A-11. The preceding command line will work correctly only if the ABC123.txt file is in the current directory. If it is in a different directory, you will need to reflect that in the path for the file that you enter at the command line.

The next section combines the techniques that you have seen so far to find a combination of literally expressed characters and a sequence of characters.

Figure A-11

Matching Sequences of Different Characters

A common task in simple regular expressions is to find a combination of literally specified single characters plus a sequence of characters.

There is an almost infinite number of possibilities in terms of characters that you could test. Let's focus on a very simple list of part numbers and look for part numbers with the code DOR followed by three numeric digits. In this case, the regular expression should do the following:

Look for a match for uppercase D. If a match is found, check if the next character matches uppercase O. If that matches, next check if the following character matches uppercase R. If those three matches are present, check if the next three characters are numeric digits.

Finding Literal Characters and Sequences of Characters

The file `PartNumbers.txt` is the sample file for this example.

```
BEF123

RRG417

DOR234

DOR123

CCG991
```

First, try it in OpenOffice.org Writer, remembering that you need to use the regular expression pattern [0-9] instead of \d.

1. Open the file `PartNumbers.txt` in OpenOffice.org Writer, and open the Find and Replace Dialog box by pressing Ctrl+F.

2. Check the Regular Expression check box and the Match Case check box.

3. Enter the pattern **DOR[0-9][0-9][0-9]** in the Search For text box and click the Find All button.

The text DOR234 and DOR123 is highlighted, indicating that those are matches for the regular expression.

The regular expression engine first looks for the literal character uppercase D. Each character is examined in turn to determine if there is or is not a match.

If a match is found, the regular expression engine then looks at the next character to determine if the following character is an uppercase O. If that too matches, it looks to see if the third character is an uppercase R. If all three of those characters match, the engine next checks to see if the fourth character is a numeric digit. If so, it checks if the fifth character is a numeric digit. If that too matches, it checks if the sixth character is a numeric digit. If that too matches, the entire regular expression pattern is matched. Each match is displayed in OpenOffice.org Writer as a highlighted sequence of characters.

You can check the `PartNumbers.txt` file for lines that contain a match for the pattern

```
DOR[0-9][0-9][0-9]
```

using the `findstr` utility from the command line, as follows:

```
findstr /N DOR[0-9][0-9][0-9] PartNumbers.txt
```

As you can see in Figure A-12, lines containing the same two matching sequences of characters, DOR234 and DOR123, are matched. If the directory that contains the file `PartNumbers.txt` is not the current directory in the command window, you will need to adjust the path to the file accordingly.

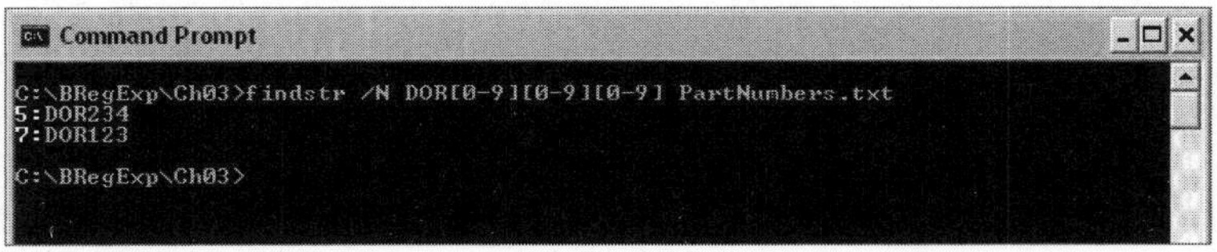

Figure A-12

The Komodo Regular Expression Toolkit can also be used to test the pattern DOR\d\d\d. As you can see in Figure A-13, the test text DOR123 matches.

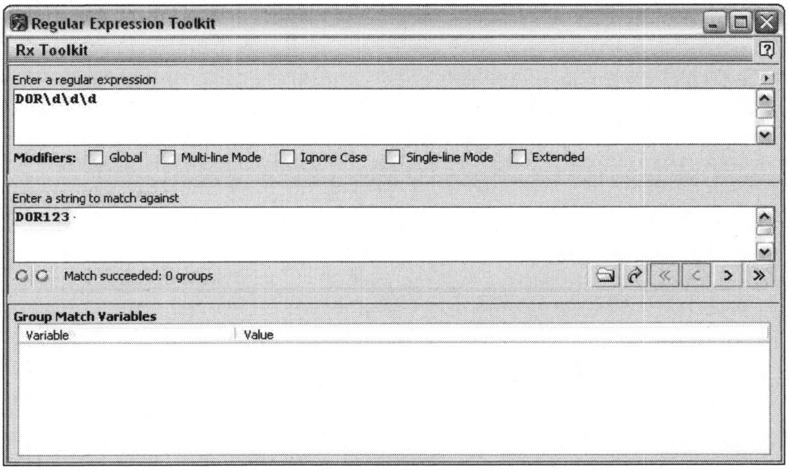

Figure A-13

Now that you have looked at how to match sequences of characters, each of which occurs exactly once, let's move on to look at matching characters that can occur a variable number of times.

Matching Optional Characters

Matching literal characters is straightforward, particularly when you are aiming to match exactly one literal character for each corresponding literal character that you include in a regular expression pattern. The next step up from that basic situation is where a single literal character may occur zero times or one time. In other words, a character is optional. Most regular expression dialects use the question mark (?) character to indicate that the preceding chunk is optional. I am using the term "chunk" loosely here to mean the thing that precedes the question mark. That chunk can be a single character or various, more complex regular expression constructs. For the moment, we will deal with the case of the single, optional character. More complex regular expression constructs, such as groups, are described in Chapter 7.

For example, suppose you are dealing with a group of documents that contain both U.S. English and British English.

You may find that words such as `color` (in U.S. English) appear as `colour` (British English) in some documents. You can express a pattern to match both words like this:

```
colou?r
```

You may want to standardize the documents so that all the spellings are U.S. English spellings.

Matching an Optional Character

Try this out using the Komodo Regular Expression Toolkit:

1. Open the Komodo Regular Expression Toolkit and clear any regular expression pattern or text that may have been retained.

2. Insert the text `colour` into the area for the text to be matched.

3. Enter the regular expression pattern `colou?r` into the area for the regular expression pattern. The text `colour` is matched, as shown in Figure A-14.

Try this regular expression pattern with text such as that shown in the sample file `Colors.txt`:

```
Red is a color.

His collar is too tight or too colouuuurful.

These are bright colours.

These are bright colors.

Calorific is a scientific term.

"Your life is very colorful," she said.
```

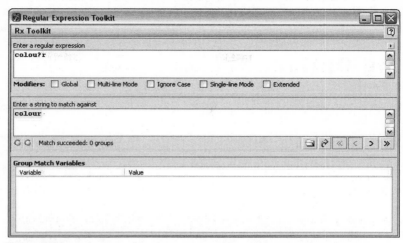

Figure A-14

The word `color` in the line `Red is a color.` will match the pattern `colou?r`.

When the regular expression engine reaches a position just before the `c` of `color`, it attempts to match a lowercase `c`. This match succeeds. It next attempts to match a lowercase `o`. That too matches. It next attempts to match a lowercase `l` and a lowercase `o`. They match as well. It then attempts to match the pattern `u?`, which means zero or one lowercase `u` characters. Because there are exactly zero lowercase `u` characters following the lowercase `o`, there is a match. The pattern `u?` matches zero characters. Finally, it attempts to match the final character in the pattern — that is, the lowercase `r`. Because the next character in the string `color` does match a lowercase `r`, the whole pattern is matched.

There is no match in the line `His collar is too tight or too colouuuurful`. The only possible match might be in the sequence of characters `colouuuurful`. The failure to match occurs when the regular expression engine attempts to match the pattern `u?`. Because the pattern `u?` means "match zero or one lowercase `u` characters," there is a match on the first `u` of `colouuuurful`. After that successful match, the regular expression engine attempts to match the final character of the pattern `colou?r` against the second lowercase `u` in `colouuuurful`. That attempt to match fails, so the attempt to match the whole pattern `colou?r` against the sequence of characters `colouuuurful` also fails.

What happens when the regular expression engine attempts to find a match in the line `These are bright colours.`?

When the regular expression engine reaches a position just before the `c` of `colours`, it attempts to match a lowercase `c`. That match succeeds. It next attempts to match a lowercase `o`, a lowercase `l`, and another lowercase `o`. These also match. It next attempts to match the pattern `u?`, which means zero or one lowercase `u` characters. Because exactly one lowercase `u` character follows the lowercase `o` in `colours`, there is a match. Finally, the regular expression engine attempts to match the final character in the pattern, the lowercase `r`. Because the next character in the string `colours` does match a lowercase `r`, the whole pattern is matched.

The `findstr` utility can also be used to test for the occurrence of the sequence of characters `color` and `colour`, but the regular expression engine in the `findstr` utility has a limitation in that it lacks a metacharacter to signify an optional character. For many purposes, the * metacharacter, which matches zero, one, or more occurrences of the preceding character, will work successfully.

To look for lines that contain matches for `colour` and `color` using the `findstr` utility, enter the following at the command line:

```
findstr /N colo*r Colors.txt
```

The preceding command line assumes that the file `Colors.txt` is in the current directory.

Figure A-15 shows the result from using the `findstr` utility on `Colors.txt`.

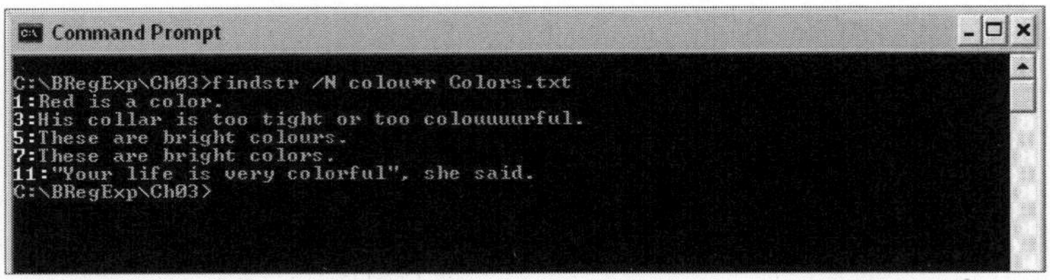

Figure A-15

Notice that lines that contain the sequences of characters `color` and `colour` are successfully matched, whether as whole words or parts of longer words. However, notice, too, that the slightly strange "word" `colouuuurful` is also matched due to the * metacharacter's allowing multiple occurrences of the lowercase letter u. In most practical situations, such bizarre "words" won't be an issue for you, and the * quantifier will be an appropriate substitute for the ? quantifier when using the `findstr` utility. In some situations, where you want to match precisely zero or one specific characters, the `findstr` utility may not provide the functionality that you need, because it would also match a character sequence such as `colonifier`.

Having seen how we can use a single optional character in a regular expression pattern, let's look at how you can use multiple optional characters in a single regular expression pattern.

Matching Multiple Optional Characters

Many English words have multiple forms. Sometimes, it may be necessary to match all of the forms of a word. Matching all those forms can require using multiple optional characters in a regular expression pattern.

Consider the various forms of the word `color` (U.S. English) and `colour` (British English). They include the following:

```
color (U.S. English, singular noun)
```

```
colour (British English, singular noun)

colors (U.S. English, plural noun)

colours (British English, plural noun)

color's (U.S. English, possessive singular)

colour's (British English, possessive singular)

colors' (U.S. English, possessive plural)

colours' (British English, possessive plural)
```

The following regular expression pattern, which includes three optional characters, can match all eight of these word forms:

```
colou?r'?s?'?
```

If you tried to express this in a semiformal way, you might have the following problem definition:

Match the U.S. English and British English forms of `color` **(**`colour`**), including the singular noun, the plural noun, and the singular possessive and the plural possessive.**

Let's try it out, and then I will explain why it works and what limitations it potentially has.

Matching Multiple Optional Characters

Use the sample file `Colors2.txt` to explore this example:

```
These colors are bright.

Some colors feel warm. Other colours feel cold.

A color's temperature can be important in creating reaction to an image.

These colours' temperatures are important in this discussion.

Red is a vivid colour.
```

To test the regular expression, follow these steps:

1. Open OpenOffice.org Writer, and open the file `Colors2.txt`.

2. Use the keyboard shortcut Ctrl+F to open the Find and Replace dialog box.

3. Check the Regular Expressions check box and the Match Case check box.

4. In the Search for text box, enter the regular expression pattern **colou?r'?s?'?** and click the Find All button. If all has gone well, you should see the matches shown in Figure A-16.

Appendix A: Simple Regular Expressions

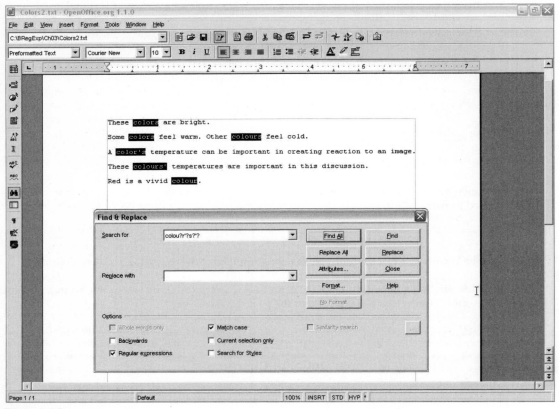

Figure A-16

As you can see, all the sample forms of the word of interest have been matched.

In this description, I will focus initially on matching of the forms of the word `colour/color`.

How does the pattern `colou?r'?s?'?` match the word `color`? Assume that the regular expression engine is at the position immediately before the first letter of `color`. It first attempts to match lowercase `c`, because one lowercase `c` must be matched. That matches. Attempts are then made to match a subsequent lowercase `o`, `l`, and `o`. These all also match. Then an attempt is made to match an optional lowercase `u`. In other words, zero or one occurrences of the lowercase character `u` is needed. Because there are zero occurrences of lowercase `u`, there is a match. Next, an attempt is made to match lowercase `r`. The lowercase `r` in `color` matches. Then an attempt is made to match an optional apostrophe. Because there is no occurrence of an apostrophe, there is a match. Next, the regular expression engine attempts to match an optional lowercase `s` — in other words, to match zero or one occurrences of lowercase `s`. Because there is no occurrence of lowercase `s`, again, there is a match. Finally, an attempt is made to match an optional apostrophe. Because there is no occurrence of an apostrophe, another match is found. Because a match exists for all the components of the regular expression pattern, there is a match for the whole regular expression pattern `colour?r'?s?'?`.

Now, how does the pattern `colou?r'?s'?` match the word `colour`? Assume that the regular expression engine is at the position immediately before the first letter of `colour`. It first attempts to match lowercase c, because one lowercase c must be matched. That matches. Next, attempts are made to match a subsequent lowercase o, l, and another o. These also match. Then an attempt is made to match an optional lowercase u. In other words, zero or one occurrences of the lowercase character u are needed. Because there is one occurrence of lowercase u, there is a match. Next, an attempt is made to match lowercase r. The lowercase r in `colour` matches. Next, the engine attempts to match an optional apostrophe. Because there is no occurrence of an apostrophe, there is a match. Next, the regular expression engine attempts to match an optional lowercase s — in other words, to match zero or one occurrences of lowercase s. Because there is no occurrence of lowercase s, a match exists. Finally, an attempt is made to match an optional apostrophe. Because there is no occurrence of an apostrophe, there is a match. All the components of the regular expression pattern have a match; therefore, the entire regular expression pattern `colour?r'?s'?` matches.

Work through the other six word forms shown earlier, and you'll find that each of the word forms does, in fact, match the regular expression pattern.

The pattern `colou?r'?s'?` matches all eight of the word forms that were listed earlier, but will the pattern match the following sequence of characters?

```
colour's'
```

Can you see that it does match? Can you see why it matches the pattern? If each of the three optional characters in the regular expression is present, the preceding sequence of characters matches. That rather odd sequence of characters likely won't exist in your sample document, so the possibility of false matches (reduced specificity) won't be an issue for you.

How can you avoid the problem caused by such odd sequences of characters as `colour's'`? You want to be able to express something like this:

Match a lowercase c. If a match is present, attempt to match a lowercase o. If that match is present, attempt to match a lowercase l. If there is a match, attempt to match a lowercase o. If a match exists, attempt to match an optional lowercase u. If there is a match, attempt to match a lowercase r. If there is a match, attempt to match an optional apostrophe. And if a match exists here, attempt to match an optional lowercase s. If the earlier optional apostrophe was not present, attempt to match an optional apostrophe.

With the techniques that you have seen so far, you aren't able to express ideas such as "match something only if it is not preceded by something else." That sort of approach might help achieve higher specificity at the expense of increased complexity. Techniques where matching depends on such issues are presented in Chapter 9.

Other Cardinality Operators

Testing for matches only for optional characters can be very useful, as you saw in the `colors` example, but it would be pretty limiting if that were the only quantifier available to a developer. Most regular expression implementations provide two other cardinality operators (also called *quantifiers*): the * operator and the + operator, which are described in the following sections.

The * Quantifier

The * operator refers to zero or more occurrences of the pattern to which it is related. In other words, a character or group of characters is optional but may occur more than once. Zero occurrences of the chunk that precedes the * quantifier should match. A single occurrence of that chunk should also match. So should two occurrences, three occurrences, and ten occurrences. In principle, an unlimited number of occurrences will also match.

Let's try this out in an example using OpenOffice.org Writer.

Matching Zero or More Occurrences

The sample file, `Parts.txt`, contains a listing of part numbers that have two alphabetic characters followed by zero or more numeric digits. In our simple sample file, the maximum number of numeric digits is three, but because the * quantifier will match three occurrences, we can use it to match the sample part numbers. If there is a good reason why it is important that a maximum of three numeric digits can occur, we can express that notion by using an alternative syntax, which we will look at a little later in this chapter. Each of the part numbers in this example consists of the sequence of uppercase characters ABC followed by zero or more numeric digits:

```
ABC

ABC123

ABC12

ABC889

ABC8899

ABC34
```

We can express what we want to do as follows:

Match an uppercase A. If there is a match, attempt to match an uppercase B. If there is a match, attempt to match an uppercase C. If all three uppercase characters match, attempt to match zero or more numeric digits.

Because all the part numbers begin with the literal characters ABC, you can use the pattern

```
ABC[0-9]*
```

to match part numbers that correspond to the description in the problem definition.

1. Open OpenOffice.org Writer, and open the sample file `Parts.txt`.
2. Use Ctrl+F to open the Find and Replace dialog box.
3. Check the Regular Expression check box and the Match Case check box.
4. Enter the regular expression pattern `ABC[0-9]*` in the Search For text box.
5. Click the Find All button, and inspect the matches that are highlighted.

Figure A-17 shows the matches in OpenOffice.org Writer. As you can see, all of the part numbers match the pattern.

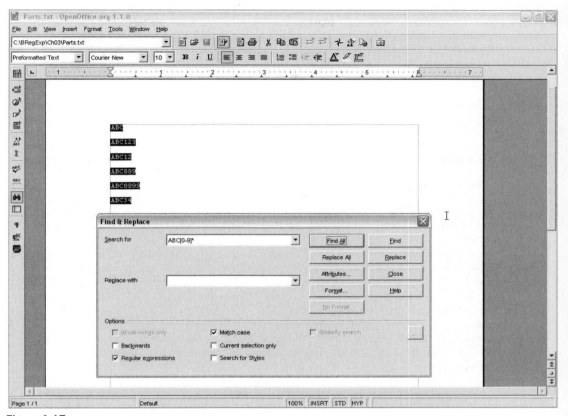

Figure A-17

Before we work through a couple of the matches, let's briefly look at part of the regular expression pattern, [0-9]*. The asterisk applies to the character class [0-9], which I call a *chunk*.

Why does the first part number ABC match? When the regular expression engine is at the position immediately before the A of ABC, it attempts to match the next character in the part number with an uppercase A. Because the first character of the part number ABC is an uppercase A, there is a match. Next, an attempt is made to match an uppercase B. That too matches, as does an attempt to match an uppercase C. At that stage, the first three characters in the regular expression pattern have been matched. Finally, an attempt is made to match the pattern [0-9]*, which means "Match zero or more numeric characters." Because the character after C is a newline character, there are no numeric digits. Because there are exactly zero numeric digits after the uppercase C of ABC, there is a match (of zero numeric digits). Because all components of the pattern match, the whole pattern matches.

Why does the part number ABC8899 also match? When the regular expression engine is at the position immediately before the A of ABC8899, it attempts to match the next character in the part number with an uppercase A. Because the first character of the part number ABC8899 is an uppercase A, there is a match. Next, attempts are made to match an uppercase B and an uppercase C. These too match. At that stage, the first three characters in the regular expression pattern have been matched. Finally, an attempt is made to match the pattern [0-9]*, which means "Match zero or more numeric characters." Four numeric digits follow the uppercase C. Because there are exactly four numeric digits after the uppercase C of ABC, there is a match (of four numeric digits, which meets the criterion "zero or more numeric digits"). Because all components of the pattern match, the whole pattern matches.

Work through the other part numbers step by step, and you'll find that each ought to match the pattern ABC[0-9]*.

The + Quantifier

There are many situations where you will want to be certain that a character or group of characters is present at least once but also allow for the possibility that the character occurs more than once. The + cardinality operator is designed for that situation. The + operator means "Match one or more occurrences of the chunk that precedes me."

Take a look at the example with Parts.txt, but look for matches that include at least one numeric digit. You want to find part numbers that begin with the uppercase characters ABC and then have one or more numeric digits.

You can express the problem definition like this:

Match an uppercase A. If there is a match, attempt to match an uppercase B. If there is a match, attempt to match an uppercase C. If all three uppercase characters match, attempt to match one or more numeric digits.

Use the following pattern to express that problem definition:

```
ABC[0-9]+
```

Matching One or More Numeric Digits

1. Open OpenOffice.org Writer, and open the sample file Parts.txt.
2. Use Ctrl+F to open the Find and Replace dialog box.
3. Check the Regular Expressions and Match Case check boxes.
4. Enter the pattern ABC[0-9]+ in the Search For text box; click the Find All button; and inspect the matching part numbers that are highlighted, as shown in Figure A-18.

As you can see, the only change from the result of using the pattern ABC[0-9]* is that the pattern ABC[0-9]+ fails to match the part number ABC.

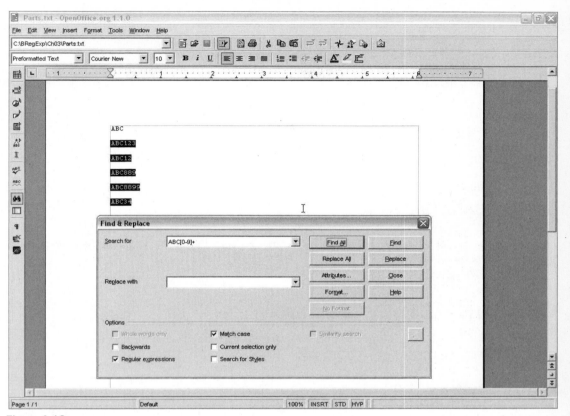

Figure A-18

When the regular expression engine is at the position immediately before the uppercase A of the part number ABC, it attempts to match an uppercase A. That matches. Next, subsequent attempts are made to match an uppercase B and an uppercase C. They too match. At that stage, the first three characters in the regular expression pattern have been matched. Finally, an attempt is made to match the pattern [0-9]+, which means "Match one or more numeric characters." There are zero numeric digits following the uppercase C. Because there are exactly zero numeric digits after the uppercase C of ABC, there is no match (zero numeric digits fails to match the criterion "one or more numeric digits," specified by the + quantifier). Because the final component of the pattern fails to match, the whole pattern fails to match.

Why does the part number ABC8899 match? When the regular expression engine is at the position immediately before the A of ABC8899, it attempts to match the next character in the part number with an uppercase A. Because the first character of the part number ABC8899 is an uppercase A, there is a match. Next, attempts are made to match an uppercase B and an uppercase C. They too match. At that stage, the first three characters in the regular expression pattern have been matched. Finally, an attempt is made to match the pattern [0-9]+, which means "Match one or more numeric characters." Four numeric digits follow the uppercase C of ABC, so there is a match (of four numeric digits, which meets the criterion "one or more numeric digits"). Because all components of the pattern match, the whole pattern matches.

Before moving on to look at the curly-brace quantifier syntax, here's a brief review of the quantifiers already discussed, as listed in the following table:

Quantifier	Definition
?	0 or 1 occurrences
*	0 or more occurrences
+	1 or more occurrences

These quantifiers can often be useful, but there are times when you will want to express ideas such as "Match something that occurs at least twice but can occur an unlimited number of times" or "Match something that can occur at least three times but no more than six times."

You also saw earlier that you can express a repeating character by simply repeating the character in a regular expression pattern.

The Curly-Brace Syntax

If you want to specify large numbers of occurrences, you can use a curly-brace syntax to specify an exact number of occurrences.

The {n} Syntax

Suppose that you want to match part numbers with sequences of characters that have exactly three numeric digits. You can write the pattern as

```
ABC[0-9][0-9][0-9]
```

by simply repeating the character class for a numeric digit. Alternatively, you can use the curly-brace syntax and write

```
ABC[0-9]{3}
```

to achieve the same result.

Most regular expression engines support a syntax that can express ideas like that. The syntax uses curly braces to specify minimum and maximum numbers of occurrences.

The {n,m} Syntax

The * operator that was described a little earlier in this chapter effectively means "Match a minimum of zero occurrences and a maximum occurrence, which is unbounded." Similarly, the + quantifier means "Match a minimum of one occurrence and a maximum occurrence, which is unbounded."

Using curly braces and numbers inside them allows the developer to create occurrence quantifiers that cannot be specified when using the ?, *, or + quantifiers.

The following subsections look at three variants that use the curly-brace syntax. First, let's look at the syntax that specifies "Match zero or up to [a specified number] of occurrences."

{0,m}

The {0,m} syntax allows you to specify that a minimum of zero occurrences can be matched (specified by the first numeric digit after the opening curly brace) and that a maximum of m occurrences can be matched (specified by the second numeric digit, which is separated from the minimum occurrence indicator by a comma and which precedes the closing curly brace).

To match a minimum of zero occurrences and a maximum of one occurrence, you would use the pattern

```
{0,1}
```

which has the same meaning as the ? quantifier.

To specify matching of a minimum of zero occurrences and a maximum of three occurrences, you would use the pattern

```
{0,3}
```

which you couldn't express using the ?, *, or + quantifiers.

Suppose that you want to specify that you want to match the sequence of characters ABC followed by a minimum of zero numeric digits or a maximum of two numeric digits.

You can semiformally express that as the following problem definition:

Match an uppercase A. **If there is a match, attempt to match an uppercase** B. **If there is a match, attempt to match an uppercase** C. **If all three uppercase characters match, attempt to match a minimum of zero or a maximum of two numeric digits.**

The following pattern does what you need:

```
ABC[0-9]{0,2}
```

Appendix A: Simple Regular Expressions

The ABC simply matches a sequence of the corresponding literal characters. The [0-9] indicates that a numeric digit is to be matched, and the {0,2} is a quantifier that indicates a minimum of zero occurrences of the preceding chunk (which is [0-9], representing a numeric digit) and a maximum of two occurrences of the preceding chunk is to be matched.

Match Zero to Two Occurrences

1. Open OpenOffice.org Writer, and open the sample file Parts.txt.

2. Use Ctrl+F to open the Find and Replace dialog box.

3. Check the Regular Expressions and Match Case check boxes.

4. Enter the regular expression pattern **ABC[0-9]{0,2}** in the Search For text box; click the Find All button; and inspect the matches that are displayed in highlighted text, as shown in Figure A-19.

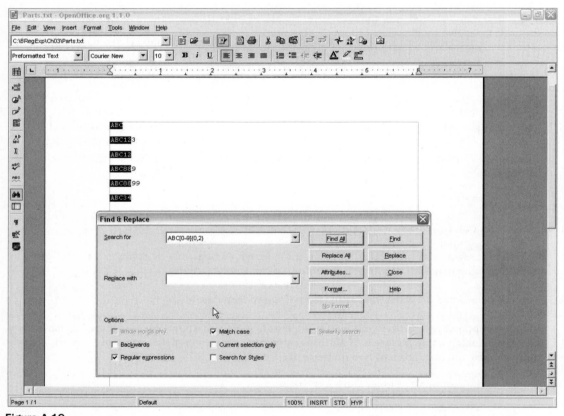

Figure A-19

Notice that on some lines, only parts of a part number are matched. If you are puzzled as to why that is, refer back to the problem definition. You are to match a specified sequence of characters. You haven't specified that you want to match a part number, simply a sequence of characters.

How does it work with the match for the part number ABC? When the regular expression engine is at the position immediately before the uppercase A of the part number ABC, it attempts to match an uppercase A. That matches. Next, an attempt is made to match an uppercase B. That too matches. Next, an attempt is made to match an uppercase C. That too matches. At that stage, the first three characters in the regular expression pattern have been matched. Finally, an attempt is made to match the pattern [0-9]{0,2}, which means "Match a minimum of zero and a maximum of two numeric characters." Zero numeric digits follow the uppercase C in ABC. Because there are exactly zero numeric digits after the uppercase C of ABC, there is a match (zero numeric digits matches the criterion "a minimum of zero numeric digits" specified by the minimum-occurrence specifier of the {0,2} quantifier). Because the final component of the pattern matches, the whole pattern matches.

What happens when matching is attempted on the line that contains the part number ABC8899? Why do the first five characters of the part number ABC8899 match? When the regular expression engine is at the position immediately before the A of ABC8899, it attempts to match the next character in the part number with an uppercase A and finds a match. Next, an attempt is made to match an uppercase B. That too matches. Then an attempt is made to match an uppercase C, which also matches. At that stage, the first three characters in the regular expression pattern have been matched. Finally, an attempt is made to match the pattern [0-9]{0,2}, which means "Match a minimum of zero and a maximum of two numeric characters." Four numeric digits follow the uppercase C. Only two of those numeric digits are needed for a successful match. Because there are four numeric digits after the uppercase C of ABC, there is a match (of two numeric digits, which meets the criterion "a maximum of two numeric digits"), but the final two numeric digits of ABC8899 are not needed to form a match, so they are not highlighted. Because all components of the pattern match, the whole pattern matches.

{n,m}

The minimum-occurrence specifier in the curly-brace syntax doesn't have to be 0. It can be any number you like, provided it is not larger than the maximum-occurrence specifier.

Let's look for one to three occurrences of a numeric digit. You can specify this in a problem definition as follows:

Match an uppercase A. If there is a match, attempt to match an uppercase B. If there is a match, attempt to match an uppercase C. If all three uppercase characters match, attempt to match a minimum of one and a maximum of three numeric digits.

So if you wanted to match one to three occurrences of a numeric digit in Parts.txt, you would use the following pattern:

```
ABC[0-9]{1,3}
```

Figure A-20 shows the matches in OpenOffice.org Writer. Notice that the part number ABC does not match, because it has zero numeric digits, and you are looking for matches that have one through three numeric digits. Notice, too, that only the first three numeric digits of ABC8899 form part of the match.

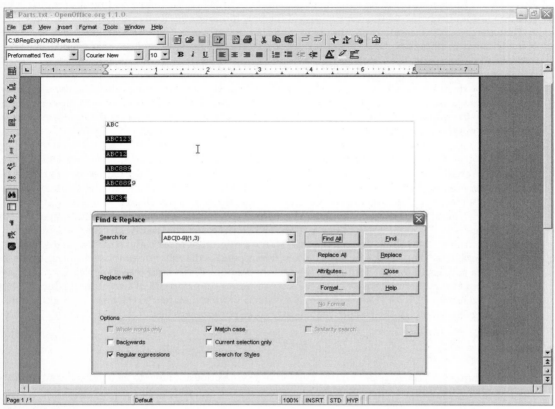

Figure A-20

{n,}

Sometimes, you will want there to be an unlimited number of occurrences. You can specify an unlimited maximum number of occurrences by omitting the maximum-occurrence specifier inside the curly braces.

To specify at least two occurrences and an unlimited maximum, you could use the following problem definition:

Match an uppercase A. **If there is a match, attempt to match an uppercase** B. **If there is a match, attempt to match an uppercase** C. **If all three uppercase characters match, attempt to match a minimum of two occurrences and an unlimited maximum occurrence of three numeric digits.**

You can express that using the following pattern:

```
ABC[0-9]{2,}
```

Figure A-21 shows the appearance in OpenOffice.org Writer. Notice that now all four numeric digits in ABC8899 form part of the match, because the maximum occurrences that can form part of a match are unlimited.

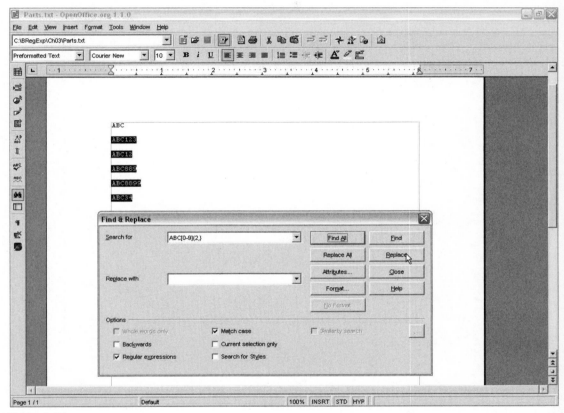

Figure A-21

Exercises

These exercises allow you to test your understanding of the regular expression syntax covered in this chapter.

1. Using DoubledR.txt as a sample file, try out regular expression patterns that match other doubled letters in the file. For example, there are doubled lowercase s, m, and l. Use different syntax options to match exactly two occurrences of a character.

2. Create a regular expression pattern that tests for part numbers that have two alphabetic characters in sequence — uppercase A followed by uppercase B followed by two numeric digits.

3. Modify the file UpperL.html so that the regular expression pattern to be matched is the. Open the file in a browser, and test various pieces of text against the specified regular expression pattern.

Glossary

This glossary contains a list of terms that may be useful to a web developer or search engine marketer reading this book. Glossary entries contained within other entries are presented in *italics*.

200   A web server *status code* that indicates the requested URL has been retrieved successfully. See Chapter 4 for more details.

301   A type of *redirect* sent by a web server that indicates the content of a URL has been relocated permanently. See Chapter 4 for more details.

302   A type of *redirect* sent by a web server that indicates the content of a URL has been relocated temporarily. See Chapter 4 for more details.

404   A web server *status code* returned when the requested URL does not exist on the server. See Chapter 4 for more details.

500   A web server *status code* returned when the server is encountering temporary technical problems. See Chapter 4 for more details.

Accessibility   The ease of use exhibited by a web site with regard to users who have disabilities or impairments.

Ad-hoc query   A search request that retrieves information without knowledge of the underlying storage structures of the database.

Aggregator   See *feed reader*.

AJAX   An acronym for *Asynchronous JavaScript and XML*. It is a technology that uses *DOM*, *JavaScript*, and the XMLHttpRequest object to create interactive web applications within a web page. With an AJAX application, users do not navigate through different pages of content — instead, the application executes (and displays updated content when necessary) inside a single web page. For a practical tutorial of AJAX with ASP.NET, we recommend Cristian Darie's *Microsoft AJAX Library Essentials* (Packt Publishing, 2007). SEO implications of AJAX are discussed in Chapter 6.

Glossary

Algorithm   A set of instructions that directs a computer to complete a task or solve a problem; in search engines, a series of such algorithms is used to create the list of search results for a particular user query, ranking the results in order of relevance.

Anchor text   The text a user clicks when he or she follows a link; in HTML it is the text contained by `<a>...</a>`.

Apache   A popular open-source web server; it is the web server used in this book.

Application programming interface (API)   Functions of a computer program that can be accessed and used by other programs. For example, many shipping companies use application programming interfaces to allow applications to query shipping prices over the Internet.

ASP.NET   A development framework created by Microsoft for creating dynamic web applications and web services. It is part of Microsoft's .NET platform and shares very little with "classic" ASP. The server-side code can be written in numerous languages, including C# and *VB.NET*.

ASPNET.MDF   A database file generated by ASP.NET to store user membership and profile information.

Asymmetric encryption   An encryption method that uses different keys for encrypting and decrypting the data. Each party has a public key and a private key, which are always generated in pairs. To send data to a recipient, one encrypts that data using the recipient's public key. That data can be then decrypted only using the associated private key, which is only known by the recipient. The *HTTPS* protocol, and digital certificates and signatures, use asymmetric encryption.

Asynchronous JavaScript and XML   See *AJAX*.

Atom   A *web feed* standard based on *XML*. For more details, see Chapter 7.

Authentication   A security-related process that identifies a human user, process, or program into a secured system. The most common method of authentication is by asking for a username and password, but many others have been implemented.

Authorization   A security-related process that decides the privileges of a human user, process, or program that has been authenticated.

BigDaddy   An update to Google's ranking algorithms for web sites that occurred in early 2006. It is similar in scope to the *Florida* update.

Black hat   The use of techniques that to varying degrees do not follow the guidelines of search engines and may also exploit the work or property of others. For more details, see Chapter 8.

Blog   A content management system that presents articles in reverse chronological order. Blogs are explored in Chapter 16 when you set one up using *WordPress*.

Bot   See *spider*.

Breadcrumb navigation   Navigational links appearing on a web page that show the path taken to reach that particular page; for example, "home ➪ products ➪ cookies."

C# A programming language, with a syntax similar to that of Java and C++, used to create programs for the .NET Framework. The extension used for C# source files is `.cs`.

Cookie A feature supported by modern web browsers that allows web sites to store data on a visitor's machine for later retrieval. Typically cookies are used by web applications to store user identification data, or user preferences, so that the visitor can be identified on subsequent visits to a web site.

Cascading Style Sheets A language that defines the presentation and aesthetics of a markup language such as HTML.

Class A blueprint for an object in object-oriented programming.

Click-through The act of a user clicking a particular ad or *SERP*.

Click-through rate The ratio of click-throughs per number of visitors who view the advertisement or *SERP*.

Cloaking The (sometimes deceptive) practice of delivering different content to a search engine than to human visitors browsing a web site.

Code behind An ASP.NET feature that allows writing the code of a *Web Form*, *Web User Control*, or *Master Page*, in a separate file. The code-behind file has the same name as the file with which it is associated, and it contains an additional extension that reflects the language used for the code. For example, the code-behind file for `Default.aspx`, if written in C#, will be named `Default.aspx.cs`.

Content theft The practice of stealing another individual's web content.

Conversion rate The ratio of conversions or sales per the number of visitors.

Constructor A special method in a class that is executed when the class is instantiated.

CSS See *Cascading Style Sheets*.

CTR See *click-through rate*.

Custom control In *ASP.NET*, a custom control is a custom-built reusable component that can be included in *Web Forms*, similar to the controls included in the .NET Framework, such as `TextBox`, `Calendar`, `GridView`, and so on.

Data escaping Altering the text and other data received from a non-trusted source, such as a comment added with a form on your web site, so that it doesn't cause any unwanted side effects when that data is further processed by your application.

DELETE Basic SQL command used to delete one or more rows from a data table.

Delist To remove a web site from a search engine's index.

Directory A human-edited catalog of web sites organized into categories; examples include the Yahoo! directory and DMOZ.

DNS   Acronym for *Domain Name Server*.

Document Object Model   The representation of a hierarchical structure such as that of an *XML* or HTML document. Most programming languages provide a Document Object Model (DOM) object that allows loading and manipulating such structures. In particular, *AJAX* web applications use DOM to create web applications inside of a web page.

DOM   See *Document Object Model*.

Domain Name Server   A server that stores various data about domain names and translates them to their designated IP addresses.

Duplicate content   Substantially identical content located on different web pages.

Encapsulation   A concept of *object-oriented programming* that refers to the clear separation between an object's exposed functionality (what the object does) and its internal structure (the implementation details).

Extensible Markup Language   Better known as XML, this is a general-purpose text-based document structure that facilitates the sharing of data across diverse applications. See `http://en.wikipedia.org/wiki/Xml` for more information.

Feed   See *web feed*.

Feed reader   An application that reads and displays web feeds for human consumption.

.FLA   A source script file used to generate Flash .SWF files.

Flash   A technology developed by Adobe that can be used to add animation and interactive content to web pages using vector graphics.

Florida   An update to Google's ranking *algorithms* for web sites that occurred in late 2003.

Foreign key   An *RDBMS* concept that refers to a column or group of columns in a data table that point to the *primary key* of another data table, creating a link between the tables. Technically, the foreign key is implemented by the database as a rule that ensures the link isn't broken.

Geo-targeting   The practice of providing different content depending on a user's or spider's physical location on Earth.

Global.asax   Known as the "ASP.NET application file," `Global.asax` contains handlers that respond to application-wide events, such as `Application_Start`, `Application_BeginRequest`, and so on.

Google Sandbox   The virtual "purgatory" that many newly launched sites must pass through in order to rank well in Google. This concept is described in Chapter 2.

Hashing   The process of obtaining a unique value that represents another value by applying a mathematical function to it. The two most popular hashing algorithms are MD5 (Message Digest 5 — `http://en.wikipedia.org/wiki/MD5`) and SHA (Secure Hash Algorithm — `http://en.wikipedia.org/wiki/SHA-1`).

HTTP   HyperText Transfer Protocol is the protocol used to exchange information between web clients and web servers.

HTTPS   HyperText Transfer Protocol Secure is a secure version of HTTP that encrypts transmitted data, so that a party that intercepts all the communication cannot re-create the original messages.

HTTP status codes   Numeric codes (such as 200, 301, etc.) that provide information regarding the state of an HTTP request. You can use them, for example, to indicate that the information requested is not available or has been moved.

Inbound link   A link to your web site from an external web site.

IP address   The unique numerical address of a particular computer or network device on the Internet; it can be analogized to a phone number in purpose.

IP delivery   The practice of using the IP address of the connecting computer, whether robot or human, and sending different content based on that. It is the technology behind both *geo-targeting* and *cloaking*.

Inheritance   A feature commonly supported by *OOP* languages such as *C#*, *VB.NET*, Java, C++, and others, that allows creating a new class by inheriting the behavior of an already existing class. The new class is also known as subclass, or derived class. The original class is also known as base class, or superclass. The .NET Framework supports single inheritance, meaning that a class can derive from exactly one other class. In .NET, all classes are derived from the class `Object`.

INSERT   Basic SQL command used to add a row to a table.

JavaScript   A scripting language implemented by all modern web browsers, best known for its use as a client-side programming language embedded within web pages. Some common uses of JavaScript are to open popup windows, validate data on Web Forms, and more recently to create *AJAX* applications.

Link bait   Any content or feature within a web site that is designed to bait viewers to place links to it from other web sites.

Link equity   The equity, or value, transferred to another URL by a particular link. This concept is discussed in Chapter 2.

Link farm   A web page or set of web pages that is contrived for the express purpose of manipulating link popularity by strategically interlinking web sites.

Keyword density   A metric that calculates how frequently a certain keyword appears in web page copy to calculate relevance to a query.

Keyword stuffing   Excessive and contrived keyword repetition for the purpose of manipulating search results.

Managed stored procedure   A *stored procedure* written in a .NET language such as *C#* or *VB.NET*, which is compiled and stored inside *SQL Server*. Managed stored procedures are supported starting with SQL Server 2005, and they're useful when you need to perform complex mathematical operations or complex logic that can't be easily (or efficiently) implemented with *T-SQL*.

Master Page   A new feature in ASP.NET 2.0, the Master Page is a template that can be used to implement ASP.NET *Web Forms*. Master Pages are files with the `.master` extension, and support features such as *code behind*.

Matt Cutts   An outspoken Google engineer who runs a *blog* at `http://www.mattcutts.com/blog`.

Method overloading   A useful feature of many modern programming languages, including the .NET languages, that allow creating multiple methods with the same name in a class, but having differing types or numbers of parameters.

mod_rewrite   An *Apache* module that performs *URL rewriting*. See Chapter 3 for more details.

MySQL   A free open-source relational database that uses *SQL* to specify requests or queries for data contained therein.

Natural   See *organic*.

Nofollow   An attribute that can be applied to links to specify that search engines shouldn't count them as a vote, with regard to *link equity*, for the specified URL. The concept is discussed in Chapter 8.

Object-oriented programming (OOP)   A feature implemented by modern programming languages that allows the programmer to create types (*classes*) that are modeled after real-world entities. An instance of a class is an *object*, which is a self-contained entity that has state and behavior, just like a real-world object. Typical features of OOP languages are *encapsulation*, *inheritance*, and *polymorphism*.

Organic   An adjective that describes the results from unpaid results in a search engine.

Outbound link   A link from a web page to an external web site.

Overloading   See *method overloading*.

PageRank (PR)   An algorithm patented by Google that measures a particular page's importance relative to other pages included in the search engine's index. It was invented in the late 1990s by Larry Page and Sergey Brin.

Pay Per Click (PPC)   An advertising method whereby advertisers competitively bid for clicks resulting particular keywords or contextually placed advertisement blocks. These advertisements are called "sponsored ads" and appear above or next to the organic results in *SERP*s.

PHP   A programming language designed primarily for producing dynamic web pages, originally written by Rasmus Lerdorf. PHP is a recursive acronym of "PHP: Hypertext Preprocessor."

Polymorphism   An *OOP* concept that refers to the ability to make use of objects by only knowing a base class from which they derive.

Postback   An *ASP.NET* mechanism that implements event-driven programming, similar to that in desktop applications, in web applications. In other words, a web page becomes an application that reacts to the visitor clicking on buttons, changing values, and so on. This paradigm isn't meant to replace the normal web site navigation using links, but it comes in very handy when there is functionality that needs to happen on a single web page. When a postback event occurs, such as clicking a button on the page, the page is submitted to the server, the event is handled at server-side, and then the page is reloaded in a new state. Modern web applications use *AJAX* to enhance the user experience in scenarios when waiting for a page reload is undesirable.

Primary key   An *RDBMS* concept that refers to the column, or group of columns in a data table, that uniquely identify the rows in that table. For this reason, the primary key column is often referred to as "the ID column (or columns)."

RDBMS   Acronym for Relational Database Management System. Refers to a software application that is designed to efficiently store, manipulate, and retrieve data. Typically, RDBMSs support a dialect of *SQL*, which can be used to interact with the database server. Microsoft SQL Server is an RDBMS.

Redirect   The process of redirecting requests for a web page to another page. Redirecting is discussed in Chapter 4.

REFERER   A header sent by a web browser indicating where it arrived from — or where it was referred from. Our misspelling of "referer" is deliberate and in the specification.

Regex   See *regular expression.*

Regular expression   A string written in a special language that matches text patterns. Regular expressions are used in text manipulation and are discussed in Chapter 3 and Appendix A.

Return on investment (ROI)   A metric for the benefit attained by a particular investment.

Robot   In the context of this book, a robot refers to a *spider.*

robots.txt   A text file located in the root directory of a web site that adheres to the robots.txt standard, described at http://www.robotstxt.org. The standard specifies files that should not be accessed by a search engine *spider.*

ROI   Acronym for *return on investment.*

RSS   A *web feed* standard based on *XML*. For more details, see Chapter 7.

Screen scraping   The practice of using a program to parse out information from an HTML document.

Search engine optimization   The subset of search engine marketing that aims to improve the *organic* rankings of a web site for relevant keywords.

SELECT   Basic SQL command used to read one or more rows from a data table.

SEM   An acronym for search engine marketing or search engine marketer.

SEO   An acronym for search engine optimization.

SEO copywriting   The practice of authoring content in such a way that it not only reads well for the surfer, but additionally targets specific search terms in search engines.

Glossary

SERP   An acronym for search engine results page.

Sitemap   A file that provides an easy way for both humans and search engines to reference pages of your web site from one central location. Sitemaps are covered in Chapter 9.

Social bookmarking   Offers users convenient storage of their bookmarks remotely for access from any location. Examples of web sites that offer this service include del.icio.us, digg, reddit, and so on Social bookmarking is covered in Chapter 7.

Spam (search engine)   Web page(s) that are contrived to rank well in search engines but actually contain no valuable content.

Spider   A computer program that performs the process of *spidering*.

Spider trap   A set of web pages that cause a web spider to make an infinite number of requests without providing any substantial content and/or cause it to crash.

Spidering   The process of traversing and storing the content of a web site performed by the *spider*.

Spoofing   Sending of incorrect information deliberately.

SQL   An acronym for *Structured Query Language*.

SQL Server   Microsoft's *RDBMS* product.

Status code   See *HTTP status codes*.

Stored procedure   A procedure stored inside the database server. Each database server supports one or more languages that can be used to write stored procedures. The language used to write stored procedures for SQL Server is named *T-SQL*. SQL Server 2005 also supports writing *managed stored procedures* in .NET languages such as *C#* and *VB.NET*.

Structured Query Language   A computer language used to create, update, select, and delete data from (relational) databases.

Supplemental index   A secondary index provided by Google that is widely believed to contain content that it regards as less important. See more details in Chapter 2.

Supplemental result   A result in the *supplemental index*.

.SWF   A vector graphics format created by Macromedia (now owned by Adobe) used to publish animations and interactive applications on the web. Although technically incorrect, SWF files are frequently referred to as "Flash movies."

Symmetric encryption   An encryption method that uses the same password, or key, for encrypting and decrypting the data. Popular symmetric encryption algorithms include Rijndael, Blowfish, and Serpent.

T-SQL   The dialect of *SQL* understood by SQL Server.

Transact-SQL   See *T-SQL*.

UPDATE   Basic SQL command used to modify one or more rows of a data table.

URL rewriting   The practice that translates incoming URL requests to requests for other URLs. You use URL rewriting to serve pages with search-engine friendly URLs from dynamic scripts written in ASP.NET and other server-side web development technologies. This topic is discussed in Chapter 3.

Usability   The ease of use exhibited by a web site.

User agent   Any user or web spider accessing a web site; also refers to the string sent by a user's web browser or a web spider indicating what or who it is, that is, "Mozilla/5.0 (Windows; U; Windows NT 5.1; en-US; rv:1.8.1) Gecko/20061010 Firefox/2.0."

Validator control   ASP.NET ships with six validation controls that can be used to enforce the validity of values in a page before the page can be submitted to the server. The validation controls are: `RequiredFieldValidator`, `RangeValidator`, `RegularExpressionValidator`, `CompareValidator`, `CustomValidator`, and `ValidationSummary`. These controls work by generating JavaScript code on the server. Because JavaScript can be disabled at the client side, the validation controls are only a usability enhancement. To enforce security, the status of the validator controls need to be verified as the server side as well by reading the value of `Page.IsValid`.

Viewstate   An ASP.NET technique that persists the state of the controls in a Web Form during *postback* events.

Viral marketing   Marketing techniques that use social phenomena to spread a message through self-replicating viral processes — not unlike those of computer viruses.

Visual Basic .NET   A programming language, with a syntax similar to that of Visual Basic, used to create programs for the .NET Framework. The language of choice for most .NET developers is *C#*, but Visual Basic .NET is also frequently used because of its syntax resemblance with the versions of Visual Basic that were used by older versions of ASP for writing the server-side code, and with the popular (albeit obsolete) Visual Basic 6. The extension used for VB.NET source code files is `.vb`.

VB.NET   See *Visual Basic .NET*.

Web analytics   A software package that tracks various web site data and statistics used for analyzing and interpreting results of marketing efforts.

Web.config   Configuration file written in XML format, used by ASP.NET web applications to store various application settings.

Web feed   Provides automated access to content contained by a web site via some sort of software application. *XML* is typically used to transport the information in a structured format.

Web log   See *blog*.

Web client   A software program that can be used to send HTTP requests to *web servers*, and visualize the received data.

Glossary

Web Form   The basic page type in ASP.NET web applications. The Web Form is a file that contains HTML markup and server-side code to generate dynamic content. The extension for Web form files is `.aspx`.

Web User Control   A simple yet efficient technique for implementing component reuse in ASP.NET web applications. Web User Controls are similar to Web Forms, except they cannot be requested directly by web clients. Instead, they are supposed to be included in existing Web Forms. Web User Controls files have the `.ascx` extension.

Web server   A software program that understands the HTTP protocol, and replies to HTTP requests received from *web clients*.

Web spider   See *spider*.

Web syndication   Permits and facilitates other web sites to publish your web content.

White hat   Describes the use of techniques that follow the guidelines of a search engine.

WordPress   A popular open-source blogging application written in *PHP*.

XML   See Extensible Markup Language.

Index

SYMBOLS

R